Political Philosophy

Text and Context

Political Philosophy
Text and Context

B.N. Ray

2014
Kaveri Books
New Delhi - 110 002

First Published in 2014

ISBN: 978-81-7479-152-8 (PB)
ISBN: 978-81-7479-153-5 (HB)

Published by
Kaveri Books
4832/24, Ansari Road
New Delhi - 110 002 (India)
Ph.: 011-2328 8140, 2324 5799
E-mail: kaveribooks@vsnl.com
E-mail: kaveribooks@gmail.com
website: www.kaveribooks.com

Laser Typesetting by
Aarati Computers, Delhi - 110 009

Printed at
Chawla Offset Printers, Delhi

PRINTED IN INDIA

This book is dedicated to
my former teachers
who inculcated in me the spirit of love,
compassion and respect for the Other

Preface

We might begin with a simple definition of political philosophy as the application of the tools of philosophical analysis to problems of politics. Philosophy asks questions about fundamentals, about justification, and typically seeks to use logical arguments to seek answers. Political philosophy, then, is concerned with questions such as "what is the nature of justice?" and "what sorts of social arrangements are best?" and "do I have an obligation to obey the law?"

Political scientists are sometimes concerned with these questions also, but as formal discipline political science has come to be devoted more to empirical matters such as models of voting behavior or comparative world politics. These are hardly insignificant; we mention the distinction simply for the purpose of clarification. In its most usual sense, political philosophy is a normative subject; it uses words like "best" and "right" and "good". Often, then, there is overlap between political philosophy and moral philosophy, for the basic concepts underlying words like that are the subject of the latter field. Nevertheless, political philosophy is its own distinctive area of inquiry, for theories about personal virtue or obligation may not answer all questions about social arrangements. We need some insights into moral philosophy to ask about the "most just government", but making progress towards an answer will take us beyond ethics. The question sifts from "how should I live my life?" to "how shall we arrange our society?"

One answer to the question of how best to arrange society is that "everyone should do as I command". This seems almost comical today, but for large bits of human history there has been little more that has served as a "guiding principle" for many societies. If my tribe has conquered yours, perhaps all in your tribe would recognize that mine should rule. But perhaps not. At some point, someone thought to ask about the justification of the power some held over others, and this remains a vexing question. The nature and justification of political authority, the proper relationship between the individual and society, the role of the divine in affairs of state – these and many other questions are the subject of the field we call political philosophy.

Not surprisingly, the ancient Greek philosophers Plato and Aristotle have much to say about these questions, but the debate continues today. It is often the case in political philosophy that questions get revised in each generation, in slightly different terms. This may be because relying merely on tradition is an unreliable guide. Still, some questions seem to have been answered with a virtual consensus: few today endorse the notion that trial-by-combat is a more reliable method of judicial inquiry than trial-by-jury, just as few defend the idea that kings have a divine right to absolute power over their subjects. Yet, although democracy has been challenged since its invention 2500 years ago, even in our own century it continues to be challenged by such recent competitors as Nazism and Communism. Within democracies, vital questions abound concerning the eternal conflict between the liberty of the individual and the will of the majority. Political philosophy remains an active site. But the debates of political philosophy are not merely academic: Contest. Ideas shape political systems. From the wars between Greece and Persia to the 20th century battles among liberalism and fascism, political philosophy has played a role in shaping the fates of nations and of people. American independence is arguably the ultimate result of a radical argument put forward by a philosopher, as was Soviet Communism. Few could dispute that political philosophy is a subject which deserves attention.

This text book has grown out of working in writing about and teaching political philosophy. This book has been written to help students see how political philosophy connects and negotiates diverse aspects of human life in ways most people do not realize. It is desired for these enrolled in first course in political philosophy and for the teachers who teach them. It can be used in conjunction with primary sources but it can also stand on its own as an introduction to political philosophy. The overall aim of this book is to discuss consciously the views of major Western political philosophers in order to demonstrate how their views about politics and society are critical to understanding the politics of our own time. It should enable students to develop a solid appreciation of how important political a solid appreciation of how important political philosophy is, whether they want a revolution wish to change the constitution or just wait to understand how to improve human condition.

A political philosophy textbook need not be merely a channel transmitting information from book to readers. I strongly believe that an introduction to social and political philosophy can be a serious intervention into that discipline and that an historically focused introduction is a sounder route to political philosophy. A text can promote active learning that excites and engages students and fosters pleasure in philosophical enquiry. It can demonstrate that philosophical study is not a hindrance to understanding or pursuing practical politics. On the contrary philosophy and politics must invite and interact as Aristotle observed may centuries earlier. There will always be many philosophers than any political philosophy text can cover, but the aim is to present as broad a rage of thinker as possible: form Plato to Rousseau, Nozick and Wollstonecraft, then Hegel and Marx to John Rawls, Herbert Marcuse, Habermas and to the postmoderns Foucault and Judith Butler. I hope the students will begin to appreciate the depth and breadth of the field and that the range of philosophers will allow them not only to learn about each philosopher and his/her ideas but to explore relation between faith, religion, science, and skepticism that have persisted throughout history of political thought. This book addresses newer issues as well as many of the traditional themes taught in the standard introduction courses. Gender issues for example are relatively recent theme in the secondary literature. All the authors I have read whose insight helped me understand more fully the ideas of the masters, many of them are citied in the reference. Many of my students through their questions and comments have provoked me to rethink many point and issues and have motivated me to write the best possible work for their successors.

Finally, I welcome comments from both those who find this book worth value and those suggest improvement.

My goal in assembling this collection was to facilitate this attention. There have been many collections of political philosophy, but they tend to be either well-served in classical sources, with poor representation of contemporary debates, or vice versa. My intention is a comprehensive collection, in one volume, of essential selections of political philosophy from the ancient world to the contemporary. Readings are presented in chronological order, grouped by period. Each reading is accompanied by a brief biographical sketch of the philosopher, and each period is prefaced by a general historical overview, but I have endeavored to keep my own editorializing out. The thinkers represented here are perfectly capable of speaking for themselves, as are the professors who may be using this as textbook. Since the readers, mostly students, need to have an in-depth encounter with these significant philosophers, the selections ought to be approached on their own terms. Some guidance is called for, of course but as students are likely to have such a guide in their teachers, the editor believes that adding additional commentary will tend to create confusion. A general bibliography is attached should the reader wish to pursue any of these philosophers.

Makar Sankranti
14 January, 2013

B.N. Ray

Contents

Introduction

Hang up philosophy!

Unless philosophy can make you a Juliet—*Shakespeare*

We might begin with a simple definition of "political philosophy" as the application of the tools of philosophical analysis to problems of politics. Philosophy asks questions about fundamentals, about justification, and typically seeks to use logical arguments to seek answers. Political philosophy, then, is concerned with questions such as "what is the nature of justice?" and "what sorts of social arrangements are best?" and "do I have an obligation to obey the law?"

Political scientists are sometimes concerned with these questions also, but as formal discipline political science has come to be devoted more to empirical matters such as models of voting behavior or comparative world politics. These are hardly insignificant; we mention the distinction simply for the purpose of clarification. There are also some who think that political philosophy is concerned with something else, namely, how philosophers should deal with political regimes, but this meaning is a bit and used only in certain academic contexts.

In its most usual sense, political philosophy is a normative subject; it uses words like "best" and "right" and "good". Often, then, there is overlap between political philosophy and moral philosophy, for the basic concepts underlying words like that are the subject of the latter field. Nevertheless, political philosophy is its own distinctive area of inquiry, for theories about personal virtue or obligation may not answer all questions about social arrangements. We need some insights into moral philosophy to ask about the most just government, but making progress towards an answer will take us beyond ethics. The question sifts from "how should I live my life?" to "how shall we arrange our society?"

One answer to the question of how best to arrange society is that "everyone should do as I command". This seems almost comical today, but for large bits of human history there has been little more that has served as a guiding principle for many societies. If my tribe has conquered yours, perhaps all in your tribe would recognize that mine should rule. But perhaps not. At some point, someone thought to ask about the justification of the power some held over others, and this remains a vexing question. The nature and justification of political authority, the proper relationship between the individual and society, the role of the divine in affairs of state – these and many other questions are the subject of the field we call political philosophy.

Not surprisingly, the ancient Greek philosophers Plato and Aristotle have much to say about these questions, but the debate continues today. It is often the case in philosophy that questions get revised in each generation, in slightly different terms. This may be because relying merely on tradition is an unreliable guide. Still, some questions seem to have been answered with a virtual consensus: few today endorse the notion that trial-by-combat is a more reliable method of judicial inquiry than trial-by-jury, just as few defend the idea that kings have a divine right to absolute power over their subjects. Yet, although democracy has been challenged since its invention 2500 years ago, even in our own century it continues to be challenged by such recent competitors as Nazism and Communism. Within democracies, vital questions abound concerning the eternal conflict between the liberty of the individual and the will of the majority. Political philosophy remains an active field. But the debates of political philosophy are not merely academic: lives hang in the balance. Ideas shape political systems. From the wars between Greece and Persia to the 20th century battles among liberalism and fascism, political theory has played a role in shaping the fates of nations and of people. American independence is arguably the ultimate result of a radical argument put forward by a philosopher, as was Soviet Communism. Few could dispute that political philosophy is a subject which deserves attention.

"Man was born free and he is everywhere in chains... How can this be made legitimate?" Jean-Jacques Rousseau's profound observation and question express the fundamental concerns of political philosophy. Accordingly, political philosophy is primarily a normative project, one whose main focus is on the principles that guide the evaluation and reform of political and economic institutions that have pervasive effects on our lives. Government, bureaucracy, law, police, property, markets, the welfare state and courts have profound effects on all our lives. And while these institutions enhance our freedom and benefit almost all of us in a great variety of ways, they also impose costs and restrict our freedom in many ways as well. The protection of the property of a person guarantees the freedom of the property holder, for example, but it also restricts the freedom of those who do not hold this property. The efforts to ensure a reasonable distribution of wealth require that taxes be imposed on some to benefit others. Indeed, the whole scheme of institutions guaranteeing security is costly and so requires each to make a contribution to its maintenance.

The question for us as members of societies is which of these types of institutions are ethically defensible? And how should we reform institutions if they are ethically defective? This is a significant part of the stuff of political debates in democratic societies. But this raises the question about what the appropriate normative standards are by which we make these assessments. The assessments we make are at least partly based in more general principles, but we disagree often about the basic principles as much as about the policy questions. One does political philosophy when one articulates and rationally defends some of these principles and criticizes others.

There is much disagreement concerning the legitimacy of each one of the activities modern states engage in, raising the suspicion in each case, that they are merely the misguided efforts of some or the thievery of others. Many argue, for example, that there is not enough redistribution of wealth in society or there is too much inequality and that as a consequence the protection of private property is in effect the protection of a privileged class of persons. Others argue that there is too much redistribution and that the government that carries out these activities is engaged in simple thievery no matter how fine sounding may be. A theory of distributive justice attempts to elaborate and defend principles by which we can adjudicate these issues by determining the correct answers to the general question of what justice requires regarding the distribution of wealth.

Furthermore, when there is such pervasive disagreement about how society should be organized, we must then ask who ought to decide such contentious issues? Traditionally many argued that the wisest ought o decide, but in the modern world it is generally assumed that people ought to be serve limits on what democracies can decide, leaving the leftover areas of social life to be determined by individuals themselves. But how extensive should these limits be? Who ought to decide this matter? Theories of democracy and constitutionalism attempt to answer these questions in rationally defensible ways.

Moreover, one of the profound questions of political philosophy concerns how to deal with the centuries-long injustices done to minorities, women and others, especially since the injustices of the past have had a tremendous impact on the present. These injustices and their current effects often remain unacknowledged or at least ignored by the larger society and thus create fresh new injustices in the present. The experiences of minorities are belittled and their plights blamed on them. What is the just response to the great injustice of this sort? Again, the activity of political philosophy expresses the hope that these questions can be given generally defensible answers.

Finally, the focus of political philosophy has expanded in the last thirty years beyond its initial focus on the assessment of the nation-state to include questions about the nature of global justice and the place of the nation-state in the larger global order. Some have argued that the principles that were thought to apply to individual political societies in fact apply to the world as a whole. Why, these thinkers ask, should we focus on issues of poverty only in our own societies? Why shouldn't we be even more concerned with global poverty, which is often much more serious? These cosmopolitan views are criticized by those who think that there is still an important place for the modern state in our moral appraisals of political power. They argue that citizens have special obligations to their compatriots that they do not have towards others and that these obligations include those of distributive justice. But all theorists agree that the assessment of the modern state and its politics must now be carried out with an eye to its position in the larger global order. Many theorists, then, are interested in developing conceptions of human rights that take into account the interests of all human beings and that set minimal standards for the assessment of the activities of states towards people in other countries. Still there is much disagreement about the nature and basis of human among contemporary theorists.

For most philosophers, political theory involves a commitment to the idea that the questions above have objectively valid answers and that the issues can be understood and progress can be made on them by means of rational argument and good judgment. They approach the issues with an eye towards clarifying the central concepts and problems. They advance alternative systematic theories of the principles of justice and the common good. And they defend theorists by means of rational arguments in favor of the theory and against alternatives. To be sure, even this commitment should be brought under scrutiny when we think as philosophers.

How should political philosophy proceed? What mode of thought should predominate in theoretical exchanges about such complex and tortuous controversies as are the subject matter of politics? The legacy of the European Enlightenment, and the modernist philosophical framework it helped spawn, has long suggested that "reason" in some form provide the fundamental basis for moral principle and thus, by extension, the justification of political principles. However, much nineteenth- and twentieth-century political and philosophical thought insisted that we reappraise the role of reason in the justification of political positions especially given the pervasive human tendency to be irrational, moved by subconscious motives, given to rationalizations and subterfuge, and so on, not to mention the fact that various injustices that were supported by reason in those Enlightenment and later thinkers themselves.

Stephen White, in his examination of the aftermath of these challenges, surveys ways that being "reasonable" might now substitute for a traditional foundational understanding of the grounding of principles in untethered "reason". He proceeds to examine the way "reasonableness" functions in four areas of political discussion: the justification of basic social and political structures; the foundations of ethical-political judgments: and the struggle for recognition of identity. He considers the ways that seeing ideal rationality as a personal and social (and philosophical) ideas has, in the past, led to all manners of exclusion and domination. He traces the idea of "reasonableness" as a substitute for the traditional idea of reason as the foundation of political power in ways that is more sensitive to our many and deep differences as well as our mortality and fmitude. White's essay differs from most of the others here both in style and perspective; this is due to his focus on ways that paradigm methodologies in political philosophy have been questioned.

One of the key issues in political philosophy is the relationship between ethical theorizing and social science. This issue pervades many of the discussions in political philosophy. But it is nowhere more in evidence than in John Rawls's political philosophy. On Rawls's view many of the fundamental principles of justice depend for their validity on facts about human nature and society. For instance, Rawls asserts that the virtue of justice only arises in the context of the circumstances of justice in which humans are only moderately altruistic and there is moderate scarcity of the things that people want. Furthermore, Rawls argues that the principles of justice are those that would be chosen by individuals in a suitable set of circumstances and assuming knowledge of the general facts about human nature and society. More generally, many have argued that principles of justice must be feasible in order for them to be valid. Thus, facts about feasibility constrain the choice of principles. So the complete carrying out of the project of elaborating and justifying fundamental principles of justice requires a good deal of social science and psychology.

G.A. Cohen has questioned this frequently cited methodological constraint. He argues that the fundamental principles of political philosophy must be fact insensitive. By this he means that the truth or validity of fundamental principles of political philosophy must hold regardless of the facts. To the extent that facts play a role in these principles, it is a conditional one. That is, facts affect the conditions under which principles are to be applied, they may also be present in principles as conditions for requirements. But any fact that appears to play a fundamental role does this only because there is a deeper grounding principle that explains this role. Ultimately,

Cohen argues that this grounding relation must terminate in fact insensitive principles.

Samuel Freeman has responded to Cohen's challenge by defending the Rawlsian account of the relation of facts to principles of justice. His reply depends on making a distinction between fundamental principles of conduct such as principles of justice and fundamental justificatory principles such as the principle of impartiality, and the freedom and equality of persons, which determine for John Rawls the need for and the nature of the initial position in which persons are to agree on principles of justices but are not themselves fundamental in the sense that they are not grounded in any other principles of conduct even though they are grounded in facts and fundamental justificatory principles, which are not principles of conduct though they are normative principles.

This exchange raises the broader question of what kinds of facts might be relevant to the shape and legitimacy of normative political principles. Facts about the historical and sociological conditions of democratic societies, to which such normative principles are to apply, might include, for example, a record of poverty, social hierarchies, violence, and division. Actual constitutional democracies that even pretend to be fully inclusive and egalitarian, after all, are very recent phenomena. This speaks to a broader issue of whether political philosophy should proceed in an ideal fashion, where past and ongoing patterns of injustice, domination, and violence are ignored or bracketed in order to specify the precise nature of normative principles. Are the principles that would be justified under relatively ideal conditions the same as would be required in real world settings where centuries of inequality and oppression have left their marks and continue unabated in many settings?

However, when one does turn to the specification and justification of normative principles for a society, one paradigm has dominated the landscape in many ways, at least since the seventieth century in Europe and continuing to the present day, and that is liberalism. There are many forms of liberalism and several fundamental components to it, but the domination of this framework for normative political principles in recent decades notable and indeed is even taken for granted by liberalism's several critics. It is fitting, then, that this paradigm be represented in full force, including many of the central issues raised about and within it in recent work in political philosophy. Liberalism refers generally to the broad approach to the justification of social and political power that sees such a power as legitimate only if it is based on popular sovereignty, the rule of law, and the protection of basic rights and liberties of individuals, whether basic rights are seen as derivative from universal moral principles or simply the required postulates of a political compromise based on the freedom and equality of citizens. Several issues in political philosophy arise concerning the core elements of this paradigm. One such element is the idea that insofar as just political institutions must meet with the popular approval of those living under them, they must remain neutral toward all of the various value frameworks and moral views those citizens follow. This is supposedly in opposition to the more ancient view that the purpose of state institutions is to advance the virtue or good of the citizenry, where those concepts are defined objectively and apart from citizen consent. But the question of whether state neutrality is feasible and what its implications are is a prominent one in recent philosophical work.

Gerald Gaus defends a strong version of liberal neutrality, which he traces form a view of morality generally and concepts of freedom and equality in particular. He argues that all coercion of one person by another person or state without sufficient justification is prima facie morally wrong, and that to justify correction to another moral free and equal person we must provide sufficient justification from her rational and reflective point of view. This principle states that in treating all others in ways that may involve coercing them we must be neutral between our own and their evaluative standards, their moral point of view. Then, if we assume that states must follow moral dictates that apply to persons, then a particular of liberal political neutrality follows, namely that state politics must be neutral between justifiable point of view of all citizens. His arguments for these claims are painstaking, and the conclusions he draws are dramatic, namely, that very few state policies are in fact justifiable by these standards, since very few of them could plausibly be reasonable and reflective given people's deep differences in moral outlook and ranking of values.

Neutrality is typically pitted against perfectionism, which is generally the view that state policies, rather than claiming some kind of neutral position vis-à-vis moral value, should actually promote the most worthwhile values and ideals for their citizens.

Stephen Wall defends such a view. He claims that liberal neutralists such as Gaus as well as political liberals like Rawls and others cannot consistently justify their view that disagreement about conceptions of the good can give way to consensus about procedures for determining the right. Wall questions whether there we can ever devise procedures that are justifiable from a broad spectrum of citizen points of view and that have specific content without relying on perfectionist values in the end. Wall and Gaus may not be as far apart as they appear, as both agree that a purified conception of liberal neutrality leads to very much in the way of justified state policy. But Wall favors the alternative to liberal neutrality, namely that the state should promote lives of its citizens that are in fact "worthwhile". Some values, Wall claims, are justified on objective grounds, even if some people do not grasp those grounds.

Principles of distributive justice have been at the heart of debates in political philosophy in the second half of the twentieth century and the early twenty-first century. The basic questions of distributive justice concern how the good things of social life such as wealth, power, or honors ought to be distributed. In the modern era many have asked a somewhat more abstract question of distributive justice: how ought happiness or opportunity or other intrinsically good things in human life be distributive? And in modern political debates, many have argued that the great inequalities of wealth or opportunities we see are morally indefensible and arbitrary.

The classical tradition of political philosophy in Plato and Aristotle articulated and defended principles concerning the just distribution of goods in society. Aristotle argued that wealth and political honors should be distributed in accordance with merit. The more virtuous persons in political society deserved to have more political power than the less virtuous. The scholastic natural law tradition carried on Aristotle's tradition of distribution according to merit but theoretical discussions of distributive justice waned in the seventeenth century. Hobbes thought that considerations of distributive justice were not of fundamental importance, and Locke makes no mention of distributive justice, though the satisfaction of needs plays a central role in his thought. The idea begins to make reappearance in theatrical discussions with John Stuart Mill and Karl Marx, who is responsible for articulating the deeply egalitarian principle: "To each according to his needs and from each according to his ability".

The person most responsible for the revival of interest in the theoretical grounding and elaboration of principles of distributive justice in the second half of the twentieth century is John Rawls in his *A Theory of Justice*. Rawls thinks of the whole of social justice as being concerned with questions of distribution. He articulates two central principles of distributive justice. The first principle is that each person is to have the maximal amount of basic liberty consistent with an equal basic liberty for all. The second asserts that each is to have fair equality of opportunity and that inequalities of wealth and power are justified only if they work to the advantage of the worst off. Rawls's arguments and principles have been taken by many as reasons for reducing the levels of inequality of wealth and power in society subject to the restriction that we must not include in the basic liberties of persons.

Contemporary debates about distributive justice focus on two sorts of questions. The first is whether distributive justice is a genuine part of justice at all. Libertarians have famously argued that there really is no such thing as distributive justice as a distinct moral set of principles. Robert Nozick in his book for example, argues that the distribution of goods is just to the extent that it comes about through a process of voluntary exchange among persons who have property rights to the things they exchange. Any concern to redistribute goods so that the distribution accords more with some principle of distributive justice, he claimed, would involve a deep interference in human freedom to which each has a fundamental natural right. Eric Mack attempts to give a philosophical grounding to an account of distributive justice that continues in the Nozickian line of analysis. Mack follows Nozick in seeing rights to self-ownership and companion rights to private property as the cornerstone of distributive justice. Seeing people as "separate", on his view, means taking seriously the independent importance that any person's well being has for her as compared to the importance it typically has for others. Mack argues that taking seriously this special importance will be meaningful only if we correspondingly recognize, at the social level, special rights-based protections against others interfering with one's pursuit of one's good. Without these second sorts of protections, the first sort of regard for the importance of people's pursuing their own good in their own way has no real weight. This, for him, establishes the fundamental right of self-ownership that justice must always respect.

But Mack proceeds from these basic ethical considerations to specifically libertarian conclusions, namely that protecting people's rights to non-interference and by extension their right to full private property rights as an extension of this basic self-ownership is the central tenet of distributive justice. No further attempt to equalize people's chances at achieving well-being or in any other way promoting the public good should proceed unless these basic rights are respected. The "practice of private property", as he puts it will protect individuals from the intrusions by others that basic self-ownership forbids.

This attention to basic self-ownership – that we all have fundamental moral rights against all others to move and use our bodies, develop our talents, and otherwise pursue our goods, within the bounds of others' rights of the same sort – also grounds Peter Vallentyne approach to justice. But Vallentyne takes a turn from here, in that he suggests that the protection of self-ownership rights of the sort Mack lays out is consistent with a number of different positions on the principles governing the overall distribution of goods. The "right-libertarian" stance combines individual self-ownership with individual capitalist property rights in the basic principles of distributive justice, resulting in a prominent role of free markets and minimal state interference in capitalist economic activity in the society. But Vallentyne rejects this position, and pursues instead the "left-liberation" strategy of claiming that justice requires the protection of individual rights to self-ownership along with equal opportunity, which insists any individual claim of property ownership must be consistent with others having an opportunity for well-being that is at least as good as the opportunity for well being that the first person has in acquiring the property. This is a strict egalitarian approach to the distribution of resources built upon the kind of moral individualism that theorists such as Mack emphasize.

Vallentyne's position illustrates the way that in many accounts of distributive justice, equality plays the central role in conceptions of justice in modern political philosophy. Historically, the principle of equal distribution is associated with democracy. Citizens in

Athens and other Greek city-states claimed rights to an equal amount of political power on the basis of equal citizenship. And Aristotle cites this principle of equality as the foundation of democracy. But he criticized the idea of abstract Universal equality on the grounds that the more virtuous deserved greater power than the less virtuous. To be sure, no one in ancient Greece argued for universal equality, women and slaves were to be excluded from political power by both the democrats and by Aristotle. On Aristotle's view, distributive justice was to be understood as proportionate equality. That is, each person was to receive in proportion to his merit so that the proportion of benefit to merit is the same. And this conception of distributive justice was to be the dominant conception through the scholastic period.

Though Rawls did not defend an egalitarian principle, the principles he does defend are close to egalitarian ones. The first principle is a principle of equal liberty and the second principle includes a principle of equal opportunity and a principle that takes equality of wealth and power to be the baseline from which departures must be justified. And Rawls is the main source for one of the principle contemporary arguments for equality. Rawls argues the differences in people's meritorious qualities should not serve as the basis for difference in the distribution of social goods. The reason for this is that differential meritorious qualities are primarily the result of factors for which the persons who have them are not responsible. To think that I can deserve greater rewards for qualities for which I cannot be held responsible is to think that I can deserve more good things than another merely as a result of my greater good luck, which seems quite arbitrary. Indeed, a large part of a person's ability to navigate successfully in the modern world is due to good family background and education other environmental factors available to some and not to others. These are factors for which the person in question is not responsible. Rawls taken this argument one step further when he says that the natural talents I am born with that make a great difference in how well my life goes are also features that I am not responsible for. I am born with them. The final step in this argument is to deny that even differential efforts ought to be the basis of differential rewards. Rawls argues that the amount of effort I am willing to put forth is itself in significant part a function of environmental factors and natural talent. So even differences in effort could often be attributed to differences in background conditions for which persons do not have responsibility.

Larry Temkin defending the principle of equality as a comparative principle of distribution takes this kind of Rawlsian argument as given. He tentatively endorses the formulation that one person's life should not go worse than another's life through no fault of his own. Only qualities or actions for which people can be held responsible are legitimate bases for differential rewards. Temkin generalizes the basic idea by saying that departures from equality must be fair and that no one ought to suffer unfair disadvantage relative to others. This is in order to capture the idea that it is not unfair that a criminal who has not been caught by the police suffers disadvantage through no fault of his own.

Temkin then discusses the question of what equality should be equality of. The most traditional account of equality has been of equality of wealth or income. But most have rejected this kind of metric of equality on the grounds that some people are much needier than others because of health problems or disabilities for which they are not responsible. The natural conclusion seems to be that each should have equality of well-being. But the worry here is that some persons may exploit a concern for equality of well-being and develop highly expensive tastes, which require the redistribution of resources to them. So this has led some to prefer equality of opportunity for well-being or equality of resources so that people have the opportunities to achieve the same level of well-being but they also have the opportunities to achieve the same level of well-being but they also have the opportunities to pursue more expensive projects without being able to impose the costs on others. Temkin's position is to endorse a pluralism with respect to these different kinds of equality, a pluralism that accords with a more general moral pluralism that he also endorses. One of the main, indeed perhaps the main objection to the principle of equality is what is called the leveling down objection. Some have thought that a commitment to a principle of equal distribution implies that one must always prefer an equal distribution of good to an unequal distribution even if everyone is better off in the unequal distribution. Not all egalitarians accept that the principle of equality has this implication. Temkin does accept it, though, he argues that it is not an objection, it only shows that the principle of equality is not the only principle of morality. He claims that our aversion to leveling down is not explained by a rejection of the principle of equality, it is explained by the fact that in addition to a principle of equality we also think it is morally important to advance well-being. And he says the principle that enjoins advancing well-being overrides the principle of equality in this instance.

John Kekes argues against the principle of equality. His principle objection is to the idea that persons are owned equal concern and respect, sometimes taken as a key ground of the principle of equality. On his account the idea that persons are moral equals is highly implausible. He complains first that no idea one has offered any justification for this principle of equal moral status and most seem to think that none is needed. This complaint is sharpened by the observation that we do not think of people as equals in many important circumstances. Parents do not treat their children as the equals of other children; citizen do not treat foreigners as the equals of fellow citizens; and criminals are not treated as equals with ordinary law-abiding citizens. Kekes considers a number of possible ways of blunting the force of this kind of objection and finds them all wanting. He also objects to egalitarianism on the ground that it seems to criticize what is a necessity for the social organization of the vast majority of developed societies. Moreover, he argues that the only genuine source of appeal for equality is not a concern for equality per se but a compassion for those who are badly off.

Kekes defends what he calls a reasonable alternative to egalitarianism. It starts from the observation that certain conventional rules are necessary for the maintenance and flourishing of societies. He enumerates three central kinds of rules those pertaining to family and special relationships, those pertaining to compliance with promises and contracts and those protecting the security of persons. These conventional rules are such that those who abide by them deserve praise and those who violate them deserve punishment. Furthermore these rules also subvert equality by creating special obligations towards family members and persons to whom one has promised things or made contractual relations with. And these inequalities are essential to the maintenance of society, so Kekes argues that egalitarianism subverts societies and is therefore dangerous.

The ideal of democracy was first explicitly articulated, as far as we know, in ancient Greek city-states around the sixth century before the Christian era. In these societies all free males were equal citizens, and women, slaves and laborers were excluded. Even this modest form of democracy was undermined in the ancient world by the development of large empires and by the work of philosophers who argued that power ought to be in the hands of the most virtuous or the most knowledge. The arguments of Plato and Aristotle were for the most part unanswered for over 2,000 years. This answer came, though, with the idea that those governed by the power of a sovereign ought to be the ultimate source of that sovereign's legitimacy. The idea of popular sovereignty was developed by a few medieval thinkers but the rise of democratic thinking must wait until John Locke, Jean-Jacques Rousseau and John Stuart Mill to reach its function.

One of the major issues to be dealt with in the theoretical development of democracy is how to accommodate the demands of equal citizenship with a large nation-state. Rousseau thought that equal citizenship was only possible in a small city-sate. James Madison agreed with him but thought that some kind of citizen participation was possible in large nation-states and indeed he argued that in some respects it could be more successful than city-state republics. John Stuart Mill is however the most important thinker to try to show the demands of active citizenship could be made compatible with and indeed enhanced by the large nation-state.

In contemporary theorizing there are two main sources of debate concerning the normative underpinnings of democracy. The first is whether democracy is merely instrumentally justified or whether there is some intrinsic merit to democratic ways of making decisions. Some have thought that if democracy and indeed any political institutions are justified they must be justified by reference to the consequences such political institutions have for the society in which they rule. Hobbes, for example, thought that political institutions were to be evaluated solely according to their propensity to establish social peace in the society and argued that monarchy was superior to democracy in this respect. But one could evaluate democracy or political institutions more generally in terms of the quality of legislation that is produced, the quality of the relationships that arise in such societies and the quality of character traits that are generated in such a society.

Richard Arneson and Russell Hardin both argue forcefully for an exclusively instrumentalist approach to the evaluation of democracy. Arneson's master argument is that whenever a person exercises power over others the legitimacy of that exercise of power must be evaluated in terms of the consequences it has for the rights and interests of the persons over whom power is exercised. Arneson also argues against the idea that democracy has intrinsic value by defending the idea that inequality of power is a necessary feature of any political society in which a division of labor is necessary and in which the input of any particular citizen is extremely small. This is important because the usual reasons given for thinking that democracy is instrinsically valuable is that it realizes a kind of equality among citizen in the making of collective decisions. Arneson also thinks that we do not require democratic decision-making in voluntary associations in societies and seem perfectly happy with the hierarchies we live with in corporations, universities and churches. He argues that if we really thought equality in the process of collective decision-making were required, we would require it in these associations.

Elizabeth Anderson argues, to the contrary, that democracy has intrinsic value. That is, it is important not only that we have our interests advanced in our political societies but that we advance them ourselves and don't have them handed on al platter to us. Our participation is essential. Anderson makes an analogy with shopping. She limits most of us don't merely want to have our interests in having consumer goods satisfied, we want to go about getting the things for ourselves, with all the deliberation and experimentation that this involves. Anderson's argument is not primarily based on equality but rather on a deep interest in participation. She places the democratic process narrowly conceived within the context of a larger democratic society in which people treat other as equals in ongoing processes of cooperation and experimentation.

This textbook does not provide anything like a comprehensive history of political philosophy, or even a partial history, refracted through the work of its master thinkers. It offer, instead, philosophical investigations of some of these thinkers ideas; with special attention paid to views of theirs that reveal the scope and limits of the philosophical tradition they did so much to forge. However, there is an obvious danger in treating our twenty four philosophers as if they were participants in a single, unfolding conversation. Philosophers, like everyone else, are creatures of their time and place. It can be misleading, therefore, to ignore the context within which philosophical positions arise. On the other hand, there is no doubt that our authors knew a great deal about the history of political philosophy, and that whatever else was of concern to them, they were intent on intervening into discussions shaped, in part, by the interventions of their predecessors. In at least some instances, therefore, it is not only instructive but also fair, from an historical point of view, to present the views of the later authors on our list as if they were indeed engaging in a dialogue with those who came before them. In doing so, however, care must be taken not to distort positions or arguments for the sake of some philosophical or pedagogical point.

In ordinary speech and also in some more formal contexts, the term philosophy designates a comprehensive set of beliefs about ourselves, our relations with others, our being in the world, and any of a number of other, less general, concerns. However, this usage invites misunderstanding, especially when dealing with philosophers. Let us say, then, that a philosophy is better viewed as the product of something one does, philosophizing, than as a collection of beliefs. To do philosophy is to try to make sense of aspects of human experience by identifying puzzlements, formulating them in ways that make their resolution tractable, and then, but only then, arriving at positions that address the questions philosophizing leads us to ask.

Puzzlements that give rise to activity of this sort are mainly conceptual in nature. When we already know what sort of discovery would lay out puzzlement to rest, there is seldom any need for philosophical activity. But there is philosophizing to be done when the conceptual resources available to us seem inadequate, when we are nuclear about what would count as an answer to questions we are not quite sure how to formulate. In these circumstances, new information will not help. What is required instead is more fundamental – a rethinking of our conceptual moorings, a reconceptualization of our concerns.

Some philosophical questions appear to have a timeless quality. The puzzlement they articulate seems so universal and the obstacles in the way of dissipating that puzzlement seem s intractable that they may always be with us. Introductory philosophy courses are typically organized around questions of this kind. They investigate problems - the existence of God, the relation between minds and bodies, the problem of free will, the nature of the good, and so on. Perhaps these questions really are timeless. But however this may be, in political philosophy, few, if any, problems even appear to have a timeless character. The concerns of political philosophers are too connected to transitory real world social and political phenomena to assume such as aspect. Sometimes, however, political philosophers ignore this fact. When they do, misunderstandings inevitably follow. In dealing with therefore, it is important not to lose sight of how their views are historically situated. To fail to do so is to risk misconstruing their positions and the rationales that support them.

The fact that the problems of political philosophy are ineluctably historical invites the construction of an historical narrative that is sufficiently rich to make sense of the emergence and subsequent career of these problems. But some attention must be paid to the rise and subsidence of the puzzlements to which the philosophical activity of philosophers responds. Real world political and social transformations have played a crucial role in shaping their work, and indeed in the making of modern political philosophy generally. That the rise of the nation state in the seventeenth and eighteenth centuries made problems pertaining to political authority and political obligation central to political philosophy, and that the consolidation of this historically particular kind of political entity in the nineteenth and twentieth centuries caused attention to. In the eighteenth and nineteenth centuries, as the state form of political organization came to seem less puzzling, questions pertaining to the rightful limits, if any, of political authority became primary concern. And finally, that the struggles of the working class and others for their rightful place in the social order throughout the nineteenth and twentieth centuries made the problem of justice a central philosophical concern.

In general, conceptual puzzlements of the sort that call for philosophical responses arise in consequence of changes that upset received ways of thinking – not, of course, in everyone's mind but in the minds of the comparatively few far-sighted thinkers who recognize the implications of these changes. Thus one would expect that there would not be much philosophical activity in societies in which events seldom, if ever, threaten traditional understandings, societies in which events seldom, if ever, threaten traditional understandings, societies in which conceptual moorings are effectively secure. Societies of this kind, traditional societies, have been the norm throughout human history. As expected, they have fostered very little philosophical activity. Members of traditional societies do, of course, have philosophies in the ordinary sense of the term. They have beliefs that help the make sense of lived experience. But traditional societies have few, if any philosophers in the sense in question here; few people who do philosophy.

The rise of the new sciences of nature in the seventeenth century posed great challenge to received ways of thinking. What is conventionally called modern philosophy, the philosophical movement that is conventionally said to have begun with Descartes and that continues to this day, was in part, induced by this new way of apprehending nature. It is not surprising, therefore, that questions about what we can know and about what there is, epistemological and metaphysical questions, have been the principal concerns of Western philosophy throughout its history. Typically, issues pertaining to society and politics have played a more peripheral role, even when they arise in response to puzzlements generated by social and political transformations of momentous importance. This is why epistemology and metaphysics, not social and political philosophy, constitute Western philosophy's core. In this respect, Hobbes's example as illustrative. Even as he philosophized about politics and society, he was concerned to make his views accord with the vision and practice of the new sciences of nature, as he understood them. Hobbes wanted a theory of the state that would be systematically integrated into a more general, materialist account of being, a metaphysical stance that the thought the new sciences of nature made rationally compelling.

But Hobbes and other seventeenth and eighteenth century political thinkers were also responding to far-reaching transformations in European social and political life. Evidently, technological development, what Marx would call the development of "productive forces", and the emerging capitalist organization of European society, had much to do with the great transformations that brought modern political philosophy into being. So too, as Rawls would insist, did the Protestant Reformation and the wars of religion that followed in its aftermath.

The first of these phenomena is the rise of the modern state. Political authority itself, the right to compel compliance through the use or threat of force, is undoubtedly a universal of human social life. Few, if any, human groupings have persisted for very long without authority relations of some kind, relations that are properly political in the sense that they are ultimately coercive in nature. What was new in early modern Europe was the concentration of political authority into a single institutional nexus. In feudal Europe, authority relations were scattered and diffuse. This was the norm nearly everywhere else as well. To be sure, on the premodern period, empires of various sorts existed. Typically, they were large, sometimes very large. Where empires existed, hierarchically organized bureaucracies maintained a semblance of control over subject populations, aided by military garrisons loyal to the central authorities. This form of political organization was more common in Asia than in Europe – though, following the Roman example, Europe too had empires from time to time, even if, like the Holy Roman Empire, they existed more often in theory than in practice. But it was only with the rise of the state from of political organization that the right to compel compliance became fixed in a single, centrally controlled mechanism of administration and coercion. Thus sovereignty in its distinctively modern sense, supreme authority over a given territory or population, emerged. Sovereignty was, at first, "incarnated" in individuals – indeed, in monarchs, as Hobbes supposed. After the English revolutions of the seventeenth century, parliamentary institutions assumed this role to some extent, at least in England; a fact registered in Locke's political philosophy. By Rousseau's time, a full fledged notion of popular sovereignty, of the people themselves as sovereign was widely intimated. Rousseau gave this idea theatrical expression. It would therefore be only slightly glib to say that the principal concern of each of these authors was to get sovereignty.

The second of the great transformations to which modern political philosophy was a response was more social than political. With the dissolution of feudal solidarities, the wearing away of the communal bonds that joined people together in premodern times - or, what comes to the same thing, with the emergence of economies organized mainly through exchange relations – the individual was born. Here too, Hobbes's example is telling. Hobbes's account of sovereignty takes for granted the atomization of social relations that resulted from feudal disintegration. His point of departure was what might be called the atomic individual. This use of atomic is, of course, metaphorical. But the description is apt. as remarked, a goal of Hobbes's was to develop a political philosophy joined systematically to a metaphysics that reflects the findings of modern science. Hobbes thought that the new sciences of nature implied a metaphysics relevantly similar to that of ancient Greek and Roman atomism. For the atomists, atoms, indivisible, units of matter, were both the fundamental constituents of material things and also radically independent entities. The second atomist tenet was as important to Hobbes as the first. Everything that is essential to a particular atom is, in the atomist's view, in the atom itself. What an atom essentially is therefore has nothing to do with its relations with other atoms; it could be alone in the universe and still be the atom that it is. Of course, atoms do not, in fact, stand alone; they exist in multitudes and enter into a host of relation with other atoms. But these relations are always external; they never affect what philosophers would call the atom's "identity conditions". This was how Hobbes viewed human societies. For him, individuals, individuals conceived apart from their relations with other individuals, provide the proper starting-point for thinking about social and political arrangements. These individuals ae the radically independent, fundamental constituents of political life. In this respect, as in many others, Hobbes dramatized stakly what each of our authors, with the partial exception of Marx, assumed. Modern political philosophy, following Hobbes's lead, accords paramount importance to individuals and their interests, often to the exclusion of everything else.

Thus a necessary condition for the political philosophies of thinkers, including even Marx's was the emergence of the individual. Needless to say, everyone everywhere has always recognized that human beings have distinct bodies and minds. But, until the modern period, this did not impinge on theories of social and political institutions in the way that it has after Hobbes. The fundamental constituents of premodern societies – families, clans, tribes, and, in European feudal societies, relations based on ecclesiastical status and on fealty and other forms of personal loyalty – no longer serve as a basis for thinking about political arrangements. Their place has been taken over by the individual. Thus it has become part of the common sense of our intellectual culture that, for virtually all normative and explanatory purposes, individuals precede society. This way of thinking would have seemed strange, if not incomprehensible, to people in other times and places. But it as a core component of the underlying conceptual framework, the deep structure, of modern political thought.

The idea that political institutions are justified to the degree that they accord with individuals interests is an assumption that all strains of modern political philosophy share. It plays a role in the thought of each of our authors – including Marx, who was more a critic of modern political philosophy than a practitioner of it, but whose reflections on politics nevertheless developed themes implicit in the work of several of the other philosophers discussed in this volume. Because it is so pervasive and because its implications are so far-reaching, it will be useful to think of this idea as a fixed point in modern political philosophy. The idea that what matters exclusively are individuals and their interests has become so deeply emtrenched that it is seldom expressly endorsed or even acknowledged. It functions instead as a guiding metaphor, a piece of imagery that different philosophers adapt in their own characteristic ways. The assumption is actually a composite of two distinct background positions – the individualism and the idea that political philosophy is, so to speak, interest-driven. In principle, there could be interest driven accounts of political arrangements that are not individualistic in Hobbes' sense.

At the present time, we seem to be witnessing the emergence of just such understandings, especially in multinational states without clear constitutional settlements. Thus it is sometimes said nowadays that , for some purposes, what matters fundamentally is the interest of particular communities within states rather than the interests of individuals within these communities. This thought is most commonly raised in debates around constitutional matters and is therefore typically expressed in terms of rights – as when it is claimed, for example, that some linguistic communities have language rights.

Claims of this sort are not reducible to claims about individual's rights. To say, for example, that the francophone community in Quebee has a right to have the French language protected within Quebee and throughout Canada is not the same thing as to say that individual Quebeckers or Canadians ought to have the right to speak French. The latter, individualistic right is assured so long as neither Quebec nor Canada prescribe the speaking of French. On the other hand, the former right for its implementation, requires the active intervention of some agency, the state presumably, to assure that French will be the dominant language in Quebec and an official language in the rest of Canada. Thus the francophone community in Quebec might be thought to have an interest that is irreducible to the interests of the individuals who comprise it. Similar claims have lately been made with respect to national self determination, and to such diffuse interests as peace, economic development, and environmental integrity. Even more radical positions have been advanced by some environmentalists, again in the form of rights claims. Thus it has been said that plants and animals, individually or in groups, and even landscapes and other parts of nature have rights. In these instances, too, rights talk usually articulates claims about interests. But the interests are not those of Hobbesian individuals. They are not even interests of human beings. Political philosophies that acknowledge contentions of these kinds and that accord them normative force are appropriately described as interest-driven. But they are not individualistic in the Hobbesian sense. It is conceivable and even likely that, in the future, these and other departures from the prevailing orthodoxy will become commonplace. Perhaps too, contemporary uses of the concept of rights and other devices of interest-driven normative political philosophies will someday seem more problematic than is now the case.

It has so far been emphasized how discontinuities is knowledge and in lived experience give rise to philosophical activity. But, in the political domain, there are important continuities too. The conviction that politics is a positive good for human beings and the competing view of politics as, at best, a necessary evil are both longstanding. They predate and also survive the epochal social transformations that gave rise to modern political philosophy. The idea that politics is an indispensable component of a fully human life and therefore a positive good was a conviction of Aristotle's and indeed of ancient

Greek political thought generally. It will be convenient to call it the classical view. The idea that politics is a necessary evil dates back at least to the rise of Christian political theory in the fourth century AD, when Christianity became an official religion of the Roman Empire. I will therefore call it the Christian View. Hobbes was a Christian in this sense and s was Locke, though to a less extreme degree. Rousseau was not. By the nineteenth century, the difference between these very different conceptions of political life had become blurred. Thus one finds elements of both classical and Christian political theory in Mill's work and also in Rawls's. Marx, however, like Rousseau, stands in the classical tradition. It is fair to say that, on the whole, modern political philosophy has been more Christian than classical.

On the Christina view, in its pre-Hobbesian form, human beings are so corrupted by Original Sin that they are incapable, by their own efforts, of doing good for themselves or for each other; incapable of achieving the earthly excellence classical writers extolled. Rather the good for human kind lies outside this world, in the world to come; and access to it depends entirely on unmerited grace. Were human beings left to their own devices, their lives would degenerate into a devastating "war of all against all". But this condition is contrary to God's will, as St. Augustine, the greatest, of the Christian political philosophers, maintained. It threatens to upset Providential design. God therefore established political institutions to save human beings form themselves. Fallen humanity cannot attain excellence through them. But, through their workings, God insures that order will prevail, thereby allowing providential design to unfold. To this end, repressive political institutions, mechanisms of coercion, are indispensable. Unless persons are made unfree to do what they want, the evil that lurks within would engulf human society, undoing any semblance of peace.

It is instructive to think of the modern theory of the state as a secular variant of this ancient teaching. Needless to say, none of our authors is committed literally to the doctrine of Original Sin. But insofar as they are Hobbesians, they do not think that human nature is such that its free expression would lead to a devastating war of all against all. This is a fate to be avoided if at all possible – not because it is contrary to what Providence requires, as in the original Christian conception, but because it is radically detrimental to individuals interests. The secular version of Christian political theory has no place for divinely established institutional arrangements. They themselves, not God, must connect a remedy.

Hobbes, Rousseau, and Locke emphatically agree that individuals interests are at risk when individuals are entirely free to act on their own desires. The problem for then, therefore, is to conceive a way in which individuals can make themselves unfree to do so, as their interests require. Rousseau put this thought to use ingeniously – in behalf of the classical conviction that political institutions are indispensable components of the good life for human beings. But Hobbes and, to a lesser degree, Locke and the liberals that followed them, including even Mill and Rawls, regard it as unfortunate, and therefore regard its "solution", the state as an imposition upon humankind, an evil – albeit a necessary evil, in the sense that is absence would be even worse than its presence is. For St. Augustine, political institutions were simultaneously a punishment for Original Sin, but also, because they prevent a war of all against all, a partial remedy for its consequences. Modern political philosophers, because they are Hobbesian statists, share this conviction, whether they realize it or not. Even Rousseau by endorsing a Hobbesian rationale for sovereignty, participates in the consensus view. Thus a Christian sensibility pervades modern political philosophy, extending even into the thinking of its most classical exponent.

Political philosophers from Plato to the post moderns have used terms such as justice, authority, law and government. Does this validate the view of philosopher Alfred North Whitehead that Western thought consists of a series of footnotes to Plato? In a sense there is some continuity in the enterprise of political philosophy, since it has often consisted o the effort to understand the role of humans within the cosmos. But has the use of common terms varied so much over time that they meant different things to different thinkers? That would confirm the statement attributed to Heraclitus, an ancient Greek philosopher, that all is in flux, as demonstrated by the fact that "It is not possible to step twice into the same river".

Given an awareness of the past, we see that both are in a sense correct: Continual change is a constant fact of life. Understanding and reflecting on the development, change, and renewal of key ideas-the inventions of political philosophers-keeps alive the possibilities for both greater political progress and human freedom in a world where Thrasymachus and his successors, in common with the old tribal and imperial regimes, would rather we focus on the here and now and stop try-questioning and even forget the inventors of ideas, thus yielding to the power of their tyranny as the only option for the future.

New political ideas can thus provide a perspective that tells us much about the meaning of life and the role politics and related thought play in helping establish a more meaningful life, as each of us understand it. In this way they not help us make sense of a changing world; they also give a sense of direction for identifying where change is called for. However, they cannot show us the actual future; that is something we have to build, day by day.

This book has provided a comparative framework for understanding and evaluating the ideas that comprise Western political philosophy. The ancient philosopher Plato raised some hard questions about justice and order and demonstrated how consideration of such questions can lead to standards for judging actual governments. Aristotle considered the role of balanced government, traditional community, and the hierarchical relationship between different kinds of communities in defining the public interest.

While most medieval thinkers focused on the religions community as the center of political thought and action, the early moderns deemphasized the role of community in favor of the individual. Machiavelli advocated individual liberty in a new setting called the nation-state, composed of virtuous citizens and officials, which would promote private freedom. Hobbes stressed the need of a clearly defined sovereign authority to minimize criminal violence and a political contract to define government's powers and limits. Locke understood the importance of "property", a civil society that required a social contract, and a responsible legislature.

The neomoderns argued that the early modern focus on the individual did not provide real freedom but actually corrupted individuals by removing them from their "natural" social context. Their inventions focused on a new form of community that would overcome poverty and alienation. Thus Rousseau stressed political equality and the need for a general will as the basis for a new, smaller political community, one in which wealth would play no part in governmental policy making. Marx pointed to the role of economics throughout history as the fundamental precondition for a community that would realize history's goal of economic justice for all. Finally, the late modern John Stuart Mill sought to reconcile the emphasis of early and neomodern thinkers by considering the social value as well as the personal significance of individual liberty: modernity and its ideological offshoots, liberalism, democracy, and socialism are symptomatic of slave morality. All endorse the position of the weak and deny the life affirming values of human nature the master morality once endorsed. Modern politics is the victory of the slaves over the masters, the rabble over the leaders, and the triumph of a set of dehumanizing values over human nature, resulting in the denial of freedom and the production o weak and resentful individuals.

The tranvaluation of values is the origin of what Nietzsche describes as the crisis of modernity. This is a crisis of nihilism, of denying the reality of human existence and wrongly seeking to provide a rational foundation for morality. According to Nietzsche ; the project of the Enlightenment and modernity has not been so modest: with s stiff seriousness that inspires laughter, all our philosophers demanded something far more exalted, presumptuous, and solemn for themselves as soon as they approached the study of morality: they wanted to supply a rational foundation for morality – and every philosopher so far has believed that he has provided such a foundation.

The enterprise of political philosophy over time emerges from a very human need: to reconcile the tension each of us feels in choosing between several perhaps incompatible politically relevant ideals. A central tension this book has focused on is the proper balance the roles of the individual and the collective. It would seem that, by nature, we need both to be fully human.

Each philosopher has inflected the tenor of political philosophy and induced a new sense of what can be included under its banner. I too hope to tilt the trajectory of scholarly attention, in my case toward contemporary public problems and events that plague, surprise, and inspire. I incline this way because, what is invaluable about the (historical, conceptual, poetic) art of thinking called political philosophy is that it aspires to help us live better – to identify, invent, and pursue paths through which a more vital, less violent, more sustainable collective life might unfold. This is a political theory sympathetic to John Dewey's belief that "philosophy recovers itself when it ceases to be a device for dealing with the problems of philosophers and becomes a method, cultivated by philosophers, for dealing with the problems of men". The hope here is that careful theoretical reflection upon the concepts, ideals, narratives, perceptions, arguments, comportments, spatial arrangements, and moods of public life can, however, indirectly and tentatively, but build a better world. Political philosophy must include rigorous argument, but at its best it also moves its readers and inspires creative ways of inhabiting politics.

Because everyday life mixes the political, the aesthetic, the economic, the sensuous, and the bioethical, I am also drawn toward scholarship that experiments with vocabularies, themes, and modes of inquiry from other disciplines. There is fine political-theoretical work being done, for example, in human geography, literature and rhetoric, anthropology, visual culture, and architectural studies, to name just a few.

Teachers of political philosophy know how philosophy can make a difference to the lives of students. In cultivating capacity for meta-level thinking, in rendering familiar political terms strange by placing them within wider cultural, philosophical, linguistic, scientific histories, theory opens doors of perception and political imagination. We welcome the essays that make this difference-to-life more explicit, the essays that practice that delicate art of rising above but then re-engaging the messy, dangerous, and exhilarating domain of politics.

1

Leo Strauss

Leo Strauss (1899-1973), was born and educated in Germany and emigrated to the United States in 1938. He taught political science and philosophy at the New School for Social Research, and later became Professor of Political philosophy at the University of Chicago and at Claremont Men's College. From 1969 to his death he was the Scott Buchanan Scholar in Residence at Saint John's in Annapolis, MD. Strauss' influential theories are still discussed today. His major publications include *The City and Man* (1964), *Natural Right and History* (1965), and *What Is Political Philosophy?* (1959), from which the following is taken. —Editor

What is Political Philosophy?

The meaning of political philosophy and its meaningful character is as evident today as it always has been since the time when political philosophy came to light in Athens. All political action aims at either preservation or change. When desiring to preserve, we wish to prevent a change to the worse; when desiring to change, we wish to bring about something better. All political action is then guided by some thought of better and worse. But thought of better or worse implies thought of the good. The awareness of the good which guides all our actions has the character of opinion: it is no longer questioned but, on reflection, it proves to be questionable. The very fact that we can question it directs us towards such a thought of the good as is no longer questionable - towards a thought which is no longer opinion but knowledge. All political action has then it itself a directedness towards knowledge of the good: of the good life, or of the good society. For the good society is the complete political good.

If this directedness becomes explicit, if men make it their explicit goal to acquire knowledge of the good life and of the good society, political philosophy emerges. By calling this pursuit political philosophy, we imply that it forms a part of a larger whole: of philosophy; or that political philosophy is a branch of philosophy. In the expression "political philosophy", "philosophy" indicates the manner of treatment: a treatment which both goes to the roots and is comprehensive; "political" indicates both the subject matter and the function: political philosophy deals with political matters in a manner that is meant to be relevant for political life; therefore its subject must be identical with the goal, the ultimate goal of political action. The theme of political philosophy is mankind's great objectives, freedom and government or empire - objectives which are capable of lifting all men beyond their poor selves. Political philosophy is that branch of philosophy which is closet to political life, to non-philosophic life, to human life.

Only in his *Politics* does Aristotle make use of oaths - the almost inevitable accompaniment of passionate speech.

Since political philosophy is a branch of philosophy, even the most provisional explanation of what political philosophy is cannot dispense with an explanation, however provisional, of what philosophy is. Philosophy, as quest for wisdom, is quest for universal knowledge, for knowledge of the whole. The quest would not be necessary if such knowledge were immediately available. The absence of knowledge of the whole does not mean, however, that men do not have thoughts about the whole: philosophy is necessarily preceded by opinions about the whole. It is, therefore, the attempt to replace opinions about the whole by knowledge of the whole. Instead of "the whole" the philosophers also say "all things": the whole is not a pure ether or an unrelieved darkness in which one cannot distinguish one part from the other, or in which one cannot discern anything. Quest for knowledge of "all things" means quest for knowledge of God, the world, and man - or rather quest for knowledge of the natures of all things: the natures in their totality are "the whole".

Philosophy is essentially not possession of the truth, but quest for the truth. The distinctive trait of the philosopher is that "he knows that he knows nothing", and that his insight into our ignorance concerning the most important things induces him to strive with all his power for knowledge. He would cease to be a philosopher by evading the questions concerning these things or by disregarding them because they cannot be answered. It may be that as regards the possible answers to these questions the pros and cons will always be in a more or less even balance, and therefore that philosophy will never go beyond the stage of discussion or disputation and will never reach the stage of decision. This would not make philosophy futile. For the clear grasp of a fundamental question requires understanding of the nature of the subject matter with which the question is concerned. Genuine knowledge of a fundamental question, thorough understanding of it, is better than blindness to it, or indifference to it, be that indifference or blindness accompanied by knowledge of the answers to a vast number of peripheral or ephemeral questions or not.

Of philosophy thus understood, political philosophy is a branch. Political philosophy will then be the attempt to replace opinion about the nature of political things by knowledge of the nature of political things. Political things are by their nature subject to approval and disapproval, to choice and. rejection, to praise and blame. It is of their essence not to be neutral but to raise a claim to men's obedience, allegiance, decision or judgment. One does not understood them as what they are, as political things, if one does not take seriously their explicit or implicit claim to be judged in terms of goodness or badness, of justice or injustice, i.e., if one does not measure them by some standard of goodness or justice. To judge soundly one must know the true standards. If political philosophy wishes to do justice to its subject matter, it must strive for genuine knowledge of these standards. Political philosophy is the attempt truly to know both the nature of political things and the right, or the good, political order.

Political philosophy ought to be distinguished from political thought in general. In our times, they are frequently identified. People have gone so far in debasing the name of philosophy as to speak of the philosophies of vulgar impostors. By political thought we understood the reflection on, or the exposition of, political ideas, and by a political idea we may understood any politically significant "phantasm, notion, species, or whatever it is about which the mind can be employed in thinking" concerning the political fundamentals. Hence, all political philosophy is political thought but not all political thought is political philosophy. Political thought is, as such, indifferent to the distinction between opinion and knowledge; but political philosophy is the conscious, coherent and relentless effort to replace opinions about the political fundamentals by knowledge regarding them. Political thought may not be more, and may not even intend to be more, than the expounding or the defense of a firmly held conviction or of an invigorating myth; but it is essential to political philosophy to be set in motion, and be kept in motion, by the disquieting awareness of the fundamental difference between conviction, or belief, and knowledge. A political thinker who is not a philosopher is primarily interested in, or attached to, the truth. Political thought which is not political philosophy find its adequate expression in laws and codes, in poems and stories, in tracts and public speeches inter alia; the proper form of presenting political philosophy is the treatise. Political thought is as old as the human race; the first man who uttered a word like "father" or an expression like "thou shalt not..." was the first political thinker; but political philosophy appeared at a knowable time in the recorded past.

By political theory, people frequently understand today comprehensive reflections on the political situation which lead up to the suggestion of a broad policy. Such reflections appeal in the last resort to principles accepted by public opinion or a considerable part of it; i.e., they dogmatically assume principles which can wel! be questioned. Works of political theory in this sense would be Pinsker's *Automancipation* and Herzl's *Judenstaat*. Pinsker's Automancipation carries as its motto the words: "If I am not for myself, who will be for me? And if not now, when?" it omits the words: "And if I am only for myself, what am I?" Pinsker's silent rejection of the thought expressed in the omitted words is a crucial premise of the argument developed in his tract. Pinsker does not justify this rejection. For a justification, one would have to turn to the 3rd and the 16th chapters of Spinoza's *Tractus thelogicopoliticus, to a work of a political philosopher.*

We are compelled to distinguish political philosophy from political theology. By political theology we understand political teachings which are based on divine revelation. Political philosophy is limited to what is accessible to the unassisted human mind. As regards social philosophy, it has the same subject matter as political philosophy, but it regards it form a different points of view. Political philosophy rests on the premise that the political association -one's country or one's nation - is the most comprehensive or the most authoritative association, whereas social philosophy conceives of the political association as a part of a larger whole which it designates by the term "society".

Finally, we must discuss the relation of political philosophy to political science. "Political science" is an ambiguous term: it designates such investigations of political things as are guided by the model of natural science, and it designates the work which is being done by the members of political science departments. As regards the former, or what we may call "scientific" political science, it conceives of itself as the way towards genuine knowledge of political things. Just as genuine knowledge of natural things began when people turned from sterile and vain speculation to empirical and experimental study, the genuine knowledge of political things will begin when political philosophy will have given way completely to the scientific study of politics. Just as natural science stands on its own feet, and at most supplies unintentionally materials for the speculations of natural philosophers, political science stands on its own feet, and at most supplies unintentionally materials for the speculations of political of political philosophers. Considering the contrast between the solidity of the one pursuit and the pitiful pretentiousness characteristic of the other, it is however more reasonable to dismiss the vague and inane speculations of political philosophy altogether than to go on paying lip service to a wholly discredited and decrepit tradition. The sciences, both natural and political, are frankly non-philosophic. They need philosophy of a kind: methodology or logic. But these philosophic disciplines have obviously nothing in common with political philosophy. "Scientific" political science is in fact incompatible with political philosophy.

All political knowledge is surrounded by political opinion and interspersed with it. By political opinion we understand here opinion as distinguished from knowledge of political things: errors, guesses, beliefs, prejudices, forecasts, and so on. It is of the essence of political life to be guided by a mixture of political knowledge and political opinion. Hence, all political life is accompanied by more or less coherent and more or less strenuous efforts to replace political opinion by political knowledge. Even governments which lay claim to more than human knowledge are known to employ spies.

The character of political knowledge and of the demands made on it has been profoundly affected by a fairly recent change in the character of society. In former epochs, intelligent men could acquire the political knowledge, the political understanding they needed, by listening to wise old men or, which is the same thing, by reading good historians, as well as by looking around and by devoting themselves to public affairs. These ways of acquiring political knowledge are no longer sufficient because we live in "dynamic mass societies", i.e., in societies which are characterized by both immense complexity and rapid than in former times. Under these conditions it becomes necessary that a number of men should devote themselves entirely to the task of collecting and digesting knowledge of political things. It is this activity which today is frequently called political science. It does not emerge if it has not been realized among other things that even such political matters as have no bearing on the situation of the day deserve to be studied, and that their study must be carried on with the greatest possible care: a specific care which is designed to counteract the specific fallacies to which our judgment on political things is exposed. Furthermore, the men we speak of invest much toil in giving political knowledge the form of teachings which can be transmitted in classrooms. Moreover, while even the most unscrupulous politician must constantly try to replace in his own mind political opinion by political knowledge in order to be successful, the scholarly student of political things will go beyond this by trying to state the results of his investigations in public without any concealment and without partisanship: he will act the part of the enlightened and patriotic citizen who has no axe of his own to grind. Or, differently expressed, the scholarly quest for political knowledge is essentially animated by a moral impulse, the love of truth. But however one may conceive of the difference between the scholarly and the non-scholarly quest for political knowledge, and however important these differences may be, the scholarly and the non-scholarly quest for political knowledge are identical in the decisive respect: their center of reference is the given political situation, and even in most cases the given political situation in the individual's own country. It is true that a botanist in Israel pays special attention to the flora of Canada. But this difference, which is not more than the outcome of a convenient and even indispensable division of labor, has an entirely different character than the only apparently similar difference between the preoccupation of the Israeli political scientist and the Canadian political scientist. It is only when the Here and Now ceases to be the center of reference that a philosophic or scientific approach to politics can emerge.

All knowledge of political things implies assumptions concerning the nature of political things; i.e., assumptions which concern not merely the given political situation, but political life or human life as such. One cannot know anything about a war going on at a given time without having some notion, however dim and hazy, of war as such and its place within human life as such. One cannot see a policeman as a policeman without having made as assumption about law and government as such. The assumptions concerning the nature of political things, which are implied in all knowledge of political things, have the character of opinions. It is only when these assumptions are made the theme of critical and coherent analysis that a philosophic or scientific approach to politics emerges.

The cognitive status of political knowledge is not different from that of the knowledge possessed by the shepherd, the husband, the general, or the cook. Yet the pursuits of these types of man do not give rise to a pastoral, martial, military, or culinary philosophy because their ultimate goals are sufficiently clear and unambiguous. The ultimate political goal, on the other hand, urgently calls for coherent reflection. The goal of the general is victory, whereas the goal of the statesman is the common good. What victory means is not essentially controversial, but the meaning of the common good is essentially controversial. The ambiguity of the political goal is due to its comprehensive character. Thus the temptation arises to deny, or to evade, the comprehensive character of politics and to treat politics as one compartment among many. But this temptation must be resisted if it is necessary to face our situation as human beings, i.e., the whole situation...

II. The Classical Solution

When we describe the political philosophy of Plato and of Aristotle as classical political philosophy, we imply that it is the classic form of political philosophy. The classic was once said to be characterized by noble simplicity and quiet grandeur. This suggestion guides us in the right direction. It is an attempt to articulate what was formerly also called the "natural" character of classical thought. "Natural" is here understood in contradistinction to what is merely human, all too human. A human being is said to be natural if he is guided by nature rather than by convention, or by inherited opinion, or by tradition, to say nothing of mere whims. Classical political philosophy is non-traditional, because it belongs to the fertile moment when all political traditions were shaken, and there was not yet in existence a tradition of political philosophy. In all later epochs, the philosophers study of political things was mediated by a tradition of political philosophy which acted like a screen between the philosopher and political things, regardless of whether the individual philosopher cherished or rejected that tradition. From this it follows that the classical philosophers see the political things with a freshness and directions which have never been equaled. They look at political things in the perspective of the enlightened citizen or statesman. They see things clearly which the enlightened citizens or statesmen do not see clearly, or do not see at all. But this has no other reason but the fact that they look further afield in the same direction as the enlightened citizens or statesman. They do not look at political things from outside, as spectators of political life. They speak the language of the citizens or statesman: they hardly use a single term which is not familiar to the market place. Hence their political philosophy is comprehensive; it is both political theory and political skill; it is an open minded to the legal and institutional aspects of political life as it is to that which transcends the legal and institutional; it is equally free from the narrowness of the lawyer, the brutality of the technician, the vagaries of the visionary, and the baseness of the opportunist. It reproduces, and raises to its perfection, the magnanimous flexibility of the true statesman, who crushes the insolent and spares the vanquished. It is free from all fanaticism because it knows that evil cannot be eradicated and therefore that one's expectations from politics must be moderate. The spirit which animates it may be described as serenity or sublime sobriety.

Compared with classical political philosophy, all later political thought, whatever else its merits may be, and in particular modern political thought, has a derivative character. This means that in later times there has occurred an estrangement from the simple and primary issues,. This has given to political philosophy the character of "abstractness", and has therefore engendered the view that the philosophic movement must be a movement, not form opinion to knowledge, not from the here and now to what is always or eternal, but from the abstract towards the concrete. It was thought that by virtue of this movement towards the concrete, recent philosophy has overcome the limitations not only of modern political philosophy, but of classical political philosophy as well. It was overlooked, however, that this change of orientation perpetuated the original defect of modern philosophy because it accepted abstractions as its staring point, and that the concrete at which one eventually arrived was not at all the truly concrete, but still an abstraction....

(From *What is Political Philosophy*? by Leo Strauss, The Free Press, 1959)

2

Plato

In the history of Western philosophy Socrates' most famous student, Plato (BC. 428-347BC), elevated the human intellect by a prodigious leap. Plato was interested in practically every subject, and each came to our mind intelligently on philosophical topics and problems. Platonic metaphysics formed the model for Christian theology for fifteen centuries. This model was surpassed only when translations of Aristotle's works were rediscovered by European philosophers and theologians in the thirteenth century A.D. After this rediscovery, Aristotle's metaphysics came to predominate in Christian thinking, although Christianity is still Platonic in many, many ways.

Plato was the nickname of an Athenian whose true name was Aristocles. The nickname, which means "broad shoulders", struck, and so did this man's philosophy. Few individuals, if any, have had more influence on Western thought than Plato. Plato initially studied with Cratylus, who was a follower of Heraclitus, and then Socrates. He was also influenced by the Pythagoreans, from whom he may have derived his great respect for mathematics. Plato thought that the study of mathematics was a necessary introduction to philosophy, and it is said that he expelled from his Academy students who had difficulty with mathematical concepts. Plato founded his Academy in 387, and it was the first multisubject, multiteacher institution of higher learning in Western civilization. The Academy survived for nine centuries, until the emperor Justinian closed it to protect Christian truth.

Plato's dialogues are divided into three groups. According to recent respected scholarship, the earliest include most importantly the *Apology*, which depicts and philosophically examines Socrates' trial and execution; the Meno, which is concerned with whether virtue can be taught; the *Gorgias*, which concerns the nature of right and wrong; and the first book of the Republic. The dialogues from the middle period include the remaining books of the *Republic, Phaedo, Symposium, Phaedrus, Cratylus, Parmenides, and Theaetetus.* In the most famous of these, the *Republic*, Plato explains and interrelates his conceptions of justice, the ideal state, and the Theory of Forms. Plato's later dialogues include most notably the *Timaeus*, which is Plato's account of the creation of the universe; the *Sophist*, which examines the nature of nonbeing; and the *Laws*, which is concerned with what laws a good constitution should contain. The *Laws* is Plato's longest dialogue and the only dialogue in which Socrates is not present.

Plato's metaphysics is known as the Theory of Forms, and it is discussed in several of the two dozen compositions we have referred to as Plato's dialogues. According to Plato's Theory of Forms, what is truly real is not the objects we encounter in sensory experience but, rather, Forms, and these can only be grasped intellectually. Therefore, once you know what Plato's Forms are, you will understand the Theory of Forms and the essentials of Platonic metaphysics. Unfortunately, it is not safe to assume Plato had exactly the same thing in mind throughout his life when he spoke of the Forms. Nevertheless, Plato's concept is pretty clear and can be illustrated with an example or two.

The Greeks were excellent geometers, which is not surprising, because they invented the subject as a systematic science. Now, when a Greek geometer demonstrated some property of, say, circularity, he was not demonstrating the property of something that could actually be found in the physical world. After all, you do not find circularity in the physical world: what you find are things – various round objects – that approach perfect circularity but are not perfectly circular. Even if you are drawing circles with an excellent compass and are paying close attention to what you are drawing, your "circle" is not perfectly circular. Thus, when a geometer discovered a property of circularity, for example, he was discovering something about an ideal thing. Circularity does not exist in the physical world. Circularity, then, is an example of a Form.

Here is another example. Consider two beautiful objects: a beautiful statue and a beautiful house. These are two very different objects' but they have something in common – they both qualify as beautiful. Beauty is another example of a Form. Notice that beauty, like circularity, is not something you encounter directly in the physical world. What you encounter in the physical world is always some object or other, a house or a statue or whatever, which may or may not be beautiful. But beauty itself is not something you see rather, you see objects that to varying degrees possess beauty or, as Plato said, "participate" in the Form beauty. Beauty, like circularity, is an ideal thing, not a concrete thing.

You may be tempted to suppose that the Forms are just ideas or concepts in someone's mind. But this might be a mistake. Before any people were around, there were circular things, logs, and round stones and so on – that is, things that came close in varying degrees to being perfectly circular. If there were circular things when there were no people around, it would seem that circularity is not just an idea in people's heads. It may be more difficult to suppose that there were beautiful things before there were people to think of things of beautiful, but this difficulty might only be due to assuming that "beauty is in the eyes of the beholder". Whether that assumption truly is justified is actually an unsettled question. Sometimes Plato's Forms are referred to as *Ideas*, and the Theory of Forms is also said to be the Theory of Ideas. But *Idea* is misleading because, as you can see, Plato's Forms are not the sort of ideas that exist in people. We will stick with the word Forms.

Forms have certain important and unusual features. We will begin by asking, How old is circularity? Immediately on hearing the question, you will realize that circularity has not any age. Circular things, have some age or other. But circularity itself has no age. The same thing is true of beauty, the Form. So we can see that the Forms are ageless, that is, eternal. They are also unchanging. A beautiful house may change due to alternations or aging, but that couldn't happen to beauty itself. Finally, the forms are unmoving *and* indivisible. Indeed, what sense would it make even to suppose that they might move or be physically divided?

When you think of these various characteristics of Forms and remember as well that Plato equated the Forms with true reality, you may begin to see why we stated that Plato's metaphysics formed the model for Christian theology. You may also be reminded, we hope, of what Parmenides said about true being (i.e.., that it is eternal, unmoving, unchanging, and indivisible). Of course, you should also remember that for Parmenides there is only one being, but for Plato there are many Forms.

Many people scold philosophers, mathematicians, and other thinkers for being concerned with abstractions and concepts. "That's all very interesting", they say about some philosophical or mathematical theory, "but I'm more interested in the real world". By "real world" they mean the world you experience with your senses. On the face of it, at least, Plato makes a convincing case that world is not the real world at all.

Another reason-knowledge is not just sense perception-is that you can retain knowledge even after you are no longer sensing a thing.

Finally, and even more important, in Plato's view true knowledge is knowledge of what is. Because the objects of sense perception are always changing (remember Heraclitus), sense perception and knowledge cannot be one and the same. True knowledge, Plato was certain, must be concerned with what is truly real. This means, of course, that the objects of true knowledge are the Forms because the objects of sense perception are real only to the extent that they "participate" in the Forms.

This, then, is essentially Plato's theory of knowledge, and he elaborated on it in the *Republic* – especially in a passage known as the Theory of the Divided Line and in the Myth of the Cave.

The Theory of the Divided Line is used by Plato to contrast knowledge, on one hand, with mere belief or opinion, on the other. Plato illustrates his theory by dividing a line in two parts. The upper part of the line stands for knowledge, and the lower part stands for belief or opinion. Knowledge is concerned with absolutes – absolute beauty, absolute good, and so forth – in short, with the Forms. And this is not. If your "knowledge" of beauty or goodness or circularity or the like is limited to this or that beautiful car or good deed or round plate, then you really do not have knowledge of absolute beauty, goodness, or circularity. At the best you have a bunch of opinions that, as they are as likely as not to be riddled with error, come closer to ignorance than to true knowledge.

In Plato's Divided Line, the upper part of the line respresents knowledge and the lower part represents opinion. Plato also subdivided the knowledge section of the line into two parts and did the same for the opinion section. What is essential to remember is that, according to Plato, the highest form of knowledge is that obtained through the use of reason because perfect beauty or absolute goodness or the ideal triangle cannot be perceived. Knowledge is true ultimately because it is knowledge of what is. Plato believed that is not enough to know the truth; rather, a person must also become that truth. This is where Plato's epistemology, or theory of truth, becomes ontology or theory of being. To know, for Plato, is to be. The more you know, the more you are and the better you are.

Plato began with the Myth of the Cave, which shows how and why human beings are in the dark about the truth of things. And this ignorance is almost universal – even Socrates admits that he has no knowledge. What allow humans eventually to come into the light of day regarding the truth of things is the Forms. Each individual has in his or her immortal soul a perfect set of Forms that can be remembered, and only this constitutes true knowledge.

In the *Republic*, Plato uses a vivid allegory to explain his two-realm philosophy. He invites us to imagine a cave in which some prisoners are bound so that they can look only at the wall in front of them. Behind them is a fire whose light casts shadows of various objects on the wall in front of the prisoners. Because the prisoners cannot see the objects themselves, they regard the shadows they see as the true reality. One of the prisoners eventually escapes from the cave and, in the light of the sun, sees real objects for the first time, becoming aware of the big difference between them and the shadow images he had always taken for reality.

The cave, obviously, represents the world we see and experience with our senses, and the world of sunlight represents the realm of Forms. The prisoners represent ordinary people, who, in taking the sensible world to be the real world, are condemned to darkness, error, ignorance, and illusion. The escaped prisoner represents the philosopher, who has seen light, truth, beauty, knowledge, and true reality. Of course, if the philosopher returns to the cave to tell the prisoners how things really are, they will think he is mad. This difficulty is sometimes faced by those who have seen the truth and decide to tell others about it.

Plato was aware that there is a sense in which the objects we see and touch are real. Even appearances are real appearances. But Plato's position is that the objects we see and touch have a lesser reality because they can only approximate their Form and thus are always to some extent flawed. Any particular beautiful thing will always be deficient in beauty compared with the Form beauty. And, as any particular beautiful thing owes whatever degree of beauty it has to the Form beauty, the Form is the source of what limited reality as a beautiful thing the thing has.

Thus, Plato introduced into Western thought a two-realms concept. On one hand, there is the realm of particular, changing, sense-perceptible or sensible things. This is realm likened to a cave. It is the realm of flawed and lesser entities. Consequently, it is also, for those who concern themselves with sensible things, a source of error, illusion, and ignorance. On the other hand, there is the realm of Forms – eternal, fixed, and perfect – the source of all reality and of all true knowledge. This Platonic dualism was incorporated into Christianity and transmitted through the ages to our thought today, where it lingers still and affects our views on virtually every subject.

Plato believed in two radically separate spheres: the realm of shadows or imperfect, changing beings and the realm of perfect, eternal, unchanging Forms. The problem is, how do we get out of the cave to the perfect world of Forms? In his dialogue *The Symposium,* Plato postulated the notion of love as the way in which a person can go from the state of imperfection and ignorance to the state of perfection and true knowledge. He defined love as a longing for and a striving to attain the object of longing. Love is that which seeks to possess the beautiful and to recreate in beauty. Human beings love to love: they truly come alive only in seeking a beloved, whether that beloved is another human being or an idea or health or money. For Plato, love is meant to be the force that brings all things together and makes them beautiful. It is the way by which all beings, but especially human beings, can ascend to higher stages of self-realization and perfection. Plato's love begins as an experience of lacking something. Love provokes both thought and effort in the pursuit of what is lacking. The deeper the thought, the greater the love.

Plato initially mirrored the Athenian view that the deepest human relationships were between two men, usually an older man and a younger one. Women were not only considered the weaker sex but were also thought to be superficial, excitable, and superstitious. Marriage had as its purpose the reproduction and raising of children, and physical lovemaking was considered a low form of love. Plato's love does not exclude physical beauty, but "Platonic love" begins at a higher stage of development, namely, with the sharing of beautiful thoughts with a beautiful person. Plato believed that this kind of love should be experienced while a person is young. In this intellectual or spiritual love that begins the ascent of love, which may eventually lead to the permanent possession of absolute beauty or goodness.

The love for just one other human, even if that person is as noble as a Socrates, remains a limited form of intellectual eros. It is but the first step in the ascent of philosophical love to absolute beauty. To reach the higher stages of love means entering what are called the mysteries. Plato has Socrates recount a theory of love given to him by a woman named Diotima. Socrates implies that few may be able to follow this line of reasoning, which he himself has difficulty of comprehending, but Diotima's theory of love was this: The higher forms of love express the will to immorality and the will to produce immortal "children", not merely physical children. All love seeks to possess beauty and to reproduce in beauty, but the creation of immoral children (like the writings of Homer) can grant the author immortality. A first step beyond merely loving a beautiful person and begetting beautiful thoughts lies in the realization that beauty in all things is one and the same and that all love is one. A further step involves the recognition of the superiority of intellectual or spiritual beauty over physical beauty. Then love must expand beyond preoccupations with a particular person to an appreciation of the beauty of moral practices and laws. An individual is part of larger social groupings, each with accompanying obligations. Love here takes the form of appreciating and aptly participating in organizations such as a city-state like Athens. Yet no matter how wide a person's involvement is in the moral and social spheres of love, this still does not represent the highest and most inclusive love. A person begins to glimpse the all-inclusive, all-uniting kind of love by first seeing the beauty of knowledge as a whole or at least many of the different forms of knowledge. This leads to an appreciation and love of the whole realm of beauty or the integrated beauty of everything there is. In the happiness of viewing such vast beauty, a person will have beautiful thoughts and be able to speak beautiful words. Eventually such a person may be able to make the final step to the beauty and truth, which is beyond all mortal things.

The last and highest stage of love lies in the discovery of the ultimate mystery, absolute beauty itself. The beauty of this being contains no change of any kind. It was never born and will never die, nor will it increase or decrease. It is not good in one part and bad in another. It is perfect and one with itself forever. All imperfect things participate in this Beauty, thereby receiving a modicum of fulfillment and self-realization. Plato indicated that once a person has seen Absolute Beauty, then such a fortunate person would no longer be dazzled by mere physical beauty or the other rubbish of mortality. This, for human beings, is the ultimate kind of immortality, he thought.

Thus, love for Plato is the ultimate way of knowing and realizing truth. For mortals, love is a process of seeking higher stages which beget immortal children. The greater the love, the more it will contain an intellectual component. The lifelong longing and pursuit seeks ever higher stages of love so that it can eventually lead to the possession of absolute beauty. This is the pursuit that motivates the highest sorts of human beings and that transforms entire civilizations. To love the highest is to be become the best.

According to Plato's *Republic*, the human soul has three different elements, one consisting of raw appetites, another consisting of drives such as anger and ambition, and a third consisting of thought or intellect. In the virtuous or just person, each of these three elements fulfills its own unique function and does so under the governance of reason. Likewise, according to Plato, in the ideal or just state there are also three elements, each of which fulfills its unique function and does so in accordance with the dictates of reason. The lowest element in the soul – the appetitive element – corresponds in the well-ordered state to the class of craftsmen. The soul's drive element corresponds in the state to the class of police-soldiers, who are auxiliaries to the intellectual, rational element of the soul.

The governing class, according to Plato, comprises a select few highly educated and profoundly rational individuals, including women so qualified. An individual becomes a member of a class by birth, but he or she will move to a higher or lower class according to aptitude.

In the healthy state, said Plato, as in the well-ordered soul, the rational element is in control. Thus, for Plato, the ideal state is a class-structured aristocracy ruled by philosopher-kings. Unlike the craftsmen, the ruling elite and their auxiliaries, who jointly are the guardians of society, have neither private property nor even private families: property, wives and children are all possessions held in common. Reproduction among the guardians is arranged always to improve the bloodline of their posterity in intelligence, courage, and other qualities apt for leadership. The guardians not only must be trained appropriately for soldiering but also must be given a rigorous intellectual education that, for the few whose unique abilities allow it, prepares them for advanced work in mathematics and dialectic. These few, at age fifty and after many years of public service, advance to membership in the ruling aristocracy and to leadership of the state. Such is Plato's vision of the ideal political structure.

It is important to be aware that from Plato's perspective, the state, like the person, is a living organism whose well-being must be sought by its subjects. Although he assumed that the healthy state is best for the individuals in it, Plato also believed that the health or well-being requires the proper functioning and coordination of the elements of the soul under the overarching rule of reason, the state's health or wealth-being lies in the proper functioning and coordination of its elements under the rule of the reasoning elite. The ideal state, according to Plato, is well ordered in this way, and its being well ordered in this way is something that is intrinsically desirable.

In Book VIII of the *Republic*, Plato identified five forms of government. The preferred form, of course, is an aristocracy, governed by rational philosopher-kings. According to Plato, however, even if this ideal state could be achieved, it would in time degenerate into a timocracy, in which the ruling class is motivated by love of honor rather than by love for the common good. A timocracy in turn gives way to a plutocracy, which is ruled by men who primarily desire riches. Under a plutocracy, society becomes divided between two classes, the rich and the poor, Plato thought. Nevertheless, this form of government, Plato said, is preferable to the next degeneration, democracy, which results because a society cannot hold wealth in honor and at the same time establish self-control in its citizens. With Plato's democracy, people's impulses are unrestrained, and the result is lack of order and direction. Mobocracy is what we would call Plato's "democracy" today. Tyranny, the last form of government in Plato's classification, results when the democratic mob submits itself to a strongman, each person selfishly figuring to gain from the tyrant's rule and believing that the tyrant will end democracy's evil. In fact, Plato thought, the tyrant, will himself become a slave to his wretched craving for power and self-indulgence. Plato was not always an optimist!

—Editor

Timarchy

'Like this. –It will be difficult to bring about any change for the worse in a state so constituted; but since all created things must decay, even a social order of this kind cannot last for all time, but will decline. And its dissolution will be as follows. Not only for plants that grow in the earth, but for animals that live on it, there I are seasons of fertility and infertility of both mind and body, seasons which come when their periodic motions come full circle, a period of longer duration for the long-lived, shorter for the shim-lived. And though the Rulers you have trained for your city are wise, reason and observation will not always enable them to hit on the right and wrong times for breeding; some time they will miss them and then children will be begotten amiss.

'Once internal strife has started, the two elements pull in,' different directions; the iron and bronze towards private profit and property in land and houses and gold and silver, the other two, the silver and gold, having true riches in their own hearts, towards excellence and the traditional order of things. The violence of their' opposition is resolved in a compromise under which they distribute land and houses to private ownership, while the subjects whom they once guarded as Freemen and friends, and to whom they owed their maintenance, arc reduced to the status of serfs and menials, and they devote themselves to war and holding the population in subjection.'

'Its own peculiar characteristics, on the other hand, will be, for example, a fear of admitting intelligent people to office, because intelligence is no longer combined with simplicity and sincerity; it will prefer the simpler, hearty types, who prefer war to peace. It will admire the tricks and stratagems which are needed in war, which will be its constant occupation.'

'A feature it will share with oligarchy,' I went on, 'will be its love of money. There will be a fierce and secret passion for gold and silver, now that there are private strongrooms to hide it in, and now that there are the four walls of their private houses–expensive nests in which they can spend lavishly on their wives and anything else they choose.'

'They will also be mean about money, because though they love it they may not acquire it openly, but they will be ready enough to spend other people's money for their own satisfaction. They will enjoy their pleasures in secret, avoiding the law like truant children; the reason being that they have been educated by force rather than persuasion, owing to neglect of the true principles of a rational philosophic education and an overvaluation of physical it the expense of intellectual training.'

He must be rather more self-willed, and rattier less well-educated though not without an interest in the arts; ready to listen, but quite incapable of expressing himself. He will be harsh L-to his slaves, because his imperfect education has left him without a proper sense of his superiority to them; he will be polite to his fellow-freemen and obey the authorities readily. He will be ambitious to hold office himself, regarding as qualifications for it not the ability to speak or anything like that, but military achievements and soldierly qualities, and he'll be fond of exercise and hunting.'

'When he's young,' I continued, 'he will despise money, but the older he grows the keener he will get about it. His nature has a touch of avarice and there are flaws in his character because he has lost his best safeguard.'

'And this is roughly how he's produced. Suppose a young man, whose father is a good man but lives in a badly run state and avoids office and honours and law-suits and all the bother attached them, being quite content with a back seat to save himself trouble.'

'When he hears his mother complaining that her husband isn't one of the bosses, and that she is slighted by other women because of it; she sees that her husband is not very keen on making money, but avoids the wranglings and bickerings of politics and the law, which he treats very lightly, and keeps his own counsel, while he doesn't take her unduly seriously, though he does not neglect her. All this annoys her and she says that the boy's father isn't a real man and is far too easy-going, and drones on with ail the usual complaints women make in the circumstances.'

'And, as you know,' I went on, 'servants who seem quite loyal will sometimes repeat the same sort of thing to the children behind their master's back. And if they see the father failing to prosecute someone who owes him money or has done him some wrong, they tell the son that when he grows up he must have his rights and be more of a man than his father. The boy hears the same sort of lining outside and sees how those who mind their own business publicly called silly and not thought much of, while those who 'don't get all the honour and glory. He hears and sees all this, and on the other hand listens to what his father has to say, and sees his way of life from close to and contrasts it with other people's; as a result he is torn in two directions, his father's influence fostering the growth of his rational nature, and that of the others his desire and his ambition.' And since he's not really at heart a bad chap, 'but has merely got into bad company, he takes a middle course between the two, and resigns control of himself to the middle element and its competitive spirit, and so becomes an arrogant and ambitious man.'

Oligarchy

A society in which wealth is the criterion of merit and the wealthy are in control. The appearance of a 'drone' class of criminals and malcontents.

'Well, I suppose that the next kind of society is an oligarchy,'

'And what sort of regime do you mean by an oligarchy?'

'A society where it is wealth that counts,' I said, 'and in which political power is in the hands of the rich and the poor have no share of it.'

'I understand.'

'We must first describe how oligarchy originates from timocracy–though heaven knows,' I added, 'it's obvious enough even to a blind man.'

'The accumulation of wealth in private hands is what destroys timarchy. The men find ways to become extravagant, and for this reason pervert the law and disobey it, and the women follow their example.'

'And mutual observation and jealousy stamps the same character on the ruling class as a whole.'

'The further they go in the process of accumulating wealth, the more they value it and the less they value goodness. For aren't wealth and goodness related like two objects in a balance, so that when one rises the other must fall?'

'So the higher the prestige of wealth and the wealthy, the lower that of goodness and good men will be.'

'And so there is a transition from the ambitious, competitive type of man to the money-loving businessman, honour and admiration and office are reserved for the rich, and the poor arc despised.'

'At this stage they introduce legislation, the characteristic mark an oligarchy, which prescribes a certain minimum amount of property greater or less according to the narrowness of the oligarchy as a necessary qualification for office, a measure they force through by armed violence, if they have not already got their way by terrorism. Do you agree?'

'That it inevitably splits society into two factions, the rich and the poor, who live in the same place and are always plotting against each other.'

'Its probable inability to wage war is another discreditable Mature. The oligarchs can't do this because they must either arm the people, whom they fear worse than the enemy, or, if they don't, have the thinness of their ranks' shown up by the stress of battle; and at the same time they arc too grasping to want to pay the expenses of a war.'

'Then we come to the worst defect of all, which makes its first appearance in this form of society.'

That a man can sell all he has to another and live on as a member of society without any real function; he's neither businessman nor craftsman nor cavalryman nor infantryman, but merely one of the so-called indigent poor.'

'It's the first form of society in which this happens,' he agreed.

And there is certainly nothing to prevent it in oligarchies; otherwise you would not get the sharp division between the very rich and the very poor.'

The Oligarchic Character

The timarchic man has a son who at first admires his father and follows in his footsteps; then he sees him suddenly wrecked in some political disaster–he has, perhaps, spent all his substance and energy in some military command or other position of authority, to be brought into court by informers and put to death, or exiled, or outlawed with the loss of all his property.'

'That might well happen.'

'The son sees all this,' I continued, 'and, frightened by his sufferings and the loss of property, incontinently dethrones courage and ambition from the place they have held in his heart. Reduced to poverty, and forced to earn his living, by slow and painful economy and hard work he succeeds in amassing a fortune; so won't he proceed to elevate the element of desire and profit-seeking to the throne, and let it govern like an oriental despot with tiara, chain, and sword?'

'Yes.'

'While reason and ambition squat in servitude at its feet, reason forbidden to make any calculation or inquiry but how to make more money, ambition forbidden to admire or value anything but wealth and the wealthy, or to compete for anything but the acquisition of wealth and whatever leads to it.'

'There's no transition quicker or more violent than that from ambition to avarice,' he said.

'And. being a mean fellow, he's a poor competitor personally for any success or ambitious achievement in public life; he's unwilling to spend money in the struggle for distinction, and scared of stirring up a whole lot of expensive desires to fight on the side of his ambition. So, like a true oligarch, he fights with only part of himself, and though he loses the battle he saves his money.'

Democracy

Equality of political opportunity and freedom or the individual to do as he likes arc, for Plato and Aristotle, the salient characteristics of democracy. Plato is writing, of course, about democracy in the ancient city-state, and J Athens particularly in mind.

'Our next subject, I suppose, is democracy. When we know how it originates, and what it is like, we can again identify and pass judgement on the corresponding individual.'

'Because the rulers, owing their power to wealth as they do, are unwilling to curtail by law the extravagance of the young, and prevent them squandering their money and ruining themselves; for it is by loans to such spendthrifts or by buying up their property that they hope to increase their own wealth and influence.'

'It should then be clear that love of money and adequate self-discipline in its citizens are two things that can't coexist in any society; one or the other must be neglected.'

That's pretty clear.'

'This neglect and the encouragement of extravagance in an oligarchy often reduces to poverty men born for better things.'

'Some of them arc in debt, some disfranchised, some both, and they settle down, armed with their stings, and with hatred in their hearts, to plot against those who have deprived them of their property and against the rest of society, and to long for revolution.'

'Meanwhile the money-makers, bent on their business, don't appear to notice them, but continue to inject their poisoned loans wherever they can find a victim, and to demand high rates of interest on the sum lent, with the result that the drones and beggars multiply.'

'Yet even when the evil becomes flagrant they will do nothing to quench it, either by preventing men from disposing of their property as they like, or alternatively by other suitable legislation.'

'What legislation?'

'But as it is the oligarchs reduce their subjects to the state we have described, while as for themselves and their dependants their young men live in luxury and idleness, physical and mental, become idle, and lose their ability to resist pain or pleasure.'

'Indeed they do.'

'Such being the state of rulers and ruled, what will happen when they come up against each other in the streets or in the of business, at a festival or on a campaign, serving in the navy or army? When they see each other in moments of danger, the rich man will no longer be able to despise the poor man; the poor man will be lean and sunburnt, and find himself fighting next to some rich man whose sheltered life and superfluous flesh make him puff and blow and quite unable to cope. Won't he conclude that people like this are rich because their subjects are cowards, and won't he say to his fellows, when he meets them in private, "This lot are no good; we've got them where we want e them"?'

'Then democracy originates when the poor win, kill or exile their opponents, and give the rest equal civil rights and opportunities of office, appointment to office being as a rule by lot.'

'Would you agree, first, that people will be free? There is liberty and freedom of speech in plenty, and every individual is free to do as he likes.'

'That's what they say.'

Granted that freedom, won't everyone arrange his life as pleases him best?'

'Obviously.'

'And so there will be in this society the greatest variety of individual character?'

'There's bound to be.'

'I dare say that a democracy is the most attractive of all Societies,' I said. 'The diversity of its characters, like the different colours in a patterned dress, make it look very attractive. Indeed,' I added, 'perhaps most people would, for this reason, judge it to be the best form of society, like women and children when they see gaily coloured things.'

'It contains every possible type, because of the wide freedom it allows, and anyone engaged in founding a state, as we are doing, should perhaps be made to pay a visit to a democracy and choose hat he likes from the variety of models it displays, before he proceeds to make his own foundation.'

'Then in democracy,' I went on, 'there's no compulsion cither to exercise authority if you are capable of it, or to submit to authority if you don't want to; you needn't fight if there's a war, or you can wage a private war in peacetime if you don't like peace, and if there's any law that debars you from political or judicial office, you will none the less take cither if they come your way. It's a wonderfully pleasant way of carrying on in the short run, isn't it?'

Then they're very considerate in applying the high principles we laid down when founding our state; so far from interpreting them strictly, they really look down on them. We said that no one who had not exceptional gifts could grow into a good man unless he were brought up from childhood in a good environment and trained in good habits. Democracy with a grandiose gesture sweeps all this away and doesn't mind what the habits and background of its politicians are; provided they profess themselves the people's friends, they are duly honoured.'

'These, then, and similar characteristics are those of democracy. It's an agreeable anarchic form of society, with plenty of variety, which treats all men as equal, whether they are equal or not.'

The Democratic Character

'Then let us look at the corresponding individual. Should we first look at his origin, as we did with the society?'

'And back he goes to live with the Lotus-eaters. If his family send help to the economical element in him, the pretentious invaders shut the gates of the citadel, and will not admit the relieving force, nor will they listen to the individual representations of old and trusted friends. They make themselves masters by force of arms, they call shame silliness and drive it into disgrace and exile; they call self-control cowardice and expel it with abuse; and they call on a lot of useless desires to help them banish economy and moderation, which they maintain are mere provincial parsimony.

'For the rest of his life he spends as much money, time and trouble on the unnecessary desires as on the necessary. If he's lucky and doesn't get carried to extremes, the tumult will subside as he gets older, some of the exiles will be received back, and the invaders won't have it all their own way. He'll establish a kind of equality of pleasures, and will give the pleasure of the moment its turn of complete control till it is satisfied, and then move on to another, so that none is underprivileged and all have their fair share of encouragement.'

'It anyone tells him that some pleasures, because they spring from good desires, are to be encouraged and approved, and others, springing from evil desires, to be disciplined and repressed, he won't listen or open his citadel's doors to the truth, but shakes his head and says all pleasures are equal and should have equal rights.'

'In fact,' I said, 'he lives from day to day, indulging the pleasure of tin moment. One day it's wine, women and song, the next wrier to drink and a strict diet; one day it's hard physical training, the next indolence and careless ease, and then a period of philosophic study. Often he takes to politics and keeps jumping to his feet and saying or doing whatever comes into his head. Sometimes all his ambitions and efforts arc military, 'sometimes they are all directed to success in business.'

'Life, and he reckons his way of living is pleasant, free and happy, and sticks to it through thick and thin.'

'Yes,' I said, 'and I think that the versatility of the individual, and the attractiveness of his combination of a wide variety of characteristics, match the variety of the democratic society. It's a life Which many men and women would envy, it contains patterns of so many constitutions and ways of life.'

'This, then, is the individual corresponding to the democratic iciety, and we can fairly call him the democratic man.

'Areed.'

Tyranny

'Well, my dear Adeimantus, what is the nature of tyranny? It's obvious, I suppose, that it arises out of democracy.'

'Then isn't it true that tyranny arises out of democracy in the same sort of way that democracy arises out of oligarchy?'

'The main objective of oligarchy, for the sake of which it was established, was, I think we agreed, wealth.'

I have used the traditional 'tyrant' and 'tyranny' to translate the Greek words of which they are in fact, transliterations. As Cornford points out, the essential feature of the Greek 'tyrant' was that he was an absolute and sole ruler, and he accordingly uses the more neutral word 'despot'. But already in Plato's day the use of the word implied a certain moral disapproval, and tyrant is therefore a suitable translation.

'And its fall was due to the excessive desire for wealth, which led to the neglect of all other considerations for the sake of making money.'

'Then does not democracy set itself an objective, and is not excessive desire for this its downfall?'

'Liberty, I said. 'You must have heard it said that this is the greatest merit of a democratic society, and that for that reason it's the only society fit for a man of free spirit to live in.'

'Then, as I was just saying, an excessive desire for liberty at the expense of everything else is what undermines democracy and leads to the demand for tyranny.'

'A democratic society in its thirst for liberty may fall under the influence of bad leaders, who intoxicate it with excessive quantities of the neat spirit; and then, unless the authorities are very mild and give it a lot of liberty, it will curse them for oligarchs and punish them.'

'It goes on to abuse as servile and contemptible those who obey the authorities and reserves its approval, in private life as well as public, for rulers who behave like subjects and subjects who behave like rulers. In such a society the principle of liberty is bound to go to extremes, is it not?'

'What is more,' I said, 'it will permeate private life and in the end infect even the domestic animals with anarchy.'

'Well,' I said, 'it becomes the thing for father and son to change places, the father standing in awe of his son, and the son neither respecting nor fearing his parents, in order to assert what he calls his independence; and there's no distinction between citizen and alien and foreigner.'

'They do,' I said, 'and there are other more trivial things. The teacher fears and panders to his pupils, who in turn despise their teachers and attendants; and the young as a whole imitate their elders, argue with them and set themselves up against them, while 'their elders try to avoid the reputation of being disagreeable or strict by aping the young and mixing with them on terms of easy good fellowship.'

'The extreme of popular liberty is reached in this kind of society when slaves - male and female - have the same liberty as I their owners - not to mention the complete equality and liberty in I the relations between the sexes.'

'Right,' I said; 'you shall. You would never believe — unless you id seen it for yourself - how much more liberty the domestic animals have in a democracy. The dog comes to resemble its mistress, as the proverb has it, and the same is true of the horses and donkeys as well. They are in the habit of walking about the streets with a grand freedom, and bump into people they meet if they don't get out of their way. Everything is full of this, spirit of liberty.'

'What it all adds up to is this,' I said; 'you find that the minds of the citizens become so sensitive that the least vestige of restraint is resented as intolerable, till finally, as you know, in their determination to have no master they disregard all laws, written or unwritten.'

'Well, this is the root from which tyranny springs,' I said; 'a fine and vigorous beginning.'

'The same disease which afflicted and finally destroyed oligarchy afflicts democracy, in which it has more scope, still more virulently and enslaves it. Indeed, any extreme is liable to produce a violent reaction; this is as true of the weather and plants and animals as of political societies.'

'So from in extreme of liberty one is likely to get, in the individual and in society, a reaction to an extreme of subjection.

'And if that is so, we should expect tyranny to result from democracy, the most savage subjection from an excess of liberty.'

'But I haven't answered your question, which was, what is the disease whose growth enslaves democracy and oligarchy alike?'

'You remember me talking about a class of thriftless idlers, whom I compared to drones, their, energetic leaders to drones with stings, the more inert mass of followers to drones without stings.'

'Whenever these two elements appear in society they cause trouble,' I said, 'as phlegm and bile do in the body. The good doctor and the good lawgiver must make provision against both in advance, just as the bee-keeper who knows his job will try to prevent drones being bred at all, and if they arc bred cut them out at once, cells and all.

'Let us suppose a democratic society falls into three groups, as indeed it docs. First comes the group we have mentioned, larger than in an oligarchy because of the freedom it gets.'

'Granted.'

'And indeed a good deal more energetic.'

'How is that?'

'In an oligarchy it is despised and kept from power, and so lacks practice and strength. In a democracy practically all the leaders are drawn from it. Its more energetic elements do the talking and acting, the remainder sit buzzing on the benches and won't let anyone else speak, so that all public business, with trifling exceptions, is in their hands.'

Then there's a second group which continually emerges from mass.

Everyone's on the make, but the steadiest characters will generally be most successful in making money.'

'And the drones find them a plentiful and most convenient Source to extract honey from.'

'And so this group, on which the drones batten, are called the rich.'

'The third group is the mass of the people, who earn their own ' living, take little interest in politics, and aren't very well off. They are the largest class in a democracy, and once assembled are supreme.'

'Yes,' he said, 'but they won't assemble often unless they are given their share of honey.'

'They get their share all right,' I replied. 'Their leaders rob the rich keep as much of the proceeds as they can for themselves, and is tribute the rest to the people.' 'Yes, that's how they get their share.'

'Those whom they've plundered are forced to defend themselves, by speaking in the Assembly and doing the best they can elsewhere.'

'They are then accused by their rivals of plotting against the people and being reactionaries and oligarchs, even though in fact they may have no revolutionary intentions.'

'In the end, when they see the people trying to wrong them, not with intent, but out of ignorance and because they've been misled by the slanders spread by their leaders, why then they've no choice but to turn oligarchs in earnest, not because they want to, but again because the drones' stings have poisoned them.

'There follow impeachments and trials in which the two parties bring each other to court.'

'In this struggle don't the people normally put forward a single popular leader, whom they nurse to greatness?'

'Then it should be clear,' I said, 'that this leadership is the root from which tyranny invariably springs.'

'That the man who tastes a single piece of human flesh, mixed in with the rest of the sacrifice, is fated to become a wolf. Surely you've heard the tale?'

'Yes, I have.'

'The same thing happens with the popular leader. The mob will do anything he tells them, and the temptation to shed a bather's blood is too strong, He brings the usual unjust charges 'against him, takes him to court and murders him, thus destroying a human life, and getting an unholy taste of the blood of his fellows. Exiles, executions, hints of cancellation of debts and redistribution of land follow, till their instigator is inevitably and fatally bound either to be destroyed by his enemies, or to change from man to wolf and make himself tyrant.'

'It is he who leads the class war against the owners of property.'

And if he's exiled, and then returns in spite of his enemies, he returns a finished tyrant.'

'And if they are unable to banish him, or set the citizens against him and kill him, they form a secret conspiracy to assassinate him.

'Then follows the notorious gambit which all tyrants produce at this stage of their career, the demand for a personal bodyguard to preserve their champion for the people.'

''Then shall we describe the happy condition of this man, and of 'he state in which a creature like him is bred?'

'In his early days he has a smile and a kind word for everyone; he says he's no tyrant, makes large promises, public and private, frees debtors, distributes land to the people and to his own followers, and puts on a generally mild and kindly air.'

'But I think we shall find that when he has disposed of his foreign enemies by treaty or destruction, and has no more to fear from them, he will in the first place continue to stir up war in order that the people may continue to need a leader.

'And the high level of war taxation will also enable him to reduce them to poverty and force them to attend to earning their daily bread rather than to plotting against him.'

Finally if he suspects anyone of having ideas of freedom and not submitting to his rule, he can find an excuse to get rid of them by handing them over to the enemy. For all these reasons a tyrant must always be provoking war.'

'But all this lays him open to unpopularity.'

'So won't some of the holder characters among those who helped him to power, and now hold positions of influence, begin to speak freely to him and to each other, and blame him for what is happening?'

Then, if he is to retain power, he must root them out, all of them, till there's not a man of any consequence left, whether friend or foe.'

'So he must keep a sharp eye out for men of courage or vision or intelligence or wealth; for, whether he likes it or not, it is his happy ate to be their constant enemy and to intrigue until he has purged them from the state.'

Tie remarked.

'Yes,' I returned, 'and the reverse of a purge in the medical sense. For the doctor removes the poison and leaves the healthy elements in the body, while the tyrant does the opposite.'

'He is compelled to make the happy choice,' I said, 'between a life with companions' most of whom are worthless and all of whom hate him, and an inevitable death,'

'And the greater the unpopularity of this policy, the larger and the more trustworthy must his bodyguard be.'

'By robbing the citizens of their slaves, freeing them, and enrolling them in his bodyguard.'

'What an enviable lot the tyrant's is,' I exclaimed, 'if these are the trusty friends he must employ after destroying his earlier supporters.'

'And I suppose these newly made citizens, whose company he keeps, admire him very much, though all decent men detest and avoid him.'

'No option?' I said. 'But what if they get annoyed and say that it's not right for a father to keep his son when he's grown up it's the son should keep the father: and that they never intended, when they bred him and set him up, that when he grew great they should be enslaved to their own slaves, and have to keep him and his servile rabble: on the contrary, he was to be their champion and free them from the power of the wealthy and so-called upper classes? What-if they then order him and his partisans to leave the country, like a father ordering his son out of the house with his riotous friends?'

'Then,' with emphasis, 'people will find out soon enough what sort of a beast they've bred and groomed for greatness. He'll be too strong for them to turn out.'

'What?' I exclaimed. 'Do you mean that the tyrant will dare to use violence against the people who fathered him, and raise his hand against them if they oppose him?'

'So the tyrant is a parricide,' said I, 'and little comfort to his old /parent. In fact, here we have real tyranny, open and avowed, and the people find, as the saying is, that they've jumped out of the frying-pan of subjection to free men into the fire of subjection to slaves, and exchanged their excessive and untimely freedom for the harshest and bitterest of servitudes, where the slave is master.'

'Well,' I said, 'I think we can fairly claim to have given an adequate description of how democracy turns to tyranny and what tyranny is like.'

The Tyrannical Character

'We've still to describe the individual of tyrannical character and see how he develops from the democratic man, what he's like, and whether his life is a happy or miserable one.'

'I don't think our classification of the nature and number of the desires is complete. And as long as that's incomplete the object of 'our investigation will remain obscure.'

'Good. What I want to get clear about is this. I think that some of the unnecessary pleasures and desires are lawless and violent. Perhaps we are all born with them, but they are disciplined by law and by a combination of reason and the better desires till in some people they are got rid of altogether, or rendered few and feeble, though in some they retain their numbers and strength.'

'The sort that wake while we sleep, when the reasonable and humane part of us is asleep and its control relaxed, and our fierce bestial nature, full of food and drink, rouses itself and has its fling and tries to secure its own kind of satisfaction. As you know, there's nothing too bad for it and it's completely lost to all sense and shame. It doesn't shrink from attempting intercourse with a mother or anyone else, man, beast or god, or from murder or eating forbidden food. There is, in fact, no folly nor shamelessness it will not commit.'

'That's perfectly true.'

'But a man of sound and disciplined character, before he goes to sleep, has wakened his reason and given it its fill of intellectual argument and inquiry; his desires he has neither starved nor indulged, so that they sink to rest and don't plague the highest part of him with their joys and sorrows, but leave it to pursue its investigations unhampered and on its own, and to its endeavours to apprehend things still unknown to it, whether past, present or future; the third, spirited, part of him he calms and keeps from quarrels so that he sleeps with an untroubled temper. Thus he goes to rest with the other two parts of him questioned, and his reasoning clement stimulated, and is in a state to grasp the truth undisturbed by lawless dreams and visions.

'Then let's go back to the character of our democratic man. He was produced, you remember, by an early upbringing under an economical father, whose desires centred entirely on business, and who had no use for the "unnecessary" desires for either amusement or elegance.'

'But he got into the company of men with more sophisticated tastes and desires of the kind we described, took to their ways because of his dislike of his father's meanness, and was driven to all sorts of excesses; yet at heart he was a better man than his corrupters, and so effected what he thought was a very reasonable compromise between the competing attractions of the two lives, getting the best of both and avoiding both meanness and extravagance —in fact, he turned into a democratic character from an oligarchic.'

'Yes, I still think that's true.'

'Suppose, then,' I went on, 'he has in due course a son whom he brings up in his own ways.'

'Suppose it.'

'Suppose, further, that the same thing happens to the son as to the father; he's drawn towards complete licence (which his tempters call complete liberty), his father and family support moderation, and his tempters come in on the other side. And when the wicked wizards who want to make him a tyrant despair of keeping their hold on the young man by other means, they contrive to implant a master passion in him to control the idle desires that divide his time between them, like a great winged drone–unless you can think of a better description for such a passion?'

'No–that describes it very well.'

'The other desires buzz round it, loading it with incense and perfume, flowers and wine, and all the pleasures of a dissolute life, on which they feed and fatten it until at last they produce in it the sting of mania. Then the master passion runs wild and takes ' madness into its service; any opinions or desires with a decent reputation and any feelings of shame still left are killed or thrown out, until all discipline is swept away, and madness usurps its place.'

'A very complete description of the genesis of the tyrannical man.'

'Isn't this the reason,' I asked, 'why the passion of sex has for so long been called a tyrant?'

'And the madman whose mind is unhinged imagines he can control gods and men and is quite ready to try.'

'Then a precise definition of a tyrannical man is one who, either by birth or habit or both, combines the characteristics of drunkenness, lust, and madness.'

"I will,' I said. 'When a master passion within has absolute control of a man's mind, I suppose life is a round of extravagant feasts and orgies and sex and so on.'

'And there will be a formidable extra crop of desires growing day by day and night by night and needing satisfaction.'

'So whatever income he has will soon be expended,' I said, and, when he agreed, added, 'and next of course he'll start borrowing and drawing on capital.'

'When these sources fail, his large brood of fierce desires will aloud, and he will inevitably be stung to madness by them, and still more by the master passion under which they all do armed service, and will cast about to find someone to rob by force or fraud.'

'Plunder he must have from all available sources or his life will 'be torment and agony.'

'If they don't give in to him, I suppose he'll try first to get his way by fraud and deceit.'

'I suppose so.'

'And if he can't, will he proceed to robbery and violence?'

'I think he will.'

'And if his old mother and father put up a resistance and show fight, will he feel any scruple about playing the tyrant to them?'

'Do you really mean that he will strike his own mother and his ageing father, to whom he is bound by ties of birth and long affection, and, if they're all under the same roof, subordinate them to his latest mistress or his latest young favourite, who have no claims on him at all?'

'And I suppose that when he comes to the end of his father's and mother's resources, having by now a pretty considerable swarm of pleasures collected in himself, he'll start by burgling a house or holding someone up at night, and go on to clean out a temple. Meanwhile the older beliefs about honour and dishonour, which he was brought up to accept as right, will be overcome by others, once held in restraint but now freed to become the bodyguard of his master, passion. When he was still democratically minded and under the influence of the laws and his father, they only appeared in his dreams; but under the tyranny of the master passion he becomes in his waking life what he was once only occasionally in his dreams, and there's nothing, no taboo, no murder, however terrible, from which he will shrink. His passion tyrannizes over him, a despot without restraint or law, and drives him (as a tyrant drives a state) into any venture that will profit itself and its gang, a gang collected partly from the evil company he keeps and partly from impulses within himself which these same evil practices have freed from restraint. Do you think that's the sort of life he will lead?'

'They become thieves, burglars, pick-pockets, footpads, temple robbers and kidnappers; or, if they have a ready tongue, they turn I informers and false witnesses or take bribes.'

'Minor is a relative term,' I replied, 'and so far as the welfare or wickedness of the community goes, crimes like these don't come anywhere near tyranny. But when the criminals and their followers increase in numbers and become aware of their strength, the folly of the people helps them to produce a tyrant, and they pick the man who is at heart the completest and most absolute tyrant.'

"And if the people submit to him, well and good. If not, he'll punish his country, if he can, just as he punished his parents. He will bring his home country, his once dear motherland as the Cretans call it, under the control of the gang of upstart followers he introduces, and keep it in subjection to them. Which was the object of all his ambitions, was it not?'

'Men of his kind behave in the same sort of way in private life, I before they have gained power. Their companions are parasites in every way subservient to them, and they are themselves always prepared to give way and put on the most extravagant act of friendship if it suits their purpose, though once that purpose is achieved their tune changes.

'Yet his is just the sort of predicament in which the tyrant is imprisoned. He is naturally a prey to fears and passions of every sort, as we have described; and he's the only person in the state who can't travel abroad or attend the festivals the ordinary free man loves to see, much as in his heart he longs to, but must lurk in the shelter of his home, like a woman, and envy the freedom with which other men can travel and see things worth seeing.'

'The tyrannical character, therefore, whom you judged to be most wretched of men because of the harvest of evils produced by the disorder prevailing within him, is in all these ways still worse off when he ceases to be a private citizen, and is compelled by fate to become a real tyrant and to control others though he cannot control himself. It's just as if you compelled an invalid or paralytic to spend his life on military service or in athletic competitions instead of living quietly at home.'

'And so, my dear Glaucon, will you agree that the actual tyrant's condition is utterly wretched, and his life harder than the one you thought hardest?'

'So whatever people may think, the truth is that the real tyrant is really a slave of the most abject kind dependent on scoundrels. He can never satisfy his desires, and behind his multitudinous wants you can see, if you know how to survey it as a whole, the real impoverishment of his character; his life is haunted by fear and if the condition of the state he rules is any guide, as we know it is torn by suffering and misery. Do you agree?'

'Add to all that what we said before, that his power will make him still more envious, untrustworthy, unjust, friendless, and godless, a refuge and home for every iniquity, and you can see that he's a source of misery above all to himself, but also to his neighbours.'

'Come on, then,' I said, 'you must act as final judge for us, and give us your verdict how these five types the philosopher king, the timocratic, the oligarchic, the democratic and the tyrannical man–stand in order of happiness.'

'The verdict is easy,' he replied. 'I rank the competitors in the "order of their appearance, not only in happiness but also in degree of excellence.'

'Then shall we hire a herald,' I asked, 'or shall I proclaim the judgement of the son of Ariston myself—that the supremely happy man is the one who is justest and the best, that is, the philosopher king who is sovereign over himself, and that the supremely wretched man is the one who is unjustest and worst, that is again, the man who is most tyrannical and who tyrannizes completely both over himself and over his own country?'

(From *The Republic* by Plato translated by Desmond Lee, Penguin Books, 2007)

3

Aristotle

Aristotle (384BC- 322 BC) was born at Stagira, a Macedonian city some two hundred miles to the north of Athens, in the year 384 B.C. His father was friend and physician to Amentias, King of Macedon and grandfather of Alexander. Aristotle himself seems to have become a member of the great medical fraternity of Asclepiads. He had every opportunity and encouragement to develop a scientific bent of mind: he was prepared from the beginning to become the founder of science.

We have number of stories about his youth. One narrative represents him as squandering his patrimony in riotous living, joining the army to avoid starvation, returning to Stagira to practice medicine, and going to Athens at the age of thirty to study philosophy under Plato. A more dignified story takes him to Athens at the age of eighteen, and puts him at once under the tutelage of the great master; but even in this fascinating account there is sufficient echo of a reckless and irregular youth, living rapidly.

Under Plato he studied twenty years; and indeed the pervasive Platonism of Aristotle's speculations—even of those most anti-Platonic—suggests the longer period. One would like to imagine these as very happy years; a brilliant pupil guided by an incomparable teacher, walking like Greek lovers in the gardens of philosophy. But they were both geniuses; and it is notorious that geniuses accord with one another as harmoniously as dynamite with fire. Almost half a century separated them; it was difficult for understanding to bridge the gap of years and cancel the incompatibility of souls. Plato recognized the greatness of this strange new pupil from the supposedly barbarian north. Aristotle had spent money lavishly in the collection of books. He was the first, after Euripides, to gather a library; and the foundation of the principles of library classification was among his many contributions to scholarship. A more authentic quarrel seems to have arisen towards the end of Plato's life. Our ambitious youth apparently developed an "Oedipus complex" against his spiritual father for the favors and affections of philosophy, and began to hint that wisdom would not die with Plato; while the old sage spoke of his pupil as a foal that kicks his a mother after draining her dry.

The other incidents of his Athenian period are still more problematical. Some biographers tell us that Aristotle founded a school of oratory to rival Isocratic; and that he had among his pupils in this school the wealthy Hernias, who was soon to become autocrat of the city-state. After reaching this elevation Hernias invited Aristotle to his court; and in the year 344B.C. he rewarded his teacher for past favors by bestowing upon him a sister in marriage. One might suspect this as a Greek gift; but the historians hasten to assure us that Aristotle, despite his genius, lived happily enough with his wife, and spoke of her most affectionately in his will. It was just a year later that Philip, king of Macedon, called Aristotle to the court to undertake the education of Alexander. It bespeaks the rising repute of our philosopher that the greatest monarch of the time, looking about for the greatest teacher, should single out Aristotle to be the tutor of the future master of the world.

Alexander, when Aristotle came, was a wild youth of thirteen; passionate, epileptic, almost alcoholic; it was his pastime to tame horses untamable by men. The efforts of the philosopher to cool the fires of this budding volcano were not of much avail. Alexander left philosophy after two years to mount the throne and ride the world. History leaves us free to believe that his teacher, the most synthetic thinker in the history of thought; and that the conquest of order in the political realm by the pupil, and in the philosophic realm by the master, were but diverse sides of one noble and epic project—two magnificent Macedonians unifying two chaotic worlds.

Setting out to conquer Asia, Alexander left behind him, in the cities of Greece, governments favorable to him but populations resolutely hostile. The long tradition of a free and once imperial Athens made subjection—even to a brilliant world-conquering despot-intolerable; and the bitter eloquence of Remoistens kept the Assembly always on the edge of revolt against the "Macedonian party" that held the reins of city power. Now when Aristotle, after another period of travel, returned to Athens in the year 334 B.C., he very naturally associated with this Macedonian group, and took no pains to conceal his approval of Alexander's unifying rule.

Meanwhile life had become unmanageably complicated for Aritotle. He found himself on the one hand embroiled with Alexander for protesting against the execution of his nephew Calisthenics who had refused to worship Alexander as a god; and Alexander had answered the protest by hinting that it was quite within his omnipotence to put even philosopher to death. At the same time Aristotle was busy defending Alexander among the Athenians. He preferred Greek solidarity to city patriotism, and thought culture and science would flourish better when petty sovereignties and disputes were ended; and he saw in Alexander what Goethe was to see in Napoleon-the philosophic unity of a chaotic and intolerably manifold world. The Athenians, hungering for liberty, growled at Aristotle, and became bitter when Alexander had a statue of the philosopher put up in the heart of the hostile city. The angry crowds intrigued and clamored for his exile or his death.

And then, suddenly, Alexander died. Athens went wild with patriotic joy; the Macedonian party was overthrown, and Athenian independence was proclaimed. Antipatter, successor of Alexander and intimate friend of Aristotle, marched upon the rebellious city. Most of the Macedonian party fled. Eurymedon, a chief priest, brought in an indictment against Aristotle, charging him with having taught that prayer and sacrifice were of no avail. Aristotle saw himself fated to be tried by juries and crowd incomparably more hostile than those that had murdered Socrates. Very wisely, he left the city, saying that he would not give Athens a chance to sin a second time against philosophy. There was no cowardice in this; an accused person at Athens had always the option of preferring exile. Arrived at Chalices, Aristotle fell ill; it has been reported that the old philosopher, in utter disappointment with the turn of all things against him, committed suicide by drinking hemlock. However, induced, his illness proved fatal; and a few months after leaving Athens the lonely Aristotle died in 322BC.

Aristotle worked within the severest limitations. He was an astronomer without a telescope, a biologist without a laboratory, a physiologist and psychologist without apparatus. He was a natural historian who had to rely for his data partly on hearsay and tradition, partly on the miscellaneous specimens and prodigies that reached him from the itinerant agents of Alexander the Great. In an age when written records were few, he devoted himself to placing phenomena in historical and causal perspective. Aristotle was also among the first to study comparative government to analyze the life history of institutions. In his attempt to relate the individual to the state, and education to law, he became an ethical theorist of prime importance.

He was a literary and dramatic critic of rare insight. And underlying all these achievements was this: he was a logician of subtlety and strength, and a searcher after the knowledge that transcends and exists independent of all other knowledge. He called this knowledge "first philosophy" or "wisdom," and it has since become known as metaphysics.

Many of the questions Aristotle asked—about the nature of man and society, science and knowledge and art—are very much alive today. But it cannot be denied that some of the answers he gave are no longer valid. His aristocratic bias and his relative insularity now seem to vitiate some of his conclusions about ethical, social, and political goals, while his particular scientific conclusions have since been denied by fact and experience. The keystone of Aristotle's logic, the syllogism now has little real function, even though for centuries it was regarded as one of the more potent instruments of human inquiry. Similarly, Aristotle's doctrine of causes, which he considered his chief and distinctive contribution to philosophy, has lost its usefulness, even though its schematic and semantic beauty is still appealing.

–Editor

The State Exists by Nature

Now in this as in other fields we shall get the best view of things if we look at their natural growth from their beginnings. First, those which are incapable of existing without each other must unite as a pair, For example, (a) male and female, for breeding (and this not from choice; rather, as in the other animals too and in plants, the urge to leave behind another such as one is oneself is natural); (b) that which naturally rules and that which is ruled, for preservation. For that which can use its intellect to look ahead is by nature ruler and by nature master, while that which has the bodily strength to labour is ruled, and is by nature a slave. Hence master and slave benefit from the same thing.

So it is by nature that a distinction has been made between female and slave. ' For nature produces nothing skimpily (like the Delphic knife that smiths make), but one thing for one purpose; for every tool will be made best if it sub serves not many tasks but one. Non-Greeks, however, assign to female and slave the same status. This is because they do not have that which naturally rules: their association comes to be that of a male slave and a female slave. Hence, as the poets say, 'It is proper that Greeks should rule non-Greeks', on the assumption that non-Greek and slave are by nature identical.

Thus it was from these two associations that a household first arose, and Hes-iod was right in his poetry when he said, 'first of all a house and a wife and an ox' to draw the plough.' (The ox is the poor man's slave.) So the association formed according to nature for the satisfaction of the purposes of every day is a household, the members of which Charondas calls 'bread-fellows', and Epimenides the Cretan 'stable-companions'.

The first association, from several households, for the satisfaction of other than daily purposes, is a village. The village seems to be by nature in the highest degree, as a colony of a household-children and grandchildren, whom some people call 'homogalactic'. This is why states were at first ruled by kings (as are the nations to this day): they were formed from persons who were under kingly rule. For every household is under the kingly rule of its most senior member; so" too the colonies, because of the kinship. This is what is mentioned in Homer; 'Each one lays down the law to children and wives.' For they were scattered; and that is how they dwelt in ancient times. For this reason the gods too are said by everyone to be governed by a king-namely because men themselves were originally ruled by kings and some are so still. Men model the gods' forms on themselves, and similarly their way of life too.

The complete association, from several villages, is the state, which at once reaches the limit of total self-sufficiency, so to say. Whereas it comes into existence for the sake of life, it exists for the sake of the good life. Therefore every state exists by nature, since the first associations did too. For this association is their end, and nature is an end; for whatever each thing is in character when its coming into existence has been completed, that is what we call the nature of each thing-of a man, for instance, or a horse or a house. Moreover the aim, i.e. the end, is best; and self-sufficiency is both end and best.

These considerations make it clear, then, that the state is one of those things which exist by nature, and that man is by nature an animal fit for a state. Anyone who by his nature and not by ill-luck has no state is either a wretch or superhuman; he is also like the man condemned by Homer as having 'no brotherhood, no law, no hearth'; for he is at once such by nature and keen to go to war, being isolated like a piece in a game of *pettoi*.

Connected with these matters is the following question: are we to say that the goodness of a good man and a good citizen are the same, or not? If this ought to be examined, we must first get some outline of the goodness of the citizen. We say, then, that the citizen, like the sailor, is one of the partners in a society. Sailors are unlike each other in capacity: one is an oarsman, another a helmsman, another a bowman, and others have other such names; but it is clear that, while the most precise account of each one's goodness will be peculiar to himself, there will also be some common account fitting them all alike. The safety of the voyage is the business of them all, for each of the sailors aims at that. Similarly the citizens, though unlike each other, have the safety of the society as their business; and their society is the constitution. Hence the goodness of the citizen must be relative to the constitution; and, since there are several kinds of constitution, there clearly cannot be one single goodness of the good citizen, namely perfect goodness. But the good man, we say, has one single goodness, namely perfect goodness. Plainly, therefore, it is possible to be a good citizen and yet not possess the goodness of a good man.

One can go into the same argument by raising the question in another way, namely with regard to the best constitution. For, if it is impossible for a city to consist entirely of good men, it is nevertheless necessary that each should do his own job well, and do it out of goodness; but, since it is impossible for the citizens to be all alike, there would not be one single goodness of a citizen and a good man. This is because the goodness of the good citizen must belong to them all (only so can the city be the best), whereas the goodness of the good man cannot do so, since the citizens in the good city cannot all be good men.

Moreover, the city consists of unlike members. As an animal consists of soul and body, and a soul of reason and desire, and a household of man and woman, and a proprietorship of master and slave, so a city consists of all these and of other unlike forms in addition. Necessarily, therefore, the goodness of all the citizens is no more identical than is that of the leader and the sideman in a chorus.

That it is not always the same is plain from these considerations. But will there be anyone in whom the goodness of a citizen and the goodness of a man do coincide? We say that the good ruler is also a good and wise man, but that the citizen need not be wise. Some say that the very upbringing of a ruler is different. The sons of kings appear to be brought up on the arts of riding and war. And Euripides says implying that a ruler has a special upbringing. If then the goodness of a good ruler is identical with that of a good man, while the subject also is a citizen, the goodness of a man would be identical with that of a certain citizen but not with that of every citizen. The goodness of a ruler and of a citizen are not the same. Perhaps this is why Jason said he was hungry when not a tyrant; he did not know how to be a private man.

Furthermore, we praise the power to rule and to obey, and it seems that the goodness of an approved citizen consists in being able both to rule and to obey well. If therefore we make the goodness of the man to consist in ruling, but that of the citizen in both, the two would not be equally praiseworthy. Since then there are occasions when they seem different, and ruler and subject should not learn the same things, while the citizen should know and share in both, the consequence becomes clear.

One problem concerning the citizen remains: Is it really the case that the citizen is he who has the right to take part in the government, or should we call workmen also citizens?

If we are to include these persons also, who have no part in governing, such goodness cannot belong to every citizen, this man being a citizen. But, if such a person is not a citizen, in what class are we to put him? He is not a resident foreigner, nor a stranger.

Can we not say that there is no absurdity here? He is in the same position as slaves and freedmen. It is certain that we must not call citizens all those without whom there would be no city. Even children are not citizens in the some way as adults. Adults are citizens simply; but children are only hypothetically so. They are citizens, but imperfect ones.

In ancient times the working class was slave or foreign in some places, which is why most of them are so today; and the best city will not make a workman a citizen. If, however, he too is a citizen, then we must say that the goodness we spoke of does not belong to every citizen, nor to every free man, but only to those who are released from necessary services. Those who provide necessary services for one man are slaves. Those who do it for the community are workmen and labourers.

(From *Politics* by Aristotle (trans) E. Barker, Oxford University Press, Oxford, 1979)

Friendship and Politics

For no one would choose to live without friends even if he had all the other goods. For in fact rich people mid holders of powerful positions, even more than other people, seem to need friends. For how would one benefit from such prosperity if one had no opportunity for beneficence, which is most often displayed, and most highly praised, in relation to friends? And how would one guard and protect prosperity without friends, when it is all the more precarious the greater it is? In poverty also, and in the other misfortunes, people think friends are the only refuge.

Moreover, the young need it to keep them from error. The old need it to care for them and support the actions that fail because of weakness. And those in their prime need it, to do fine actions; for 'when two go together ...', they are more capable of understanding and acting.

Further, a parent would seem to have a natural friendship for a child, and a child for a parent, not only among human beings but also among birds and most kinds of animals. Members of the same race, and human beings most of all, have a natural friendship for each other; that is why we praise friends of humanity. And in our travels we can see how every human being is akin and beloved to a human being.

Moreover, friendship would seem to hold cities together, and legislators would seem to be more concerned about it than about justice. For concord would seem to be similar to friendship and they aim at concord above all, while they try above all to expel civil conflict, which is enmity.

Further, if people are friends, they have no need of justice, but if they are just they need friendship in addition; and the justice that is most just seems to belong to friendship....

...Hence friendship has three species, corresponding to the three objects of love. For each object of love has a corresponding type of mutual loving, combined with awareness of it, and those who love each other wish goods to each other in so far as they love each other.

Those who love each other for utility love the other not in himself, but in so far as they gain some good for themselves from him. The same is true of those who love for pleasure; for they like a witty person not because of his character, but because he is pleasant to themselves.

And so those who love for utility or pleasure are fond of a friend because of what is good or pleasant for themselves, not in so far as the beloved is who he is, | but in so far as he is useful or pleasant.

I Hence these friendships as well [as the friends] are coincidental, since the beloved is loved not in so far as he is who he is, but in so far as he provides some good or pleasure.

And so these sorts of friendships are easily dissolved, when the friends do not remain similar [to what they were]; for if someone is no longer pleasant or useful, the other stops loving him.

What is useful does not remain the same, but is different at different times. Hence, when the cause of their being friends is removed, the friendship is dissolved too, on the assumption that the friendship aims at these [useful results]. This sort of friendship seems to arise especially among older people, since at that age they pursue what is advantageous, not what is pleasant, and also among those in their prime or youth who pursue what is expedient.

Nor do such people live together very much. For sometimes they do not even find each other pleasant. Hence they have no further need to meet in this way if they are not advantageous [to each other]; for each finds the other pleasant [only to the extent that he expects some good from him. The friendship of hosts and guests is taken to be of this type too.

The cause of friendship between young people seems to be pleasure. For their lives are guided by their feelings, and they pursue above all what is pleasant for themselves and what is near at hand. But as they grow up [what they find] pleasant changes too. Hence they arc quick to become friends, and quick to stop; for their friendship shifts with [what they find] pleasant, and the change in sue pleasure is quick. Young people are prone to erotic passion, since this mostly follows feelings, and is caused by pleasure; that is why they love and quickly stop, often changing in a single day.

These people wish to spend their days together and to live together; for this is how they gain [the good things] corresponding to their friendship.

But complete friendship is the friendship of good people similar in virtue; for they wish goods in the same way to each other in so far as they are good, and they are good in themselves. (Hence they wish goods to each other for each other's own sake.] Now those who wish goods to their friend for the friend's own sake are friends most of all; for they have this attitude because of the friend himself, not coincidentally. Hence these peoples friendship lasts as long as they are good; and virtue is enduring.

Each of them is both good unconditionally and good for his friend, since good people are both unconditionally good and advantageous for each other. They are pleasant in the same ways too, since good people are pleasant both unconditionally and for each other. [They are pleasant for each other] because each person finds his own actions and actions of that kind pleasant, and the actions of good people are (he same or similar.

It is reasonable that this sort of friendship is enduring, since it embraces in itself all the features that friends must have. For the cause of every friendship is good or pleasure, either unconditional or for the lover; and every friendship reflects some similarity. And all the features we have mentioned are found in this friendship because of [the nature of] the friends themselves. For they are similar in this way [i.e. in being good]. Moreover, their friendship also has the other things — what is unconditionally good and what is unconditionally pleasant; and these arc lovable most of all. Hence loving and friendship are found most of all and at their best in these friends.

[These kinds of friendships are likely to be rare, since such people are few. Moreover, they need time to grow accustomed to each other; for, as the proverb says, they cannot know each other before they have shared the traditional [peck of] salt, and they cannot accept each other or be friends until each appears lovable to the other and gains the others confidence. Those who are quick to treat each other in friendly ways wish to be friends, but are not friends, unless they art also lovable, and know this. For though the wish for friendship comes quickly, friendship "does not.

This sort of friendship, then, is complete both in time and in the other ways. In every way each friend gets the same things and similar things from each, and this is what must be true of friends. Friendship for pleasure bears some resemblance to this complete sort, since good people are also pleasant to each other. And friendship for utility also resembles it, since good people art also useful to each other. . . .

As we said at the beginning, friendship and justice would seem to have the same area of concern and to be found in the same people. For in every community there seems to be some sort of justice, and some type of friendship also. At any rate, fellow-voyagers and fellow-soldiers are called friends, and so are members of other communities. And the extent of their community is the extent of their friendship, since it is also the extent of the justice found there. The proverb 'What friends have is common' is correct, since friendship involves community. But while brothers and companions have everything in common, what people have in common in other types of community is limited, more in some communities and less in others, since some friendships are also closer than others, some less close.

There are three species of political system (politeia), and an equal number of deviations, which are a sort of corruption of them. The first political system is kingship; the second aristocracy; and since the third rests on property it appears proper to call it a timocratic system, though most people usually Call it a polity (politeia). The best of these is kingship and the worst timocracy.

The deviation from kingship is tyranny. For, though both are monarchies, they show the widest difference, since the tyrant considers his own advantage, but the king considers the advantage of his subjects. For someone is a king only if he is self-sufficient and superior in all goods; and since such a person needs nothing more, he will consider the subjects' benefit, not his own. For a king who is not like this would be only some sort of titular king. Tyranny is contrary to this; for the tyrant pursues his own good....

Friendship appears in each of the political systems, to the extent that justice appears also. A king's friendship to his subjects involves superior beneficence. For he benefits his subjects, since he is good and attends to them to ensure that they do well, as a shepherd attends to his sheep; hence Homer also called Agamemnon shepherd of the peoples.

Paternal friendship resembles this, but differs in conferring a greater benefit, since the father is the cause of his children's being, which seems to be the greatest benefit, and other nurture and education. These benefits are also ascribed to ancestors; and by nature father is ruler over sons, ancestors over descendants, and king over subjects.

All these are friendships of superiority; that is why parents are also honoured. And what is just in these friendships is not the same in each case, but corresponds to worth; for so does the friendship.

The friendship of man to woman is the same as in an aristocracy. For it reflects virtue, in assigning more good to the better, and assigning what is fit ting to each. The same is true for what is just here.

The friendship of brothers is similar to that of companions, since they an equal and of an age, and such people usually have the same feelings and characters. Friendship in a timocracy is similar to this. For there the citizens are meant to be equal and decent, and so rule in turn and on equal terms. The same is true, then, of their friendship.

In the deviations, however, justice is found only to a slight degree; and hence] the same is true of friendship. There is least of it in the worst deviation; for in a tyranny there is little or no friendship.

For where ruler and ruled have nothing in common, they have no friendship, since they have no justice either. This is true for a craftsman in relation to his tool, and for the soul in relation to the body. For in all these cases the user benefits what he uses, but there is neither friendship nor justice towards soulless things.

Nor is there any towards a horse or cow, or towards a slave, in so far as he is a slave. For master and slave have nothing in common, since a slave is a tool with a soul, while a tool is a slave without a soul. In so far as he is a slave, then, there is no friendship with him.

But there is friendship with him in so far as he is a human being. For every human being seems to have some relations of justice with everyone who is capable of community in law and agreement. Hence there is also friendship, to the extent that a slave is a human being.

Hence there are friendships and justice to only a slight degree in tyrannies also, but to a much larger degree in democracies; for there people are equal, and so have much in common.

(From *Nichomachean Ethics,* **Book Eight** by Aristotle translated by Terence Irwin, Hackett Publishing Company, Indianpolis. 1985)

Justice and Injustice

The questions we must examine about justice and injustice are these: What sorts of actions are they concerned with? What sort of mean is justice? What are the extremes between which justice is intermediate? Let us examine them by the same type of investigation that we used in the topics discussed before...

Let us, then, find the number of ways an unjust person is spoken of. Both the lawless person and the greedy and unfair person seem to be unjust; and so, dearly, both the lawful and the fair person will be just. Hence what is just will be both what is lawful and what is fair, and what is unjust will be both what is lawless and what is unfair.

Since the unjust person is greedy, he will be concerned with goods—not with all goods, but only with those involved in good and bad fortune, goods which, are, [considered] unconditionally, always good, but for this or that person not; always good. Though human beings pray for these and pursue them, they are wrong; the right thing is to pray that what is good unconditionally will also be good for us, but to choose [only] what is good for us.

Now the unjust person [who chooses these goods] does not choose more in every case; in the case of what is bad unconditionally he actually chooses less. But since what is less bad also seems to be good in a way, and greed aims at more of what is good, he seems to be greedy. In fact he is unfair; for unfairness includes [all these actions], and is a common feature [of his choice of the greater good and of the lesser evil].

Since, as we saw, the lawless person is unjustified and the lawful person is just, it dearly follows that whatever is lawful is in some way just for the provisions of legislative science are lawful, and we say that each of them is just. Now in every matter they deal with the laws aim either at the common benefit of all or at the benefit of those in control, whose control rests on virtue or on some other such basis. And so in one way what we call just is whatever produces and maintains happiness and its parts for a political community.

Now the law instructs us to do the actions of a brave person—not to leave the battle-line, e.g., or to flee, or to throw away our weapons; of a temperate person—not to commit adultery or wanton aggression; of a mild person—not to strike or revile another; and similarly requires actions that express the other virtues, and prohibits those that express the vices. The correctly established law does this correctly, and the less carefully framed one does this worse.

This type of justice, then, is complete virtue, not complete virtue unconditionally, but complete virtue in relation to another. And this is why justice often seems to be supreme among the virtues, and "neither the evening star nor the morning star is so marvelous," and the proverb says "And in justice all virtue is summed up."

Moreover, justice is complete virtue to the highest degree because it is the complete exercise of complete virtue. And it is the complete exercise because the person who has justice is able to exercise virtue in relation to another, not only in: what concerns himself; for many are able to exercise virtue in dieir own concerns but unable in what relates to another.

And hence Bias seems to have been correct in saying that ruling will reveal the man, since a ruler is automatically related to another, and in a community. And for the same reason justice is the only virtue that seems to be another person's good, because it is related to another; for it does what benefits another, either the ruler or the fellow-member of the community.

The worst person, therefore, is the one who exercises his vice towards himself and his friends as well [as towards others]. And the best person is not the one who exercises virtue [only] towards himself, but the one who [also] exercises it in relation to another, since this is a difficult task.

This type of justice, then, is the whole, not a part, of virtue, and the injustice contrary to it is the whole, not a part, of vice.

At the same time our discussion mikes clear the difference between virtue and this type of justices. For virtue is the same as justice, but what it is to be virtue is not the same as what it is to be justice. Rather, in so far as virtue is related to another, it is justice, and in so far as it is a certain sort of state unconditionally it is virtue.

But we are looking for the type of justice, since we say there is one, that consist!* in a part of virtue, and correspondingly for the type of injustice that is a part [of vice].

Here is evidence that there is this type of justice and injustice:

First, if someone's activities express the other vices—if, e.g., cowardice made him throw away his shield, or irritability made him revile someone, or ungenerosity made him fail to help someone with money—what he does is unjust, but not greedy. But when one acts from greed, in many cases his action expresses none of these vices—certainly not all of them; but it still expresses some type of wickedness, since we blame him, and [in particular] it expresses injustice. Hence there is another type of injustice that is a part of the whole, and a way for a thing to be unjust that is a part of the whole that is contrary to law.

Moreover, if A commits adultery for profit and makes a profit, while B commits adultery because of his appetite, and spends money on it to his own loss, B seems intemperate rather than greedy, while A seems unjust, not intemperate. Clearly, then, this is because A acts to make a profit.

Further, we can refer ever)' other unjust action to some vice—to intemperance if he committed adul^tery, to cowardice if he deserted his comrade in the battle-line, to anger if he struck someone. But if he made an [unjust] profit, can refer it to no other vice except injustice.

Hence evidently (a) there is another type of injustice, special injustice, besides the whole of injustice; and (b) it is synonymous with the whole, since the definition is in the same genus. For (b) both have their area of competence in relation to another. But (a) special injustice is concerned with honour or wealth or safety, or whatever single name will include all these, and aims at the pleasure that results from making a profit; but the concern of injustice as a whole is whatever concerns the excellent person.

Clearly, then, there is more than one type of justice, and there is another type besides [the type that is] the whole of virtue; but we must still grasp what it is, and what sort of thing it is.

What is unjust is divided into what is lawless and what is unfair, and what is just into what is lawful and what is fair, The [general] injustice previously described, then, is concerned with what is lawless. Hut what is unfair is not the same as what is lawless, but related to it as part to whole, since whatever is unfair is lawless, but not everything lawless is unfair. Hence also the type of injustice and the way for a thing to be unjust [that expresses unfairness] are not the same as the type [that expresses lawlessness], but differ as parts from wholes. For this injustice [as unfairness] is a part of the whole of injustice, and similarly justice [as fairness] is a part of the whole of justice.

Hence we must describe special [as well as general] justice and injustice, and equally this way for a thing to be just or unjust.

Let us, then, set to one side the type of justice and injustice dun corresponds to the whole of virtue, justice being the exercise- of the whole of virtue, and injustice of the whole of vice, in relation to another.

And it is evident how we must distinguish the way for a thing to be just or unjust that expresses this type of justice and injustice; for the majority of lawful actions, we might say, are the actions resulting from virtue as a whole. For the law instructs us to express each virtue, and forbids us to express each vice, in how we live. Moreover, the actions producing the whole of virtue are the lawful actions that the laws prescribe for education promoting the common good.

We must wait till later, however, to determine whether the education that makes an individual an unconditionally good man is a task for political science or for another science; for, presumably, being a good man is not the same as being every sort of good citizen.

Special justice, however, and the corresponding way for something to be just [must be divided.

One species is found in the distribution of honours or wealth or anything else that can be divided among members of a community who share in a political system; for here it is possible for one member to have a share equal or unequal to another's.

Another species concerns rectification in transactions. This species has two parts, since one sort of transaction is voluntary, and one involuntary. Voluntary transactions include selling, buying, lending, pledging, renting, depositing, hiring out—these are called voluntary because the origin of these transactions is voluntary. Some involuntary ones are. secret, e.g. theft, adultery, poisoning, pimping, slave-deception, murder by treachery, false witness; others are forcible, e.g. assault, imprisonment, murder, plunder, mutilation, slander, insult.

Since the unjust person is unfair, and what is unjust is unfair, there is clearly an intermediate between the unfair [extremes], and this is what is fair; for in any action where too much and too little are possible, the fair [amount] is also possible. And so if what is unjust is unfair, what is just is fair (ison), as seems true to everyone even without argument.

And since what is equal (ison) [and fair] is intermediate, what is just is some sort of intermediate. And since what is equal involves at least two things [equal to each other], it follows that what is just must be intermediate and equal, and related to some people. In so far as it is intermediate, it must be between too much and too little; in so far as it is equal, it involves two things; and in so far as it is just, it is just for some people. Hence what is just requires four things at least; the people for whom it is just are two, and the [equal] things that are involved are two.

Equality for the people involved will be the same as for the things involved, since [in a just arrangement] the relation between the people will be the same as the relation between the things involved. For if the people involved are not equal, they will not [justly] receive equal shares; indeed, whenever equals receive unequal shares, or unequals equal shares, in a distribution, that is the source of quarrels and accusations.

This is also clear from considering what fits a person's worth. For everyone agrees that what is just in distributions must fit some sort of worth, but whit they call worth is not the same; supporters of democracy say it is free citizen ship, some supporters of oligarchy say it is wealth, others good birth, while supporters of aristocracy say it is virtue.

Hence what is just [since it requires equal shares for equal people] is in some way proportionate....

We have previously described, then, the relation of reciprocity to what is just. We must now notice that we are looking not only for what is just unconditionally but also for what is just in a political association. This is found among associates in a life aiming at sell-sufficiency, who are free and either proportionate or numerically equal.

Hence those who lack these features have nothing politically just in their relations, though they have something just in so far as it is similar [to what is politically just].

For what is just is found among those who have law in their relations. Where there is law, there is injustice, since the judicial process is judgment that distinguishes what is just from what is unjust. Where there is injustice there is also doing injustice, though where there is doing injustice there need not also He injustice. And doing injustice is awarding to oneself too many of the things that, [considered] unconditionally, are good, and too few of the things that, [considered] unconditionally, are bad.

This is why we allow only reason, not a human being, to be ruler; for a human being awards himself too many goods and becomes a tyrant, but a ruler is a guardian of what is just and hence of what is equal [and so must not award himself too many goods].

If a ruler is just, he seems to profit nothing by it. For since he does not award himself more of what, [considered] unconditionally, is good if it is not proportionate to him, he seems to labour for another's benefit; that is why justice is said, as we also remarked before, to be another person's good. Hence some payment [for ruling] should be given; this is honour and privilege, and the people who are unsatisfied by these are the ones who become tyrants.

What is just for a master and a father is similar to this, not the same. For there is no unconditional injustice in relation to what is one's own; ones own possession, or one's child until it is old enough and separated, is as though it were a part of oneself, and no one decides to harm himself. Hence there is no injustice in relation to them, and so nothing politically unjust or just either. For we found that what is politically just must conform to law, and apply to those who arc naturally suited for law, hence 10 (hose who have equality in ruling and being ruled. [Approximation to this equality] explains why relations with a wife more than children or possessions allow something to count as just—for that is what is just in households; still, this too is different from what is politically just.

One part of what is politically just is natural, and the other part legal. What is natural is what has the same validity everywhere alike, independent of its seeming so or not. What is legal is what originally makes no difference [whether it is 'done] one way or another, but makes a difference whenever people have laid down the rule—e.g. that a mina is the price of a ransom, or that a goat rather than two sheep should be sacrificed; and also laws passed for particular cases, e.g. that sacrifices should be offered to Brasidas, and enactments by decree.

Now it seems to some people that everything just is merely legal, since what is natural is unchangeable and equally valid everywhere—fire, e.g, burns both here and in Persia—while they see that what is just changes [from city to city)]

This is not so, though in a way it is so. With us, though presumably not at all with the gods, there is such a thing as what is natural, but still all is changeable; despite the change there is such a thing as what is natural and what is not.

What sort of thing that [is changeable and hence] admits of being otherwise is natural, and what sort is not natural, but legal and conventional, if both natural and legal arc changeable? It is clear in other cases also, and the same distinction [between the natural and the unchangeable] will apply; for the right hand, e.g., is naturally superior, even through it is possible for everyone to become ambidextrous.

The sorts of things that are just by convention and expediency are like measures. For measures for wine and for corn are not of equal size everywhere, but in whole-sale markets they are bigger, and in retail smaller. Similarly/the things that are just by human [enactment] and not by nature differ from place to place, since politicals systems also differ; still, only one system is by nature the best everywhere....

(From *Nichomachean Ethics,* **Book Five** by Aristotle translated by Terence Irwin, Hackett Publishing Company, Indianpolis. 1985)

4

Cicero

Marcus Tullius Cicero (106 BC-43 BC) is the Roman orator, statesman, and philosopher as representative of a historically important ancient attempt to develop a normative anthropology with cosmic significance. In particular, Cicero appeals to the Stoic account of human beings as loci of the divine reason that governs the whole universe or cosmos as cosmopolis – in a way analogous to that in which human reason should govern the polis or res publica.

By the 90s, when Cicero came to Rome as a teenager, young men of wealth and standing were beginning to be educated in more than the traditional elements of law and public speaking. In the dialogue *On the Orator* written in 55 BC, Cicero documents the growing acquaintance of Roman senators with Greek philosophy and rhetoric; by 100, it was not unusual for magistrates on their way to govern eastern provinces to stop in Athens to listen to philosopher' explain the simpler dialogues of Plato; Cicero himself, when he found it politically prudent to leave Rome in the early 70s, went to Rhodes to study philosophy and rhetoric. That encounter with Greek learning had a lasting effect. His speeches reveal, a deep and extensive knowledge of Greek philosophy, poetry, history, and art; and although his philosophical works often proclaim distrust of Greek learning for its own sake. Inconsistentlyhe attempted to shape it to the needs and values of Roman society.

By the time he returned from exile in 57 to his frustratingly powerless position in Rome, therefore, it is not altogether surprising that he turned from political action to writing. The 50s were a time of extraordinarily broad and complex engagement with Greek ideas in Rome: Pompey's vast conquests in the Greek east in the 60s encouraged what Sulla's brutal siege of Athens in 88 had begun, an exodus of leading Greek intellectuals to Rome. Some came willingly to the new financial, military, and now cultural capital of the Mediterranean; others, like Virgil's Greek teacher Panhenius, came as enslaved prisoners of war. The Epicurean Philodemus was the house of Cicero's enemy Piso one of Caesar's fathers-in-law and was well known lo Cicero. The invasion of Greek intellectuals had a powerful effect on Roman philosophers and scholars beginning in the 50s: both Catullus, writing learned poetry in the manner of the Alexandrians, and Lucretius, expounding Epicureanism in Latin verse, were the beneficiaries of Greek learning and exercised an immense influence on Latin poetry in the next generations.

Although Cicero came from a wealthy, provincial aristocratic family in central Italy, he was a "new man" or parvenu in Roman politics. Nonetheless, he enjoyed a spectacular career as a legal advocate and politician, becoming consul at an unusually young age in 63 B.C. In his successful attempt to thwart the conspiracy of Cataline, he had the conspirators extralegally executed and later, in 58 B.C.., he was forced into exile for sixteen months as a result. With the aid of the Roman general Pompey, Cicero was soon able to resume his political career. In the decade following his return from exile, he composed political and legal works, most notably the *De re publica and De legibus,* which were loosely modeled on Plato's *Republic* and *Laws*, respectively.

Pompey, with Crassus and Julius Caeser, formed the First Triumvirate, but an ensuing civil war ultimately resulted in the dictatorship of Julius Caesar. After the fall of the Roman republic and rise of Caesar, Cicero largely withdrew from politics and produced a series of literary and philosophical works beginning in about 46 B.C. After Caesar's assassination in 44 B.C., Cicero hoped for the reestablishment of republican rule. As a leader of the republican movement, he attacked Mark Antony, a leader of the Caesarian faction, in a series of fourteen speeches (the *Philippics*). Cicero's political hopes were dashed with the formation in 43 B.C. of the Second Triumvirate, consisting of Antony, Lepidus, and Caesar's great-nephew, Octavius (who later become Augustus Caesar). Cicero was proscribed as an enemy of the state and killed by Antony's soldiers later that same year.

The standard modern view is that, while Cicero was of great importance in translating Greek philosophical concepts into Latin terminology, he himself was not much of a philosopher. Although it would be fanciful to include Cicero among those in the very first rank of philosophy, he possessed considerable philosophical intelligence and was an able and sophisticated exponent of philosophical ideas. Like other intellectually inclined young men of his age and class, he received training in Greek philosophy. As a young man, he had been exposed to the teaching of Philo, then head of Academy Plato, and of the Stoic Diodotus. After his first marriage in 79, Cicero traveled extensively in Greece and the eastern Mediterranean, where he heard the Academic philosopher Antiochus and the Stoic Posidonius. In view of Cicero's philosophical antecedents, then, it is not surprising that he officially identified himself as an adherent of the New Academy. But, like that of Philo, his skepticism was an urbane, sophisticated antidogmatism. He was particularly influenced by Stoicism in his moral, political, and legal thought.

The Latin term res publica literally translates as "public thing", "public property", or "public business". In the first book of his Republic, Cicero characterizes it as the res of the public. But a public or people populus is not any kind of human gathering, congregating in any matter, but a numerous gathering brought together by agreement with respect to what is right for of law and community of interest. The primary reason for its coming together is not so much weakness as a sort of innate desire on the part of human being to from communities. For our species is not made up of solitary individuals or lonely wanderers.

Cicero then proceeds to give a standard account of different kinds of constitution in terms of the number of persons involved in political decision-making: monarchy, aristocracy, democracy. The strengths and weakness of each of these pure forms of constitution are discussed by Cicero's character Scipio, who prefers monarchy. However, Scipio adds that monarchy is itself surpassed by an even and judicious blend of the three simple forms at their best. A state should possess an element of regal supremacy, something else should be assigned and allotted to the authority of aristocrats; and certain affairs should be reserved for the judgment and desires of the masses. Such a constitution has, in the first place, a widespread element of equality which free men cannot long do without. Secondly, it has stability; for although those three original forms easily degenerate into their corrupt versions producing a despot instead of a king, an oligarchy instead of an aristocracy, and a disorganized rabble instead of a democracy and although those simple forms often change into others, such things rarely happen in a political structure with represents a combination and a judicious mixture – unless, the politicians are deeply corrupt.

It is not surprising that Scipio, evidently speaking for Cicero, regards the Roman form of government, "the one which our fathers received from their forebears and have handed down to us, as an instantiation of this superior, mixed constitution. In other places, Cicero sometimes uses the term *res publica* specifically for the form of government of the late Roman republic, often in the course of lamenting its displacement by despotic rule. Indeed, as an eloquent defender of the government and society of the Roman republic that Cicero has been primarily known in later history.

In his *De Legibus*, Cicero explicitly dismisses what, for the Roman of his time, would have been the two most salient positivist sources of law: the ancient Twelve Tablets and the edicts issued by urban praetor on his assumption of office. The former was a codification of criminal and civil law dating from about 450 B.C.; the latter statements issued by chief magistrates, detailing forms and procedures for the administration of civil law and building upon similar edicts by their predecessors in office. According to Cicero in order to understand law, we must clarify the nature of what is right [*ius*], and that has to be deduced from the nature of man. Then we must consider the laws by which states ought to be governed, and finally deal with the laws and enactments which peoples have compiled and written down.

The strategy outlined by Cicero is that the principles of what is right (*ius*) are to be located in law (*lex*). And the essence of law is to be found in nature – both the nature of the universe as a whole and in the particular nature of the human part of the universe: law is the highest reason inherent in nature, which enjoins what ought to be done and forbids the opposite. When that reason is fully formed and completed in the human mind, it, too, is law. So for the most learned authorities law for enjoins right action and to forbid wrong-doing, is wisdom or practical rationality or prudential.

Cicero, however, inverts this order: it is lex that is deeper and grounds *ius*, in its general sense. The answers to both questions, lie in his Stoic conception of the whole universe as a *cosmopolis*, ruled by an immanent Reason with a capital R, which dictates the details of each successive world history. In orthodox Stoicism, each of these histories or cycles is identical in detail to all the others – because, since Reason is responsible for each history, there would be no reason for differences among cycles. Reason gets it right each and every time. Since the universe is analogized to a human polis or respublica it is natural enough to think of objective moral correctness or rightness as founded in the statues of that all-encompassing cosmopolis. He also thinks of human persons as sharing, along with any other rational inhabitants of the universe, in the divine Reason that is immanent in that universe and that gives the universe the rational, intelligible nature of a cosmos.

The cultivation of human reason, according to Cicero's Stoic doctrine, leads to our recognition of what is fine, noble, or morally good. This process is allied with something like the identification of each person's own, true individual good with the common good – in the sense of the good of all rational beings – through the Stoic technical concept of "sociation" or "appropriation".The essential unity of all human beings, and of what the good is for human beings, is a Stoic theme that is stressed by Cicero. This is sufficient proof that there is no essential difference within mankind. Reason in fact – the one thing in which we are superior to the beasts... - that is certainly common to us all.

There are two propositions concerning ancient ethical thought that are now widely regarded as truisms. The first is that ancient ethics is more or less universally "virtue ethics". That is, ancient ethical theory is primarily focused on the virtues and vices: the character traits that make a human person a morally good person and their contraries rather than the duties, obligations, and rights that are proper to human beings. The second proposition is that the classical natural-law theory of ethics and politics – that derives especially from St. Thomas Aquinas in the thirteenth century A.D. – is a Christianized development of ancient moral theory, particularly that of Aristotle.

The first point that needs to be made is that the "rule-bound" character of classical natural-law theory has been exaggerated by later writers. Nonetheless, the transformation from virtue to law is striking. An important element in that transformation, is to be found in Cicero's use of the Stoic tradition in his moral and political writings. Human beings have the ability to participate in the universal, cosmic reason directed towards action. Because of human nature's being what it is, human practical reason manifests itself through the four cardinal virtues of wisdom, fortitude, justice, and temperance. The application of these virtues within the context of a person's living his life in community with his fellows involves the discernment and performance of offices or duties . And, finally, practical wisdom must effect the formation of political structures, human or "positive" law, and systems of teaching that codify certain of these duties. "There is", Cicero says, "no doubt that, as the law should correct wickedness and promote goodness, a code of conduct may be derived from it".

In his *On Duties,* Cicero discuses the kinds of behavior that ought to manifest the virtues different circumstances. Justice is founded in the desire for self-preservation. is first transformed to a desire of a person "to devote himself to providing whatever may contribute to the comfort and sustenance not only of himself, but also of his wife, his children, and others whom he holds dear and ought to protect". Then, it is transformed into a like concern for all humans as beings who are capable of partaking in reason. Thus, justice is the part of practical reason involved "with preserving fellowship among men, with assigning to each his own, and faithfulness to agreements one has made".

Wisdom and practical rationality are initially conflated as pertaining to "the search for truth and its investigation as, peculiar to man". Very shortly thereafter in the text, Cicero makes a quite un-Aristotelian assertion of the primacy of practical rationality. A fault or vice opposed to reason is "that some men bestow excessive devotion and effort upon matters that are both abstruse and difficult, and unnecessary". It is, Cicero claims, contrary to duty to be drawn by such a devotion away from practical achievements: all the praise that belongs to virtue lies in action. On the other hand, there is often a break from it, and we are given many opportunities to return to our studies. Besides, the activity of the mind, which is never at rest, can maintain in us our pursuit of learning even without effort on our part. It is practical rationality's connection with human community and society that he later involves as the reason why the application of reason to distinctively human matters "should be ranked above mere learning. As an aside, it is interesting to note that the Stoic-Ciceronian divinity, Reason immanent in the cosmos, is essentially practical.

Cicero laments that Caesar overturned all the laws of goods and men for the sake of the pre-eminence that he had imagined for himself in his mistaken fancy. There is something troubling in this kind of case, in that the desire for honour, command, power and glory usually exists in the greatest spirit and most brilliant intellectual talent. Therefore one must be all the more careful not to do wrong in this way.

Cicero's conception of the fourth cardinal virtue, temperance, is also broad – but not so distinctly modern. Temperance is the aspect of the morally good or honourable that is concerned with order and limit in everything that is said and done. This virtue possesses what might be called, from the contemporary perspective, a peculiarly aesthetic character. The order and limit – conceived in aesthetic terms, as a kind of beauty – in human behavior to which this virtue pertains is closely allied with the human ability to discern similar qualities in nature. No other animal, therefore, perceives the beauty, the loveliness, the congruence of the parts, of the things that sight perceives. Nature and reason transfer this by analogy from the eyes to the mind, thinking that beauty, constancy and order should be preserved, and much more so, in one's decisions and in one's deeds.

Cicero is clear that the preeminent virtue is wisdom or rationality. Since this virtue pertains to the investigation and discovery of what is true, it is the common virtue of all rational beings. As for the other three virtues, he says that "their aim is necessities: they are to procure and conserve whatever is required for the action of life". Action vitae here connotes more than just life in its biological sense of being born, taking nutrition, growing, maturing, reproducing, aging, and dying. It connotes the distinctively human life assigned to us by nature and reason: "preserving the fellowship and bounding between men", allowing excellence and greatness of spirit to shine out, "conserveing honorableness and seemliness when we apply some limit and order to the things with which we deal in our life.

We might describe Cicero, who here follows the lead of the Stoics, as "rationalizing" the moral virtues and as "legalizing" ethics. According to Aristotle, the connection between the moral and intellectual virtues is indirect and, it might seem, essentially passive. While the intellectual virtues are cultivated by teaching, the moral virtues are acquired by habitation and training. They are, for Aristotle, those habits of character that make an agent amenable to direction by reason; and in this respect at least, Aristotle's conception of the moral virtues resembles Plato's conception of the virtues other than reason. For Cicero, however, the moral virtues are more directly expressions of rationality with respect to the nature, rational and social, of human beings. Since human rationality is an expression of divine Reason, viewed in terms of the lex governing the whole cosmopolis, there is a sense in which Cicero "legalizes" ethics. This phenomenon is less a matter of viewing ethical matters as a matter of a code of proscriptions and prescriptions than it is of seeing moral and ethical matters as developing from a universal, authoritative source, Reason with a capital R.

With respect to law in the sense of what is now termed positive law, it is thus not surprising that Cicero should be strongly committed to legal moralism, the doctrine that in order for positive law to qualify as "law" it is has to reflect law in the fullest, normative sense, that is, Reason. Well then, as the divine mind is the highest law so, in the case of a human being, when it is fully developed, that is law; and it is fully developed in the mind of the wise man [the Stoic sage]. Those laws, however, which have been formulated in various terms to meet the temporary needs of communities, enjoy the name of law thanks to popular approval rather than actual fact...From this it is reasonable to infer that those who framed harmful and unjust rules for their communities, acting in a way quite contrary to their claim and promises, introduced measures which were anything but laws. So, when it comes to interpreting the word, it is clear that inherent in the very name of law is the sense and idea of choosing what is just and true.

It turns out, then, that politics is not for Cicero a local affair – at least not politics as a normative ideal embodied in the Ciceronian notion of a res publica. Magistrates should observe the rule of law. But the relevant law is not necessarily a particular code, or the decress of their predecessors. As magistrates are subject to the laws, the people are subject to the magistrates. In fact it is true to say that a magistrate is a speaking law, and law a silent magistrate. Nothing is so closely bound up with the decress and terms of nature as authority. Without that no house or state or clan can survive – nor the human race, nor the whole of nature, nor the very universe itself. For the universe obeys God; land and sea abide by the laws of the universe, and human life is subject to the command of the supreme law.

Cicero rose to eminence as a public speaker and as a supporter of moderate reform within the traditional social order based on landed wealth and hierarchical defence; his early speeches attack corruption and abuse of power within the system rather than the system itself. His success was based in part on his rhetorical and political skills, in part on his reassuring conservation at a time of extraordinary military ad social upheaval. Elected as a safe alternative to Catiline, the bankrupt and unsavory aristocrat whose electoral failure drove him to conspiracy and revolution, he managed very briefly to unite the discordant elements of Roman society in the face of the genuine danger posed by Cataline.

Early in December 63 BCE, the consul Cicero, having unmasked the conspiracy of Catiline and supervised the execution of several of the leading conspirators, was hailed as Father of his Country and escorted home by a crowd of grateful romans from all ranks of society; a public thanksgiving was decreed in his honour, the first such award ever made for nonmilitary service to the state. The actions that deserved honor, however, were the source of all downfall even more rapid than his rise. Legitimate fear of armed insurrection led Cicero to execute citizens in 63 on the basis of a resolution of the senate, without a formal trial. In the violent factional politics of the late 60s and early 50s, his actions in 63 left Cicero vulnerable to his enemies; the coalition which he had created against Catiline dissolved in the face of mob violence and rampant corruption; and he was sent into exile in 58 at the instigation of the tribune Publius Clodius Pulcher - only to be recalled eighteen months later when political circumstances changed. Cicero relied on his own abilities at a time when the possession of money and armed troops, had far more political effect than eloquence, decency, or parliamentary skill; although honored for his eloquence and expertise, he remained without real influence through the turbulence that preceded the civil war between Pompey and Caesar; and having half-heartedly chosen to support Pompey, he had virtually no place in public life under Caesar's dictatorship in the 40s. Only at he end of his life, after the assassination of Caesar on 15 March 44, did Cicero regain some measure of power, leading the senate in its support of Brutus and Cassius against Antony. But in the bewildering military and political circumstances of 44-43, Cicero's mistaken judgment that he could control and use the young heir of Caesar. Augustus had fatal consequences: at the formation of the Second Triumvirate Antony, the young Caesar, and us Lepidus in November 43, he was proscribed. After he was killed on 7 December 43, his head and hands were cut off and placed on the Rostrum in Rome, a sign of the ruthlessness of the triumvirs and a symbol of the end of traditional republican politics.

In this cultural climate, and with his extensive knowledge of Greek rhetoric and philosophy, Cicero was similarly moved to adapt the learning of Greece to the traditional culture of Rome. In the period between 55 and his reluctant departure to govern the province of Cilicia in the spring of 51, Cicero wrote three dialogues *On the Orator* adapted and replied to the Corpus and Phuedrus; *On the Commonwealth* is his version of the Republic; and *On the Laws* which was left incomplete is modeled on Plato's Laws. After the Civil war, his literary production increased in speed and diminished in elegance: two more works on rhetoric and a long series of studies, which Cicero himself claimed falsely were simply transcripts of Greek works, on epistemology, ethics, and religion. While in these dialogues Cicero adapted his models through the use of Roman examples and issues, it was only after the death of Caesar, at the same time that he wrote the *Philippics* attacking Antony, that he returned to writing about the immediate concerns of Roman public life: the treatise *On Duties* written at the end of 44 was for centuries his most widely read and influential work.

Although in all his philosophical works Cicero made extensive use of the writings of Hellenistic philosophers, above all the Stoics and in the dialogues written after the Civil War he generally employed the form of Aristotelian dialogue - set speeches expounding different philosophical points of view rather than Socratic conversation – it was Plato to whom he: was first attracted as a literary and stylistic model, even though he found Plato's views on rhetoric and government both wrong and unrealistic, The use of strongly characterized speakers of divergent views in a fully realized dramatic setting - particularly true of the Plutonic dialogues Cicero most extensively employed, *Gorgias, Phaedrus, Republic,* and *Laws* - was eminently suitable for Cicero's project in the 50s, an attempt to transpose Greek ideas about public life into a Roman context and to provide a more rigorous philosophical model for Roman public behavior and institutions than had previously existed.

In *On the Orator* there are clear indications of Cicero's larger concerns with the political context of ethical values and with the importance of the orator as the true statesman; above all, it displays Cicero's belief that it is through the character and political wisdom of particular individuals - in *On the Orator* seen as an element of rhetoric itself- that the larger goals of society can best be fostered and maintained. In *On the Commonwealth,* he attempted to give a fuller account of the values and nature of public life. Although *On the Commonwealth* seems to have been a canonical text in antiquity and was widely known until the fifth century CE, it cannot be shown to have existed entire after that, and it survives only in fragmentary form. Two things clearly take place in the dialogue: there is a move from historical arguments about constitutional form to arguments from nature; and there is similarly a move from considering good government in terms of its practical effectiveness and stability to examining it in terms of its moral values

On the Commonwealth was the first, and perhaps the only, serious attempt by a Roman to analyze the structure and values of republican government and imperial rule. In adapting Platonc and Aristotelian theories based on the small, self-contained, and relatively homogeneous society of the polis to the conditions of the Roman imperium, Cicero made use of Stoic ideas of the cosmpolis and of natural law to develop a complex and ambitious argument, linking the traditional values and institutions of republican Rome on the one hand to Aristotelian ideas of civic virtue and on the other to the order of the universe itself. Stoic moral theory made it possible for Cicero to construct an image of society ruled not by a Platonic intellectual elite which alone had access to truth through dialectic and the knowledge of the Forms, but by all those whose recognition of their own moral capacities, as a part of a cosmic whole, led them to contribute to the creation and preservation of a society which reflected and incorporated the natural justice of the universe. As the preface to *On the Commonwealth* make clear, Cicero framed the dialogue as an exhortation to public service and an explanation of the goals and rewards of civic life; he rejects Epicurean withdrawal into private life as well as Platonic and Aristotolian ideas of the superiority of contemplation to action. Political institutions, as in Aristotle, serve not only political ends but moral ones; but in Cicero's universe they also provide a necessary link between social order and the natural law. Perhaps the most striking argument in *On the Commonwealth* is Cicero's attempt in Book 4 to explain the traditional institutions of Roman society in terms of Stoic moral theory, giving a philosophical basis to inherited social practices. Similarly, by demonstrating that the traditional Roman constitution was the only moral form of government and grounding it in the ethical structure of the cosmos in Book 3, Cicero offers a philosophical justification for Roman imperialism and claims to universal rule.

In this connection, however, it is important to recognize that Cicero is very far from advancing an argument in favor of Roman nationalism any more than the emphasis on the role of the statesman a call for monarchy. For both national and individual behavior, Cicero's cosmic framework supplies an absolute standard with which to judge the moral worth of actions and, in the case of nations, an indication of whether or not they deserve to survive. Aristotle had argued that good government are those in which power is exercised in the interest of the governed rather than the rulers; Cicero extends this to include rule over subject peoples as well and gives a moral and political dimension to Aristotle's ideas about natural slavery. It is essential for Cicero that a commonwealth or an empire be above all a moral community; he makes it very clear not only that lapses in moral government will inevitably lead to political collapse, but also that Rome itself, in both its internal government and its conduct of empire, has fallen away from the standard which it once maintained.

On the Commonwealth is the last known Roman philosophical work completed before the outbreak of the civil war between Caesar and Pompey which effectively ended republican government at Rome, and Cicero was well aware that the social and political structure which he idealized in his dialogue had collapsed: indeed, he says as much in the preface to Book 5. What he offers in *On the Commonwealth* is less a practical program for political reform than a philosophical rationale for what had been lost, together with an explanation of why it had failed. It is an explanation based not on the economic and social changes in Rome that had in fact placed intolerable stress on the structure of republican government, but on Cicero's belief in the moral obligations of statesmen and of states. It was perhaps an unfashionable and certainly ineffective approach to the problems of civic life even when it was written, and the contradictions in Cicero's own account seem to acknowledge that. In the dialogue, Scipio is presented as the sole possible savior of ancestral virtue; his sudden death only signals Cicero's sense of the impossibility of maintaining the form of government he so admired and his recognition that the ideal presented in the dialogue was, like Plato's Republic, an ideal and not reality.

Because the complete text of *C:n the Commonwealth* was lost between about 600 and 1819, its direct influence on modern political theory is virtually nonexistent. Nonetheless, portions of it, preserved by other writers, were widely known. *The Dream of Scipio* was known and used by writers including Dante throughout the Middle Ages.

— Editor

Forms of Governments

From that arises a government either of an aristocracy or of a faction, or tyrannical or monarchic or, quite frequently, popular, and similarly from that usually arises another of those There are remarkable revolutions and almost cycles of changes and alterations in commonwealths; to recognize them is the part of a wise man, and to anticipate them when they are about to occur, holding a course and keeping it under his control while governing, is the part of a truly great citizen and nearly divine man. My own opinion, therefore, is that there is a fourth type of commonwealth that is most to be desired, one that is blended and mixed from these first three types that I have mentioned

Laelius : I know that is your view, Africanu, and I have heard it from you often; but still, if it isn't too much trouble, I would like to know which of these three types of commonwealth you think best. It will be of some use to know.

Scipio: And the character of any commonwealth corresponds to the nature or the desire of its ruling power. And so in no other state than that in which the people has the highest power does liberty have any home liberty, than which nothing can be sweeter, and which, if it is not equal, is not even liberty. And how can it be equal (I won't speak about monarchy, in which slavery is not even hidden or ambiguous) in those states in which everyone is free in name only? They vote, they entrust commands and offices, they are canvassed and asked for their support, but they give what must be given even if they are unwilling, and they are asked to give what they do not have themselves. They have nit share in power, in public deliberation, or in the panels of select judges, all of which are apportioned on the basis of pedigree or wealth. In a free people, as at Rhodes or Athens, there is no citizen who.

If one or several wealthy men arise from the people, then they say that these faults come from their scorn and haughtiness, as the cowardly and weak give way to the arrogance of the wealthy. But if the people holds to its own rights, they deny that there is anything more outstanding, more free, more blessed: they are masters of the laws and the courts, of war and peace, of treaties, of the status and wealth of every individual. They think that this commonwealth (that is, the "concern of the people") is the only one properly so named; and sc it is usual for the "concern of the people" to be liberated from the domination of kings and aristocrats, and not for kings or the power and wealth of an aristocracy to be sought by a free people. Furthermore, they say that this type of free people should not be condemned because of the failings of an undisciplined populace: when the people is harmonious and judges everything in terms of its safety and liberty there is nothing more unchanging or more stable. It is easiest, they say, for harmony to obtain in a commonwealth in which everyone has the same interest: from a variety of interests, when different things are advantageous for different people, discord arises And so, when the senate gains control of affairs, the condition of the state is never stable, and that is all the more true of monarchies: as Ennius said, "there is no holy bond or trust" in a monarchy. And therefore, since law is the bond of civil society, and rights under law are equal then by what right can a society of citizens be held together when the status of citizens is not the same? Even if equality of property is not appealing, and if the mental abilities of all cannot he equal, certainly the rights of all who are citizens of the same commonwealth ought to be equal. What is a state if not the association of citizens under law?

They believe that other commonwealths should not even be given the names that they themselves prefer. Why should I call "king," using the title of Jupiter the Best, a man who yearns for power and sole rule, lording over an oppressed populace, rather than "tyrant"? It is possible for tyrant to be as merciful as a king can be harsh, so that there is this difference only for their subjects, whether they are slaves to a mild master or a harsh one: it is in any case impossible for them not be to slaves. How could Sparta, at the time when it was thought to have the best-ordered commonwealth, make sure that it had good and just kings, when they had to accept as king whoever was born in the royal family? And who could endure aristocrats, "the best people," who have taken that name for themselves not by the concession of the people but by their own self-election? How is one of them judged "best"? by learning, skill, education? So you say : but when has that ever been the criterion for being an aristocrat?

If it chooses its leaders by chance, it will be overturned as quickly as a ship that has one of its passengers chosen by lot as helms-man. But if a free people chooses the men to whom to entrust itself (and it will chose he best people if it wants to be safe), then surely the safety of the citizens' is found in the deliberations of the best men. That is particularly true because nature has made sure not only that men outstanding for virtue and courage rule over weaker people, but that the weaker people willingly obey the best. But they say that this ideal condition is overturned by men's bad judgments: through their ignorance of virtue (which not only appears in few men but is judged and recognized by few) they think that men of wealth and property, or men of noble birth, are "best." By this common error, when the wealth of a few replaces virtue in control of the commonwealth, those leaders cling doggedly to the name of "best citizens," but in fact they lack the substance for that very reason. For wealth, or reputation, or resources, if they are empty of prudence and of a method of living and of ruling over others, are filled with disgrace and insolent pride; and there is no uglier form of state than that in which the richest are thought to be the best. But when virtue rules over the commonwealth, what could be more glorious? Then the man who commands others is himself enslaved to no desires when he himself embraces all the things to which he educates and exhorts his citizens, and he imposes no laws on the populace which he does not himself obey but offers his own life as a law to his citizens. If one such person could adequately accomplish everything, then there would be no need of more; if everyone could see what is best and could agree on it, then no one would seek selected leaders. The difficulty of making policy transferred control from a king to a group of people, and the rash folly of popular governments has transferred it from the multitude to the few. In this way, the aristocrats hold the middle ground between the weakness of a single person and the rashness of many. Nothing can be more moderate than this, and when the aristocrats look after the commonwealth then the populace is of necessity most blessed: they arc free of every care and thought, having handed over their tranquility to others who must guard it and must make sure that the people do not believe that their interests are being neglected by their leaders. For legal equality - the object of free peoples-cannot be preserved: the people themselves, no matter how uncontrolled they may be, give great rewards to many individuals, and they pay great attention to the selection of men and honors. And what people call equality is in fact very unfair. When the same degree of honor is given to the best and the worst (and such must exist in any population), then equity itself is highly inequitable. But that is something that can not happen in states that are ruled by the best citizens.

Laelius: What do you think, Scipio? Which one of these three forms do you most approve?

Scipio:You are right to ask which one of the three I most approve, since I approve of none of them by itself, separately. I prefer to the individual forms the type that is an alloy of all three. But if I had to express approval of one of the simple forms, then I would choose monarchy ... is named at this point, the name of king appears almost fatherly, someone looking after his citizens as if they were his children, and preserving them more eagerly than . . . to be supported by the diligence of one man, the best and greatest. Here are the aristocrats, who claim that they can do this same job better and say that there is more judgment in the deliberations of several people than of one, but the same equity and honor. And here is the populace shouting loudly that they will not obey one person or a few; that even for wild animals there is nothing sweeter than liberty, and that everyone is deprived of it, whether it is a king or aristocrats to whom they are enslave' . And so kings captivate us by their affection, aristocrats by their judgment and the people by its liberty, so that in comparing them it is hard to pick the most desirable.

Laelius: That makes sense; but the rest of the subject can hardly be explained if you leave this question unanswered.

Scipio: Then we should imitate Aratus: in undertaking to speak about great matters he believes that one must begin from Jupiter.

Laelius: Why Jupiter? How is this subject anything like that poem?

Scipio: Only that we should duly take our starting point from him, whom all men, learned and unlearned, agree is the one king of all gods and men.

Laelius : Why?

Scipio: Why do you think? The reason is in front of your eyes. The leaders of commonwealths may have thought that it would be useful for civic life that people should believe that there is one king in the sky who turns all Olympus with his nod, as Homer says, and that he is both king and father of all; there is much authority and many witnesses (everyone, in fact) to show that all nations have acquiesced in the decision of their leaders that nothing is better than a king, because they believe that all the gods are ruled by the will of One. On the oilier hand, it may be that, as we have been taught, this belief is one of the errors of the uneducated and a kind of myth. In any case, we should listen to the common instructors of educated men, who have seen as if with their eyes things that we scarcely know from hearing about them.

Laelius: What are your examples?

Scipio: Well, dont's you see that because of the relentess arrogence of a single man, Traquinius, the name of king became hated by our people?

Laelius: I see it

Scipio: So you see this (something I expect to say more about as our discussion goes on), 81 that when Tarquinius was expelled, the novelty of freedom made the people amazingly unrestrained in their pleasure: that was when innocent people were driven into exile and many people's property was plundered; annual consuls were established, the faces were lowered before the people, there was a right appeal for every kind of crime, there were secessions of the plebs: in short, that was when most things were arranged so that the people had total control.

Laelius: All that is true.

Scipio: Peace and tranquility are like a ship or a minor illness: you can be undisciplined when there is on danger. But when the sea hets rough or the disease gets worse, the sailor or the sick man calls for one person's help. So too, at home and in peace, our pepole give orders ot the magistrates themselves-they theratem, refuse to obey, ask for one magistrate's help against another, and appeal to the pepole; but in our they obey their leaders as they-would a king: safety matters more than one's own desires. And in major ware, our people wanted all the power to be in the hands of one individual without a colleague, whose very title indicates the exten of his power: he is called a dictator because he is appointed, but in our augural books, Laelius, you see that he is called "master of the people."

Scipio: They thought that life, honor, and glory were given to them by the justice of king. The same goodwill would have lasted among their descendants, if the kings had retainde the same character; but you see that because of the injustice of one of them that entire form of the commonwealth was destroyed.

Laelius: I see it and want to learn the patterns of changes not just in our commonwealth but in all commonwealths.

Scipio; When I have said what I think about the type of commonwealth I most admire, I must speak with greater precision about the transfomations of commonwealths, even though I think that will not take place easily in the best, type But the alteration of the monarchic form is the first and must certain: when a king begins to be unjust, the form is immediately destroyed, and that same person is a tyrant, the worst form, but closest to the best. If the aristocracy gets rid of him (which generally happens), the commonwealth has the second of the three forms; it is almost monarchic, that is, a senatorial council of leaders taking good care of the people. If the people themselves kill or expel the tyrant, the government is reasonably restrained, so long as it is intelligent and perceptive: they rejoice in their accomplishment, and want to protect the commonwealth that they have set up. But when either the people bring force to bear on a just king and deprive him of his throne or even (as happens more frequently) have tasted the blood of the aristocracy and subordinated the entire commonwealth to their own desires, do not make the mistake of thinking that any huge ocean or fire is harder to calm than the violence of a mob out of control. Plato has eloquently described this condition; it is hard to put it into Latin, but I will try to do it anyway.

"When," he says, "the insatiable throats of the people the parched with thirst for liberty, and through the aid of evil ministers have drained in their thirst a pure draught of liberty instead of a moderate mixture, then unless the magistrates and the leaders are very mild and lenient and serve up liberty to them generously, the people persecute, attack, and accuse them, calling them over powerful kings or tyrants." I think that all this is familiar to you.

Laelius: Very familiar.

Scipio: What follows is this: "Those who obey the leaders are attacked by the people and called willing slaves; but they shower with praise and give exorbitant honors to magistrates who act like private citizens and private citizens who act as if there were no difference between private citizens and magistrates. In such a commonwealth everything is inevitably filled with liberty: private homes have no master, and this evil extends even to animals; ultimately fathers fear their sons, sons neglect their fathers, all sense of shame is lost, and they are utterly free. There is no difference between citizen and foreigner, the teacher fears his pupils and fawns on them, pupils scorn their teachers, the young take on the gravity of old men, while old men are reduced to children's games, so as not to be hateful or tiresome. Slaves behave with too much freedom, women have the same rights as their husbands, and even dogs and horses and asses go about sc freely in this atmosphere of liberty that people have to get out of their way in the streets. The final outcome of this extreme license,'1 he says, "is that the minds of citizens become so delicate and sensitive that if the least authority is brought to bear on them they are angered and unable to endure it; the result is that they begin to ignore the laws as well, so that they are utterly without any master."

Laelius: Your translation of what Plato said is completely accurate.

Scipio: To return to my source: he says that this excessive license, which they think; the only true liberty, is the stock from which tyrants grow, so to speak. For just as the excessive power of the aristocracy causes their fall, so too liberty itself makes slaves out of this excessively free populace. Anything that is too successful - in weather, or harvests, or human bodies generally turns into its opposite, and that is particularly true of commonwealths: extreme liberty, both of the people at large and of particular individuals, results in extreme slavery. From this pure liberty arises a tyrant, the most unjust and harshest form of slavery. For from this unruly, or rather monstrous, populace some leader is usually chosen against those aristocrats who have already been beaten down and driven from their place: someone bold, corrupt, vigorous in attacking people who have often served the commonwealth well; someone who buys the people's good will using others' property as well as his own. As a private citizen, he fears for his safety, and so he is given power which is renewed; he is protected by bodyguards, like Pisistratus in Athens; and finally he emerges as tyrant cver those very people who promoted him. If, as often happens a tyrant is overthrown by respectable people, the state is restored; if by men of daring, it becomes an oligarchy, which is just another form of tyranny. The same type of regime can often emerge from a good aristocratic government, when corruption turns the leaders themselves from the right path. In this way, they snatch the government from one another as if it were a ball: tyrants from kings, aristocrats or the people from them, and from them oligarchies or tyrants. No form of commonwealth is ever maintained for very long.

Since that is the case, of the three primary forms my own preference is for monarchy; but monarchy itself is surpassed by a government which is balanced and compounded from the three primary forms of commonwealth. I approve of having something outstanding and monarchic in a commonwealth; of there being something else assigned to the authority of aristocrats; of some things being set aside for the judgment and wishes of the people. This structure has, in the first place, a certain degree of equality, which free people cannot do without for very long; it also has solidity, in that those primary forms arc easily turned into the opposite vices, so that a master arises in place of a king, a faction in place of aristocracy, a confused mob in place of the people; and these types themselves are often replaced by new ones. That does not occur in this combined and moderately blended form of commonwealth unless there are great flaws in its leaders. There is no reason for revolution when each person is firmly set in his own rank, without the possibility of sudden collapse.

But 1 am afraid, Laelius and all you other good and wise friends, that if I continue too long in this vein, I will seem to speak like some instructor or lecturer instead of a fellow inquirer into this subject." So I will turn to some thing everyone knows, and which we started looking for some time ago. I will state my own opinion and belief and judgment that no commonwealth, in either its organization or its structure or its conduct and training, can be compared to the one our fathers received from their ancestors and have passed on to us. And if you agree, since you want to hear from me what you know yourselves, I will explain both the character and the superiority of our commonwealth. My description of our commonwealth will serve as the pattern to which I will tailor what I have to say concerning the best form of state. If I can carry this our completely, then I will, in my opinion, have thoroughly fulfilled the task which Laelius gave me.

Laelius: The task is yours, Scipio, and yours alone. Who could speak about the institutions of our ancestors better than you, who an: descended from the most distinguished ancestors? Who could speak better about the best form of the state? And if we ever get such a state, who could be more distinguished in it than yon?

Scipio's Dream

Sciplo: After I had come to Africa, as you know, as military tribune to the fourth legion when Manilius here was consul, my first desire was to meet King Masinissa, a close friend of my family for the best of reasons." When I came to him, the old man embraced me and wept; and after a little he looked up to the sky and said: "I offer thanks to you, great Sun, and to you the other heavenly gods, because before I depart from this life I see in my kingdom and in my own home Publius Cornelius Scipio, whose very name revives me: the memory of that best and most unconquerable of men never departs from my mind." Then I asked him about his kingdom, and he asked me about our commonwealth; the day passed with much conversation between us.

Later, after dining royally, we stretched our conversation late into the night; the old man spoke of nothing but Africanus and called to mind not only all his actions but also his words. Then we went to bed; and as I was exhausted from the trip and from slaying awake so lair, I was griped by a deeper sleep than usual. At this point - and I believe that it was the result of what we had said: our thoughts and words often bring forth in sleep something like Ennuis' report of Homer, about whom he obviously used to think and speak a great deal when he was awake' - Africanus showed himself to me in the appearance which I knew better from his portrait than from having seen him.' When I recognized him, I shuddered; but he said, "Stay calm and don't be afraid, Scipio, and remember what I tell you."

"Do you see that city, which I forced to obey the Roman people but which now renews its earlier wars and is incapable of remaining peaceful?' (He was pointing at Carthage from a spot high up and filled with stars, that was bright and glorious.) "You are coming to besiege it now as little more than a simple soldier, but within two years you will destroy it as consul, and you will receive on your own account the name which you have already inherited from me. But after you have destroyed Carthage, have celebrated a triumph, and have been censor, and after you have as an ambassador visited Egyptt Syria, Asia, and Greece, you will be elected consul for the second time in your absence and you will bring to a conclusion a major war by destroying Numantia. But after you ride up the Capitol in your triumphal chariot, you will encounter the commonwealth in a state of disorder because of the plans of my grandson.' At this point, Africanus, you will have to display to your country the brilliance of your mind and talent and judgment. But I see at this point a double path of fate: when your span of years has traversed seven times eight turns and returns of the sun, and these two numbers, each of which is considered perfect for various reasons, have made up the sum of your fare by their natural circling, the whole state will turn to you alone and to your name: the senate, all upstanding citizens, the allies, and the Latins will look to you; you will be the one person on whom the safety of the state rests. To be brief: you will have to restore the commonwealth as dictator – if you escape the impious hands of those close to you."

At this point Laelius shouted out, and all the others groaned deeply, but Scipio smiled gently and said: Hush, please! or you will wake me up. Listen for a short time to the rest.

"But so that you may be all the more eager, Africanus, to protect the commonwealth, know this: for all those who have saved, aided, or increased the fatherland there is a specific place set aside in the sky where they may enjoy eternity in blessedness. There is nothing that can happen on earth that is more pleasing to that leading god who rules the whole world than those councils and assemblages of men associated through law which are called states; the guides and preservers of these have set out from here, and here they return."

At this point, even though I was terrified not so much by the fear of death as of treachery on the part of my own people, I still asked him whether he was alive, along with my father Paullus and the others whom we think of as dead. "Yes indeed," he said, "these people are alive; they have escaped from the chains of the body as if from a prison, and what is called life among you is in fact death.1" Don't you sec your father Paullus approaching you?" And when I saw him, I wept heavily, but he embraced me and kissed me and told me not to weep.

As soon as I could quell my tears and began to be able to speak, I said: "I ask you, best and most sacred of fathers, since this is life, as Africanus tells me, why am I delaying on earth: Why don't I hurry to come here to you;'"

"That isn't the way things are," he said. "Unless the god, whose precinct is all that you behold, frees you from the guardianship of your , you have no access to this place.' Men are created under these terms, that they are to took after that globe which you see in the middle of this precinct, which is called earth; and they are given a soul from those eternal fires which you call constellations and stars, which are spherical globes endowed with divine minds and accomplish their rotations and revolutions with amazing speed. And so, Publius, both you and all pious people must keep your soul in the guardianship of the body, and you must not depart from human life without the order of him who gave you your soul: you must not seem to run away from the human duty assigned by the god. But Scipio, you should be like your grandfather here and like me your father it cultivating justice and piety; it is important in relation to your parents and family, but most important in relation to your fatherland. That way if life is the way to the heavens and to this gathering of those who have ceased to live and after having been released from the body now inhabit the place you see" (it was a bright circle shining among the stars with a most radiant whiteness), "which you have learned from the Greeks to name the Milky Way." And from that point, as I studied everything, it all seemed to me glorious and marvelous. There were stars which we never see from this place, and their size was such as we have never suspected; the smallest one was the fine furthest from the heavens and closest to earth and shone with borrowed light.

The globes of the stars easily surpassed the size of the earth, and earth itself now seemed so small to me that I was ashamed of our empire, which touches only it link- speck of it.

And as I kept looking, Africans asked me: "I wonder how long your mind will be fixed on the ground? Don't you see the precinct into which you have come? Everything is linked, you see, in nine circles or rathier spheres. One of them, the outer one, is the sphere of the heavens which, embraces all the rest; it is the highest god himself protecting and limiting the rest, and in it are fixed the eternal revolving courses of the stars. Within that are seven which revolve in the opposite direction from the heavens. The first sphere belongs to the planet which humans call Saturn's;" then the light giving favor and safety to men called Jupiter's; then the red one hateful to earth which you call Mars'; then the one below, roughly in the center, belongs to the Sun, the ruler, leader and guide of the remaining celestial bodies, the mind and balance of the universe, so large that it traverses and fills all with its light. The orbits of Venus and of Mercury follow it like attendants, and in the lowest sphere the Moon revolves, lit by the rays of the Sun. Below that there is nothing that is not mortal and perishable concept the souls given to the human raw by the gift of the gods; Moon everything is eternal. The sphere that is ninth, in the middle, Earth; it is stationary and the lowest one, and all weights are borne towards it of their own accord."

I was staring dumbfounded at all this, but when recovered myself I said: "Tell me: what is the sound which fills my cars, so great and so sweet?"

"This is the sound that is caused by the action and motion of the spheres themselves. Its harmony is based on uneven intervals, but the inequality of intervals is proportional and based on reason, and by blending high notes with low itself causes balanced music." Such vast motions cannot proceed without sound, and the furthest in one direction naturally nukes a deep note, and the furthest in the other a high one. For that reason the highest sphere of the heavens with the stars in ii, which turns very rapidly, moves with a high and agitated sound, and the lowest sphere of the Moon with a very deep one - the ninth, the Earth, is unmoving and always stays in the same place, embracing the center of the universe. But those eight orbits, of which two have the same pitch, create seven sounds distinguished by their intervals; and that number is really at the heart of the matter. Learned men who have imitated it with stringed instruments and song have opened for themselves their return to this place, just like others who have used outstanding intelligence to cultivate divine studies in their human lives. Men's ears have been filled with this sound and consequently grown deaf to it. You have no duller sense than hearing, just as at the point where the Nile plunges from high mountain at the place called Cataract, the race of men that lives there is completely deaf because of the magnitude of the sound. The sound made by the rapid revolution of the universe is so great that human ears cannot grasp it, just as you are unable to look directly into the Sun, because your sight and sense are overcome by its rays."

Although I marveled at all this, I still kept bringing my eyes back to earth. Then Africarros said: "I realize that you are still looking at the home and dwelling of men; but if it seems to you as small as in fact it is, you must always look at these heavenly bodies and scorn what is human. What fame can you achieve in what men say, or what glory can you achieve that is worth seeking? You see that humans inhabit small and scattered portions of the earth, and that huge emptiness separates the blotches of human habitation. The people who inhabit the earth are not feels, who remembers, who looks ahead, who rules and guides and moves the body of which he is in command just as that leading god does for the universe. And just as the eternal god moves the universe, which is partly mortal, MI too Joes I he eternal soul move the fragile body. What is always in motion is eternal; but whatever brings motion to something else and is itself stirred up from elsewhere, when that motion ceases must necessarily cease its life. Therefore only what moves itself, because it never ceases itself, also never ceases to move; and if is in fact the source and beginning of motion for everything else that moves. There is no origin of beginning, but everything arises from a beginning, and the beginning itself can be born from nothing else - if it arose from elsewhere, it would not be a beginning. But if it never starts, it also never stops: for if the beginning is extinguished it will not be reborn from something else, nor will it create something else from itself, since it is necessary that everything start from a beginning. Thus the beginning of motion comes from that which is moved by itself; and it can neither be born nor die; otherwise the whole heaven and all nature would collapse and come to a stop and there would be no force that it could find to move it from the start. And since it is clear that is moved by itself is eternal who could deny that the soul has such nature? Whatever is moved by an external force is inanimate; but whatever is animate is stirred by its own internal motion. That is the special nature and force of the soul. And if it is the one thing of all which moves itself, then it is certainly not born and is therefore eternal. Use your soul in the best activities! And the best concerns are those that involve the safety of the fatherland; the soul which is aroused and exercised by them will fly more swiftly to this, its dwelling and home. It will do so all the more swiftly if even when it is enclosed in the body it project? outward and by contemplating those things that are outside it draws itself as much, as possible from the body. The souls of men who have surrendered themselves to the pleasures of the body and have made themselves into the servants of those pleasures, and at the urging of desires that are directed by pleasure have broken the laws of gods and men - those souls, when they have departed from the body, circle around the earth and only after having been harried for many generations do they return to this place."

He departed, and I awoke.

(From *On the Commonwealth and the Laws* by Cicero. Edited by James E.G. Zetzel, Cambridge University Press, UK, 1999)

5

St. Augustine

St. Augustine (354-430 AD) was born in 354 in the North African town of Thagaste what is now in Algeria. His mother Monica was a Christian but his father Patricius remained a pagan. Given the forceful personality of Monica, Augustine and his brother and sister became believers early on, but Augustine, as he vividly describes in his masterful *Confessions,* soon strayed from the fold. First at the neighboring university of Madaura and then at the university at Carthage, he succumbed to the pleasures of the flesh, living to the hilt the bawdy and sensual life of a student. Later he began to cohabit with a concubine and fathered a son by her. But there was more to the young Augustine than the pleasure-seeker and libertine. Attracted to the intellectual life by the work of Cicero, he soon fell under the influence of a heretical Christian sect called the Manichaeans. The Manichaeans preached a dualistic doctrine in which the forces of good (God) are pitted against the forces of evil (the Devil). It seemed to the young Augustine that this doctrine provided the best explanation available for the existence of evil in the world, including his own ever apparent sin. How could a good God be responsible for so much evil? Is it not more reasonable to think that an independent force of evil exists in the world and competes with God?

After his student days, Augustine became a teacher of rhetoric at Carthage and then moved to Rome to continue his academic career. Never far away lurked the indomitable Monica, worked there hoping and attempting to dissuade him from his sinful and heretical life. It was in Rome that Augustine was introduced to the work of the Neoplatonists, the result being that he began to question and then to abandon the Manichaean and Ciceronian views he had previously held. More positively, under the influence of the Neoplatonists he began to appreciate the reality of the immaterial dimension of life and world. The writings of the Neoplatonists directed his attention inward, to his soul, to his innermost, intangible being, and to the reality of the spiritual realm. Augustine was particularly attracted to Plotinus for resolution of the problem of evil, the problem of reconciling the existence of evil in the world with the reality of a good and omnipotent deity. Plotinus's theory of evil as privation claims that evil is not something that exists as a positive factor in the world but signifies only a lack of being resulting from the inferior status of the created world. By denying that evil is some entity for whose existence God must be held responsible and blamed, Plotinus demonstrates that God is wholly good.

Later, when Augustine took a professorship at Milan, he was introduced to the great Christian bishop Ambrose, with whom he was greatly impressed both intellectually and spiritually. It was in this context that he underwent his famous conversion to Christianity. The conversion occurred in a garden, where he overheard a child say, "pick it up and read it, pick it up and read it'. He took this to mean the Bible, and on opening it to one of St Paul's epistles, he read: "No reveling or drunkenness, no debauchery or vice, no quarrels or jealousies. Let Christ Jesus himself be the armour that you wear; give no more thought to satisfying the bodily appetites". He immediately came to see that no effort of will or intellect could save him from sin, and the realization dawned that his only hope lay through the power of God's grace. He came to understand that by God's grace he could turn his attention wholly to God and away from worldly desires and ambitions. He soon returned to North Africa in 388 where before long he was installed as the Christian Bishop of the town of Hippo. He remained in this post until his death many years later 430, serving both as a beloved pastor and as a highly esteemed Christian intellectual who was in the vanguard of many efforts to stem the tide of heretical doctrine. He was a prodigious and prolific writer, and he left us with an enormous body of books and pamphlets which have become seminal works of early Christian literature. In addition to his *Confessions,* his *The City of God* still ranks as one of the classics of Western civilization.

The attempt by Christian thinkers in the West to provide an account of the nature of political society draws upon a number of different sources. Christianity was born into a world dominated by Roman institutions, including Roman law, and by Greek philosophical concepts. Roman ideas on the nature of the civitas defined political society as a community under 'the rule of law'. Plato and Aristotle, on the other hand, saw the polis as an agency of moral education and formation since for them it was impossible to live a fully human life outside society. Only beasts and gods, Aristotle said, live outside the polis: beasts because they are sub-human and gods because they are superhuman. For the Greeks the civil law must always be in accordance with the moral law, otherwise tyranny ensues. Tyranny is that form of government where the naked will and power of the ruler prevails - in other words, where might is right.

The Christians of the first three centuries took an ambivalent attitude to the Roman State. Some were convinced that the end of the world and the advent of the kingdom of God were ineritable so that for them it was not a pressing concern to elaborate a Christian theory of the State. Others identified the State with the anti-Christian and pagan Roman State and rejected it completely. For them the Church, the community of believers, was the only true society. Just as the Christian philosophers had no need of pagan wisdom since the Scriptures were sufficient for them, so also Christians had no need of Greek and Roman political concepts and institutions. The 'City of God', the Church, was sufficient for them. Theocracy and fideism tend to go hand in hand. Other Christians recognized the role of the State and groped tentatively towards some kind of theory about the relationship that ought to obtain between the Church and the State -the supernatural society and the natural society - just as in the sphere of knowledge certain Christian thinkers attempted to define the relationship between what is known by 'faith' through revelation and what is known by 'natural reason' alone.

With the advent of the medieval period, we enter the world of Christianity. The West did not however, entirely abandon the modes of thought developed and perfected in ancient Greece. The two greatest Christian thinkers of all times, St. Augustine in the fourth and fifth centuries and St. Thomas Aquinas in the thirteenth, developed theologies and philosophies that attempted syntheses of the Christian message with Greek philosophy. Augustine was heavily influenced by Plato and the Platonist thinkers who followed him, especially the great Neoplatonist philosopher Plotinus. And Aquinas resurrected Aristotle and incorporated his thought into an explicit amalgam of Aristotelian and Christian beliefs. In one way or another, all of the medieval philosophers were concerned with issues whose origins were Greek. But, of course, the main driving element in the philosophies of Augustine and Aquinas as well as of the other thinkers of this period is the Christian message itself, the doctrine of the one eternal God who is creator of the world and of humanity, the loving God who sent his son Jesus Christ to save human beings from sin, and the judgmental God who assigns his human creatures to heaven or hell as a result of the kinds of lives they live during their earthly sojourns. The Platonic and Aristotelian concepts are used to articulate and interpret this message. They also provide it with universal scope or application. Augustine, Aquinas, and the other medieval thinkers see their philosophies as offering truths about humankind in general.

The Church, as an institution, may represent the values of the City of God, and the State those of the city of men, the occupants of each institution do not divide so neatly. There are members of the Church who belong to the city of man, and there are state officials who can be part of the City of God. The Church could never be equated with the heavenly city; even proximally, due to its mixed composition. Some members were predestined for heaven, others for damnation. Further, the elect and the damned were called by God, not by the Church, so the Church had no authority to designate who fits each category.

All states were created by divine providence. The Roman Empire is "good according to the standards of city of man, the kingdom of Satan, is what has emerged on earth through history. It is from its inception the result of human sin. Original Sin led to the creation and separation of two cities. Original Sin subjects "human nature to all the process of decay which we see and feel, and consequently to the earthly city". But as it was created to serve man's glory and pride, not the glory of God, Rome cannot be regarded as anything close to the City of God. Rome's purpose on earth, then, is to "suppress the grievous evils of many nations", reducing all evil and sin to the basic one of pride which can then be destroyed by the second coming of Jesus.

As the City of God is represented by Jerusalem, the City of Man is typified by Babylon and Rome. To sin is to violate God's laws, to revolt against the Creator. It becomes an attempt to destroy the essential unity of the universe. The first, or Original Sin was a declaration of defiance thrown in the face of God. It was an abuse of free will, a turning away from God's light and toward the darkness of pride and self-love. In the city of man, love of self and lust for power dominate. It is marked by the absence of justice. Remove justice, and what are kingdoms but gangs of criminals on a large scale? A gang is a group of men under the command of a leader, bound by a compact of association, in which the plunder is divided according to an agreed-upon convention. Those who rely on reason alone in a search for justice on earth have clearly chosen the earthly city. They have rejected God for "self-love reaching the point of contempt for God . . ." and are condemned to perpetual torment with the devil.

Christian doctrine holds that Christ died for men's sins and offered them the hope of salvation. The City of God is, of course, a true republic, a commonwealth not found on earth, and Christ was its founder. The inhabitants of this commonwealth are united by the love of Jesus for all creatures on earth, for his followers, their membership in the society of God's elect, and their indifference to things to this world, including politics. It is an organic body in which each participant shares in the rituals, such as baptism and the Eucharist, and in the love they feel for each other and for God. In the heavenly city, love of God extends even to the denigration of self. It provides all the necessary conditions for the reign of justice. That is, it is dedicated to advancing the cause of God. There the soul rules the body in all men who belong to this City and obey God, and the reason faithfully rules the vices in a lawful system of subordination and the individual righteous man lives on the basis of faith.

The City of God is composed of those individuals predestined in the mind of God to dwell eternally with him in heaven. They are members of a society of seekers who are clearly directed to a higher purpose. The City of God is an international conspiracy of those loyal to God's wishes. It is not a conspiracy in the sense that it involves secrecy, for it does not. All people are equally invited to join. Rather it is a conspiracy in that there is one group, the members of the heavenly city, who work for goals and with methods that those who are allied with the earthly city cannot. And the latter make a choice not to join the former, both by their immoral goals and their sinful actions. Only those who have faith in God's promise can be saved. This even includes those who lived before Christ's arrival on earth. As long as they were touched by God's grace and led godly lives, they, too, could join the elect in heaven. The dedication on earth. Consequently, the social was clearly superior to the political. Those who are not part of the heavenly city includes subjects of all nations, people who converse in all languages and differ in many ways: manners, laws, and forms of government.

They may not know the purpose of all that happens to them, such as accidents, reversals of fortune, or illness, but their faith reminds them that there is a divine meaning in all things, and it points to complete happiness in the hereafter. Better to accept the world as it as – God's creation – and focus on God's kingdom in the afterlife. As only some will be saved, and as there is no way to know who they might be, everyone lives in doubt and fear. Acceptance of one's fate and faith in God provide the only way out of uncertainty. This working of God's will may seem arbitrary or unfair to humans because its ultimate purposes are known only to God, but his will is always just and lawful.

Of course we must wait for the life-to-come to secure true justice and perfect peace.

All the commandments of God, then, are embraced in love, of which the apostle says: "Now the end of the commandment is charity, out of a pure heart, and of a good conscience, and of faith unfeigned." Thus the end of every commandment is charity, that is, every commandment has love for its aim. . . . This love embraces both the love of God and the love of our neighbor, and "on these two commandments hang all the law and the prophets." we may add the Gospel and the apostles. For it is from these that we hear this voice: The end of the commandment is charily, and God is love.

In loving God, Augustine tells us, we love truth. On the attainment of true knowledge, people will discover as he did that, "where I found truth, there I found my God, who is truth itself." Individuals come to know truth through inner experience and conviction. Moreover, they must make an effort of will to prepare the mind to receive truth. Augustine maintains that one cannot obtain true knowledge without faith: One should first believe in order to understand; The intellectual knowledge of God, however, does not by itself suffice for the perfect and ultimate comprehension of Him which is our happiness. For this, one must go beyond reason to mystical vision, the spiritual seeing of God which transcends reason. Faith, knowledge, and mystical vision may be conceived as progressive steps on the way to the transcendental understanding of God, who is the essence of all truth.

Knowledge of God is indispensable to our blessedness, but, Augustine holds, it is false pride for people to believe that they can know God by their own efforts. Only when God by His grace illuminates the mind can it grasp the truth. Similarly, salvation can be achieved only through God's grace. In the Augustinian theology, each person is predestined by God either to salvation or to damnation. Since all people are stained with original sins they deserve only punishment. Consequently, salvation is a free gift of God bestowed upon the chosen few. Without divine grace, neither faith nor good works can assure salvation. No human mind can penetrate the mystery of God's wisdom in electing some but not others to be saved. Trusting in God's goodness, and despite the fact that we cannot judge whether we will be saved or not, we are obligated to seek God and to live according to His commandments.

The whole history of humanity from the fall of Adam and Eve to the Last Judgment is depicted as a conflict between the "City of God" and the "City of Man." Those who live in the earthly city pursue material interests and carnal pleasures. They suffer not only the frustrations brought about by their false beliefs while on earth, but also endure the everlasting alienation from God which is the punishment of the sinful. By contrast, the citizens of the City of God form a "mystical and unanimous society of saints in Heaven and believers on Earth." Through the redemptive mission of Jesus Christ, they enjoy both spiritual peace on earth and the eternal blessedness of the vision of God which is humanity's true happiness.

In the support and defense of Christian doctrine, Augustine is obliged to resolve some of the most troublesome metaphysical problems of ethics. Among these, perhaps the most crucial challenge to the effectiveness of his ethical theory and a natural point of entry into his entire moral philosophy is the so-called problem of evil, namely, how to reconcile the existence of evil in the world with the omnipotence and benevolence of God. The paradoxical nature of this problem is clearly evident from the formulation of it attributed to the Greek philosopher, Epicurus:

Either God would remove evil out of this world, and cannot; or He can, and will not; or, He has not the power nor will; or, lastly, He has both the power and will. If He has the will, and not the power, this shows weakness, which is contrary to the nature of God. If He has the power, and not the will it is malignity, and this is no less contrary to His nature. If He is neither able nor willing, he is both impotent and malignant, and consequently cannot be God. If He be both willing and able whence comes evil, or why does He not prevent it? As a starting point for his treatment of the problem of evil, Augustine insist "that God is perfectly good and all things come from Him. Since God in His goodness cannot create anything evil, it follows that evil cannot be a positive characteristic of things. However, the things which God creates are less than wholly good, and they are evil only insofar as they lack goodness.

Nevertheless, it still remains to resolve another part of the problem of evil. If God is able to do all things, why does He permit us to choose evil? Or, if God h free to do whatsoever He will, why should He will evil? Augustine argues that since God is all-powerful, He can prevent evil if He so wills, so that His permitting evil must reflect His goodness in some way. He explains that God's mercy and justice are served by presenting individuals with a choice between good and evil. Whichever we choose, God's will ultimately is fulfilled, and even evil choices are turned to good account by Him. In our preset imperfect state, we cannot always perceive the wisdom of God's ways, but Augustine is confident that in the fullness of faith, all will become clear.

Although Augustine has resolved here and elsewhere the problem of evil to his satisfaction, another traditional paradox arises when it is considered that God knows in advance what choices we will make. Divine foreknowledge must be reconciled with our freedom to choose good or evil. Because all things have causes, it would appear that if God knows in advance what is to happen, all that happens is determined, and individuals cannot have free will. Then, if we are not free, punishment and reward are both unjust and ineffective. On the other hand, if we are free to choose our own courses of action, God cannot have foreknowledge of human behavior, and consequently cannot be omniscient.

Augustine sets about the task of showing how it is possible to retain the belief both divine prescience and human freewill. Granting that every event has a cause, he points out that human will is one of the causes of its actions. Hence, the causal power of the will is part of the overall causal order of events foreknown by God, The paradox is effectively resolved by the distinction between the knowledge of a cause and the cause itself: God's knowing in advance that an event will necessarily occur is not the same as His causing it to occur. It follows, then, that people are themselves responsible for their misfortunes; they are free to choose, and they choose evil. For Augustine, however, an evil will itself is a defective one. Just as he defines evil as the absence of good, so too he characterises an evil will as one which fails to choose the good.

Augustine's rational justification of the Christian belief in an individual's moral responsibility and the presence of moral evil in the world constitutes a philosophical background for his description of the City of God and the City of Man. Those who choose good he calls them citizens of the City of God, and those who choose evil are called citizens of the City of Man. To live in the heavenly city, one must follow the spirit as well as the letter of the teachings of Jesus; those who pursue the pleasures of the body or accept idolatrous or heretical beliefs must be said to "live after the flesh" in the earthly city.

It must be realized, Augustine points out, that supreme good and evil refer to eternity, not to the brief moment of this life. Those who seek happiness in this world and through their own efforts cannot be either truly happy or truly moral. Not only those who pursue the carnal pleasures, but also those who rely upon reason as the foundation of morality, are in error. Unaided by divine guidance, reason cannot provide a cure for the evils of life.

When we appreciate the feebleness of unaided human reason, we see that faith, hope, and love are the fundamental virtues of the true Christian, who seeks peace and happiness through God. The virtues of prudence, temperance, justice, and fortitude which the rationalistic Greek philosophers value so highly are nothing more than prideful vices unless they are used in the service of the true religion.

Everyone earnestly desires peace, but the misdirected methods of the City of Man fail to achieve it. Those who dwell in God's city know that peace is not achieved by war, but by love. Hence, everyone should obey and teach the precepts of Jesus, "Love God" and "Love thy neighbor as thyself."

It is not possible to judge from our earthly history whether we are blessed or not, for in the mingled web of human affairs, God's judgment is present, though it cannot be discerned. We must accept without complaint the knowledge that the good may suffer earthly misfortunes, while the wicked may enjoy life,

The Last Judgment will be a day of reckoning where virtue and vice will be clearly seen and just reward and punishment meted out. The City of Man will be dissolved and its citizens condemned to eternal death. This is not the ordinary death in which the soul leaves the body, but a "second death," in which God abandons the soul. While eternal punishment is a harsh judgment, like enormity of our sin merits it. But God in His goodness is not only just, but also merciful, for He sent to us His only Son through whom the citizens of the City of God are saved.

The final vision of God, permitted to those who have lived in righteousness and been blessed with God's grace, is the reward of our faith.

His vast description of the cities of God and of Man completed, Augustine expresses the hope that he has communicated the meaning of the love of God through giving a true account of the true religion. Augustine's ideas are based on a synthesis of classical and Biblical ways of understanding, with primacy given to faith. But the synthesis is far from systematic. This is understandable, since almost all his works were written to deal with pressing issues of the day. He regards the world in oppositional terms. For him things are either black or white, earthly or heavenly, good or evil. Human nature posits love versus lust. Human affairs pit ethics against politics. There is no gray. None of these dualisms, he feels, can be reconciled. All must remain as strict opposites until Judgment Day. Only then will God unite all dualisms, all conflicts, all differences. At the same time, these dualisms serve to sharpen his defense of Christianity against its pagan and heretical critics.

—Editor

Human Nature and the Two Cities

God, desiring not only that the human race might be able by their similarity of nature to associate with one another, but also that they might be bound together in harmony and peace by the ties of relationship, was pleased to derive all men from one individual. And He created men with such a nature that the members of the race should nothave died, had not the first two (of whom one was created out of nothing, and the other out of him) merited this with their disobedience; for by them so great a sin was committed, that by it the human nature was altered for the worse, and was transmitted also to their posterity.

That the whole human race has been condemned in its first origin, this life itself, if life it is to be called, bears witness by the host of cruel ills with which it is filled. Is not this proved by the profound and dreadful ignorance which produces all the errors that enfold the children of Adam, and from which no man can be delivered without toil, pain, and fear? Is it not proved by his love of so many vain and hurtful things, which produces gnawing cares, disquiet, griefs, fears, wild joys, quarrels, law-suits, wars, treasons, angers, hatreds, deceit, flattery, fraud, theft, robbery, perfidy, pride, ambition, envy, murders, parricides, cruelty, ferocity, wickedness, luxury, insolence, impudence, shamelessness, fornications, adulteries, incests, and the numberless uncleannesses and unnatural acts of both sexes, which it is shameful so much as to mention; sacrileges, heresies, blasphemies, perjuries, oppressidn-of the innocent, calumnies, plots, falsehoods, false witnessings,-unrighteous judgments, violent deeds; plunderings, and innumerable other crimes that do not easily come to mind, but that never absent themselves from the actuality of human existence? These are indeed the crimes of wicked men, yet they spring from that root of error and misplaced love which is bòrn with every son of Adam. For who is there that has not observed with what profound ignorance, manifesting itself even in infancy, and with what superfluity of foolish desires, beginning to appear in boyhood, man comes into this life, so that, were he left to live as he pleased, and to do what-ever he pleased, he would plunge into all, or certainly into many of those crimes and iniquities which 1 mentioned, and could not mention?

But because God does not wholly desert those whom He condemns, nor shuts up in His anger His tender mercies, the human race is restrained by law and education, which keep guard against the ignorance that besets us, and oppose the assaults of vice, but are themselves full of labour and sorrow. For what mean those multificarious threat which are used to restrain the folly of children? What mean pedagogues, masters, the birch, the strap, the cane, the schooling which Scripture says must be given a child, "beating him on the sides lest he wax stubborn" and it be hardly possible or not possible at all to subdue him? Why all these punishments, save to overcome ignorance and bridle evil desires—these evils with which we come into the world? For why is it that we remember with difficulty, and without difficulty forget? learn with difficulty, and without difficulty remain ignorant? are diligent with difficulty, and without difficulty are indolent? Does not this show that vitiated nature inclines and tends to by its own weight, and what succour it needs if it is to be delivered? Inactivity, sloth, laziness, negligence, are vices which shun labour, since labour, though useful, is itself a punishment.

But, besides the punishments of childhood, without which there would be no learning of what the parents wish—and the parents rarely wish anything useful to be taught—who can describe, who can conceive the number and severity of the punishments which afflict the human race—pains which are not only the accompaniment of the wickedness of godless men, but are a part of the human condition and the common misery—what fear and what grief are caused by bereavement and mourning, by losses and condemnations, by fraud and false-hood, by false suspicions, and all the crimes and wicked deeds of other men? For at their hands we suffer robbery, captivity, chains, imprisonment, exile, torture, mutilation, loss of sight, the violation of chastity to satisfy the lust of the oppressor, and many other dreadful evils. What numberless casualties threaten our bodies from without—extremes of heat and cold, storms, floods, inundations, lightning, thunder, hail, earthquakes, houses falling; or from the stumbling, or shying, or vice of horses; from countless poisons in fruits, water, air, animals; from the painful or even deadly bites of wild animals; from the madness which a mad dog communicates, so that even the animal which of all others is most gentle and friendly to its own master, becomes an object of intenser fear than a lion or dragon, and the man whom it has by chance infected with this pestilential contagion becomes so rabid, that his parents, wife, children, dread him more than any wild beast! What disasters are suffered by those who travel by land or sea! What man can go out of his own house without being exposed on all hands to unforeseen accidents? Returning home sound in limb, he slips on his own door-step, breaks his leg, and never recovers. What can seem safer than a man sitting in his chair? Eli the priest fell from his, and broke his neck. How many accidents do farmers, or rather all men, fear that the crops may suffer from the weather, or the soil, or the ravages of destructive animals? Commonly they feel safe when the crops are gathered and housed. Yet, to my certain knowledge, sudden floods have driven the labourers away, and swept the barns clean of the finest harvest. Is innocence a sufficient protection against the various assaults of demons? That no man might think so, even baptized infants, who are certainly unsurpassed in innocence, are sometimes so tormented, that God, who permits it, teaches us hereby to bewail the calamities of this life, and to desire the felicity of the life to come. As to bodily diseases, they are so numerous that they cannot all be contained even in medical books. And in very many, or almost all of them, the cures and remedies are themselves tortures, so that men are delivered from a pain that destroys by a cure that pains. Has not the madness of thirst driven men to drink human urine, and even their own? Has not hunger driven men to eat human flesh, and that the flesh not of bodies found dead, but of bodies slain for the purpose? Have not the fierce pangs of famine driven mothers to eat their own children, incredibly savage as it seems? In fine, sleep itself, which is justly called repose, how little of repose there sometimes is in it when disturbed with dreams and visions; and with what terror is the wretched mind overwhelmed by the appearances of things which are so presented, and which, as it were, so stand out before the senses, that we cannot distinguish them from realities! How wretchedly do false appearances distract men in certain diseases! With what astonishing variety of appearances are even healthy men sometimes deceived by evil spirits, who produce these delusions for the sake of perplexing the senses of their victims, if they cannot succeed in seducing them to their side!

From this hell upon earth, 'the deserved penalty of sin would have hurled all headlong even into the second death, of which there is no end, had not the undeserved grace of God saved some therefrom. And thus it has come to pass, that though there are very many and great nations all over the earth, whose rites and customs, speech, arms, and dress, are distinguished by marked differences, yet there are no more than two kinds of human society, which we may justly call two cities, according to the language of our Scriptures. The one consists of those who wish to live after the flesh, the other of those who wish to live after the spirit.

First, we must see what it is to live after the flesh, and what to live after the spirit. For any one who either does not recollect, or does not sufficiently weigh, the language of sacred Scripture, may, on first hearing what we have said, suppose that the Epicurean philosophers live after the flesh, because they place man's highest good in bodily pleasure; and that those others do so who have been of opinion that in some form or other bodily good is man's supreme good: and that the mass of men do so who, without dogmatizing or philosophizing on the subject, are so prone to lust that they cannot delight in any pleasure save such as they receive from bodily sensations: and he may suppose that the Stoics, who place the supreme good of men in the soul, live after the spirit; for what is man's soul, if not spirit? But in the sense of the divine Scripture both are proved to live after the flesh. For by flesh it means not only the body of a terrestrial and mortal animal, as when it says, "All flesh is not the same flesh, but there is one kind of flesh of men, another flesh of beasts, another of fishes, another of birds," but it uses this word in many other significations.... If we are to ascertain what it is to live after the flesh (which is certainly evil, though the nature of flesh is not itself evil), we must carefully examine that passage of the epistle which the Apostle Paul wrote to the Galatians, in which he says, "Now the works of the flesh are manifest, which are these: adultery, fornication, uncleanness, lasciviousness, idolatry, witchcraft, hatred, variance, emulations, wrath, strife, seditions, heresies, envyings, murders, drunkenness, revel-lings, and such like: of the which I tell you before, as 1 have also told you in time past, that they which do such things shall not inherit the Kingdom of God." This whole passage of the apostolic epistle being considered, so far as it bears on the matter in hand, will be sufficient to answer the question, what it is to live after the flesh.

In enunciating this proposition of ours, then, that because some live according to the flesh and others according to the spirit there have arisen two diverse and conflicting cities, we might equally well have said, "because some live according to man, others according to God." For Paul says very plainly to the Corinthians, "For whereas there is among you envying and strife, are ye not carnal, and walk according to man?" So that to walk according to man and to be carnal are the same; for by flesh, that is, by a part of man, man is meant.

But the character of the human will is of moment;... for the man who lives according to God, and not according to man, ought to be a lover of good, and therefore a hater of evil. And since no one is evil by nature, but whosoever is evil is evil by vice, he who lives according to God ought to cherish toward evil men a perfect hatred, so that he shall neither hate the man because of his vice, nor love the vice because of the man. For the vice being cursed, all that ought to be loved, and nothing that ought to be hated, will remain.

He who resolves to love God, and to love his neighbor as himself, not according to man but according to God, is on account of this love said to be of a good will; and this is in Scripture more commonly called charity, but it is also, even in the same books: '-ailed love.... The right will is, therefore, well-directed love, and the wrong will is ill-directed love. Love yearning to have what is loved, is desire; and having and enjoying it, is joy; fleeing what is opposed to it, is fear; and feeling what is opposed to it, when it has befallen it, is sadness. Now these motions are evil if the love is evil, good if the love is good.

Two cities have been formed, therefore, by two loves: the earthly by love of self, even to contempt of God; the heavenly by love of God, even to contempt of self. The former glories in itself, the latter in the Lord. For the one seeks glory from men; but the greatest glory of the other is God, the witness of conscience. The one lifts up its head in its own glory; the other says to its God, "Thou art my glory, and the lifter up of mine head." In the one, the princes and the nations it subdues are ruled by the love of ruling; in the other, the princes and the subjects serve one another in love, the latter obeying, while the former take thought for all. The one delights in its own strength, represented in the persons of its rulers; the other says to its God, "I will love Thee, O Lord, my strength." And therefore the wise men of the one city, living according to man, have sought for profit to their own bodies or souls, or body, and those who have known God "glorified Him not as God, neither were thankful, but became vain in their imaginations, and their foolish hearts were darkened; professing themselves to be wise"—that is, glorying in their own wisdom, and being possessed by pride—"they became fools, and changed glory of the incorruptible God into an image made like to corruptible man, and to birds, and four-footed beasts, and creeping things." For they were either leaders or followers of the people in adoring images, "and worshipped and served the creature more than the Creator, who is blessed for ever." But in the other city there is no human wisdom, but only godliness, which offers due worship to the true God, and looks for its reward in the society of the saints, of holy angels as well as holy men, "that God may be all in all." And when these two cities severally achieve what they wish, they live in peace, each after its kind....

True Justice: Not of this World

Justinus, who wrote Greek or rather foreign history in Latin, and briefly, like Trogus Pompeius whom he followed, begins his work thus. "In the beginning of the affairs of peoples and nations the government was in the hands of kings, who were raised to the height of this majesty not by courting the people, but by the knowledge good men had of their moderation. The people were held bound by no laws; the decisions of the princes were instead of laws. It was the custom to guard rather than to extend the boundaries of the empire; and kingdoms were kept within the bounds of each ruler's native land. Ninus king of the Assyrians first of all, through new lust of empire, changed the old and, as it were, ancestral custom of nations. He first made war on his neighbours, and wholly subdued as far as to the frontiers of Libya the nations as yet untrained to resist." And a little after he says: "Ninus established by constant possession the great-ness of the authority he had gained. Having mastered his nearest neighbours, he went on to others, strengthened by the accession of forces, and by making each fresh victory the instrument of that which followed, subdued the nations of the whole East." Now, with whatever fidelity to fact either he or Trogus may in general have written—for that they sometimes told lies is shown by other more trustworthy writers—yet it is agreed among other authors, that the kingdom of the Assyrians was extended far and wide by King

Ninus. And it lasted so long, that the Roman empire has not yet attained the same age; for, as those write who have treated of chronological history, this kingdom endured for twelve hundred and forty years from the first year in which Ninus began to reign, until it was transferred to the Medes. But to make war on your neighbours, and thence to proceed to others, and through mere lust of dominion to crush and subdue people who do you no harm, what else is this to be called than great robbery?

Indeed, without justice, what are kingdoms but great robberies? For what are robberies themselves, but little kingdoms? The band itself is made up of men; it is ruled by the authority of a prince, it is knit together by the pact of the confederacy; the booty is divided by the law agreed on. If, by the admittance of abandoned men, this evil increases to such a degree that it holds places, fixes abodes, takes possession of cities, and subdues peoples, it assumes the more plainly the name of a kingdom, because the reality is now manifestly conferred on it, not by the removal of covetousness, but by the addition of impunity. Indeed, that was an apt and true reply which was given to Alexander the Great by a pirate who had been seized. For when that king had asked the man what he meant by keeping hostile possession of the sea, he answered with bold pride, "What thou meanest by seizing the whole earth; but because I do it with a petty ship, I am called a robber, whilst thou who dost it with a great fleet art styled emperor."

(From *The Political Writings of St. Augustine*, edited by Henry Palucci, translation by N. Lods Gateway Editors, 1985.)

6

Thomas Acquinas

Thomas Aquinas (1225-1274) was born in Roccasecca, Italy near Naples. The son of a count and a member of a long-established feudal family, he outraged his family members when he entered the Dominican Order. At one point they went so far as to kidnap him and hold him prisoner in order to prevent his ordination. He studied and then taught theology in Paris, and his later career as a theologian included stays in Italy and then Paris again. Some of his writings were condemned by the Church soon after his death in 1274, but shortly thereafter, given the shifting winds of religious politics, he was canonized. He is reputed to have been the first person raised to sainthood by virtue of his teachings and his thought rather than by virtue of the performance of miracles. His philosophy is considered to be one of the glories of the high Middle Ages, and he ranks even today as one of the most important philosophers in the history of Western civilization.

It is obvious in reading Aquinas that he was considerably under the influence of Aristotle. His admiration for Aristotle was so great that he referred to this Greek thinker simply as 'The Philosopher'. Aquinas's own philosophy is a synthesis of Christian doctrine and Aristotelian thought. It has been claimed by some that his philosophy is merely eclectic and hence unoriginal, but this judgment ignores the genius involved in elaborating a systematic theory in which Aristotelian naturalism sits comfortably with the otherworldly attitudes of Christianity. As Aquinas saw it, Aristotle's work gives us deep insight into the secular dimension of human nature and the natural world. This secular view is not so much false as limited. Aristotle had no conception of the personal, providential God of Christianity, his deity being an entity who engages eternally in pure thought and pure thought alone. To attain an understanding of the

Christian God, revelation is also required and hence pure or natural philosophy is not enough. Since, the natural power of understanding is not sufficient to see the essence of God, this power of understanding must come to it by divine grace. But admitting this does not diminish the importance of Aristotle's thought in understanding the natural order.

St. Thomas Aquinas was the greatest of these Christian theologians and the major architect of this philosophical triumph. He produced a synthesis of ideas from Aristotle and Christianity that eventually became official church canon, or doctrine binding on all believers. Born into an aristocratic family in Italy, at age fourteen he left his studies at a monastery and for the next six years was at the University of Naples. The church had banned the teaching of Aristotle's philosophy at religious institutions, but Naples was an imperial, or public, university. Aquinas was exposed not only to the ideas of the Greek thinker but also, through a teacher who knew Arabic, to Islamic commentaries on Aristotle. Wanting a more significant career for him, Aquinas's father was opposed to his desire to join the Dominicans to poverty. He was kidnapped and imprisoned in the family castle for a year, but he could not swayed from his choice of orders, and he was finally released to follow his chosen path. After attending universities in Paris and Cologne, he returned to Paris, where he wrote and taught for virtually the rest of his brief life.

His major work, the multivolume *Summa Theological*, is a systematic account of Christian theology based on a philosophical methodology. It is a great work whose approach and content epitomize the best of medieval thought. Aquinas writes with great certainty. All questions raised are answered. None are postponed or require further consideration. At the end of this dialectic process of question, false proposition and true answer, truth does not stem from rational argument but from the authoritative positions cited. Only after the true position is set forth is reason used to explain how it is supported by a quoted authority. Of his other principal works, the four books of the Summa Contra Gentiles are a defense of Christianity addressed to Muslims and Jews. The authentic parts of *On Kingship* were written for the King of Cyprus as a tutorial on how to rule as a good monarch.

Some pundits may discount Aquinas's life work as simply a commentary on Aristotle. But apart from the inapplicability of the term simply to his extraordinarily complex and nuanced writings, his synthesis of classical and Christian philosophy gave the medieval world a profoundly new set of ideas on which to order people's lives and their governments. On at least two major issues, Aquinas goes beyond Aristotle could never have contemplated: the relationship of church and state. However, Aquinas's thoughts on this subject were influenced by Aristotle's discussion of human happiness.

Aquinas's crowning achievement as a political thinker was to fashion a synthesis of Aristotelian, Roman, and Christian elements into systematic philosophy. In uniting classical ideas with Christian thought he was also able to solve the specific political problem of how to relate church and state. As a result of his synthesis, the ancient connection between virtue and politics was reestablished. The attempt of Christians to understand their own group life provided a new and sorely needed source of ideas for Western political thought. Even when Aquinas examined spiritual questions, politics pervaded. Whether he was discussing thenature of Divine Providence, the status of angels, the church or sacraments, essentially political categories were recurrent: authority power, membership, community, common good, law, and monarchical rule.

Aquinas creates a new theory of government to link the spiritual to the temporal and politics to theology. He does so by visualizing a different sort of political community in which a kind of dual citizenship becomes meaningful once again. This is not the dual citizenship of Cicero, although there are parallels. Cicero's distinction of men as citizens of their polis and citizens of universal community becomes, in the scheme of Aquinas, a mass of subjects in their small communities with a higher loyalty to those bodies, religious and political, which point them to a universal fellowship of believers.

The government of any city-state or kingdom is best ordered when somebody appointed by virtue of personal excellence presides over everyone, with subordinates similarly governing by virtue of and in accordance with their true merits, and yet rulership belongs to everyone because anyone is eligible to be elected and each ruler is elected by everyone.

Aquinas's debt to Aristotle is perhaps even more apparent in his ethics than in other parts of his philosophy. As one commentator has put it, the theological ethics of Aristotle was, in general, sound, and that the Greek philosopher's way of thinking provided a philosophical backbone for a Christian ethics. Aquinas, like Aristotle, begins ethical inquiry with the question what is the good for human beings. Thus the notion of goodness is central to his ethics, as is the conviction that action is always aimed at an end or good, and ultimately aimed at the greatest, highest, most final good. But Aquinas's answer to the question of the good for human beings, while still very much Aristotelian in nature, has an obvious religious connotation, for the final good for a person turns out to be his perfection. Human perfection is what human fulfillment becomes when it is viewed as attaining a higher level of existence that puts human beings in touch with God and brings to completion God's plan for them. Life is seen by both Aristotle and Aquinas as a striving after the good, an attempt to achieve one's final end which alone brings fulfillment, the realization of one's potentialities, and happiness. But whereas for Aristotle one attains this end and lives the happy life in the natural world, among one's fellow citizens, for Aquinas the earthly life is but a preliminary step on the way to true happiness, achieved in the next life through union with God.

In his reading of human life and human nature, Aquinas reveals his religious perspective most clearly when he argues that nothing in the natural world totally satisfies our desires. A life of worldly goods, even a life of worldly virtue, leaves one dissatisfied and incomplete, with a sense that one has not made the most of one's life and not truly fulfilled one's inner nature and true purpose in life. Our desires remain unsatisfied by all temporal goods and accomplishments, and hence these desires reach beyond the temporal domain. Human beings are most strongly drawn to what fulfills and perfects them. As Aquinas puts it: Because in all things whatsoever there is an appetite for completion, the final end to which each moves marks its own perfect and fulfilling good. It turns out that this final end for human beings is God himself. Our ultimate end is uncreated good, namely God, who alone can fill our will to the brim because of his infinite goodness. We desire, most ultimately, to be united with God, to become one with him, to find our own joy and completion in him. Thus, complete and self- sufficient happiness is possible for us only in the next life when, through the grace of God, we are united with him, behold him, and enjoy his infinite goodness. God alone, the infinite good, will quiet the human heart.

But in this life, as we live in preparation for the next, it is human reason, which provides the tutelage and guidance required to attain earthly happiness. Although reason cannot grasp man's supernatural end or define the life by which it is to be attained, it can enable a human being to live the type of natural life ordained for him by God. And the picture Aquinas gives us of his life is essentially Aristotelian in nature. Human beings have a property or characteristic which sets them apart from all other things in the created universe: they are rational. The proper life for them to lead, then, is the life of reason. Reason is able to discern the ethical principles by means of which God intends us to live our lives. Furthermore, in living the life of reason, we are enabled to fulfill our potentialities, to actualize the modes of existence, which moves us closer to our final end, God.

Reason permits us to grasp human nature and to live a life that accords with it. In doing so, reason puts us in touch with natural law, the law that reflects in human nature the eternal law of God.

—Editor

Does God Exist?

Obj. 1. It seems that there is no God. For if one of two opposing entities were to exist without limitation the other would be totally destroyed. But the word, God, means something that is infinitely good. Therefore if there were a God, evil would not exist. But we encounter evil in the world. Therefore there is no God.

Qbj. 2. Furthermore what can be explained by a few causes should not be explained by many. But it seems that everything we see in the world can be explained by other causes withou t, assuming that God exists, because natural things are explained by natural causes, while those that are done for a purpose are the products of human reason and will. Therefore there is no need to sup pose that God exists.

On the contrary, God says in the Scripture, "I am who am." I answer that the existence of God can be proved in five ways:

The first; and most obvious way is the argument from motion. It is certain and evident to our senses that things are in motion in this world. Everything chat moves is moved by something else, for nothing can move unless it has the potentiality of acquiring the perfection of that towards which it moves. To move something is to act, since to move is to make actual what is potential. Now nothing can be changed from a state of potentiality to actuality except by something that itself is in a state of actuality. A fire that is actually hot makes wood that is potentially hot become actually hot, and so moves and changes it. Now it is impossible for the same thing to be both in actuality and in potentiality at the same time and in the same respect — only in different respects. What is actually hot cannot at the same time be potentially hot, although it is potentially cold. Therefore it is impossible for a thing to be both the mover and the thing moved in the same way, or for it to move itself. Therefore everything that moves must be moved by something else. If that by which it is moved also moves, it must itself be moved by something else and that by something else again. But things can not go on forever because then there would be no first mover, and consequently no subsequent mover since intermediate things move only from the motion they receive from the first mover—just as a staff moves only because it is moved be a hand. Therefore, it is necessary to go back to some first mover who is not moved by anyone, and this ever-one understands as God.

The second way is from the nature of an efficient cause. In the world of the senses we find that there is a sequence of efficient causes, but we never fine something that causes itself, and it is impossible to do because it would precede itself—which is impossible. Now the series of finite causes cannot go on co 'infinity became in every series of causes the first cause is the cause of the intermediate cause and intermediate causes cause the last cause, whether the intermediate causes are many or only one. However if you take away a cause you also take away it effect. If there is no first cause among the efficient causes, there will be no last or intermediate cause. But if we proceed to infinity in the series of causes there will be no first cause and therefore no final or intermediate effects would exist-which is obviously not true. Thus it is necessary to posit some first efficient cause which all men call god.

The third way is based on what can exist (\possibility) and what must exist (necessity). It is the following: We find things in nature that can exist or not exist, since things are found to come into existence (be generated) and to cease to exist (be corrupted) and therefore it is possible for them to exist or not exist. Now it is impossible for such things always to have existed, for if it is possible for something not to exist, at some time it did not exist. Therefore if it is possible for everything not to exist, at one .time nothing was in existence. But if this is true then nothing would exist even now, since that which does not exist only begins to exist through something else that is in existence. But if nothing was in existence it was impossible for anything to begin to exist, and so nothing would exist now—which is obviously not true. Everything cannot be [merely possible but there must be some necessary being in existence. Something is a necessary) being either as a result of the action or another or not. However it is impossible to go on to infinity in [the series of necessary beings that must exist because they are caused by another, as we have already proved above in the case of efficient causes. We must therefore posit a [necessary] being that must exist in itself and does not owe its existence to anything else, but is the reason that other things must be. This all men call God.

The fourth way is based on the gradations that exist in things. We find in the world that some things are more or less true, or good, or noble and so on. The description of "more" or "less" is given to things to the degree that they approach the superlative in various ways. For example a thing is said to be hotter as it approaches more closely what is hottest. Therefore there is something that is the most true, and best, and most noble, and consequently most fully in being, for the things that are the greatest in truth are the greatest in being, as is said in the Metaphysics. Now the superlative in and classification (genus) is the cause of all the things in that classification. Fire, for example, which is the hottest of all things is the cause of everything that is hot, as is said in the same book. Therefore there is something that is the cause or being and goodness and whatever perfection everything has, and this we call God.

The fifth way is based on the order (gobernatio) in the universe. We see that things that lack consciousness such as bodies in nature function purposively. This is evident from the fact that they always, or nearly always, function in the same wav so as to achieve what is be it, Therefore it is evident that they achieve their end, not by chance but by design. But things that do not possess consciousness tend towards an end only because they are directed by a being that possesses consciousness and intelligence, in the same way that an arrow must be aimed by an archer. Therefore there is an intelligent being who directs all things to their goal, and we say that this is God.

Reply to Obj. 1. Augustine says. "Since God is the supremely highest good he would not allow evil to exist in his creation unless he were so all powerful and good that he could even make good out of evil. Thus it is part of the infinite goodness of God that he permits evils to exist so that he can bring good from them.

Reply to Obj. 2. Since nature acts for a given end at the direction of a higher agent, the things that take place in nature go back to God as their first cause. Similarly what is done for a purpose must go back to some higher cause which is not the reason and will of man because these are changeable and can cease to exist. Everything that is changeable and perishable must eo back to an unchangeable and necessary first cause that is unchangeable and self-existent (per se neceaarium).

How We Know God

Can We Know God in this Life by Natural Reason?

Our natural knowledge begins from the senses. Therefore our natural knowledge can only extend as far as it can be led by the objects of the senses. On the basis of sensory objects our intellect can not go so far as to see the essence of God, because sensory creatures are effects of God which are no: equal in power to their cause. Hence we cannot know the full power of God on the basis of the objects of the senses and consequently we cannot see his essence. However because they are effects that are dependent on a cause, we can be led from them to know that God exists, and to know the characteristics that he must possess as the first cause of all things that transcends everything caused by him. Hence we know about his relationship to his creatures that he is the cause of all, and that creatures differ from him in that he is not a part of the things that he has caused, and that they are separate from him not because of any deficiency on his part but because of his transcendence.

Do We Know God Better through Grace than through Natural Reason?

We have a more perfect knowledge of God through grace than through natural reason. This is true for the following reason: The knowledge we have by natural reason requires two things, images derived from the objects of the senses and the natural light of the intellect which enables us to abstract intelligible concepts from them. In both these operations human knowledge is assisted by the revelation of grace. The natural light of the intellect is strengthened by the infusion of the light of grace, and by the action of God images are sometimes placed in the imaginations of men that better express divine things than those which we naturally receive from the senses.

Although by the revelation of grace in this life we do not know what God is and so are joined to him as to one who is not known, we still know him more fully because many of his most excellent works are demonstrated to us, and because through divine grace we attribute to him many things that, the natural reason cannot attain—as, for example, that God is three and one.

Resisting Tyrannical Government

A tyrannical government is not just, because it is directed, not to the common good, but to the private good of the ruler, as the Philosopher states (Politics, 111. 5; Ethics, VIII. 10). Consequently there is no sedition in disturbing a government of this kind, unless indeed the tyrant's rule be disturbed so inordinately, that his subjects suffer greater harm from the consequent disturbance than from the tyrant's government. Indeed it is the tyrant rather that is guilty of sedition, since he encourages discord and sedition among his subjects, that he may lord over them more securely; for this is tyranny, being conducive to the private good of the ruler, and to the injury of the multitude.

In order for a war to be just, three things are necessary; First, the authority of the Sovereign by whose command the war is to be waged. For it is not the business of a private individual to declare war, because he can seek for redress of his rights from the tribunal of his superior. Moreover it is not the business of a private individual to summon together the people, which has to be done in wartime. And as (he care of the common weal is committed to those who are in authority, it is their business to watch over the common weal of the city, kingdom or province subject to them. And just as it is lawful for them to have recourse to the sword; in defending that common weal against internal disturbances, when they punish: evil-doers, according to the words of the Apostle (Rom. xiii. 4): He holdeth not the sword in vain: for he is God's minister, an avenger to execute wrath upon hirnl Mat doth evik so too, it is their business to have recourse to the sword of war in; defending the common weal against external enemies. Hence it is said to those who are in authority: Rescue the poor: and deliver the needy out of the hand of the sinner, and for this reason Augustine says: The natural order conducive to peace among mortals demands that the power to declare and counsel war should be in the hands of those who hold the supreme authority,

Secondly, a just cause is required, namely that those who are attacked should be attacked because they deserve it on account of some fault. Wherefore Augustine, says; A just war is wont to be described as one that avenges wrongs, when a nation or state has to be punished, for refusing to make amends for the wrongs inflicted by its subjects, or to restore what it has seized unjustly.

Thirdly, it is necessary that the belligerents should have a rightful intention, so that they intend the advancement of good, or the avoidance of evil. Hence Augustine says: True religion looks upon as peaceful those wars that are waged not for motives of aggrandisement, or cruelty, but with the object of securing peace, of punishing evil-doers, and of uplifting the good. For it may hap | pen that the war is declared by the legitimate authority, and for a just cause, and yet be rendered unlawful through a wicked intention. Hence Augustine says (Contra Faust, xxii. 74): The passion for inflicting harm, the cruel thirst for vengeance, an unpacific and relentless spirit, the fever of revolt, the lust of power, and suchlike things, all these are rightly condemned in war.

(From *Summa Theologica* by Thomas Acquinas, Benziger Brothers, Inc. 1948.)

7

Niccolo Machiavelli

Niccolo Machiavelli (1469-1527) descended from a Florentine family, which had risen to major public office during the fourteenth century, but he was not a member of the Great Council or could hope to be elected to the civic magistracies. Machiavelli was concerned intimately and passionately with the political life of his time. His father was a Florentine lawyer of ancient family and moderate means and he grew up during the golden age of Florentine culture under Lorenzo Medici. When the French rode into the city unopposed, Machiavelli was still an unknown young man yet unnoticed by his literary contemporaries and apparently with no writing of his own to show. The events of the last years of the fifteenth century made a deep and lasting impression on him. He saw the collapse of the Medici and was impressed by the instability of a government not based on the good will of the people. He witnessed the strife of the Florentine factions during the stormy period of Savonarola's domination and realized the need for powerful government based on internal unity. Very soon, he was to wrestle political problems at close hand.

We know comparatively little about Machiavelli's family life. About 1502 he married a Marietta Cosine by whom he had six children. She seems to have been devoted to him ands probably to have been sadly neglected by a husband whose heart was in political affairs. It is doubtful if he was as loose -living as he has been supposed. One notorious letter which he wrote to his friend Francesco Vector describing an encounter with a hideous prostitute was perhaps more a literary adventure than anything else. He was certainly a man of strong emotions far removed from the cold calculating deceiver of the legend. But if he could be passionate when aroused, the general impression left by his life and work is of a man withdrawn from the crowd standing aside with a slight contemptuous smile on his face. It is surely possible to reconcile an intellectual aloofness and arrogance with a restless urge for active participation in political life.

We have a picture of young Machiavelli as a man of middle height, slender figure, sparkling eyes, dark hair rather a small head, a slightly aquiline nose, a tightly closed mouth. All about him bore the impress of a very acute observer and thinker but not that of one ankle to wield much influence over other. He could not cagily rid himself of the sarcastic expression continually playing round his mouth and flashing from his eyes which gave him the air of a cold and impassible calculator while nevertheless he was frequently ruled by his powerful imagination some time led away by it to an extent befitting the most fantastic of visionaries.

He was a man too capable of great exertions. Because of its shrewd psychological insight, its prophetic quality and its hard vehement prose *The Prince* has never lost the power to shock. The artist in Machiavelli as much as the analyst is often responsible for the shocks. He loved antithesis and generalization; he was intuitive rather than logical. He constantly dramatized his remarks and exaggerated his conclusions for the sake of impact. His delight in bold sweeping statements, his admiration of efficiency at all costs and his admonitions to the Italian princes to respond to foreign ruthlessness with equal toughness almost account for the indignation which the book has aroused throghout the centurics.

The Florentines followed the sensible practice of giving state employment to men of letters. In 1498 when he was about thirty he was appointed secretary and second chancellor becoming in effect a fairly senior civil servant whose duty it was to serve the executive committees of the government; his work brought him mainly diplomatic responsibilities although he was also employed on administrative and military errands. Machiavelli held office fourteen years until the downfall of the republic in 1512. Machiavelli was not an outstandingly successful diplomat. In any case, despite the importance of those to whom he was sent he was never in a position to negotiate with decisive authority. But he traveled widely and kept his eyes open and in his letters, dispatches and commentaries of this period can be found the ideas based on shrewd observation which he later developed in his major works. In particular, he showed his genius for grasping the fundamental political condition of the states he visited basing characteristic generalizations on a multitude of carefully observed details. It was during this period too that he became increasingly obsessed by the need for Florence to control a strong militia of her own instead of relying on mercenary troops or the fluctuating help of allies.

In November 1512 after he had already hopefully written letters of advice on government to the Medici his movements were restricted. A few months later suspected of being involved in a conspiracy against the new rulers he was imprisoned and tortured but subsequently exonerated and released. He retired to his small family property at San Casino he could just see the buildings of Florence from there and wonder what was going on and an intense period of literary activity began.

He was also introduced to the Medici household and his hopes of office revived. After carrying out a few commercial commissions of little importance, he at last enjoyed a brief return to public life. He visited Rome where he received a subsidy from Pope Clement for writing the history of Florence. He failed to persuade the Pope to do anything practical about his plan for establishing a militia but was then give responsibility for a scheme to fortify the walls of Florence. Ironically his craving for official employment meant that when the republic was restored Machiavelli was to some extent identified with the Medici and was therefore suspected and ignored. Soon after he fell ill with violent stomach trouble and he died in June 1527. According to his son, he left his family in considerderable poverty.

The language of *The Prince* is not as modern as many of its sentiments. Some words and phrases are repeated frequently in all Machiavelli's writings: words like Onore, Gloria, Fortuna, Necessity and Virtue. These are key words both for Machiavelli and for other Renaissance writers. They are often too employed very judiciously as for example in chapter VIII of *The Prince* where Machiavelli uses the word *onore* again and again with mounting irony to describe how Oliver Otto tricked his uncle. A great deal has been written about the Renaissance concept of Virtue, But Machiavelli like his contemporaries seems to have used it freely and loosely nearly always in antithesis to Fortuna sometime with the sense of will power, sometimes efficiency, sometimes even with the sense of virtue.

Decade was swept away. During the years of enforced political idleness he produced a series of works which place him securely among the masters of Italian prose. His versatility and erudition were considerable and it is now commonplace to say that *The Prince* alone unjustly carries the burden of representing his genius. But it is not so unfair that he should be judged by *The Prince* which after all is his supreme masterpiece and which contains the essence of his political thought. It is also a book, which still arouses men's passions and around which controversy still rages. Its meaning, its purpose, even the date of its composition and whether it was first composed without its traditional dedication and last chapter are still matters on which no final unchallenged judgment has been given.

Machiavelli would spend years in enforced retirement reflecting on precisely the issue of statecraft for he had come to know the Florentines, their characters and their ambitions exceedingly well. He had also read enough ancient Roman history to insist that it should be used, indeed its successes imitated, rather than simply admired. To organize a republic or rule a kingdom requires knowledge of the character of the people to be ruled and sufficient knowledge of history so that its lessons might be applied to contemporary problems concerning the governance of men and the maintenance of states, be they princedoms or republics. In his dedicatory preface to *the Prince* he says that his dearest possession is his knowledge of the action of great men, which he has acquired in two ways: through long experience of contemporary events learnt at the cost of personal privation and danger, and through a constant reading of antiquity. Just as those who draw maps, station themselves on the plains to consider the mountains, and then take up a position on high ground in order to get a good view of the plains below, so it is necessary for a prince to know the nature of the people and to be of the people to know the nature of princes. The traditions, circumstances and character of the people would determine the nature of that state.

By the end of his career, he would have a wealth of experiences. Like other civil servants, he undertook missions as a negotiator and diplomat, within Florentine territories, elsewhere in Italy, to the papal court in Rome under Pope Alexander VI and Pope Julius II, and to the former's ambitious son Cesare Borgia, abroad to the king of France and to the Holy Roman Emperor. He proved himself to be by far the most active among the chancery officials who wanted to keep his jobs despite changes in regimes, he has been described as a political fence sitter. He also made enemies because he allowed himself to be seen as too independent and arrogant. When in 1512, Spanish troops attacked Florentine territory, the republican regime dissolved and the Medici returned to power, Machiavelli would be dismissed from office. In 1513, he was accused of a role in an anti-Medici conspiracy. He was tried, tortured and imprisoned, and upon his release he retired to his farm seven miles outside of Florence and composed a draft of the text we call *The Prince*.

Machiavelli's experience of the Florentine republic in its various reformulations had begun during the 1480s at the time when Lorenzo Medici was in position, and ended with the return in 1512 of another Medici, Galliano, who was in turn replaced by his nephew, the younger Lorenzo in 1515. *The Prince* was originally dedicated to Galliano and re-dedicated to junior Lorenzo in 1515. It was aimed at a Medici with princely ambitions. By this time, Italy had been subjected to a succession of foreign invasions and Machiavelli would include as his final chapter of *The Prince* an exhortation that such a man free Italy from the stench of foreign domination. Machiavelli would still be alive in 1527 when Rome was sacked by the forces of Charles V, King of Spain and Holy Roman Emperor and Florence revolted against the Medici, establishing a new republic. But by then he was viewed as a Medici collaborator, and he died shortly thereafter, in poverty.

Bitter factionalism within the ruling elite ensued from 1494-98, during which Florence saw the guiding influence on politics of the Medici replaced by Savonarola. It is too infrequently mentioned in general histories of the Renaissance that religion and rhetoric interacted in preaching; indeed, that religious preaching remained the universal form of contemporary oratory and was often influenced by humanist theory and practice. As a friar who not only lacked political rights as a foreigner but whose religious status prevented him from direct participation in government, Savonarola was a powerful preacher who condemned the Medici as tyrants dominating a free republic. He came to play an exceptional role in Florentine republican politics when the government invited him to advise the citizens on constitutional reform. Instead, he argued in true Dominican fashion that since neither God nor Christ were heads of state, then it must be 'the people' who were lord of Florence: 'government is in the hands of the people which is the true and legitimate Lord of our city', not the Signori but the Great Council as sovereign legislator. The Great Council, comprising some three and a half thousand citizens who themselves, their parents or grandparents, had held one of the three major offices of state, were to be advised by Savonarola. He spoke of himself as a new Moses, a prophet, legislator and disciplinary leader of his people. This was Savonarola's popular republicanism, preaching popular participation in discussion and voting to Florentines in the great Council.

Savonarola did hold skeptical view of the people's right reason. Hence, he modifies the vision of the natural rationality of the 'human legislator' in the Great Council. His language was penetrated by a prophetic quasi-royal imperative that can also be found in contemporary discourse on mixed constitutions, not least based on the Venetian model of an aristocratic republic. Savonarola first favored the Venetian model but then changed to popular government. He thought the character of the Florentine people did not suit them for monarchy, although his early preaching indicates that princely government, superficially along the lines presented by Thomas Aquinas, was his ideal. And so, like the Medici before him, who used the language of the Platonic philosopher-king to justify their arbitrary power, Savonarola appropriated for himself the regal role in the mixed government. It was through him as judge and prophet, as their Moses, that Florentines in their Great Council were, in effect, counseled by God. Like Moses, Savonarola was believed to talk with God. Led by its prophet-king, Savonarola saw this as a true republican regime.

Machiavelli had heard Savonarola's sermons and summarized the sermons for the Florentine ambassador in Rome, saying that Savonarola kept digressing and changing with the times, telling the people lies to suit them. In 1498, Savonarola's regime ended and Savonarola was tried and executed, having been excommunicated by church authorities for his criticism of Catholic corruption. During the next fourteen years, Machiavelli worked for the Republic. In 1502, the republican constitution was again modified. Soderine was elected to this position, but he refused to accept the addition of a Senate of aristocrats curtailing his position. It was Soderine regime that collapsed largely through aristocratic hostility in 1512. Machiavelli served him well and reached a position of diplomatic importance that was unusual for his social rank. While there is no evidence that Machiavelli played any role as Soderine's political agent, and there is evidence that he manicured among the various political factions, it is known that he expressed intense hatred for the aristocrats who destroyed Soderine's government.

Just before he entered the Florentine chancery, Machiavelli had heard Savonarola preach, like Moses, of the importance of arms for success, but he was aware that unlike Moses, Savonarola was an unarmed preacher who lost control of his followers after they ceased to believe him. He observed that Moses got his laws adopted by murdering men opposed to him, and Savonarola said it was necessary to murder the sons of Brutus – but he never did it. Machiavelli came to the view that oratory was necessary but not sufficient either to motivate men to action or to maintain them in that motivation. Machiavelli was on his way to formulating his theory of political success based, in part, on the lesson of violence and the need for arms. Skinner has observed that Machiavelli challenged his own humanist heritage in denouncing the humanists' failure to emphasize the significance of sheer power in political life. They misunderstood the scope of necessity. Not only is it not enough to devote oneself either to ancient or Christian virtue. The maintenance of successful government also depends on an unflinching willingness to supplement the arts of persuasion with the employment of effective military force.

The novelty in Machiavelli's writings was his attitude towards religion and morality, which distinguished him from all those who preceded him. He was scathing in his attack on the Church and its clergy for their failure to provide moral inspiration. Machiavelli was anti-Church and anti-clergy, but not anti-religion. He considered religion as necessary not only for man's social life, but also for the health and prosperity of the state. It was important within a state because of the influence it wielded over political life in general. Though an indispensable part of civic life, religion was never an end in itself. As a political tool, princes and rulers were to use religion in their power struggles effectively, but responsibly and cautiously, otherwise it could be disastrous. Religion was good only if it produced order, for peace brought forth fortune and success.

Machiavelli's political theory would eventually surface in his *Prince* and *Discourses*. These two works in particular provide two perspectives on government, princely and republican. Most analysts have observed that there are fundamental differences between these two works, Skinner arguing in particular that *The Prince* is organized around the basic value of security, and the *Discourses* around the value of liberty. Like other humanists, Machiavelli wrote a tract in the tradition of the mirrors for princes, and one on republics, both works taking up the agendas revealed in contemporary writing on monarchies and republics by civic humanists. But in shifting humanist priorities, both works display a belief that history, one's own, can teach us, if we read it correctly, that success comes not through persuasion or even good laws, in the first instance, but rather comes through the prudential deployment of force responding to necessity.

—Editor

Human Nature

All writers on civil life have pointed out that ... in constituting and legislating for a republic one must presuppose that all men are wicked and that men never do good unless necessity drives them to it. Hence.... it is said that hunger and poverty make men industrious and that laws make them good.

Princes should learn, therefore, that they begin to lose their state the moment they begin to break the laws and to disregard the ancient traditions and customs under which men have long lived ... For it is much easier to acquire the affection of good men than of the bad, and to obey laws rather than to override them.

If the present be compared with the remote past, it is easily seen that in ail cities and in all peoples there are the same desires and the same passions as there always were. So that, if one examines with diligence the past, it is easy to foresee the future of any commonwealth, and to apply those remedies which were used of old; or, if one does not find that remedies were used, to devise new ones owing to the similarity between events.

For this may he said of men generally they are ungrateful, fickle, feigners and If dissemblers, avoiders of dangers, eager for gain. While you benefit them they; are all devoted to you they would shed their blood for you they offer their possessions, their lives, and their sons, as I said before, when the need to do so is far off. But when you are hard pressed, they turn away.

Prudent men arc wont to say—and this is not rashly or without good ground—that he who would foresee what has to he, should reflect on what has been, for everything that happens in the world at any time has genuine resemblance to what happened in ancient times. This is due to the fact that the agents who bring such things about are men, and that men have, and always have had, the same passions.

I hope it will not be considered presumptuous for man of very low and humble condition to dare to discuss princely government, and to lay down rules about it. For those who draw maps place themselves on low ground, in order to understand the character of the mountains and other high points, and climb higher in order to understand properly the characters of the plains. Likewise, one needs to be a ruler properly to understand the character of the people, and to he a man of the people to understand properly the character of rulers.

No government should ever believe that it is always possible to follow safe policies. Rather, it should he realised that all courses of action involve risks: for it is in the nature of things that when one tries to avoid one danger another is always encountered. But prudence consists in knowing how to assess the dangers, and to choose the least bad course of action as being the right one to follow.

This authentic incident affords us an excellent example of how a humane and kindly act sometimes makes a much greater impression than an act of ferocity or violence; and how districts and cities into which neither arms nor the accoutrements of war, nor any other kind of human force would have been able to obtain entry, it has been possible to enter by displaying common humanity and kindness, contingence or generosity.

For when one deliberates on the safety of one's country no consideration should he paid to either justice or injustice, kindness or cruelty, or it's being praiseworthy or ignominious. On the contrary, every other consideration being postponed that advice should he whole-heartedly adopted which will save the life and preserve the freedom of one's country.

About becoming notorious for those vices without which it is difficult to preserve one's power, because, if one considers everything carefully, doing some things that *seem* virtuous may result in one's ruin, whereas doing other things that *seem* vicious may strengthen one's position and cause one to flourish

That the populace is more prudent, more stable, and of sounder judgement than the prince. Not without good reason is the voice of the populacet: likened to that of God; for the opinion of the people is remarkably accurate in its prognostications, so much so that it seems as if the populace by some hidden power discerned the evil and the good that was to befall it.

Statecraft

Many have dreamed up republics and principalities which have never in truth been known to exist; the gulf between how one should live and how one does live is so wide that a man who neglects what is actually done for what should be .one learns the way to self-destruction rather than self-preservation. The fact is that a man who wants to act virtuously in every way necessarily comes to grief among so many who are not virtuous. Therefore if a prince wants to maintain his rule he must learn how not to be virtuous, and to make use of this or not according to need.

So leaving aside imaginary things about a prince, and referring only to those which truly exist, I say that whenever men are discussed they are noted for various qualities which earn them either praise or condemnation. Some, for example, are held to be generous, and others miserly. Some are held to be benefactors, others are called grasping; some cruel, some compassionate; one man faithless, another faithful; one man effeminate and cowardly, another fierce and courageous; one man courteous, another proud; one man lascivious, another pure; one guileless, another crafty; one stubborn, another flexible; one grave, another frivolous; one religious, another skeptical; and so forth. I know everyone will agree that it would be most laudable if a prince possessed all the qualities deemed to be good among those I have enumerated. But because of conditions in the world, princes cannot have those qualities, or observe them completely. So a prince has of necessity to be so prudent that he knows how to escape the evil reputation attached to those vices which could lose him his state and how to avoid those vices which are not so dangerous, if he possible can; but if he need not worry so much about the latter. And then he must not flinch from being blamed for vices which are necessary for safeguarding the state. This is because, taking everything into account, he will find that some of the things that appear to be virtues will, if he practices them, ruin him and some of the things that appear to be vices will bring him security and prosperity.

So, starting with the first of the of Generosity and Parsimony above, I say it would be splendid if one had a reputation for generosity; none the less if you do in fact earn a reputation for generosity you will come to grief. This is because if your generosity is good and sincere it may pass unnoticed and it will not save you from being reproached for its opposite. If you want to acquire a reputation for generosity, therefore, you have to be ostentatiously lavish; and a prince acting in that fashion will soon squander all his resources, only to be forced in the end, if he wants to maintain his reputation, to lay excessive burdens on the people, to impose extortionate taxes, and to do everything else he can to raise money. This will start to make his subjects hare him, and, since he will have impoverished himself, he will be generally despised. As a result, because of this generosity of is, having injured many and rewarded few, he will be vulnerable o the first minor setback, and the first real danger he encounters will bring him to grief. When he realizes this and tries to retrace his path he will immediately be reputed a miser.

So as a prince cannot practice the virtue of generosity in such a way that he is noted for it, except to his cost, he should if he is a prudent not mind being called a miser. In time he will be recognized as being essentially a generous man, seeing that because of his parsimony his existing revenues are enough for him, he can defend himself against an aggressor, and he can embark on enterprises without burdening the people. So he proves himself generous to all those from whom he takes nothing, and they are innumerable, and miserly towards all those to whom he gives nothing, and few.

There is nothing so self-defeating as generosity: in The-act of practicing it, you lose the ability to do so, and you become either poor and despised or, seeking to escape poverty, rapacious and hated. A prince must try to avoid, above all else, being despised and hated; and generosity results in your being both. Therefore it is wiser to incur the reputation of being a miser, which invites ignominy but not hatred, than to be forced by seeking a name for generosity to incur a reputation for rapacity, which brings you hatred as well as ignominy.

Taking others of the qualities I enumerated above, I say that a prince must want to have a reputation for compassion rather than for cruelty: none the less, he must be careful that he does not make bad use of compassion. Cesarc Borgia was accounted cruel; nevertheless, this cruelty of his reformed the Romagna, brought it unity, and restored order and obedience.

So a prince must not worry if he incurs reproach for his cruelty so long as he keeps his subjects united and loyal. By making an example or two he will prove more compassionate than those who, being too compassionate, allow disorders which lead to murder and rapine. These nearly always harm the whole community, whereas executions ordered by a prince only affect individuals.

Of Clemency and Cruelty

From this arises the following question: whether it is better to be loved than feared, or the reverse. The answer is that one would like to be both the one and the other; but because it is difficult to combine them, it is far better to be feared than loved if you cannot be both. One can make this generalization about men : they are ungrateful, fickle, liars, and deceivers, they shun danger and are greedy for profit; while you treat them well, they are yours. They would shed their blood for you, risk their property, their lives, their children, so long, as I said above, as danger is remote; but when you are in danger they turn against you. Any prince who has come to depend entirely on promises and has taken no other precautions ensures his own ruin; friendship which is bought with money and not with greatness and nobility of mind is paid for, but it does not last and it yields nothing. Men worry less about doing an injury to one who makes himself feared. The bond of love is one which men, wretched creatures that, they are, break when it is to their advantage to do so; but fear is strengthened by a dread of punishment which is always effective.

The prince must none the less make himself feared in such a way that, if he is not loved, at least he escapes being hated. For fear is quite compatible with an absence of hatred; and the prince can always avoid hatred if he abstains from the property of his subjects and citizens and from their women. If even so, it proves necessary Ito execute someone, this is to be done only when there is proper justification and manifest reason for it. But above all a prince must abstain from the property of others; because men sooner forget the death of their father than the loss of their patrimony. So, on this question of being loved or feared, I conclude that since some men love as they please but fear when the prince pleases, a wise prince should rely on what he controls, not on what he cannot control. He must only endeavor, as I said, to escape being hated.

In what Manner Princes Should Keep their Faith

Everyone realizes how praiseworthy it is for a prince to honour his word and to be straightforward rather than crafty in his dealings; none the less contemporary experience shows that princes who have achieved great things have been those who have given their word lightly, who have known how to trick men with their cunning, and who, in the end, have overcome those abiding by honest principles. You must understand therefore, that there are two ways of fighting: by law or by force. The first way is natural to men, and the second to beasts. But as the first way often proves inadequate one must needs have recourse to the second. So a prince must understand how to make a nice use of the beast and the man. The ancient writers taught princes about this by an allegory, when they described how Achilles and many other princes of the ancient world were sent to be brought up by Chiron, the centaur, so that he might train them his way. All the allegory means, in making the teacher half beast and half man, is that a prince must know how to act according to the nature of both, and that he cannot survive otherwise.

Of Lion and Fox

So, as a prince is forced to know how to act like a beast, he must learn from the fox and the lion; because the lion is defenseless against traps and a fox is defenceless against wolves. Therefore one must be a fox in order to recognize traps, and a lion to frighten off wolves. Those who simply act like lions are stupid. So it follows that a prudent ruler cannot, and must not, honour his word when it places him at a disadvantage and when the reasons for which he made his promise no longer exist. If all men were good, this precept, would not be good; but because men are wretched creatures who would not keep their word to you, you need not keep your would to them. And no prince ever lacked good excuses to color his bad faith. One could give innumerable modern instances of this, showing how many pacts and promises have been maidenly and void by the bad faith of princes: those who have known best how to imitate the fox have come off best. But one must know how to colour one's actions and to be a great liar and deceiver. Men are so simple, and so much creatures of circumstance, that the deceiver will always find someone ready to be deceived.

There is one fresh example I do not want to omit. Alexander VI never did anything, or thought of anything, other than deceiving men; and he always found victims for his deceptions. None the less his deceptions always had the result he intended, because he was a past master in the art.

A prince, therefore, need not necessarily have all the good qualities but he should certainly appear to have them. 1 would even go so far as to say that if he has these qualities and always behaves accordingly he will find them harmful; if he only appears to have them they will render him service. He should appear to be compassionate, faithful to his word, kind, guileless, and devout. And indeed he should be so. But his disposition should be such that, if he needs to be the opposite, he knows how. You must realize this: that a prince, and especially a new prince, cannot observe all those things which give men a reputation for virtue, because in order to maintain his state he is often forced to act in defiance of good faith, of charity, of kindness, of religion. And so he should have a flexible disposition, varying as fortune and circum-*F* stances dictate. He should not deviate from what is good, if that is possible, but he should know how to do evil, if that is necessary.

How to be a Pretender

A prince, then, must be very careful not to say a word which does not seem inspired by the five qualities. To those seeing and bearing him, he should appear a man of compassion, a man of good faith, a man of integrity, a kind and a religious man. And there is nothing so important as to seem to have this last quality. Men in general judge by their eyes rather than by their hands; because everyone is in a position to watch, few are in a position to come in close touch with you. Everyone sees what you appear to be few experience what you really are. And those few dare not gainsay the many who are backed by the majesty of the state. In the actions of all men, and especially of princes, where there is no court of appeal, one judges by the result. So let a prince set about the task of conquering and maintaining his state; his methods will always be judged honourable and will be universally praised. The common people are always impressed by appearances and results. In this context, there are only common people, and there is no room for the few when the many are supported by the state. A certain contemporary Ferdinand of Aragon never preaches anything except peace and good faith and he is an enemy of both one and the other, and if he had ever honoured cither of them he would have lost either his standing or his state many times over.

Of Choosing His Ministers

The choosing of ministers is a matter of no little importance for a prince; and their worth depends on the sagacity of the prince himself. The first opinion that is formed of a ruler's intelligence is based on the quality of the men he has around him. When they are competent and loyal he can always be considered wise, because he has been able to recognize their competence and to keep them loyal. But when they arc otherwise, the prince is always open to adverse criticism; because his first mistake has been in the choice of his ministers.

No one who knew messer Antonio da Venafro as the minister of Pandolfo Petrucci, prince of Siena, could but conclude that Pandolfo was himself a man of great ability. There are three kinds of intelligence: one kind understands things for itself, the other appreciates what others can understand, the third understands neither for itself nor through others. This first kind is excellent, the second good, and the third kind useless. So it follows that Pandolfo, if he did not have the first kind of intelligence, at least had the second. If a prince has the discernment to recognize the good or bad in what another says and does, even though he has no acumen himself, he can see when his minister's actions are good or bad, and he can praise or correct accordingly; in this way, the minister cannot hope to deceive him and so takes care not to go wrong.

But as for how a prince can assess his minister, here is an infallible guide: when you see a minister thinking more of himself than of you, and seeking his own profit in everything he does, such a one will never be a good minister, you will never be able to trust him. This is because a man entrusted with the task of government must never think of himself but of the prince, and must never concern himself with anything except the prince's affairs. To keep his minister up to the mark the prince, on his side, must be considerate towards him, must pay him honour, enrich him, put him in his debt, share with him both honours and responsibilities. Thus the minister will see how dependent he is on the prince; and then having riches and honours to the point of surfeit he will desire no more; holding so many offices, he cannot but fear changes. When, therefore, relations between princes and their ministers are of this kind, they can have confidence in each other; «when they are otherwise, the result is always disastrous for both of them.

We have said how necessary is Army of Army prince to lay solid foundations for his power, as without such he would inevitably be ruined. The main foundations which all states must have, whether new, or old, or mixed, are good laws and good armies. And as there can be no good laws where there are not good armies, so the laws will be apt to be good where the armies are so. I The armies with which a prince defends his state are either his own, or they are mercenaries or auxiliaries, or they are mixed. Mercenary and auxiliary troops are both useless and dangerous;

and if any on attempts to found his state upon mercenaries, it will never be stable or secure; for they are disunited, ambitious am without discipline - faithless and braggarts amongst friends, but amongst enemies cowards, and have neither, fear of God nor good faith with men; so that the ruin of the prince who depends on them will be deferred only just so long as attack is delayed; in peace he will be spoliator by his mercenaries, and in war by his enemies. The reason of all this is, that mercenary troops are not influenced by affection, or by any other consideration except their small stipend, which is not enough to make them willing to die for Arimce. They are ready to serve you as soldiers so long as you are at peace; but when war comes, they will either run away or march off. There is no difficulty in. demonstrating the truth of this; for the present ruin of Italy can be attributed to nothing else but the fact that she has for many years depended upon mercenary armies, who for a time had some success, and seemed brave enough amongst themselves, but so soon as a foreign: enemy came they showed what stuff they were made of.

I will demonstrate more fully the unhappy consequences of employing mercenary armies. Their commanders are either competent, or they are not; if they are, then you cannot trust them, because their cheif will aim always be their own aggrandisement, either by imposing upon you, who are their employer, or by oppressing others beyond your intentions; and if they are incompetent, then they will certainly hasten your ruin. If now you meet these remarks by saying that the same will be the case with every commander, whether of mercenary troops or others, I reply that inasmuch as armies are employed either by princes or by republics, the prince should always in person perform the duty of commanding his army, and a republic should send one of her own citizen to command her troops, and in case he should not be successful, then they must derange him; but if he is victorious, then they must be careful to keep him within the law, so that he may not exceed his powers. Experience has shown that princes as well as republics achieve the greatest success in war when they themselves direct the movements of their own armies, whilst mercenary troops do nothing but damage; and that a republic that has armies of her own is much less easily subjected to servitude by one of her own citizens, than one that depends upon foreign troops.

Thus Rome and Sparta maintained their liberties for many centuries by having armies of their own; the Swiss are most thoroughly armed, and consequently enjoy the greatest independence and liberty.

A ruler, then, should have no other objective and no other concern, nor occupy himself with anything else except war and its methods and practices, for this pertains only to those who rule. And it is of such efficacy [virtu] that it not only maintains hereditary rulers in power but very often enables men of private status to become rulers. On the other hand, it is evident that if rulers concern themselves more with the refinements of life than with military matters, they lose power. The main reason why they lose it is their neglect of the art of war; and being proficient in this art is what enables one to gain power.

New rulers, then, never disarm their subjects; indeed, if they find them unarmed, they always provide them with weapons. For when you arm them, these weapons become your own: those whom you distrusted become loyal, those who were loyal remain so, and subjects are converted into firm adherents. Since it is not possible to provide all your subjects with arms, when you benefit those whom you arm, you will also be able to secure yourself better against the others. Since the former are treated favorably, they will be more attached to you. The latter will excuse your conduct, because they will realize the need to treat favourably those who carry more dangerous duties.

Because all the arts that are provided for in a civil community are for the sake of the common good of men, all the statutes made in it so that men will live in fear of the laws and of God would be in vain if for them there were not provided defenses, which when well ordered, preserve them, even though they themselves are not well ordered. And so, on the contrary, good customs, without military support, suffer the same sort of injury as do the rooms of a splendid and kingly palace, even though ornamented with gems and gold, when, not being roofed over, they have nothing to protect them from the rain.

How to Avoid Flatterers

I will not leave unnoticed an important subject, and an evil against which princes have much difficulty in defending themselves, if they are not extremely prudent, or have not made good choice of ministers; and this relates to flatterers, who abound in all courts. Men are generally so well pleased with themselves and their own acts, and delude themselves to such a degree, that it is with difficulty they escape from the pest of flatterers; and in their efforts to avoid them they expose themselves to the risk of being contemned. There is no other way of guarding against adulation, than to make people understand that they will not offend you by speaking the truth. On the other hand, when every one feels at liberty to tell you the truth, they will be apt to be lacking in respect to you. A prudent prince therefore should follow a middle course, choosing for ministers of his government only wise men, and to these only should he give full power to tell him the truth, and they should only be allowed to speak to him of those tailings which he asks of them, and of none other. But then the prince should ask them about everything, and should listen to their opinions and reflect upon them, and afterwards form his own resolutions. And he should bear himself towards all his advisers in such manner that each may know that the more freely he speaks, the more acceptable will he be. But outside of these he should not listen to any one, but follow the course agreed upon, and be firm in his resolves. Whoever acts otherwise will either be misled by his flatterers, or will vacillate in his decisions, because of the variety of opinions; and this will naturally result in his losing in public estimation.

I will cite one modern example to this effect. Padre Luca, in the service of the present Emperor Maximilian, is speaking of his Majesty, says that he 'counsels with no one, and yet never does anything in his own way'; which results from his following the very opposite course to that above indicated; for the emperor is a reserved man, who never communicates his secrets to any one, nor takes advice from anybody. But when he attempts to carry his plans into execution and they begin to be known, then also do they begin to be opposed by those whom he has around him; and being easily influenced, he is diverted from his own resolves. And thence it comes that he undoes one day what he has done the day before, and that one never knows what he wants or designs to do; and therefore his conclusions cannot be depended upon.

A prince nevertheless should always take counsel, but only when he wants it, and not when others wish to thrust it upon him; in fact, he should rather discourage persons from tendering him advice unsolicited by him. But he should be an extensive questioner, and a patient listener to the truth respecting the things inquired about, and should even show his anger in case any one should, for some reason, not tell him the truth.

Those who imagine that a prince who has the reputation of sagacity is not indebted for it to his own natural gifts, but to the good counsels of those who surround him, certainly deceive themselves. For it may be taken as a general and infallible rule, that a prince who is not naturally wise cannot be well advised, unless he should perchance place himself entirely in the hands of one man, who should guide him in all things, and who would have to be a man of uncommon ability. In such a case a prince might be well directed, but it would probably not last long, because his counsellor would in a short time deprive him of his state. But a prince who is not wise himself, and counsels with more than one person, will never have united counsels; for he will himself lack the ability to harmonise and combine the various counsels and suggestions. His advisers will only think of their own advantage, which the prince will neither know how to discern nor how to correct.

And things cannot well be otherwise, for men will always naturally prove bad, unless some necessity constrains them to be good. Whence we conclude that good counsels, no matter whence they may come, result wholly from the prince's own sagacity; but the wisdom of the prince never results from good counsels.

Of the Influence of Fortune in Human Affairs, and how It may be Counteracted

I am well aware that many have held and still hold the opinion, that the affairs of this world are so controlled by fortune and by the divine power that human wisdom and foresight cannot modify them; that, in fact, there is no remedy against the decrees of fate, and that therefore it is not worth while to make any effort, but to yield unconditionally to the power of fortune. This opinion has been generally accepted in our times, because of the great changes that have taken place, and are still being witnessed every day, and are beyond all human conjecture.

In reflecting upon this at times, I am myself in some measure inclined to that belief; nevertheless, as our free will is not entirely destroyed, I judge that it may be assumed as true that fortune to the extent of one half is the arbiter of our actions, but that she permits us to direct the other half, or perhaps a little less, ourselves. I compare this to a swollen river, which in its fury overflows the plains, tears up the trees and buildings, and sweeps the earth from one place and deposits it in another. Every one flies before the flood, and yields to its fury, unable to resist it; and notwithstanding this state of things, men do not when the river is in its ordinary condition provide against its overflow by dikes and walls, so that when it rises it may flow either in the channel thus provided for it, or that at any rate its violence may not be entirely unchecked, nor its effects prove so injurious. It is the same with fortune, who displays her power where there is no organised valour to resist her, and where she knows that there are no dikes or walls to control her.

If now you examine Italy, which is the seat of the changes under consideration, and has occasioned their occurrence, you will see that she is like an open country, without dikes or any other protection against inundations; and that if she had been protection with proper valour and wisdom, as is the case with Germany, Spain and France, these inundations would either not have caused the great changes which they did, or they would not have occurred at all.

These remarks I deem sufficient as regards resisting fortune in general; but confining myself now more to particular cases, I say that we see a prince fortunate one day, and ruined the next, without his nature or any of his qualities being changed. I believe this results mainly from (he causes which have been discussed at length above; namely, that the prince who relies entirely upon fortune will be ruined according as fortune varies. I believe, further, that the prince who conforms his conduct to the spirit of the times will be fortunate; and in the same way will he be unfortunate if in his actions he disregards the spirit of the times. For we see men proceed in various ways to attain the end they aim at, such as glory and riches: the one with circumspection, the other with rashness; one with violence, another with cunning; one with patience, and another with impetuosity; and all may succeed in their different ways. We also see that of two men equally prudent, the one will accomplish his designs, whilst the other fails; and in the same way we see two men succeed equally well by two entirely different methods, the one being prudent and the other rash; which is due to nothing else than the character of the times, to which they either conform in their proceedings or not. Whence it comes, as I have said, that two men by entirely different modes of action will achieve the same results; whilst of two others, proceeding precisely in the same way, the one will accomplish his end, and the other not. This also causes the difference of success; for if one man, acting with caution and patience, is also favoured by time and circumstances, he will be successful; but if these change, then will he be ruined, unless, indeed, he changes his conduct accordingly. Nor is there any man so sagacious that he will always know how to conform to such change of times and circumstances; for men do not readily deviate from the course to which their nature inclines them; and moreover, it they have generally been prosperous by following one course, they cannot persuade themselves that it would be well to depart from it. Thus the cautious man, when the moment comes for him to strike a bold blow, will not know how to do it, and thence will he fail; whilst, if he could have changed his nature with the times and circumstances, his usual good fortune would not have abandoned him.

Pope Julius II was in all his actions most impetuous; and the times and circumstances happened so conformably to that mode of proceeding that he always achieved happy results. Witness the first attempt he made upon Bologna, when Messer Giovanni Bentivogli was still living. This attempt gave umbrage to the Venetians, and also to the kings of Spain and France who held a conference on the subject. But Pope Julius, with his habitual boldness and impetuosity, assumed the direction of that expedition in person; which caused the Spaniards and: the Venetians to remain quiet in suspense, the latter from fear, and the others from a desire to recover the entire kingdom of Naples. On the other hand, the Pope drew the King of France after him; for that king, seeing that Julius had already started on the expedition, and wishing to gain his friendship for the purpose of humbling the Venetians, judged that he could not refuse him the assistance of his army without manifest injury to himself.

Pope Julius II, then, achieved by this impetuous movement what no other pontiff could have accomplished with all possible human prudence. For had he waited to start from Rome until all his plans were definitely arranged, and everything carefully organised, as every other pontiff would have done, he would certainly never have succeeded; for the king would have found a thousand excuses, and the others would have caused him a thousand apprehensions. I will not dwell upon the other actions of Julius II, which were all of similar character, and have all succeeded equally well. The shortness of his life saved him from experiencing any reverses; for if times had supervened that would have made it necessary for him to proceed with caution and prudence, he would assuredly have been ruined; for he could never have deviated from the course to which his nature inclined him.

I conclude, then, inasmuch as fortune is changeable, that men who persist obstinately in their own ways will be successful only so long as those ways coincide with those of fortune; and whenever these differ, they fail. But, on the whole, I judge impetuosity to be better than caution; for fortune is a woman, and if you wish to master her, you must strike and beat her, and you will see that she allows herself to be more easily vanquished by the rash and the violent than by those who proceed more slowly and coldly. And therefore, as a woman, she ever favours youth more than age, for youth is less cautious and more energetic, and commands fortune with greater audacity. And certainly anyone wise enough to understand the times and the types of affairs and to adapt himself to them would always have good fortune, or he would protect himself always from bad, and it would come to be true that the wise man would rule the stars and the fates.

(From *The Prince and the Discoverse* by Niccolo Machiavelli, edited by M. Loerner Random House, New York, 1950)

8

Thomas Hobbes

Thomas Hobbes (1588-1679) beyond doubt is the first great English philosopher. He is arguably the greatest of all that followed. He stands out as a titan for at least four reasons: first, the sweep and coherence of his analysis; second, the energy and vividness with which he expressed his views; third, the detailed and inventive development of argument, without reverting to rhetoric and fourth, simple, pellucid conclusions, thoroughly unsettling to both contemporaries and successors, and so virtually impossible to ignore. What cannot be denied is that Hobbes's work has been paid more sustained critical attention in the twentieth than in any preceding century, with the possible exception of his own. It can scarcely be doubted, given the attention Hobbes commands, that he speaks to us, and proves, in various ways, significant and relevant to our concerns.

Hobbes was born prematurely in 1588, his mother's labour, it is said, being brought on by news of the Armada ('Hobbes and Fear were born twins') but he survived all the vicissitudes of seventeenth-century English politics to die in his bed at the age of ninety-one in 1679. Hobbes was an Oxford man who found the prevailing Aristotelian scholastic philosophy little to his taste. He was recommended as tutor to the Cavendish who became the second Duke of Devonshire. He spent most of his life in the houses of noblemen. He discovered the new science on the Grand tour in 1610, and in the early 1620s he became the friend of Francis Bacon. Hobbes was a staunch Royalist. By 1641, when he fled to France to escape the coming Civil War, he had met Galileo and many of the most noted scientists and men of letters of his day.

Hobbes spent some of his time in exile in France (1641-51) as mathematics tutor to the future Charles II. He also worked on *Leviathan*, which was published in London on Hobbes's return to

England to make his peace with the Commonwealth. There is some mystery about why he actually came back when he did, though the probability is a combination of homesickness and his growing reputation in émigré circles for religious unorthodoxy, if not downright atheism. Charles II, in his good- natured way, always retained a soft spot for Hobbes. He was invited back to Court after the Restoration and given a royal pension of £100 a year.

Hobbes had no direct family, no wife, no progeny. Nor had his parents any standing in a country, in an era immensely conscious of class, or status. He was bright boy whose work was furthered by powerful protectors, who made good use of him. He was a man in service to the Cavendishs. He was a tutor to their young children. He was a dependent, with an intellect dazzlingly, but never proudly independent. Hobbes was, in short, a loyal retainer. He theorized both equality and subjection, but was more familiar with the second than the first. His theory could be said to reflect his condition: he knew his worth, but he also knew his place. In this, we are to distinguish between social inequality and intellectual superiority. It was Hobbes's intellect and that only which made him sovereign.

We have not enough knowledge of Hobbes's personality. But we do know that he was orderly, efficient, quick, productive, restrained and curious, with an immense interest in science. Science is an established means of escaping class hierarchies. Hobbes's most important, if not his only experience of class equality was among savants, where it was more the argument than the person that mattered. Hobbes's arguments were convenient to the powerful, even while removing from these some of their luster. On Hobbes's account, even if he was a servant and he were – then so were those who were less than sovereign. Not only did Hobbes's intellect make him equal to his betters, but he employed his intelligence to illuminate the principle of equal subjection by all strata to Leviathan. The sovereign, following Hobbes, was not sovereign due to any special virtue attaching to him or her or a few to wear the crown. No divinity hedges Hobbes's king, only a prudent and mutual need for common authority. Were Hobbes's tastes and sympathies were more bourgeois, or more aristocratic? Among those prepared to supply an answer we may identify Macpherson and Wood.

In England, Hobbes functioned as the dependent of a noble family. He voted with them, as required. He served them, as they saw fit. Hobbes's later irascibility may well have kept him out of the Royal Society. Hobbes's exclusion on class grounds is all the more plausible, if we take the Royal Society as a microcosmic representation of society as a whole.

He was more analytical than Machiavelli, more concise that Bodin, more historical than Descartes, more insightful than Spinoza, more coherent than Locke, and perhaps more 'modern' than any of them. He was able to argue powerfully on virtually any plane, scriptural, logical or historical. If Hobbes's greatness is now universally agreed, the reasons informing the conclusion vary from critic to critic to entice the next. For C.B. Macpherson, Hobbes reflected a new bourgeois market mentality. Leo Strauss, more broadly, saw Hobbes as a 'modern'. Lubienski took Hobbes to supply 'the first great effort' to turn ethics and politics into a science without the help of reason. It is in a way unfortunate for the history of political thought that the first masterpiece of social contract theory, Thomas Hobbes's *Leviathan*, should be so untypical of social contract theorising. Social contract was invented to support the case for disobedience to authority. In *Leviathan* Hobbes makes out a social contract case for the absolute government which social contract had been invented to undermine. Hobbes is a masterly political arguer because he meets and beats his opponents on their own ground. He uses social contract's own language to drive a coach through all the libertarian conclusions which previous social contract thinkers had come to. Hobbes is also subtle. He wrote at the time of the English Civil War (*Leviathan* was published in 1651), and his more acute readers soon realized that his arguments are double-edged. What would have been an argument for Cromwell's power in 1651, and again for Charles II in 1660. Hobbes pleased neither the Royalists nor the Parliamentarians, though Cromwell left him alone, and Charles II received him at court.

Hobbes's universe, human and natural, is subject to uniform explanation. No item requiring explanation can receive this without being resolved into its component parts. The ultimate components of human society, for Hobbes, are individuals. The ultimate components of the universe are atoms. And what governs these is motion. The individual moves and is moved, in the manner of one atom striking another. But the individual is moved not just physically, it is also moved psychologically perplexed by desires, passions and drives. Indeed, physical determination is largely a function of psychological direction. The chief motive which determines human action, is that of self-preservation. Whether this is to be read as a mere factual datum, or as a moral principle, is subject to dispute. But self-preservation, for Hobbes, is the underlying desideratum. The passions that incline men to peace, are fear of death; desire of such things as are necessary to "commodious living" and a hope by their industry to obtain them. And reason suggested convenient articles of peace, upon which men may be drawn to agreement. These articles are they which otherwise are called the Laws of Nature.

Although human individuals, for Hobbes, may be solipsistic, or self-contained, they are not self-sufficient. Indeed, one of the major difficulties for Hobbes is to determine how solipsistic parasitic individuals overcome their neurosis sufficiently to be able to establish orderly social relations. Hobbes's view of self-preservation is far more complex than at first appears. He is more likely to mean, not that the individual's first and only concern is and ought to be to preserve the self, but that the individual is, as a matter of fact, governed by an underlying fear of premature death and that this fact is not to be regarded as inconsistent with a proper morality. Indeed, Hobbes hoped to show how self-preservation was consistent with a morally grounded submission to the state, or how fear of authority was consistent with a morally grounded obedience to it.

Hobbes insists that both regulated and intuited trains of thought were caused, were determinate. But in some cases, the cause laid within, in other cases outside, the agent affected. Regulated thought was that which obtained when the process was regulated by some desire, some design. Humans, for Hobbes, enjoyed an enormous capacity for internalizing causes, which is to say for thinking in a highly regulated or rational way. The first problem was not to establish human causal control over nature but to set up regulated or rational communication among men. This, for Hobbes, was the job of language.

Language was not a by-producet but a precondition of human organization. For Hobbes, humans relate to one another, not so much by empathy, as Rousseau would later maintain, but by speech. It is by language, as Hobbes sees it, that we 'make known to others our wills and purposes'. Here, too, in discussing the reach of regulated thought, there is room for debate. Either Hobbes showed that (1) all dispute can be resolved rationally, or that (2) public authority has to be blindly obeyed since there can be no such authority if every subject keeps his own counsel.

Reason is a form of regulated thought available to humans. Reason is a form of language, and is not altogether independent of it. It is the instrument by which humans understand, and thus combine one with another. Language has no preordained meaning or purpose but that which individuals individually give it. Hence the importance of human nature, of human will and of social contract. A society for Hobbes is a form of verbal order. It expresses a convergence of wills. Individuals are not just social creatures, but self-interested solipsists, who enter into society as part of an express or tacit desire for personal good and gain. They accordingly do not exist for society, but society for individuals. For Hobbes, however, the ultimate achievement of human rationality is a firm recognition of the limits of rationality, and consequently of the need for authority. Rationality, for Hobbes, leads to the conclusion that order, which he assumes all humans to desire, can only be purchased at the cost of submission to some external authority. Here again there is much room for dispute as to how consistently authoritarian Hobbes's conclusion actually proves.

Hobbes's overall philosophy provides both an explanation and a justification for the emergence of the state, and for the consolidation and concentration of state power. It is in part because he does this so powerfully and coherently, and in the apparently neutral, scientific language of modernity, that Hobbes is rightly taken to be so great a figure. He establishes from the outset continuity between natural and social science. He insists upon individual difference, in the form of divergent perceptions and interests, even while insisting upon equality of human condition. It is indeed this very equality, which for Hobbes supplies the ground for a legitimate mutual fear. For Hobbes, it is this fear, which contradicts prospects of social peace and simultaneously foreshadows the logic of its accomplishment.

Since there is no natural accord, and everyone cannot be sovereign, the security to which reason and speech point is submission to some individual or group among them. Thus does Hobbes take up from Bodin the logic of the idea of sovereignty – the logic of establishing an ultimate and all-powerful arbiter. But again there are interpretive difficulties: what are the limits that Hobbes may or may not have intended to apply to sovereign authority? If the individual's own interest – self-preservation – is paramount, then how can this interest be meaningfully protected without legal constraints of any kind upon the sovereign? There is the inevitable problem about empowering a Leviathan to protect interests, which he, at the same time, cannot be legally bound to respect. There is the puzzle as to how a sovereign with no legal obligation to subjects may be consistently viewed as the equal defender of the natural rights of each and every one of them.

During the past decades the literature devoted to Hobbes has expanded rapidly both in volume and in breadth of focus, covering the most diverse topics of his natural and civil philosophy. The reasons for this preoccupation are complex and elusive. To some extent the pre-occupation may stem from the fact that Hobbes stood at the beginning of various intellectual and social trends that have culminated or have been eclipsed in our own time. According to C.B. Macpherson, Hobbes was one of the first advocates of "possessive individualism," an anthropological doctrine that concentrated on the accumulation and protection of property as man's primary motives and became a cornerstone of the market economy and modern industrial society. Taking a broader view, Jurgen Habermas identified Hobbes as one of the ancestors of technological rationalism, a rationalism that in its combination of rigorous analysis and technical invention continues to animate the "scientific revolution" of our age. These and similar interpretations undoubtedly possess great plausibility and persuasiveness, but they hardly tell the whole story. Neither Hobbes's vocabulary nor our own seems restricted to this range of discourse. While attractive to the scientific mentality of a technological era, Hobbes's voice also reaches us on a different level of frequency—the level of basic human experience. From this vantage point, one may legitimately query whether and to what extent Hobbes's idiom bears resemblance to that of contemporary existentialist literature.

After having delineated principles of analysis and the basic properties of inanimate and animate bodies, Hobbes embarks on an examination of human attitudes and dispositions in their natural state or in the absence of a civil community. Some of the propositions advanced at this point have received wide currency as distinctive trademarks of his thought, but their basis is less frequently explored. The thesis of man's "perpetual and restless desire of power after power, that ceases only in death" and the portrayal of natural human life as "solitary, poor, nasty, brutish, and short" are sometimes ascribed to the pessimism, if not the base disposition of the philosopher. His anthropology is thus reduced to a personal idiosyncrasy. To be sure, the context in which these propositions are advanced does not always enhance their persuasiveness.

In the first sketch of his philosophical position, the thesis of the dependence of human motivation and of animal motion in general on external impacts was joined almost abruptly with the conception of a restless competition and discord; the nexus remained largely implicit. Yet, the treatment of human sensation in terms of quasi-mechanical motion seemed to preclude at least the metaphysical notion of a human essence, of a preordained teleology gently directing man's path with the promise of fulfillment. Some implications of man's predicament were developed in *De Cive*. Arguing against Aristotle's view of man as a "political animal," Hobbes in the opening chapter maintained that nature had not provided man so conveniently with a goal. He insisted that man's inclinations and desires, even when ultimately directed at social commerce, did not by themselves procure peace. Civil society was, in short, the result less of natural inclination than of design and planning. The nexus between natural inclinations and human discord was explored more fully in the *Leviathan*. Thus while signals of command were found to be intelligible to most animate creatures, man was assigned the special capacity of "understanding not only his will, but his conceptions and thoughts, by the sequel and contexture of the names of things into affirmations, negations and other forms of speech." Moreover, man could go beyond the immediate confines of perception by trying to determine the likely consequences and possible uses of an object—a faculty, Hobbes writes, "of which I have not at any time seen any sign but in many only; for this is a curiosity hardly incident to the nature of any living creature that has no other passion but sensual." Coupled with this inventiveness was man's rational potential, his ability developed through training to "reduce the consequences he finds to general rules," to "reason or reckon, not only in number, but in all other things."

Largely on the basis of these arguments Hobbes then advanced his general thesis of the deficiency and restlessness of human life. The absence of a preordained essence and the incongruity between man's imagination and the world supported the conclusion that man on earth could not find ultimate fulfillment that the "felicity of this life" resided not "in the repose of a mind satisfied" nor in the attainment of an object, but rather in the "continual progress of the desire from one object to another, the attaining of the former being still but the way to the latter." The further proposition of human conflict and discord could be attached to this thesis without great difficulty, for in the pursuit of his goals man cannot avoid encountering others engaged in a similar endeavor. This general search or race, however, is dominated not only by scarcity of desired goods, but above all a scarcity of positions in front or on top, and from this scarcity derives the danger of hostility and even physical destruction. Moreover, man in the pursuit of his ends has to assure himself constantly of the necessary means, and, due to their diverse abilities, other human beings are liable to be employed as such objects or instruments or to be subdued or destroyed in case of resistance. As Hobbes suggests, there are three principal sources of human conflict—competition, diffidence, and resentment: competition to use and subdue others as objects, diffidence of being used or subdued as such, and resentment for being valued more as an object than as a person.

Bacon embodies empiricism, and subscribes to ontological individualism. But for a really thorough and systematic exposition of both we must turn to a far more formidable thinker, Thomas Hobbes. The one thing which everyone knows about Hobbes is the conclusion to his argument in *Leviathan*: that to establish human society on a basis of lasting security, it is necessary to place 'an absolute and arbitrary legislative power' in the hands of a single sovereign.

Divided authority, or divided sovereignty is a recipe for insecurity and conflict. It is this conclusion which has led to Hobbes being associated with theorists of absolutism like Bodin, and to his being charged, rather vaguely, with authoritarianism. Thomas Hobbes read Descartes' Meditations before its publication and raised several criticisms, which, together with Descartes' rejoinders, were published by Descartes. About ten years later, in 1651, Hobbes published his own major work, *Leviathan*. Hobbes was on close terms with many of the best scientists and mathematicians of the period, including most significantly Galileo, and their discoveries seemed to him imply clearly that all things are made of material practices and that all change reduces to motion. Accordingly, the basic premise of Hobbes's metaphysics is that all that exists is bodies in motion, motion being a continual relinquishing of one place and acquiring of another. Because, according to Hobbes, there are two main types of bodies, physical bodies and political bodies, there are two divisions of philosophy, natural and civil. Now, this business that all that exists is bodies in motion might sound plausible, until you consider such things as thoughts or acts of violation or emotion. Can it really be held that thought is just matter in motion? That emotions are? That hatred is? "Yes", said Hobbes.

Hobbes's strategy was to show that there is a basic mental activity, perception, or, as he called it, "sense", from which all other mental phenomena are derived and that perception itself reduces to matter in motion. Perception, he maintained, occurs as follows: Motion in the external world causes motion within us. This motion within is experienced by us as an external object (or group of objects) having certain properties. The properties do not really exist in the objects. Hobbes said; they are just the way the objects seem to us. So motion outside us causes motion within us, which is perception. If the internal motion remains for a while even after the external object is no longer present, it is then imagination or memory. And thinking, he said, is merely a sequence of these perceptions.

Now, humans, unlike animals are able to form signs or names (words) to designate perceptions, and it is the ability that allows human to reason. In Hobbes's view, reasoning is nothing but "adding and subtracting of the consequences of general names". Reasoning occurs, for example, when you see that the consequences of the name circle are, among other has been divided into two equal parts.

As for decisions and other voluntary actions, such as walking or speaking or moving our arms, these are all movements of the body that begin internally as "endeavors", caused by perceptions. When the endeavor is toward something that cause it, this is desire; when away from it, it is aversion. Love is merely desire, and hate merely aversion. We call a thing "good" when it is an object of desire and "bad" when it is an object of aversion. Deliberation is simply an alternation of desires and aversions, and will is nothing but the last desire or aversion remaining in a deliberation. We've left out the finer details of Hobbes's account, but this should show you how Hobbes tried to establish that every aspect of human psychology is a derivative of perception and that perception itself reduces to matter in motion. Thomas Hobbes drew exclusively from the Aristotelian channel. This is not surprising, for Hobbes was one of the first philosophers of the modern period in philosophy, a period marked by the emergence of experimental science, in which once again nature itself was an object of study, just as it had been for Aristotle.

Hobbes's metaphysics was a relentless materialism. All that exists, he said, are material things in motion. Immaterial substance does not exist. There are no such things as the nonphysical soul. Thoughts, emotions, feelings – all are motions of the matter within the brain, caused by moving things outside the brain. Even our reasoning and violation are purely physical processes. As for values, according to Hobbes the words good and evil simply denote that which a person desires or hates. And Hobbes, like Aristotle, the Epicureans, the Stoics, and Aquinas, believed that one has a natural "end" or objective toward which all activity is directed. Hobbes specified this object of desire as the preservation of one's life. One seeks personal survival above all other things, he held. Hobbes also said that one has a natural right to use all means necessary to defend oneself or otherwise ensure one's survival.

Thus, Hobbes was a descriptive egoist. That is, he believed that, in all conscious action, one seeks to promote one's self-interest. A story is reported about "Hobbes and the Beggar" that Hobbes was asked by a clergyman why he was giving alms to a beggar. He did so to end his own discomfort at seeing the beggar's discomfort. Beginning students in philosophy often are tempted to give a similar selfish analysis of even the most apparently unselfish actions. It is not because Jesus has commanded you to do so. Hobbes emphatically said "no". One moral that might be drawn from the story is that even the most altruistic and benevolent actions can be given egoistic interpretation. Why did Hobbes help the beggar? To relieve his own discomfort. Why do saints devote their lives to relieving the suffering of others? Because it brings them pleasure to do so. Why did the soldier sacrifice his life to save his comrades? To end the distress he felt at thinking of his friend's dying – or maybe even because it pleased him to think of others praising him after his demise. In short, because those who act to relieve their own discomfort or to bring pleasure themselves are acting for their own self-interest, all of these seemingly altruistic actions can be interpreted egoistically.

Was Hobbes also a prescriptive egoist? That is, did he also think that one ought to seek to promote one's self-interest above all else? In general, Hobbes did not attempt to determine how people ought to behave in some absolute sense; he seems intent on describing how they ought to behave if they want best to secure their natural objective. A question he left for subsequent philosophers and one that has not been resolved to this day, is this: If the universe is material, can there really be absolute values? Do well and evil, justice and injustice, exist in some absolute.

Hobbes's major work, *Leviathan*, is a classic in moral and political philosophy and encompasses as well metaphysics, epistemology, ethics, and psychology. It secured for Hobbes a prime-time place in all histories of Western thought. Hobbes maintained that the idea of incorporeal or immaterial substance was a contradiction in terms, but he denied being an atheist. Nevertheless, he certainly did not rest his ethics on the authority of the Church. And although most of the major philosophers of the modern period shrank from Hobbes's extreme materialism, they, too – most of them – sought to discover the basic principles of morality elsewhere then in scripture. Some, such as Locke, though believing that these principles are decreed by God, held, like Hobbes, that they are discoverable – and provable – by reason.

—Editor

The Natural Condition of Mankind

Nature has made men so equal, in the faculties of the body, and mind; as that thought there be found one man sometimes manifestly stronger in body, or of quicker mind than another; yet when all is reckoned together, the difference between man, and man, is not so considerable, as that one man can thereupon claim to himself any benefit, to which another may not pretend, as well as he. For as to strength of body, the weakest has strength enough to kill the strongest, either by secret machination, or by confederacy with others, that are in the same danger with himself.

And as to the faculties of the mind... I find yet a greater equality amongst men, than that of strength... That which may perhaps make such equality incredible, is but a vain conceit of one's own wisdom, which almost all men think they have in a greater degree, than the vulgar; that is, than all men but themselves, and a few others, whom by fame, or for concurring with themselves, they approve. For such is the nature of men, that howsoever they may acknowledge many others to be more witty, or more eloquent or more learned; yet they will hardly believe there be many so wise as themselves; for they set their own wit at hand, and other men's ata distance. But this proves rather that men are in that point equal, than unequal. For there is not ordinarily a greater sign of the equal distribution of anything, than every man is contented with his share.

From this equality of ability, arises equality of hope in the attaining of our ends. And therefore if any two men desire the same thing, which nevertheless they cannot both enjoy, they become enemies, and in the way to their end, which is principally their own conservation, and sometimes their delectation only, endeavour to destroy, or subdue one another. And from hence it comes to pass, that where an invader has no more to fear, than another man's single power; if one plant, sow, build, or possess a convenient seat, others may probably be expected to come prepared with forces united, to dispossess, and deprive him, not only of the fruit of his labour, but also of his life, or liberty. And the invader again is in the like danger of another.

And from this difference of one another, there is no way for any man to secure himself, so reasonable, as anticipation; that is, by force, or wiles, to master the persons of all men he can, so long, till he see no other power great enough to endanger him: and this is no more than his own conservation requires, and is generally allowed...

Again, men have no pleasure, but on the contrary a great deal of grief, in keeping company where there is no power able to over-awe them all. For every man looks that his companion should value him, at the same rate he sets upon himself: and upon all signs of contempt, or undervaluing, naturally endeavors, as far as he dares, (which amongst them that have no common power to keep them in quiet, is far enough to make them destroy each other), to extort a greater value from his condemners, by damage; and from others, by the example.

So that in the nature of man, we find three principle causes of quarrel. First, competition; secondly, difference; thirdly, glory.

The first makes men invade for gain; the second, for safety; and the third for reputation. The first use violence, to make themselves masters of other men's persons, wives, children, and cattle; the second, to defend them; the third for trifles, as a word, a smile, a different opinion, and any other sign of undervalue, either direct in their persons, or by reflection in their kindred, their friends, their nation, their profession, or their name.

Hereby it is manifest, that during the time men live without a common power to keep them all in awe, they are in that condition which is called war; and such a war, as if of every man, against every man. For WAR, consists not in battle only, or the act of fighting; but in a tract of time, wherein the will to contend by battle is sufficiently known: and therefore the notion of time, is to be considered in the nature of war; as it is the nature of weather. For as the nature of foul weather, lies not in a shower or two of rain; but in an inclination thereto of many days together; so the nature of war, consists not in actual fighting; but in the known disposition thereto, during all the time there is no assurance to the contrary. All other time is PEACE.

Whatsoever therefore is consequent to a time of war, where every man is enemy to every man.; the same is consequent to the time, wherein men live without other security, than what their own strength, and their own invention shall furnish them withal. In such condition, there is no place for industry; because the fruit thereof is uncertain: and consequently no culture of the earth; n navigation, nor use of the commodities that may be imported by sea; no commodious building; no instruments of moving, and removing, such things as require much force; no knowledge of the face of the earth; no count of time; no arts; no letters, no society; and which is worst of all, continual fear, and danger of violent death; and the life of man, solitary, poor, nasty, brutish, and short...

To this war of every man, against every man, this also is consequent; that nothing can be unjust. The notions of right and wrong, justice and injustice have there no place. Where there is no common power, there is no law, where no law, no injustice. Force, and fraud, are in war the two cardinal virtues. Justice and injustice are none of faculties neither of the body, nor mind. If they were, they might be in a man that were alone in the world, as well as his senses, and passions. They are qualities that relate to men in society, not in solitude. It is consequent also to the same condition, there be no propriety, no dominion, no mine and thine distinct; but only that to be every man's, that he can get; and for so long, as he can keep it. And thus much for the ill condition, which man by mere nature is actually placed in; though with a possibility to come out of it, consisting partly in the passions, partly in his reason.

The passions that incline men to peace, are fear of death, desire of such things as are necessary to commodious living; and a hope by their industry to obtain them. And reason suggests convenient articles of peace, upon which men may be drawn to agreement. These articles, are they, which otherwise are called the Laws of Nature: whereof I shall speak more particularly, in the two following chapters...

The First and Second Natural Laws

...And because the condition of man (as has been declared in the preceding chapter) is a condition of war of everyone against everyone; in which case everyone is governed by his own reason; and there is nothing he can make use of, that may not be a help to him, in preserving his life against his enemies; it follows that in such a condition every man has a right to everything; even to one another's body. And therefore, as long as this natural right of man to everything endures, there can be no security to any man (how strong or wise he is) of living out the time which nature ordinarily allows men to live. Add consequently it is a percept or general rule of reason, *that every man ought to endeavor peace, as far as he has hope of obtaining it; and when he cannot obtain it he may seek and use all helps and advantages of war*. The first branch of which rule contains the first and fundamental law of nature; which is *too seek peace and follow it*. The second, the sum of the Right of Nature; which is, *by all means we can, to defend ourselves*.

From this fundamental law of nature, by which men are commanded to endeavor peace, is derived this second law, that a man be willing, when others are also, as far as for peace, and defense of himself he shall think it necessary, to lay down this right to all things; and be contended with so much liberty against other men,, as he would allow other men against himself. For as long as every man holds this right of doing anything he likes; so long are all men in the condition of war. But if other men will not lay down their right, as well as he; then there is not reason for anyone to divest himself of his: For that would be to expose himself to prey (which no man is bound to) rather than to dispose himself to peace...

The mutual transferring of right, is that which men call CONTRACT...

The Causes, Generation, and Definition of a Commonwealth

The final cause, end, or design of men (who naturally love liberty and dominion over others) in the introduction of that restraint upon themselves (in which we see them live in commonwealths) is the foresight of their own preservation and of a more contended life; that is to say, of getting themselves out from that miserable condition of war, which is necessarily consequent (as has been shown) to the natural passions of men, when there is no visible power to keep them in awe, and tie them by fear of punishment to the performance of their covenants, and observation of those laws of nature set down in the fourteenth and fifteenth chapters.

For the laws of nature (as justice, equity, modesty, mercy, and, in sum, doing to others as we would be done to) of themselves, without the terror of some power to cause them to be observed, are contrary to our natural passions, that carry us to partially, pride, revenge, and the like. And covenants, without the sword, are but words, and of no strength to secure a man at all. Therefore notwithstanding the laws of nature (which everyone has then kept, when he has the will to keep them, when he can do it safely) if there be no power erected, or not great enough for our security; every man will, and may lawfully rely on his own strength and art, for caution against all other men...

The only way to erect such a common power as may be able to defend them from the invasion of foreigners and the injuries of one another and thereby to secure them in such a way as that by their own industry, and by the fruits of the earth, they may nourish themselves and live contentedly; is to confer all their power and strength upon one man or upon one assembly of men, that may reduce all their wills, by plurality of voices, unto once will: which is as much as to say, to appoint one man or assembly of men to bear their person...

This is more than consent or concord; it is a real unity of them all in one and the same person, made by covenant of every man with every man, in such manner as if every man should say to every man, I authorize and give up my right of governing myself to this man or to do this assembly of men, on this condition that you give up the right to him and authorize all his actions in like manner. This done, the multitude so united in one person, is called a Commonwealth, in Latin, Civitas. This is the generation of that great Leviathan, or rather (to speak more reverently) of that mortal god to which we owe under the immortal God our peace and defense. For by this authority, given him by every particular man in the commonwealth, he has the use of so much power and strength conferred on him, by terror thereof, he is enabled to form the wills of them all, to peace at home, and mutual aid against their enemies abroad. And in him consists the essence of the commonwealth; which (to define it) is one person, of whose acts a great multitude by mutual covenants one with another have made themselves every one the author, to the end he may use the strength and means of them all, as he shall think expedient, for their peace and common defense.

And he that caries this person, is called Sovereign, and said to have sovereign power; and everyone besides, his Subject.

The attaining to this sovereign power, is by two ways. One, by natural force; as when a man makes his children submit themselves and their children to his government, as being able to destroy them if they refuse; or by war subdues his enemies to his will, given them their lives on that condition. The other is when men agree amongst themselves, to submit to some man, or assembly of men, voluntarily on confidence to be protected by him against all others. This latter may be called a political commonwealth, or commonwealth by institution; and the former a commonwealth by acquisition.

(From *Levithan* by Thomas Hobbes, edited by Richerd Tulk Cambridge University Press, Combridge, 1991)

9

John Locke

John Locke (1632-1704) was born in 1632 and grew up with the seventeenth-century scientific revolution. He the foremost English philosopher of the early period of modern post-Cartesian philosophy was educated at Westminster School and Christ Church, Oxford. Besides studying and then teaching subjects such as logic, moral philosophy, rhetoric, and Greek, he had a deep and abiding interest in medicine, which brought him into the service of the Earl of Shaftesbury. As secretary to Shaftesbury he became involved in Protestant politics. This involvement resulted in an exile in Holland from 1683 to 1689, when, shortly after William of Orange took the thorne, he returned to England and led a life of private study and public service. He wrote widely—not only on various branches of philosophy, but also on education, economics, theology, and medicine. He is best known for his anonymously published *Two Treatises of Government* (1690) and his *Essay Concerning Human Understanding* (1690). He came from an upwardly mobile Somersetshire family who made it into the gentry class. Though not particularly forward at his books, Locke decided early on an academic career. He became a don at Christ Church College, Oxford, until he was illegally rejected for his allegedly subversive opinions in 1684. He was outwardly not much concerned with philosophy and political theory during his Oxford years, teaching some law and a lot of medicine. The young Locke even seems to have been a bit of a Tory, believing that non-resistance to established authority was the just price of political and social stability.

Locke's friendship with the first Earl of Shaftesbury, whose life he saved with a miraculous operation on the liver, changed him from a mildly subversive Oxford don into a meddler in high politics as adviser and confidant to highly placed plotters against the Divine Right monarchy of the Stuarts. He no doubt provided Shaftesbury with arguments to use in the everyday political battle of the Exclusionist Whigs who wished to exclude James II when he was still only the Duke of York from the succession to the throne on the grounds that he was a Roman Catholic against their Tory opponents in the last years of the reign of Charles II. It was probably inevitable either that Shaftesbury would eventually ask Locke's opinions on the most important political question of all, the question of the grounds for legitimate resistance to government, or that Locke's own position in Shaftesbury's circle would eventually lead him without prodding to consider that question. It was in these circumstances that Locke wrote his famous *Two Treatises of Government* (the exact date of the works is still not certain, but a good guess would be 1679-80). It was while enjoying the patronage of Shaftesbury that Locke worked on the ideas which would see the light of day as *An Essay Concerning Human Understanding*. It was also about this time that Locke turned his attention to economics, education and questions of colonial government.

Locke's *Two Treatises* were published to justify the Glorious Revolution of 1688, in which Locke was involved as the friend and adviser to a leading Whig, Lord Somers. Locke's own attitude to his famous political treatises appears to have been decidedly odd, not to say shifty. He never acknowledged his authorship of the treatises, but was very keen that they should be available in a true text. Editions were mangled by printers, and it may also be that Locke was worried that opinions more radical than his own would be attributed to him. On the other hand, it may simply be that there was an impenetrably secretive side to Locke's character which will always hide his true reasons for publicly denying his authorship of such famous books.

The Treatises, which contain Locke's political philosophy, were composed in the years of the Exclusion Crisis, during which Locke's patron, Shaftesbury, and others, sought to exclude James, then Duke of York, from the succession to the throne, and argued for government by consent and for the right to religious dissent. *The First Treatise* less studied now than the *Second*, consists mainly of criticism of Robert Filmer's *Patriarcha* (1680) of absolute monarchy and the divine right of kings. Locke found this account of political authority, according to which God granted Adam absolute and total political authority, unworkable. It could not be used to justify any actual political authority, since it is impossible to show of any particular ruler that he is one of Adam's heirs. In an alternative account *The Second Treatise* argues that though subjects do have a duty to God to obey their ruler, their ruler's power is not God-given or absolute, and it goes along with duties to his subjects. If a ruler's commands do not deserve obedience, resistance to them might be justified.

—Editor

The State of Nature

To understand political power aright, and derive it from its original, we must consider what estate all men are naturally in, and that is, a state of perfect freedom to order their actions, and dispose of their possessions and persons as they think fit, within the bounds of the law of Nature, without asking leave or depending upon the will of any other man.

A state also of equality, wherein all the power and jurisdiction is reciprocal, no one having more than another, there being nothing more evident than that creatures of the same species and rank, promiscuously born to all the same advantages of Nature, and the use of the same faculties, should also be equal one amongst another, without subordination or subjection, unless the lord and master of them all should, by any manifest declaration of his will, set one above another, and confer on him, by an evident and clear appointment, an undoubted right to dominion and sovereignty.

But though this be a state of liberty, yet it is not a state of license; though man in that state have an uncontrollable liberty to dispose of his person or possessions, yet he has not liberty to destroy himself, or so much as any creature in his possession, but where some nobler use than its bare preservation calls for it. The state of Nature has a law of Nature to govern it, which obliges every one, and reason, which is that law, teaches all mankind who will but consult it, that being all equal and independent, no one ought to harm another in his life, health, liberty or possessions; for men being all the workmanship of one omnipotent and infinitely wise Maker; all the servants of one sovereign Master, sent into the world by His order and about His business; they are His property, whose workmanship they are made to last during His, not one another's pleasure. And, being furnished with like faculties, sharing all in one community of Nature, there cannot be supposed any such subordination among us that may authorise us to destroy one another, as if we were made for one another's uses, as the inferior ranks of creatures are for ours. Every one as he is bound to preserve himself, and not to quit his station willfully, so by the like reason, when his own preservation comes not in competition, ought he as much as he can to preserve the rest of mankind, and not unless it be to do justice on an offender, take away or impair the life, or what tends to the preservation of the life, the liberty, health, limb, or goods of another.

And that all men may be restrained from invading others' rights, and from doing hurt to one another, and the law of Nature be observed, which willet the peace ankle preservation of all mankind, the execution of the law of Nature is in that state put into every man's hands, whereby every one has a right to punish the transgressors of that law to such a degree as may hinder its violation. For the law of Nature would, as all other laws that concern men in this world, be in vain if there were nobody that in the state of Nature had a power to execute that law, and thereby preserve the innocent and restrain offenders; and if any one in the state of Nature may punish another for any evil he has done, every one may do so. For in that state of perfect equality, where naturally there is no superiority of jurisdiction of one over another, what any may do in prosecution of that law, every one must needs have a right to do.

And thus, in the state of Nature, one man comes by a power over another, but yet no absolute or arbitrary power to use a criminal, when he has got him in his hands, according to the passionate heats or boundless extravagancy of his own will, but only to reattribute to him so far as calm reason and conscience dictate, what is proportionate to his transgression, which is so much as may serve for reparation and restraint, For these two are the only reasons why one man may lawfully do harm to another, which is that we call punishment. In transgressing the law of Nature, the offender declares himself to live by another rule than that of reason and common equity, which is that measure God has set to the actions of men for their mutual security, and so he becomes dangerous to mankind; the tie which is to secure them from injury and violence being slighted and broken by him, which being a trespass against the whole species, and the peace and safety of it, provided for by the Jaw of Nature, every man upon this score, by the right he hath to preserve mankind in general, may restrain, or where it is necessary, destroy things noxious to them, and so may bring such evil on any one who hath transgressed that law, as may make him repent the doing of it, and thereby deter him, and, by his example, others from doing the like mischief. And in this case, and upon this ground, every man hath a right to punish the offender, and be executioner of the law of Nature.

I doubt not but this will seem a very strange doctrine to some men; but before they condemn it, 1 desire them to resolve me by what right any prince or state can put to death or punish an alien for any crime he commits in their country? It is certain their laws, by virtue of any sanction they receive from the promulgated will of the legislature, reach not a stranger. They speak not to him, nor, if they did, is he bound to hearken to them. The legislative authority by which they are in force over the subjects of that commonwealth hath no power over him. Those who have the supreme power of making laws in England, France, or Holland are, to an Indian, but like the rest of the world—men without authority. And therefore, if by the law of Nature every man hath not a power to punish offences against it, as he soberly judges the case to require, I see not how the magistrates of any community can punish an alien of another country, since, in reference to him, they can have no more power than what every man naturally may have over another.

From these two distinct rights (the one of punishing the crime, for restraint and preventing the like offence, which right of punishing is in everybody, the other of taking reparation, which belongs only to the injured party) comes it to 'pass that the magistrate, who by being magistrate hath the common right of punishing put into his hands, can often, where the public good demands not the execution of the law, remit the punishment of criminal offences by his own authority, but yet cannot remit the satisfaction due to any private man for the damage he has received. That he who hath suffered the damage has a right to demand in his own name, and he alone can remit. The dandified person has this power of appropriating to himself the goods or service of the offender by right of self-preservation, as every man has a power to punish the crime to prevent its being committed again, by the right he has of preserving all mankind, and doing all reasonable things he can in order to that end. And thus it is that every man in the state of Nature has a power to kill a murderer, both to deter others from doing the like injury (which no reparation can compensate) by the example of the punishment that attends it from everybody, and also to secure men from the attempts of a criminal who, having renounced reason, the common rule and measure God hath given to mankind, hath, by the unjust violence and slaughter he hath committed upon one, declared war against all mankind, and therefore may be destroyed as a lion or a tiger, one of those wild savage beasts with whom, men can have no society nor security. And upon this is grounded that great law of Nature, 'Whoso shredded man's blood, by man shall his blood. And Cain was so fully convinced that every one had a right to destroy Such a criminal, that, after the murder of his brother, he cries out, 'Every one that fended me shall slay me,' so plain was it writ in the hearts of all mankind.

By the same reason may a man in the State of Nature punish the lesser breaches of than law, it will, perhaps, be demanded, with death? I answer: Each transgression may be punished to that degree, and with so much severity, as will suffice to make it an ill bargain to the offender, give him cause to repent, and terrify others from doing the like. Every offence that can be committed in the state of Nature may in the State of Nature, be also punished equally, and as far forth, as it may, in a commonwealth. For though it would be beside my present purpose to enter here into the particulars of the Law of Nature, or its measures of punishment, yet it is certain there is such a law, and that too as intelligible and plain to a rational creature and a studier of that law as the positive laws of commonwealths, nay, possibly plainer; as much as reason is easier to be understood than the fancies and intricate contrivances of men, following contrary and hidden interests put into words; for truly so are a great part of the municipal laws of countries, which are only so far right as they are founded on the law of Nature, by which they are to be regulated and interpreted.

To this strange doctrine—viz., That in the state of Nature every one has the executive power of the Law of Nature—I doubt not but it will be objected that it is unreasonable for men to be judges in their own cases, that self-love will make men partial to themselves and their friends; and, on the other side, ill-nature, passion, and revenge will carry them too far in punishing others, and hence nothing but confusion and disorder will follow, and that therefore God hath certainly appointed government to restrain the partiality and violence of men. I easily grant that civil government is the proper remedy for the inconveniences of the state of Nature, which must certainly be great where men may be judges in their own case, since it is easy to be imagined that he who was so unjust as to do his brother an injury will scarce be so just as to condemn himself for it. But I shall desire those who make this objection to remember that absolute monarchs are but men; and if government is to be the remedy of those evils which necessarily follow from men being judges in their own cases, and the state of Nature is therefore not to be endured, 1 desire to know what kind of government that is, and how much better it is than the state of Nature, where one man commanding a multitude has the liberty to be judge in his own case, and may do to all his subjects whatever he pleases without the least question or control of those, who execute his pleasure? and in whatsoever he doth, whether led by reason, mistake, or passion, must be submitted to? which men in the state of Nature are not bound to do one to another. And if he that judges, judges amiss in his own or any other case, he is answerable for it to the rest of mankind.

It is often asked as a mighty objection, where are, or ever were, there any men in such a state of Nature? To which it may suffice as an answer at present, that since all princes and rulers of 'independent' governments all through the world are in a state of Nature, it is plain the world never was, nor never will be, without numbers of men in that state. I have named all governors of 'independent' communities, whether they are, or are not, in league with others; for it is not every compact that puts an end to the state of Nature between men, but only this one of agreeing together mutually to enter into one community, and make one body politic; other promises and compacts men may make one with another, and yet still be in the state of Nature. The promises and bargains for truck, etc., between the two men in Soldania, in or between a Swiss and an Indian, in the woods of America, are binding to them, though they are perfectly in a state of Nature in reference to one another for truth, and keeping of faith belongs to men as men, and not as members of society.

And here we have the plain difference between the state of Nature and the state of war, which however some men have confounded, are as far distant as a state of peace, goodwill, mutual assistance, and preservation; and a state of enmity, malice, violence and mutual destruction are one from another. Men living together according to reason without a common superior on earth, with authority to judge between them is properly the state of Nature. But force, or a declared design of force upon the person of another, where there is no common superior on earth to appeal to for relief, is the State of war; and it is the want of such an appeal gives a man the right of war even against an aggressor, though he be in society and a fellow-subject.

The *State, of War* is a State of Enmity and Destruction and therefore declaring by Word or Action, not a passionate and hasty, but a sedate settled Design, upon /another Mans Life, *puts him in a Stale of War* with him against whom he has declared such an Intention, and so 5 has exposed his Life to the others Power to be taken away by him, or any one that joins with him in his Defence, and espouses his Quarrel: it being reasonable and just I should have a Right to destroy that which threatens me with) destruction. For *by the Fundamental Law of Nature, Man being to be preserved,* as much as possible, when a cannot be preserved, the safety of the Innocent is to be preferred: And one may destroy a Man who makes War upon him, or has discovered an Enmity to his being, for the same Reason, that he may kill a *Wolf* or a *Lyon* because such Men are not under the ties of the Common Law of Reason, have no other Rule, but that of Force and Violence, and so may be treated as Beasts of Prey, those dangerous and noxious Creatures that will be sure 20 to destroy him, whenever he falls into their Power.

And hence it is, that he who attempts to get another Man into his Absolute Power, does thereby *put himself into a Slate of War* with him; It being to be understood as a Declaration of a Design upon his Life. For I have reason to conclude, that he who would get me into his Power without my consent, would use me as pleased, when he had got me there, and destroy me when he had a fancy to it: for no body can desire to *have me in his Absolute Power,* unless it be to compel me by force to that, which is against the Right of my Freedom, *i.e.* make me a Slave. To be free from such force is the only security of my Preservation: and reason bids me look on him, as an Enemy to my Preservation, who would take away that *Freedom,* which is the Fence to it: so that he who makes an *attempt to enslave* me, thereby puts himself into a State of War with me. He that in the State of Nature, *would take away the Freedom,* that belongs to any one in that State, must necessarily be supposed to have a design to take away every thing else, that *Freedom* being the Foundation of all the rest: As he that in the State of Society, would take away the *Freedom* belonging to those of that Society or Common-wealth, must be supposed to design to take away from them every thing else, and so be looked on as *in a State of War.*

This makes it Lawful for a Man to *kill a Thief,* who has not in the least hurt him, nor declared any design upon his Life, any farther than by the use of Force, so to get him in his Power, as to take away his Money, or what he pleases from him; because using force, where he has no Right, to get me into his Power, let his pretence be what it will, have no reason to suppose, that he, who would *take away my Liberty,* would not when he had me in his Power, take away every thing else. And therefore it is Lawful for me to treat him, as one who has put himself *into a State of War* with me, *i.e.* kill him if T can; for to that hazard does he justly expose himself, whoever introduces a State of War, and is *aggressor* in it.

And here we have the plain *difference between the State of Nature, and the State of War,* which however some Men have confounded, are as far distant, as a State of Peace, Good Will, Mutual Assistance, and Preservation, and a State of Enmity, Malice, Violence, and Mutual Destruction are one from another. Men living together according to reason, without a common Superior on Earth, with Authority to judge between them is *properly the State of Nature.* But force, or a declared design of force upon the Person of another, where there is no common Superior on Earth to appeal to for relief, *is the State of War:* And 'tis the want of such an appeal gives a Man the light of War even against an *aggressor,* though he be in Society and a fellow Subject. Thus a *Thief,* whom cannot harm but by appeal to the Law, for having stolen all that I am worth, I may kill, when he sets on me to rob me, but of my Horse or Coat: because the Law, which was made for my Preservation, where it cannot interpose to secure my Life from present force, which if lost, is capable of no reparation, permits me my own Defence, and the Right of War, a liberty to kill the aggressor, because the aggressor allows not time to appeal to our common Judge, nor the decision of the Law, for remedy in a Case, where the mischief may be irreparable. *Want of a common hedge with Authority, puts all Men in a State of Nature: Force without Right, upon a Man's Person, makes a State of War,* both where there is, and is not, a common Judge.

To avoid this State of War wherein there is no appeal but to Heaven, and wherein every the least difference is apt to end, where there is no Authority to decide between the Contenders is one great *reason of Mens putting themselves into Society,* and quitting the State of Nature. For where there is an Authority, a Power on Earth, from which relief can be had by *appeal,* there the continuance of the State of War is excluded, and the Controversies is decided by that Power.

The *Natural Liberty* of Man is to he free from any Superior Power on Earth, and not to be under the Will or Legislative Authority of Man, but to have only the Law of Nature for his Rule. The *Liberty of Man, in Society,* is to be under no other Legislative Power, but that established, by consent, in the Common-wealth, nor under the Dominion of any Will, or Restraint of any Law, but what the Legislative shall enact, according to the Trust put in it.

A Liberty for every one to do what he lists, to live as he pleases, and not to be tyed by any Laws: But *Freedom of Men under Government,* is, to have a Standing Rule to live by, common to every one of that Society, and made by the Legislative Power erected in it; A Liberty to follow my own Will in all things, where the Rule prescribes not; and not to be subject to the inconstant, uncertain, unknown, Arbitrary Will of another Man. As *Freedom of Nature* is to be under no other restraint but the Law of Nature.

This *Freedom* from Absolute, Arbitrary Power, is so necessary to, and closely joined with a Man's Preservation, that he cannot part with it, but by what forfeits his Preservation and Life together. For a Man, not having the Power of his own Life, *cannot,* by Compact, or his own Consent, *enslave himself* to any one nor put himself under the Absolute, Arbitrary Power of another, to take away his Life, when he pleases. No body can give more Power than he has himself; and he that cannot take away his own Life, cannot give another power over it. Indeed having, by his fault, forfeited his own Life, by some Act that deserves Death; he, to whom he has forfeited it, may (when he has him in his Power) delay to take it, and make use of him to his own Service, and he does him no injury by it. For, whenever he finds the hardship of his Slavery out-weigh the value of his Life, 'tis in his' Power, by resisting the Will of his Master, to draw on himself the Death he desires.

This is the perfect condition of *Slavery,* which *is* nothing else, but *the State of War continued, between a lawful Conquerour, and a Captive.* For, if once *Compact* enter between them, and make an agreement for a limited 5 Power on the one side, and Obedience on the other, the State of War and *Slavery* ceases, as long as the Compact endures. For, as his been said, no Man can, by agreement, pass over to another that which he hath not in himself, a Power over his own Life.

I confess, we find among the *Jews,* as well as other Natiôns, that Men did sell themselves; but, 'tis plain, this was only to *Drudgery, not to Shivery.* For, it is evident, the Person sold was not under an Absolute, Arbitrary, Despotically Power. For the Master could not have power to kill him, at any time, whom, at a certain time, he was obliged to let go free out of his Service: and the Master of such a Servant was KO far from having an Arbitrary Power over his Life.

Whosoever therefore out of a state of Nature unites into a Community must be understood to give up all the power necessary to the ends for which they unite into Society. And this is done by barely agreeing to unite into one Political Society, which is all the Compact that is or needs be, between the Individuals that enter into or make up a commonwealth. And thus that which begins and actually constitutes any Political Society is nothing but the consent of any number of Freemen capable of a major to unite and incorporate into such a society. And this is that and that only, which did or could give beginning to any lawful Government in (he world Locke ibid: 367).

The Right of making laws with penalties of Death and consequently all less Penalties, for Regulating and Preserving of Property, and of employing the force of the Community, in the Execution of such Laws and in the defence of the Commonwealth from Foreign Inquiry and all this only for the Public Good.

Of Property

Whether we consider natural *Reason,* which tells us, that Men, being once born, have a right to their Preservation, and consequently to Meat and Drink, and such other things, as Nature affords for their Subsistence: Or *Revelation,* which gives us an account of those Grants God made of the World to *Adam,* and to *Noah,* and his Sons, 'tis very clear, that God, as King *David* says, *Psal.* CXV. xvi. *has given the Earth to the Children of Men,* given it to Mankind in common. But this being supposed, it seems to some a very great difficulty, how any one should ever come to have a *Property* in any thing: I will not content my self to answer, That if it be difficult to make out *Properly,* upon a supposition, that God gave the World to *Adam* and his Posterity in common; it is impossible that any Man, but one universal Monarch, should have any *Property,* upon a supposition, that God gave the World to *Adam,* and his Heirs in Succession, exclusive of all the rest of his Posterity. But I shall endeavour to show, how Men might come to have a *property* in several parts of that which God gave to Mankind in common, and that without any express Compact of all the Commoners.

God, who hath given the World to Men in common, hath also given them reason to make use of it to the best advantage of Life, and convenience. The Earth, and all that is therein, is given to Men for the Support and Comfort of their being. And though all the Fruits it naturally produces, and Beasts it feeds, belong to Mankind common, as they are produced by the spontaneous hand of Nature; and no body has originally a private Dominion, exclusive of the rest of Mankind, in any of them, as they are thus in their natural state: yet being given for the use of Men, there must of necessity be a means *to appropriate* them some way or other before they can be of any use, or at all beneficial to any particular Man. The Fruit, or Venison, which nourishes the wild *Indian,* who knows no Inclosure, and is still a Tenant in common, must be his, and so his, *i.e.* a part of him, that another can no longer have any right to it, before it can do him any good for the support of his Life.

Though the Earth, and all inferior Creatures be common to all Men, yet every Man has a *Property* in his own *Person,* This no Body has any Right to but himself. The *Labour* of his Body, and the *Work* of his Hands, we may say, are properly his. Whatsoever then he removes out of the State that Nature hath provided, and left it in, he hath mixed his *Labour* with, and joined to it something that is his own, and thereby makes it his *Property.* It being by him removed from the common state Nature 'placed it in, hath by this *labour* something annexed to it, that excludes the common right of other Men. For this *Labour* being the unquestionable Property of the Labourer, no Man but he can have a right to what that is once joyned to, at least where there is enough, and as good left in common for others.

He that is nourished by the Acorns be pickt up under an Oak, or the Apples he gathered from the Trees Government, who have Money and Commerce, no one can inclose or appropriate any part, without the consent of all his Fellow-Commoners: Because this is left common by Compact, *i.e.* by the Law of the Land, which is not to be violated. And though it be Common, in respect of some Men, it is not so to all Mankind; but is the joint property of this Countrey, or this Parish. Besides, the remainder, after such inclosure, would not be as good to rest of the Commoners as the whole was, when they could all make use of the whole: whereas in the beginning and first peopling of the great Common of the World, it was quite otherwise. The Law Man was under, was rather 15 *for/appropriating.* God Commanded and his Wants forced him to *labour.* That was his *Property, which* could not be taken from him wherever he had fixed it. And hence subduing or cultivating the Earth, and having Dominion, we see are joyned together. The one gave Title to the other. So that God, by commanding to subdue, gave Authority so far to *appropriate.* And the Condition of 'Humane Life, which requires Labour and Materials to work on, necessarily introduces *private Possessions.*

The measure of Property, Nature has well set, by the Extent of Mens *Labour, and the Conveniency of Life:* No Mans Labour could subdue, or appropriate all: nor could his Enjoyment consume more than a small part; so that it was impossible for any Man, this way, to in trench upon the right of another, or acquire, to himself, a Property, to the Prejudice of his Neighbour, who would still have room, for as good, and as large a Possession (after the other had taken out his) as before it was appropriated. This *measure* did confine every Man's *Possession,* to a very moderate Proportion, and such as he might appropriate to himself, without Injury to any Body in the first Ages of the World, when Men were more in danger to be lost, by wandering from their Company, in the then vast Wilderness of the Earth, than to be straitned for want of room to plant in. And the same *measure* may be allowed still, without prejudice to any Body, as full as the World seems. For supposing a Man, or Family, in the state they were at first peopling of the World by the Children of *Adam,* or *Noah;* let him plant in some in-land, vacant places of *America,* we shall find that the *Possessions* he could make himself upon the *measures* we have given, would not be very large, nor, even to this day, prejudice the rest of Mankind, or give them reason to complain, or think them selves injured by this Man's Encroachment, though the Race 2 of Men have now spread themselves to all the corners of the World, and do infinitely exceed the small number which was at the beginning. Nay, the extent of *Ground* is of so little value, *without labour,* that I have heard it affirmed, that in *Spain* it self, a Man may be permitted to 30 plough, sow, and reap, without being disturbed, upon Land he has no other Title to, but only his making use of it. But, on the contrary, the Inhabitants think themselves beholden to him, who, by his Industry on neglected, and consequently Land, has increased the stock of Corn, 3 which they wan ed. But be this as it will, which I lay no stress on; This I dare boldly affirm, That the same *Rule of Propriety, (viz,)* that every Man should have as much as he could make use of, would hold still in the World, without straitning any body, since there is Land 10 enough in the World to suffice double the Inhabitants had not the *Invention of Money,* and the tacit Agreement of Men to put a value on it, introduced by Consent larger Possessions, and a Right to them; which, how it has done, I shall, by and by, shew more at large.

Man hath by Nature a Power to preserve his property, that is his life Liberty and Estate. Men's 'Lives, Liberties and Estates I call by the general Name Property. By property I must be understood here, as in other places, to mean that Property which Men have in their Persons as well as Goods.

The condition all men are naturally in is 'a *State of perfect Freedom* to order their Actions, and dispose of their Possessions, and Persons as they think fit, within the bounds of the Law of Nature, without asking leave, or depending upon the Will of any other Man.

But this that the earth was given to mankind in common being supposed, it seems to some a very great difficulty, how any one should ever come to have a *Property* in any thing... I shall endeavour to shew, how Men might come to have a *property* in several parts of that which God gave to Mankind in common, and that without any express Compact of all the Commoners. Every man has a property in his own person. This no Body has any Right to but himself. The Labour of his body, and the work of his Hands, we may say, are properly his.

'As much as any one can make use of to any vantage or life before it spoils; so much he may by his labour fix a Property in. Whatever is beyond this, is more than his share, and belongs to others. Nothing was made by/ God for Man to spoil or destroy

But the *Chief matter of Property* being now not the Fruits of Earth, and the Beasts that subsist on it, but the *Earth it self...* I think it is plain, that *Property* in that too is acquired as the former *much Land* as a Man Tills7"Plants, Improves, Cultivates, and can use the Product of, so much is his *Property.* He by his Labour docs, as it were, inclose it from the Common.

But be this as it will, which I lay no stress on; This I dare boldly 'affirm, That the same *Rule of Propriety, (viz.)* that every Man should have as much as he could make use of, would hold still in the World, without straitning any body, since there is Land enough in the World to suffice double the Inhabitants had not the *Invention of Money,* and the tacit Agreement of Men to put a value on it, introduced (by Consent) larger Possessions, and a Right to them.

Money by compact transfers that profit that was the reward of one man's labour, into another man's pocket. That which occasions this, is the unequal distribution of money; which inequality has the same effect too upon land, that it has upon money. For as the unequal distribution of land, (you having more than you can, or will manure, and another less) brings you a tenant for your land; the same unequal distribution of money, (I having more than I can, or will employ, and another less) brings me a tenant for my money.

The chief end of trade is Riches & Power which beget each other. Riches consists in plenty of moveable, that will yield a price to foraigner, & are not like to be consumed at home, but espetially in plenty of gold & silver. Power consists in numbers of .men, & ability, to maintaine them. Trade conduces to both these by increasing stock & people & they each other.

It is plain, that Men have agreed to disproportionate and unequal Possession of the Earth, they having by a tacit and voluntary consent found out a way, how a man may fairly possess more land than he himself can use the product of, by receiving in exchange for the over plus, Gold and Silver, which may be hoarded up without injury to any one, these metalls not spoileing or decaying in the hands of the possessor. This portage of things, in an inequality of private possessions, men have made practicable *out of the bounds of Society and without compact* only by putting a value on gold and silver and tacitly agreeing Un the use of Money.

To which let me add, that he who appropriates land to himself by his labour, does not lessen but increase the common stock of mankind. For the provisions serving to the support of humane life, produced by one acre of inclose and cultivated land, are to speak much within compassed ten times more, than those, which are yielded by an acre of an equal richnesse, lyeing west in common. And therefore he, that incloses Land and has a greater plenty of the conveniences of life from ten acres, than he could have from an hundred left to Nature, may truly be said, to give ninety acres to Mankind. For his labour now supplies him with provisions out of ten acres, which were but the product of an hundred lying in common.

Thus the Grass my Horse has bit; the Turfs my Servant has cut; and the Ore I have digg'd in any place where I have a right to them in common with others, become my *Property* without the assignation or consent of any body. The *labour* that was mine, removing them out of that common state they were in, *at fixed* my *Property* in them.

Christianity should thus again be made a religion suited to vulgar capacities; and the state of mankind in this world, destined to labour and travel. The greatest part of mankind have not leisure for learning and logics, and superfine distinctions of the schools. Where the hand is used to the plough and the spade, the head is seldom elevated to sublime notions, or exercised in mysterious reasoning. 'Tis well if men of that rank (to say nothing of the other sex) can comprehend plain propositions, and a short reasoning about things familiar to their minds, and nearly allied to their daily experience. Go beyond this, and you amaze the greatest part of mankind.

The ancient philosophers, indeed, shewed the beauty of virtue; but leaving her unendowed, very few were willing to espouse her. But now there being put into the scales on her side, 'an exceeding and immortal weight of glory;' interest is come about to her, and virtue now is visibly the most enriching purchase, and by much the best bargain. The view of heaven and hell will cast a slight upon the short pleasures and pains of this present state, and give attractions and encouragements to virtue, which reason and interest, and the care of ourselves, cannot but allow and prefer. Upon this foundation, and upon this only, morality stands firm, and may defy all competition.

God, when he gave the World in common to all Mankind, commanded Man also to labour, and the penury of his Condition required it of him. God and his Reason commanded him to subdue the Earth, *i. e.* improve it for the benefit of Life, and therein lay out something upon it that was his own, his labour.

God gave the World to Men for their benefit, and the greatest Conveniencies of Life they were capable to draw from it. He gave it to the use of the Industrious and Rational, (and *Labour* was to be *his Title* to it;) not to the Fancy or Covetousness of the Quarrelsom and Contentious.

Every man, that hath any Possession, or Enjoyment, of any part of the Dominions of any Government, doth thereby give his *tacit Consent* and is as far forth obliged to Obedience to the Laws of that Government, during such Enjoyment, as any one under it; whether this his Possession be of Land, to him and his Heirs for ever, or a Lodging only for a Week; or whether it be barely travelling freely on the Highway; and in Effect, it reaches as far as the very being of any one within the Territories of that Government.

Every man, when he, at first, incorporates himself into any Commonwealth, by his uniting himself thereunto, annexed also, and submits to the Community those Possessions, which he has, or shall acquire, that do not already belong to any other Government. For it would be a direct Contradition, for any one, to enter into Society with others for the securing and regulating of Property: And yet to suppose his Land, whose Property is to be regulated by the Laws of the Society, should be exempt from the Jurisdiction of that Government, to which he himself the Proprietor of the Land, is a Subject.

Whether we consider natural reason, which tells us that men, being once born, have a right to their preservation, and consequently to meat and drink and such other things as Nature affords for their subsistence, or 'revelation,' which gives us an account of those grants God made of the world to Adam, and to Noah and his sons, it is very clear that God, as King David says (Psalm cxv. 16), 'has given the earth to the children of men,' given it to mankind in common. But, this being supposed, it seems to some a very great difficulty how any one should ever come to have a property in anything, I will not content myself to answer, that, if it be difficult to make out 'property' upon a supposition that God gave the world to Adam and his posterity in common, it is impossible that any man but one universal monarch should have any 'property' upon a supposition that God gave the world to Adam and his heirs in succession, exclusive of all the rest of his posterity; but I shall endeavour to show how men might come to have a property in several parts of that which God gave to mankind in common, and that without any express compact of all the commoners.

God, who hath given the world to men in common, hath also given them reason to make use of it to the best advantage of life and convenience. The earth and all that is therein is given to men for the support and comfort of their being. And though all the fruits it naturally produces, and beasts it feeds, belong to mankind in common, as they are produced by the spontaneous hand of Nature, and nobody has originally a private dominion exclusive of the rest of mankind in any of them, as they are thus in their natural state, yet being given for the use of men, there must of necessity be a means to appropriate them sortie way or other before they can be of any use, or at all beneficial, to any particular men. The fruit or venison which nourishes the wild Indian, who knows no enclosure, and is still a tenant in common, must be his, and so his—*i.e.*, a part of him, that another can no longer have any right to it before it can do him any good for the support of his life.

Though the earth and all inferior creatures be common to all men, yet every man has a 'property' in his own 'person.' This nobody has any right to but himself. The 'labour' of his body and the 'work' of his hands, we may say, are properly his. Whatsoever, then, he removes out of the state that Nature hath provided and left it in, he hath mixed his labour with it, and joined to it something that is his own, and thereby makes it his property. If being by him removed from the common state Nature placed it in, it hath by this labour something annexed to it that excludes the common right of other men/ For this 'labour' being the unquestionable property of the labourer, no man but he can have a right to what that is once joined to, at least where there is enough, and as good left in common for others.

He that is nourished by the acorns he picked up under an oak, or the apples he gathered from the trees in the wood, has certainly appropriated them to himself. Nobody can deny but the nourishment is his. I ask, then, when did they begin to be his? when he digested? or when he ate? or when he boiled? or when he brought them home? or when he picked them up? And it is plain, if the first gathering made them not his, nothing else could. That labour put a distinction between them and common. That added something to them more than Nature, the common mother of all, had done, and so they became his private right. And will any one say he had no right to those acorns or apples he thus appropriated because he had not the consent of all mankind to make them his? Was it a robbery thus to assume to himself what belonged to all in common? If such a consent as that was necessary, man had starved, notwithstanding the plenty God had given him. We see in commons, which remain so by compact, that it is the taking any part of what is common, and removing it out of the state Nature leaves it in, which begins the property, without which the common is of no use. And the taking of this or that part does not depend on the express consent of all the commoners, Thus, the grass my horse has bit, the turfs my servant has cut, and the ore I have digged in any place, where I have a right to them in common with others, become my property without the assignation or consent of anybody. The labour that was mine, removing them out of that common state they were in, hath fixed my property in them.

By making an explicit consent of every commoner necessary to any one's appropriating to himself any part of what is given in common, children or servants could not cut the meat which their father or master had provided for them in common without assigning to every one his particular part. Though the water running in the fountain be every one's, yet who can doubt but that in the pitcher is his only who drew it out? Mis labour hath taken it out of the hands of Nature where it was common, and belonged equally to all her children, and hath thereby appropriated it to himself.

Thus this law of reason makes the deer that Indian's who hath killed it; it is allowed to be his goods who hath bestowed his labour upon it, though, before it was the common right of every one. And amongst those who are counted the civilised part of mankind, who have made and multiplied positive laws to determine property, this original law of Nature for the beginning of property, in what was before common, still takes place, and by virtue thereof, what fish any one catches in the ocean, that great and still remaining common of mankind; or what ambergris any one takes up here is by the labour that removes it out of that common state Nature left it in, made his property who takes that pains about it. And even amongst us the hare that any one is hunting is thought his who pursues her during the chase. For being a beast that is still looked upon as common, and no man's private possession, whoever has employed so much labour any of that kind as to find and pursue her has thereby removed her 1 state of Nature wherein she was common, and hath begun a property.

It will, perhaps, be objected to this, that if gathering the acorns or of the earth, etc., makes a right to them, then any one may engross as he will. To which I answer, Not so. The same law of Nature that doe means give us property, does also bound that property too. 'God has give things richly.' Is the voice of reason confirmed by inspiration? But how He given it us—'to enjoy'? As much as any one can make use of to an; tags of life before it spoils, so much he may by his labour fix a property it ever is beyond this is more than his share, and belongs to others. North made by God for man to spoil or destroy. And thus considering the p natural provisions there was a long time in the world, and the few spend to how small a part of that provision the industry of one man could e3 self and engross it to the prejudice of others, especially keeping will bounds set by reason of what might serve for his use, there could be the room for quarrels or contentions about property so established.

But the chief matter of property being now not the fruits of the earth beasts that subsist on it, but the earth itself, as that which takes in and with it all the rest, I think it is plain that property in that too is acquired as mer. As much land as a man tills, plants, improves, cultivates, and can product of, so much is his property. He by his labour does, as it were, en from the common. Nor will it invalidate his right to say everybody else equal title to it, and therefore he cannot appropriate, he cannot enclose out the consent of all his fellow-commoners, all mankind. God, when h the world in common to all mankind, commanded man also to labour; penury of his condition required it of him. God and his reason command to subdue the earth—i.e., improve it for the benefit of life and therein I something upon it that was his own, his labour. He that, in obedience command of God, subdued, tilled, and sowed any part of it, thereby and it something that was his property, which another had no title to, nor without injury take from him.

Nor was this appropriation of any parcel of land, by improving it, any dice to any other man, since there was still enough and as good left, and than the yet unprovoked could use. So that, in effect, there was never the less left for others because of his enclosure for himself. For he that leaves as much other can make use of does as good as take nothing at all. Nobody could himself injured by the drinking of another man, though he took a draught, who had a whole river of the same water left him to quench his And the case of land and water, where there is enough of both, is perfect same.

God gave the world to men in common, but since He gave it them for their benefit and the greatest conveniences of life they were capable to draw from it, it cannot be supposed He meant it should always remain common and uncultivated. He gave it to the use of the industrious and rational (and labour was to be his title to it); not to the fancy or covetousness of the quarrelsome and contentious. He that had as good left for his improvement as was already taken up needed not complain, ought not to meddle with what was already improved by another's labour; if he did it is plain he desired the benefit of another's pains, which he had no right to, and not the ground which God had given him, in common with others, to labour on, and whereof there was as good left as that already possessed, and more than he knew what to do with, or his industry could reach to.

And thus, without supposing any private dominion and property in Adam over all the world, exclusive of all other men, which can no way be proved, nor any one's property be made out from it, but supposing the world, given as it was to the children of men in common, we see how labour could make men distinct titles to several parcels of it for their private uses, wherein there could be no doubt of right, no room for quarrel.

Nor is it so strange as, perhaps, before consideration, it may appear, that the property of labour should be able to overbalance the community of land, for it is labour indeed that puts the difference of value on everything; and let any one consider what the difference is between an acre of land planted with tobacco or sugar, sown with wheat or barley, and an acre of the same land lying in common without any husbandry upon it, and he will find that the improvement of labour makes the far greater part of the value. I think it will be but a very modest computation to say, that of the products of the earth useful to the life of man, nine-tenths are the effects of labour. Nay, if we will rightly estimate things as they come to our use, and cast up the several expenses about them—what in them is purely owing to Nature and what to labour—we shall find that in most of them ninety-nine hundredths are wholly to be put on the account of labour.

There cannot be a clearer demonstration of anything than several nations of the Americans are of this, who are rich in land and poor in all the comforts of life; whom Nature, having furnished as liberally as any other people with the materials of plenty—i.e., a fruitful soil, apt to produce in abundance what might serve for food, raiment, and delight; yet, for want of improving it by labour, have not one hundredth part of the conveniences we enjoy, and a king of a large and fruitful territory there feeds, lodges, and is clad worse than a day labourer in England.

(From *Two Treatise of Govarement* by John Locke edited by Peter Laslett, Cambridge University Press, New York, 1963)

10

Jean Jacques Rousseau

Jean Jacques Rousseau (1712-1778) – philosopher, novelist, and composer – loved many women and eventually became paranoid to the point of madness. He was born a watch-maker's son in Geneva. In his early teens he was apprenticed to an engraver but ran away from his master. When he was about sixteen, he met Baroness Louise de Warens, who became his patroness and later his lover. With her he spent most of his time until he was thirty, attempting through wide reading to remedy the deficiencies in his education. In 1742 he went to Paris by himself to make his fortune, which he failed to do, with a new system of musical notation he had invented. There he became a close associate of several important literary figures of the time, including, most significantly, Diderot (editor of the Encyclopedie, the crowning jewel of eighteenth-century rationalism). There he also met Therese Le Vasseur, an almost illiterate servant girl, who became his common-law wife.

In 1749 Rousseau won the first prize in a contest sponsored by the Academy of Dijon for his essay on the question, "Has the progress of the sciences and art contributed to the corruption or to the improvement of human conduct?" His answer, startling to the sensibilities of the French Enlightenment, was an attack on the corrupting effects of civilization and instantly made him famous. A second essay, *Discourse on the Origin* and *Foundation of Inequality among Men* (1754), which again portrayed the evils brought to man by civilization, was also highly controversial. Voltaire, to whom Rousseau had sent a copy of the work, thanked him from his "new book against the human race".

At this time Rousseau, disillusioned with Paris, went briefly to Geneva to regain his Genevan citizenship, but he soon returned to Paris and retired to the estate of yet another woman, Madame d'Epinay. Always emotional, temperamental, suspicious, and unable to maintain constant friendships, he suspected his friends- – Diderot, David Hume, d'Epinay, and others – of conspiring to ruin him. He departed and became the guest of the Duc de Luxembourg, at whose chateau he finished the novel *La Nouvelle Heloise* (1761), written under the influence of his love for the sister-in-law of Mme. d'Epinay.

The *Social Contract* and his treatise on education, *Emile*, both published the following year, were so. offensive to ecclesiastic authorities that Rousseau had to leave Paris. He fled to Neuchatel and then to Bern. Finally, in 1766 he found a haven with David Hume in England. But after a year, Rousseau, who by this time had become deeply paranoid, quarreled with Hume who he thought was plotting against him. In fact, Hume had been.trying to procure a royal pension for Rousseau. "Rousseau is surely the blackest and most atrocious villain, beyond comparison, that now exists in the world; and I am heartily ashamed of anything I ever wrote in his favor." Rousseau now returned to France and eventually to Paris, even though he was in danger of arrest. He was left undisturbed, however, and spent his last years copying music, wandering about readings his *Confessions* out loud, and insulting the curious throngs who came to look at him. Still, few philosophers have had as much impact as Rousseau on political philosophy, politics, education, or literature. According to Hobbes and Locke, people are better off in the properly constituted state than they are or were in the "state of nature". Quite a different point of view was expressed by Rousseau at least in his early political writings. In the state of nature, in which there was neither state nor civilization, people were essentially innocent, good, happy, and healthy, maintained Rousseau in his *Discourse on the Origin and Foundation of the Inequality among Men* (1754). Further, in the state of nature, he said, people enjoyed perfect freedom. But with the advent of private property, this all changed. "The first man who, having enclosed a piece of ground, bethought himself of saying This is mine, and found people simple enough to believe him, was the real founder of civil society," which brought with it the destruction of natural liberty and which, "for the advantage of a few ambitious individuals, subjected all mankind to perpetual labor, slavery and wretchedness".

To put this in some sort of perspective, Rousseau wrote this indictment of civilization in 1754. This was sixty-seven years after Newton had published his *Principia.* It was two years after Benjamin Franklin, with key and kite, had proved that lightening is electricity. Thirty years earlier, Fahrenheit had devised his thermometer. Bach had been dead four years, and it had been twenty-three years since he had completed the Brandenburg Concertos, a masterpiece of mathematical reasoning expressed in music. This, in short, was the eighteenth century, the Enlightenment, the age of light, the Age of Reason. Civilization was stuffed with benefits. Philosophers were as always critical, but Rousseau thought civilization a step backward and was regarded as insane.

But Rousseau later came to think that in the proper society people would surrender their individual liberty for a different and more important collective liberty. Through a social compact, a people may agree, in effect, to unite into a collective whole called "the state" or "the sovereign", and through the state or sovereign enact laws reflective of the general will. An important point to be aware of here is that, for Rousseau, the state or sovereign is an entity in its own right, a "moral person", a nonbiological organism that has its own life and its own will. Rousseau's concept of the general will – that is, the will of a politically united people, the will of the state – is his most important contribution to political philosophy. The general will, according to Rousseau, defines what is to be the common good and thus determines what is right and wrong and should and should not be done. And the state or sovereign expresses this general will by passing laws.

Further, the general will, the will of the people taken collectively, represents the true will of each person. Thus, insofar as the individual's actions coincide with the common will, he is acting as he "really" wants to act – and to act as you really want to act is to be free, said Rousseau. Compelling a person to accept the general will by obeying the laws of the state is "forcing him to be free", Rousseau wrote in a famous passage. So we may lose individual or natural liberty when we unite to form a collective whole, but we gain this new type of "civil" liberty, "the freedom to obey a law which we prescribe for ourselves." Thus, Rousseau wrote, "it is to law alone that men owe justice and civil liberty".

The question arises, of course: Just how do we know what the general will is? Rousseau's answer: If we, the citizens, are enlightened and are not allowed to influence one another, then a majority vote determines what the general will is. The general will is found by counting votes. When, therefore, the opinion which is contrary to my own prevails, this proves neither more nor less than that I was mistaken, and that what I thought to be the general will was not so. Rousseau, however, distinguished between the "will of all" and the general will. The former, Rousseau wrote, is indeed but a sum of private wills: but remove from these same wills the pluses and minutes that cancel each other, and then the general will remains as the sum of the differences.

According to Rousseau, it makes no sense to think of either delegating or dividing the general will. Therefore, he calculated, in the state there cannot validly be a division of powers in contrast to what Locke thought, and though we may commission some person or persons to administer or enforce the law, these individuals act only as our deputies, not as our representatives.

Rousseau maintained that the citizens of the state have the right at any time to terminate the social contract. He also held that they have the right at any time to depose the officials of the state. The implication of the right of the citizenry to terminate the social contract at any time and of their right t remove officials of the state at any time is that the citizenry have a right of revolution and a right to resume anarchy at any time. Thus, Rousseau is thought to have provided a philosophical justification for anarchy and revolution.

Rousseau's declared aim in *The Social Contract* was to give an account of rightful or legitimate political authority, authority de jure. This was not and could not have been Hobbes's aim. For Hobbes, because morality compels action only when and insofar as it is in individuals' interests that it do so, questions about the legitimacy of political authorities cannot arise in the way that they do for Rousseau. For Hobbes, de jure authority is of no concern in a state of nature. The task there is only to establish authority de facto, in fact. So long s authority claims are acknowledged, there is no gainsaying their legitimacy. What is decisive is might, the power to issue enforceable commands. We saw how Hobbes ultimately made a place for a notion of right – how, in his view, morality becomes advantageous for individuals and therefore germane to their lives after sovereignty is established. For Rousseau, in contrast, the world of might and the world of right are, from the very beginning, independent dimensions of human experience. It is the task of descriptive political science to investigate the former domain. It falls to the political philosopher to deal with questions of right – with "men as they are and laws as they might be"

Before turning to Book I, Chapter 6 of *The Social Contract*, it will be instructive to set that work aside in order to insert another line of argument, taken from Rousseau's *Discourse on the Origin of Inequality Among Men*, the so-called Second Discourse, into the account of de jure political authority that has unfolded to this point. These texts were never intended to be read as one. But it is worth doing, especially for anyone who would read Rousseau after Hobbes. The *Second*

Discourse recounts a story, set in the distant past, that is replete with insights abour political life and much else as well.

Although it is ostensibly about life in primitive times, *The Second Discourse* does not purport to provide a factual account of the lives of the first human beings. It is not a history in the contemporary sense; in fact, it is remarkably free of evidence of any kind. At its outset, Rousseau even declared that he would deal with the facts "by setting them aside", and he remained true to his word. In short, *The Second Discourse* is a philosophical fable, not a speculative history. It is a tale contrived to explore philosophical positions. As such, it takes atomic individualism seriously, more seriously even than Hobbes did. It describes the first human beings living in almost complete isolation from one another, without any settled social institutions, without language and without any recognizable culture. In this original state of nature, human beings could not have been in a state of war, so crucial to Hobbes's account. As one might expect of beings that are regarded as atoms, the first men and women led lives that were radically independent of one another. They came together to mate, and infants stayed with their mothers until they were able to fend for themselves. But beyond what was necessary for reproducing the human race, social interactions were accidental, of short duration, and rarely more than incidental to individuals' short-terms aims.

Did Rousseau also unwittingly establish a philosophical basis for totalitarianism? Some think that is the case because he said that "the articles of the social contract reduce to this single point: the total alienation of each person, and all his rights, to the whole community". If the community is regarded not just as the sum total of its members but as an entity somehow over and above the individuals in it, an entity with its own life and will that can itself do no wrong and must always be obeyed, then Rousseau's words do have an ominous ring and invoke concepts that are incorporated wholesale in the philosophy of fascism. Hitler's claim that the Further instinctively knows the desires of the Volk the people and is therefore due absolute obedience is an appeal to the general will. Also ominous is what Rousseau wrote near the end of The Social Contract. That if anyone, after he has publicly subscribed to these dogmas shall conduct himself as if he did not believe them, he is to be punished by death.

—Editor

The Effect of the Art and Science

The mind, as well as the body, has its needs: those of the body are the basis of society, those of the mind its ornaments.

So tong as government and law provide for the security and well-being of men in their common life, the arts, literature, and the sciences, less despotic though perhaps more powerful, fling garlands of flowers over the chains which weigh them down. They stifle in men's breasts that sense of original liberty, for which they seem to have been born; cause them to love their own slavery, and so make of them what is called a civilized people.

Necessity raised up thrones; the arts and sciences have made them strong- Powers of the earth, cherish all talents and protect those who cultivate them. Civilized peoples, cultivate such pursuits: to them, happy slaves, you owe that delicacy and exquisiteness of taste, which is so much your boast that sweetness of disposition and urbanity of manners which make intercourse so easy and agreeable among you—in a word, the appearance of all the virtues, without being in possession of one of them.

It was this sort of refined civilization, all the more attractive for its apparent lack of ostentation, which distinguished Athens and Rome in those most celebrated days of their splendor and magnificence; and it is doubtless in the same respect that our own age and nation will excel all periods and peoples. An air of philosophy without pedantry; an address at once natural and engaging, distant equally from Teutonic rusticity and Italian pantomime; these arc the effects of a taste acquired by liberal studies and improved by conversation with the world. What happiness would it be for those who live among us, if our external appearance were always a true mirror of our hearts; if decorum were but virtue, if the maxims we professed were the rules of our conduct; and if real philosophy were inseparable from the title of a philosopher But so many good qualities too seldom go together; virtue rarely appears in so much pomp and state.

Richness of apparel may proclaim the man of fortune, and elegance the man of taste; but true health and manliness are known by different signs. It is under the homespun of the laborers, and not beneath the gilt and tinsel of the courtier, that we should took for strength and vigor of body.

External ornaments are no less foreign to virtue, which is the strength and activity of the mind, The honest man is an athlete, who loves to wrestle stark naked; he scorns all those vile trappings, which prevent the exertion of his strength, and were, for the most part, invented only to conceal some deformity.

Before art had mounded our behaviour, and taught our passions to speak an artificial language, our morals were rude but natural; and the different ways in which we behaved proclaimed at the first glance the difference of our dispositions, Human nature was not at bottom better then than now; but men found their security in the ease with which they could see through one another, and this advantage, of which we no longer feel the value, prevented their having many vices.

In our day, now that more subtle study and a more refined taste have reduced the art of pleasing to a system, there prevails in modem manners a servile and deceptive conformity; so that one would think every mind had been cast in the same mould. Politeness requires this thing; decorum that; ceremony has its forms, and fashion its laws, and these we must always follow, never the promptings of our own nature.

We no tonger dare seem what we really are, but lie under a perpetual restraint; in the meantime the herd of men, which we call society, all act under the same circumstances exactly alike, unless very particular and powerful motives prevent them. Thus we never know with whom we have to deal; and even to know our friends we must wait for some critical and pressing occasion; that is, till it is too late; for it is on those very occasions that such knowledge is of use to us.

What a train of vices must attend this uncertainty! Sincere friendship, real esteem, and perfect confidence are banished from among men. Jealousy, suspicion, fear, coldness, reserve, hate, and fraud lie constantly concealed under that uniform and deceitful veil of politeness; that boasted candor and urbanity, for which we are indebted to the enlightened spirit of this age. We shall no longer take in vain by our oaths the name of our Creator; but we shall insult Him with our blasphemies, and our scrupulous ears will take no offence.

We have grown too modest to brag of our own merits; but we do not scruple to decry those of others. We do not grossly outrage even our enemies, but artfully calumniate them. Our hatred of other nations diminishes, but patriotism dies with it, ignorance is held in contempt; but a dangerous scepticism has succeeded it. Some vices indeed are condemned and others grown dishonorable; but we have still many that are honoured with the names of virtues, and it is become necessary that we should either have, or at least pretend to have them. Let who will extol the moderation of our modern sages, I see nothing in it but a refinement of in-temperance as unworthy of my commendation as their deceitful simplicity.

Such is the purity to which our morals have attained; this is the virtue we have made our own. Let the arts and sciences claim the share they have had in this salutary work. I shall add but one reflection more; suppose an inhabitant of some distant country should endeavour to form an idea of European morals from the state of the sciences, the perfection of the arts, the propriety of our public entertainments, the politeness of our behaviour, the affability of our conversation, our constant professions of benevolence, and from those tumultuous assemblies of people of all ranks, who seem, from morning till night, to have no other care than to oblige one another. Such a stranger, I maintain, would arrive at a totally false view of our morality.

Where there is no effect, it is idle to took for a cause: but here the effect is on as the arts and sciences have improved. Will it be said, that this is a misfortune peculiar to the present age? No, gentlemen, the evils resulting from our vain curiosity are as old as the world. The daily ebb and flow of the tides are not more regularly influenced by the moon than the morals of a people by the progress of the arts and sciences. As their light has risen above our horizon, virtue has taken flight, and the same phenomenon has been constantly observed in all times and places.

(From "A Discourse on the Arts and Science", in *The Social Contract and other Discourses, trans*. G.D.H. Cole, M. Dent, London, 1973.)

On the Origin of Inequality

Of all human sciences the most useful and most imperfect appears to me to be that of mankind: and I will venture to say, the single inscription on the Temple of Delphi contains a precept more difficult and more important thanis to found in all the huge volumes that moralists have even written. I consider the subject of the following discourse' as one of the most interesting questions philosophy can-propose, and unhappily for us, one of the moat-thorny that phitosophers can have to solve. For how shall we know the source of inequality between men, if we do not begin knowing mankind? And how shall man hope to see him self as nature made him, across all the changes which the succession of pelce and time must have produced in original constitution? How can he distinguish what is fund - mental in his nature from the changes and additions which his circumstances and the advances he has made have introduced to modify his primitive condition?

I conceive that there are two kinds of inequality among the human species; one, which I call natural or physical because it is established by nature and consists in a difference of age, health, bodily strength, and the qualities of the mind or of the soul: and another, which may be called moral or political inequality, because it depends on a kind of convention, and is established or at least authorized, by the consent of men. This latter consists of the different privileges which some men enjoy to the prejudice of others; such as that of being more rich, more honoured, more powerful, or ina position to exact obedience.

Itis useless to askwhatis the source of natural inequality because that question is answered by the simple denitition of the word. Again, still more useless to whether there is any essential connection between the in equalities; two or this would be only asking, in other words whether those who command are necessarily better that those who obey, and if strength of body or of mind, wisdom or virtue are always found in particular individuals, proportion to their power or wealth: a question fit perhaps to be discured by slaves in" the hearing of their marten but highly unbecoming to reasonable and free men in search of the truth.

The philosophers, who have inquired into the foundations of society, have all felt the necessity of going back to a state of nature; but not one of them has got there. Some of them liave not hesitated to ascribe to man, in such a state, the idea of just and unjust, without troubling themselves to show that he must be possessed of such an idea, or that it could be of any use to him. Others have spoken of the natural right of every man to keep what belongs to him, without explaining what they meant by telongs.' Others again, beginning by giving the strong authority over the weak, proceeded directly to the birth of government, without regard to the time that must have elapsed before the meaning of the words 'authority' and 'government' could have existed among men Every one of them, in short, constantly dwelling on wants, avidity, oppression, them, in short, constantly dwelling on wants, avidity, oppression, desires, and pride, has transferred to the state of nature ideas which were acquired in society; so that, in speaking of the savage, they described the social man. It has not even entered into the heads of most of our writers to doubt whether the state of nature ever existed; but it is dear from the Holy Scriptures that the first man, having received his understanding and commandments immediately from God, was not himself in such state; and that, if we give such credit to the writings of Moses as every Christian philosopher ought to give, we must deny that, even before the deluge, men were ever in the pure state of nature; unless, indeed, they fell back into it from some very extraordinary circumstance; a paradox which it would be very embarrassing to defend, and quite impossible to prove.

Let us begin then by laying all facts aside," as they do not affect the question. The investigations we may enter into in treating this subject, must not be considered as historical, but only as mere conditional and hypothetical reasonings rather calculated to explain the nature of things than to ascertain their actual origin; just like the hypotheses which .our physicists daily form respecting the formation of the world Religion commands us to believe that God Himsef>t having taken men out of a state of nature immediately after the creation, they are unequal only because it is His will they should be so.

Every animal has ideas, since it has senses; it even combines those ideas in a certain degree; and it is only in degree that man differs, in this respect, from the brute. Some philosophers have even maintained that there is a greater difference between one man and another than between some men and some beasts. It is not, therefore, so much the understanding that constitutes the specific difference between the man and the brute, as the human quality of free agency. Nature lays her commands on every animal, and the brute obeys her voice. Man receives the same impulsion, but at the same time knows himself at liberty to acquiesce or resist: and it is particularly in his consciousness of this liberty that the spirituality of his soul is displayed. For physics may explain, in some measure, the mechanism of the senses and the formation of ideas; but in the power of willing or rather of choosing, and in the feeling of this power/ nothing is to be found but acts which are purely spiritual and wholly inexplicable by the laws of mechanism.

Yet if the difficulties attending all these questions should still leave room for dispute about this difference between men and brutes, there is another very specific quality which distinguishes them, and which will admit of no dispute. This is the faculty of self-improvement, which, by the help of circumstances, gradually develops all the rest of our faculties, and is inherent in the species as in the individual: whereas a brute is, at the end of a few months, all he will ever be during his whole life, and his species, at the end of a thousand years, exactly what it was the first year of that thousand. Why is man alone liable to grow into a dotard? Is it not because he returns, in this, to his primitive state; and that, while the brute, which has acquired nothing and has therefore nothing to lose, still retains the force of instinct, man, who those, by age or accident, all that his perfectibility had enabled him to gain, falls by this means lower than the brutes themselves? It would be melancholy, were we forced to admit that this distinctive and almost unlimited faculty is the source of all human misfortunes; that it is this which, in time, draws man out of his original state, in which he would have spent his days insensibly in peace and innocence; that it is this faculty, which, successively producing in different ages his discoveries and his errors, his vices and his virtues, makes him at length a tyrant both over himself and over nature. It would be shocking to be obliged to regard as a benefactor the man who first suggested to the Oroonoko Indians the use of the boards they apply to the temples of their children, which secure to them some part at least of their imbecility and original happiness.

Savage man, left by nature solely to-the direction of instinct, or rather indemnified for what he may lack by faculties capable at first of supplying its place, and afterwards of raising him much above it, must accordingly begin with purely animal functions: thus seeing and feeling must be his first condition, which would be common to him and all other animals. To will, and not to will, to desire and to fear, must be the first, and almost the only operations of his soul, till new circumstances occasion new developments of his faculties.

Whatever moralists may hold, the human understanding is greatly indebted to the passions, which, it is universally allowed, are also much indebted to the understanding. It is by the activity of the passions that our reason is improved; for we desire knowledge only because we wish to enjoy; and it is impossible to conceive any reason why a person who has neither fears nor desires should give himself the trouble of reasoning. The passions, again, originate in our wants, and their progress depends on that of our knowledge; for we cannot desire or fear anything, except from the idea we have of it/ or from the simple impulse of nature. Now savage man, being destitute of every species of enlightenment, can have no passions save those of the latter kind: his desires never go beyond his physical wants. The only goods he recognizes in the universe are food, a female, and sleep: the only evils he fears are pain and hunger. I say pain, and not death: for no animal can know what it is to die; the knowledge of death and its terrors being one of the first acquisitions made by man in departing from an animal state. It would be easy, were it necessary, to support this opinion.

It is impossible that men should not at length have reflected on so wretched a situation, and on the calamities that overwhelmed them. The rich, in particular, must have felt how much they suffered by a constant state of war, of which they bore all the expense; and in which, though all risked their lives, they alone risked their property. Besides, however speciously they might disguise their usurpations, they knew that they were founded on precarious and false titles; so that, if others took from them by force what they themselves had gained by force, they would have no reason to complain. Even those who had been enriched by their own industry, could hardly base their proprietorship on letter's claims. It was in vain to repeat: T built this well; I gained this spot by my industry.' Who gave you your standing, it might be answered, and what right have you to demand payment of us for doing what we never asked you to do? Do you not know that numbers of your fellow-creatures are starving, for want of what you have too much of? You ought to have had the express and universal consent of mankind, before appropriating more of the common subsistence than you needed for your own maintenance. Destitute of valid reasons to justify and sufficient strength to defend himself, able to crush individuals with ease, but easily crushed himself by a troop of bandits, one against all, and incapable, on

account of mutual jealousy, of joining with his equals against numerous enemies united by the common hope of plunder, the rich man, thus urged by necessity, conceived at length the profoundest plan that ever entered the mind of man: this was to empty in his favour the forces of those who attacked him, to make allies of his adversaries, to inspire them with different maxims, and to give them other institutions as favorable to himself as the law of nature was unfavorable.

With this view, after having represented to his neighbours the horror of a situation which armed every man against the rest, and made their possessions as burdensome to them as their wants, and in which no safety could be expected either in riches or in poverty, he readily devised plausible arguments to make them dose with his design,' Let us join/ said he,' to guard the weak from oppression,, to restrain the ambitious, and secure to every man the possession of what belongs to him: let us institute rules of justice and peace, to which all without exception may be obliged to conform; rules that may in some measure make amends for the caprices of fortune, by subjecting equally the powerful and the weak to the observance of reciprocal obligations. Let us, in a word, instead of turning our forces against ourselves, collect them in a supreme power which may govern by wise laws, protect and defend all the members of the association, repulse their common enemies, and maintain eternal harmony among us.

With this view, after having represented to his neighbour the horror of a situation which armed every man against the rest and made their possessions as burdensome to them as their wants, and in which no safety could be expected either in riches or in poverty, he readily devised plausible arguments to make them close with his design.' Let us join/ said he,' to guard the weak from oppression, to restrain the ambitious, and secure to every man the possession what be longs to him: let us institute rules of justice an peace, to which all without exception may be obliged to conform; rules that may in some measure make amends for the caprices of fortune, by subjecting equally the powerful and the weak to the observance of reciprocal obligations. Let us, in a word, instead of turning our forces against ourselves, collect them in a supreme power which may govern us by wise protect an defend all the members of the association repulse their common enemies, and maintain eternal harmony among us."

Far fewer words to this purpose would have been enough to impose on men so barbarous and easily seduced; especially as they had too many disputes among themselves to do without arbitrators, and too much ambition and avarice to go long without masters. AH ran headlong to their chains, in hopes of securing their liberty; for they had just witen though to perceive the advantages of political institutions, without experience enough to enable them to foresee the dangers. The most capable of foreseeing the dangers were tie very persons who expected to benefit by them; and evenmost prudent judged it not inexpedient to sacrifice one part of their freedom to ensuer the rest; as a wounded man has his arm cut off to save the rest of his body.

Such was, or may well have been, the origin of society and which bound new fetters on the poor, and gave new powers to the rich; which irretrievably destroyed natural liberty, eternally fixed the law of property and inequality converted clever usurpation into unalterable right, and, for, the advantage of a few ambitious individuals, subjected all mankind to perpetual labour, slavery, and wretchedness.

The philosophers, who have inquired into the foundations of society, have all felt the necessity of going back to a state of nature; but not one of them has got there. Some of them have not hesitated to ascribe to man, in such a state, the idea of just and unjust, without troubling themselves to show that he must be possessed of such an idea, or that it could be of any use to him.,

We should beware, therefore, of confounding the savage man with the men we have daily before our eyes. Nature treats all the animals left to her care with a predilection that seems to show how jealousy she is of that right. The horse, the cat, the bull, and even the ass are generally of greater stature, and always more robust, and have more vigour, strength, and courage, when they run wild in the forests than when bred in the stall. By becoming domesticated, they lose half these advantages; and it seems as if all our care to feed and treat them well serves only to deprave them. It is thus with man also: as he becomes sociable and a slave, he grows weak, timid, and servile; his effeminate way of life totally enervates his strength and courage. To this it may be added that there is still a greater difference between savage and civilized man than between wild and tame beasts; for men and brutes having been treated alike by nature, the several conveniences in which men indulge themselves still more than they do their beasts, are so many additional causes of their deeper degeneracy.

It is not therefore so great a misfortunate to these primitive men, nor so great an obstacle to their preservation, that they go naked, have no dwellings, and lack all the superfluities which we think necessary. If their skins are not covered with hair, they have no need of such covering in warm climates; and, in road countries, they soon learn to appropriate the skins of the beasts they have overcome. If they have but two legs torn with, they have two arms to de-fend themselves with, and provide for their wants. Their children are slowly and with difficulty taught to walk; but their mothers are able to carry them with ease; an advantage which other animals lack, as the mother, if pursued, is forced either t& abandon her young, or to regulate her pace by theirs. Unless, in short, we suppose a singular and fortuitous concurrence of circumstances of which shall speak later, and which could well never come about, it is plain in caver state of the case, that the man who firs made himself ctothes or a dwelling was furnishing himself with things not at all necessary; for he had till then done without them, and there is no reason why he should not have been able to pull up inmanhood with tire same kind of life as had been his in infancy.

Whatever moralists may hold, the human understanding is greatly indebted to the passions, which, it is universally altowed, are also much indebted to the understanding, It is by the activity of the passions that our reason is improved; for we desire knowledge only because we wish to enjoy; and it is impossible to conceive any reason why a person who has neither fears nor desires should give himself the trouble of reasoning. The passions, again, originate in our wants, and their progress depends on that of our knowledge: for we cannot desire or fear anything, except from the idea we have of it, or from the simple impulse of nature, Now savage man, being destitute of every species of enlightenment, can have no passions save those of the latter kind: his desires never go beyond his physical wants. The only goods he recognizes in the universe are food, a female, and sleep: the only evils he fears are pain and hunger. I say pain, and not death: for no animal can know what it is to die; the knowledge of death and its terrors being one of the first acquisitions made by man in departing from an animal state.

It appears, at first view, that men in a state of nature, having no moral relations or determinate obligations one with another, could not be either good or bad, virtuous or vicious; unless we take these terms in a physical sense, and call, in an individual, those qualities vices which may be injurious to his preservation, and those virtues which contribute to it; in which case, he would have to be accounted most virtuous, who put least check on the pure impulses of nature. But without deviating from the ordinary sense of the words, it will be proper to suspend the judgment we might be led to form on such a state, and be on our guard against our prejudices, till we have weighted the matter in the scales of impartiality, and seen whether virtues or vices preponderate among civilized men: and whether their virtues do them more good than their vices do harm; till we have discovered whether the progress of the sciences sufficiently indemnifies them for the mischieis they do one another, in proportion as they are better informed of the good they ought to do; or whether they would not be, on the whole, ina much happier condition if they had nothing to fear or to hope from any one, than as they are. subjected to universal dependence, and obliged to take everything from those who engage to give them nothing in return.

Above all, let us not conclude, with Hobbes, that because man has no idea of goodness, he must be naturally wicked; that he is vicious because he does not know virtue; that he always refuses to do his feltow-creatures services which he does not think they have a night to demand; or that by virtue of the right he justly claims to all he needs, he foolishly imagines himself the sole proprietor of the whole universe. Hobbes had seen dearly the defects of all the modern definitions of natural right: but the consequences which he deduces from his own show that he understands it in an equally false sense. In reasoning on the principles he lays down, he ought to have said that the state of nature, being that in which the care for our own preservation is the least prejudicial to that of others, was consequently the best calculated to promote peace, and the most suitable for mankind. He does say the exact opposite, in consequence of having improperly admitted, as a part of savage man's care for self-preservation, the gratification of amultitude of passions which are the work of society, and have made laws necessary. A bad man, he says, is a robust child. But it remains to be proved whether man in a state of nature is this robust child:

and, should we grant chat he is, what would he infer? Why truly, that if this man, when robust and strong, were dependent on others as he is when fee-ble, there is no extravagance he would nor be guilty of; that he would beat his mother when she was too stow in giving him her breast; that he would strangle one of his younger brothers, if he should be troublesome to him, or bite the leg of another, if he put him to any inconvenience. But that man in the state of nature is both strong and dependent involves two contrary suppositions. Man is weak when he is dependent, and is his own master before he comes to be strong. Hobbes did not reflect that the same cause, which prevents a savage from making use of his reason, as our jurists hold, prevents him also from abusing his faculties, as Hobbes himself altows; so that it may be justly said that savages are not bad merely because they do not know what it is to be good: for it is neither the devetopment of the un-derstanding nor the restraint of law that hinders them from doing ill; but the peace fullness of their passions, and their ignorance of vice. There is another principle which has escaped Hobbes; which, havingbeen bestowed on mankind, to moderate, on certain occasions, the impetuosity of *amour-proprg* or, before its birth, the desire of self-preservation, tempers the ardour with which he pursues his own welfare, by an innate repugnance at seeing a f eltow-creature suffer.

The first man who, having enclosed a piece of ground, thought himself of saying' This is mine,' and found people simple enough to believe him, was the real founder of civil society. From how many crimes, wars, and murders, from how many horrors and misfortunes might not any one have saved mankind, by pulling up the stakes, or filling up the ditch, and crying to his fellows: 'B eware of listening to the impostor; you are undone if you once forget that the fruits of the earth belong to us all, and the earth itself to nobody/ But there is great probability that things had then already fome to such a pitch, that they could no longer continue as they were; for the idea of property depends on many prior ideas, which could only be acquired successively, and cannot have been formed all at once in the human mind. Man's kind must have made very considerable progress, and acquired considerable knowledge and industry which they must allso have transmitted and increased from age to age, before they arrived at this last point of the state of nature. Let us then go farther back, and endeavour to unify under a single point of view that show succession of events and discoveries in the most natural order.

Man' s first feeling was that of his own existence, and is first care that of self-preservation. The produce of the earth furnished him with all he needed, and instinct told how to use it. Hunger and other appetites made him atvarious times experience various modes of existence; among these was one which urged him to propagate species—a blind propensity that, having nothing to do with the heart, produced a merely animal act. The want once gratified, the two sexes knew each other no more; and the offspring was nothing to its mother, as soon as it could do without her.

Such was the condition of infant man; the life of an animal limited at first to mere sensations, and hardly profiting by the gifts nature bestowed on him, much less capable of entertaining a thought of forcing anything fromher. But difficulties soon presented themselves, and it became necessary to learnhow to surmount them: the height of the fress which prevented him from gathering their fruits, the competition of other animals desirous of the same fruits, and the ferocity of those who sought to deprive man himself of life, all obliged him to apply himself to bodily exercises. He had to be active, swift of foot, and vigorous in fight. Natural weapons, stones, and sticks, were easily found; he learnt to surmount the obstacles of nature, to contend in case of necessity with other animals, and to dispute for the means of subsistence even with other men, or to indemnify himself for what he was forced to give up to a stronger.

In proportion as the human race grew more numerous, men's cares increased. The difference of soils, climates, and seasons, must have introduced some differences into their manner of living. Barren years, long and sharp winters, scorching summers which parched the fruits of the earth, must have demanded a new industry. On the seashore and on banks of rivers, they invented the hook and line, and became fishermen and eaters offish. In the forests they made bows and arrows, and became huntsmen and warriors. In cold countries they clothed themselves with the skins of the beasts they had slain. The lightning, a volcano, or some chance lucky acquainted them with fire, a new resource against the rigours of winter: they next learned how to preserve this element then how to reproduce it, and finally how prepare with it the flesh of animals which before they had eaten raw.

This repeated relevance of various beings to himself, and one to another, would naturally give rise in the human mind to the perceptions of certain relations between them. Thus the relations which we denote by the terms great, small, strong, weak, swift, slow, fearful, bold, and the like, almost insensibly compared at need, must have at length produced in him a kind of reflection, or rather a mechanical prudence, which would indicate to him the precautions most necessary to his security.

The new intelligence which resulted from this devetopment increased his superiority over other animals, by making him sensible of it. He would now endeavour, therefore, to ensnare them, would play them a thousand tricks, and though many of them might surpass him in swiftness or in strength in time become the master of some and the scourge of others. Thus, the first time he looked into himself he felt the first emotion of pride.

It is difficult to conjecture how men first came to know and use iron; for it is impossible to suppose they would themselves think of digging the ore out of the mine, and preparing it for smelting, before they knew what would be the result. On the other hand, we have the less reason to suppose this discovery the effect of any accidental fire, as mines are only formed in barren places, bare of trees and plants; so that it took as if nature had taken pains to keep the fatal secret from us. There remains, therefore, only that extraordinary accident of some volcano which, by ejecting metallic substances already in fusion, suggested to the spectators the idea of imitating the natural operation. And we must further conceive them as possessed of unborn courage and foresight, to undertake so laborious a work, so distant a prospect of drawing advantage from it; yet the sequalities are united only in minds more advanced than we can suppose those of these first discoverers to have been, With regard to agriculture, the principles of it were kown long before they were put in practice; and it is indeed hardly possible that men, constantly employed in drawing their subsistence from plants and trees, should not readily acquit a knowledge of the means made use of by nature for propagation of vegetables. It was in all probability very long, however, before their industry took that turn, either because trees, which together with hunting and fishing afforded them food, did not require their attention; because they were ignorant of the use of corn, or with instruments to cultivate it; or because they lacked foresight to future needs; or lastly, because they were without means of preventing others from robbing them of the of their labour.

When they grew more industrious, it is natural to believe that they began, with the help of sharp stones and pointing sticks, to cultivate a few vegetables or roots around the huts; though it was long before they knew how to prepare corn, or were provided with the implements necessary far raising it in any large quantity; not to mention how esstialne it is for husbandry to consent to immediate loss, in order to reap a future gain—aprecaution very foreign to the of a savage' s mind;for, as I have said, he hardly foresees the morning what he will need at night.

The invention of the other arts must therefore have been necessary to compel mankind to apply themselves to agriculture. No sooner were artificers wanted to smelt and forge iron, than others were required to maintain them; the more hands that were employed in manufactures, the fewer were left to provide for the common subsistence, though the number of mouths to be furnished with food remained the same: and as some required commodities in exchange for their iron, the rest at length discovered the method of making iron serve for the multiplication of commodities. By this means the arts of husbandry and agriculture were established on the one hand, and the art of working metals and multiplying their uses on the other.

The cultivation of the earth necessarily brought about its distribution; and property, once recognized, gave rise to the first rules of justice; for, to secure each man his own, it had to be possible for each to have something. Besides, as menbegan to look forward to the future, and all had something to lose, every one had reason to apprehend that reprisals would follow any injury he might do to another. The origin is so much the more natural, as it is impossible to conceive how property can come from anything but manual labour for what else can a man add to things which he does not originally create,so as to make them hi sown property? It isthe husbandman' s labour alone that, giving him a title to the produce of the ground he has tilled, gives him a claim also to the land itself at least till harvest; and so, from year to year, a constant possession which is easily transformed into property.

In this state of affairs equality might have been sustained, and had the talents of individuals been equal and had, for example, the use of iron and the consumption of commodities always exactly balanced each other; but, as there was nothing to preserve this balance, it was soon disturbed; the stranger did most work; the most skilful turned his labour into best account; the most ingenious devised methods of diminishing his labour: the husbandman wanted more iron, or the smith more corn, and, while bothlaboured equally, the one gained a great deal by his work, while the others could hardly support himself. Thus natural inequality unfolds itself insensibly with that of combination, and the difference between men, developed by their different circumstances, becomes more sensible and permanent in its effects, and begins to have an influence, in the same proportion, over the lot of individuals.

Behold then all human faculties developed, memory and imagination in full play, *amour-propre* interested, reason active and the mind almost at the highest point of its perfection. Behold all the natural qualities in action, the rank and condition of every man assigned him; not merely his share of property and his power to serve or injure others, but also his wit, beauty, strength or skill, merit or talents: and these being the only qualities capable of commanding respect, it soon became necessary to possess or to affect them.

It now became the interest of men to appear what they really were not. To be and to seem became two totally different things; and from this distinction sprang insolent pomp and cheating trickery, with all the numerous vices that go in their train. On the other hand, free and independent as men were before, they were now, in consequence of a multiplicity of new wants, brought into subjection, as it were, to all nature, and particularly to one anothereach became in some degree a slave even in becoming the master of other men: if rich, they stood in need of the services of others; if poor, of their assistance; and even middle condition did not enable them to do without another. Man must now, therefore, have beenperpetual by employed in getting others to interest themselves in his lot, and in making them, apparently at least, if not really, find their advantage in promoting his own. Thus he must haw been sly and artful in his behaviour to some, and imperious and cruel to others;being under a kind of necessity to ill-use all the persons of whom be stood in need, when he could not frighten them into compliance, and did not judge it his interest to be useful to them. Insatiable ambition, the thirst of raising their respective fortunes, not so much from real want as from the desire to surpass others, inspired all men with a vile propensity to injure one another, and with a secret jealousy, which is the more dangerous, as it puts on the mask of benevolence, to carry its point with greater security. In a word, there arose rivalry and competition, on the one hand, and conflicting interests on the other, together with a secret desire on both of profiting at the expense of others. All these evils were the first effects of property, and the inseparable attendants of growing inequality.

It is impossible that men should not at length have reflected on so wretched a situation, and on the calamities that overwhelmed them. The rich, in particular, must have felt how much they suffered by a constant state of war, of which they bore all the expense; and in which, though all risked their lives, they alone risked their property. Besides, however speciously they might disguise their usurpations, the knew that they were founded on precarious and false titles; so that, if others took from them by force what they themselves had gained by force, they would have no reason to complain. Even those who had been enriched by their a industry, could hardly base their proprietorship on better claims. It was in vain to repeat; 'I built this well; gained this spot by my industry.' Who gave you your standing it might be answered, and what right have you to demand payment of us for doing what we never asked you to do? Do you not know that numbers of your feltow-creatures starving, for want of what you have too muchof you ought to have had the express and universal consent of kind, before appropriating more of the common subsistence than you needed for your own maintenance. Destitute of valid reasons to justify and sufficient strength to defend himself, able to crush individuals with ease, but easily crushed himself by a troop of bandits, one against all, and incapably on account of mutual jealousy, of joining with his equal against numerous enemies united by the common hope of plunder, the rich man, thus urged by necessity, conceived at length the prof oundest plan that ever entered the mind of man: this was to empty in his favour the forces of that who attacked him, to make allies of his adversaries, to inspect them with different maxims, and to give them other institution as favourable to himself as the law of nature unfavorable.

(From *The Social Contract and other Discourses* by J.J. Rausseau edited by G.D.H. Cole, M. Dent, London, 1973)

11

David Hume

The Scottish philosopher and historian David Hume (1711-1776) was initially headed toward the profession of law. After he finished his studies at Edinburgh University in his middle teens, he began an intensive program of self-education. By age twenty-eight he produced, anonymously, his most important book, in which he applied the new skepticism afforded by Newtonian science to a variety of matters ranging from the nature of knowledge to the psychological foundations of morals. Hume famous for advancing an argument against rationalistic ethics that still, today energizes the thinking of many philosophers. In political theory, Hume was skeptical about social contract theory, and argued for a different conception of justice, based on his understanding of human motivation. Hume is one of the most intriguing philosophers, whose thinking is still the subject of numerous studies and varied interpretations. He ended his work in philosophy quite early and turned, instead, to the history of Great Britain. He was never an academician and took an active role in public life, such as serving as charge d'affaires in Paris from 1763 to 1766. Despite his change in career, academic philosophers since Immanuel Kant have regarded him as a source of many philosophical challenges.

But in the eighteenth century, David Hume argued with some force that moral principles are neither divine edicts nor discoverable by reason. Home's general position regarding God, was that the order in the universe does offer some slight evidence that the universe has or had a creative force remotely analogous to human intelligence. But we certainly cannot affirm anything about the moral qualities of the creator, and we cannot derive guidelines for our own actions from speculating about his nature. Christianity, Hume regarded as superstition.

Hume held likewise that moral judgments are not the "offspring of reason." Scrutinize an act of murder as closely as you can, he said. Do you find anything in the facts of the case that reveal the act is morally wrong? The facts, he said, are simply that one person has terminated the life of another in a certain way at a particular time and place. Reasoning can disclose how long it took for death to occur, whether the victim suffered great pain, what the motives of the killer were, as well as the answers to many other factual questions such as these. But it will not show the moral wrongfulness of the act. The judgment that an act is immoral, Hume maintained, comes not from reason but from emotion. It is the same, Hume believed, with all value judgments. Is the judgment that a portrait is beautiful founded on reason? Of course not. Reason can disclose the chemical composition of the paints and canvas, the monetary value of the work, and many similar factual things. But whether the portrait is beautiful is an issue that cannot be settled by reason.

Thus, for Hume, moral judgments, and all value judgments, are based on emotion. Actions that we find morally praiseworthy or blameworthy create within us feelings of pleasure or displeasure, respectively. A fundamental principle of Hume's philosophy is that moral judgments are not the offspring of reason. A consideration that might favor Hume's thesis is that we tend to think of particularly heinous deeds—execution-style murders, for example—as "cold-blooded" and "heartless," not as irrational.This is an indication that we view the murderer as lacking in feeling rather than as deficient in reason. Is it hard to believe that an absolutely brilliant mind could commit murder? We think not. But is it hard to believe that someone with normal sensibilities could commit murder? Different in kind from aesthetic pleasures and pleasures of the palate. Humans clearly have a capacity for moral pleasure as well as for other types of pleasure: we are morally sensitive creatures. Behavior that pleases our moral sensibilities elicits our approval and is deemed good, right, just, virtuous, and noble. Behavior that offends our moral sense is deemed bad, wrong, unjust, base, and ignoble.

But just what is it about behavior that elicits our moral approval? What do virtuous, good, right, and noble acts have in common? Hume's answer was that the type of act we deem morally praiseworthy is one taken by an agent out of concern for others. The act that pleases our moral sensibilities is one that reflects a benevolent character on the part of the agent, Hume said. By "agent," philosophers mean the person who did the act.

Why does benevolence bring pleasure to us when we witness, read about, or contemplate it? A cynical answer is that we imagine ourselves benefiting from the benevolent activity, and imagining this is pleasant. Do you get a warm glow when you read about someone coming to the aid of a fellow person? Well, according to the cynical view, that is because you picture yourself on the receiving end'of the exchange.

But Hume contends that this cynical theory is unnecessarily complex, The reason you get that pleasant feeling when you read about or see someone helping someone else is that you sympathise with others. It just plainly upsets a normal person to see suffering, and it pleases a normal person to see others happy. True, there are people who suffer from the emotional equivalent of color blindness and lack the capacity to sympathize with others. But these people are not the norm.The normal human being is a sympathetic creature, maintained Hume.

This aspect of Hume's moral philosophy may well have some significance for us today. On one hand, we tend to believe that one should care for others but, on the other hand, that one must also certainly look out for onerself. And we are inclined to think that there is a problem in this because self-concern and other-concern seem mutually exclusive. But if Hume is correct, they are not. Looking out for one's own interests includes doing what brings one pleasure. And if Hume is correct, caring for others will bring one an important kind of pleasure. Indeed, if Hume is correct, when one praises an action as good, it is precisely because it brings one this kind of pleasure. It is important to notice, finally, the emphasis Hume placed on character. According to Hume, the act that pleases our moral sensibilities is one that reflects a benevolent character on the part of the agent. Hume believed that when we morally praise or condemn someone, it is the person's character we praise or condemn primarily: his or her actions we find praiseworthy or condemnatory mainly as an indication of character. This idea—that we apply moral attributes primarily to a person's character and secondarily to the person's actions—is common in the virtue-ethics tradition of Plato, Aristotle, and Aquinas. In this respect, Hume is part of that tradition.

"Morality," Hume said, "is more properly felt than judged of." Ethical standards are not fixed by reason He insisted that even if there is a God, it is impossible for us to gain moral guidance from him. Loosely speaking, therefore, ethics after Hume seems generally to have had these options. First, it might seek to establish that, despite Hume, morality can be grounded on reason or God. This was the option taken by Kant, who favored reason as the ultimate ground of morality. Second, ethics might try to find objective sources of moral standards other than reason and God. This is what the utilitarians tried to do. Third, it might try to determine how one should conduct one's affairs given the absence of objective moral standards. This is a primary concern of contemporary existentialists. Fourth, ethics might abandon the search for moral standards altogether and concentrate instead on such factual questions as, What do people believe is good and right? What does it mean to say that something is good or right? How do moral judgments differ from other kinds of judgments? What leads us to praise certain actions as moral and condemn others as immoral? These are some of the issues that captured the attention of many twentieth-century philosophers, such as G. E. Moore.

—Editor

Passions

Nothing is more usual in philosophy, and even in comman life, than to talk of the combat of passion and reason, to give the preference to reason, and to assen that men are only so far virtuous as they conform themselves to its dictates. Every rational creature, it is said, is obliged to regulate his actions by reason; and if any other motive or principle challenge the direction of his conduct, he ought to oppose it, till it be entirely subdued or at least brought to a conformity with that superior principle. On this method of thinking the greatest part of moral philosophy, ancient and modem, seems to be founded; nor is there an ampler field, as well for metaphysical arguments, as popular declamations, than this supposed pre-eminence of reason above passion. The eternity, invariableness, and divine origin of the former have been displayed to the best advantage; the blindness, uncon-stancy and deceitfulness of the latter have been, as strongly insisted on. In order to show the fallacy of all this philosophy, I shall endeavour to prove *first,* that reason alone can never be a motive to any action of the will; and secondly, that it can never oppose passion in the direction of the will.

The understanding exerts itself after two different ways, as it judges from demonstration or probability; as it regards the abstract relations of our ideas, or those relations of objects, of which experience only gives us information. I believe it scarce will be asserted, that the first species of reasoning alone is ever the cause of any action. As its proper province is the world of ideas, and as the will always places us in that of realities, demonstration and volition seem, upon that account, to be totally removed, from each other. Mathematics, indeed, are useful in all mechanical operations, and arithmetic in almost every art and profession; but it is not of themselves they have any influence. Mechanics are the art of regulating the motions of bodies *to some designed end or purpose'*, and the reason why we employ arithmetic in fixing the proportions of numbers, is only that we may discover the proportions of their influence and operation. A merchant is desirous of knowing the sum total of his accounts with any person. Why? But that he may learn what sum will have the same *effects* in paying his debt, and going to market, as all the particular articles taken together. Abstract or demon-strative reasoning, therefore, never influences any of our actions, but only as it directs our judgment concerning causes and effects; which leads us to the second operation of the understanding.

It is obvious, that when we have the prospect of pain or pleasure from any object, we feel a consequent emotion of aversion or propensity, and are carried to avoid or embrace what will give us this uneasiness or satisfaction. It is also obvious, that this emotion rests not here, but making us cast our view on every side, comprehends whatever objects are connected with its original one by the relation of cause and effect. Here then reasoning takes place to discover this rela-tion; and according as our reasoning varies, our actions receive a subsequent variation. But it is evident in this case, that the impulse arises not from reason, but is only directed by it. It is from the prospect of pain or pleasure that the aversion or propensity arises towards any object; and these emotions extend themselves to the causes and effects of that object, as they are pointed out to us by reason and experi-ence. It can never in the least concern us to know, that such objects are causes, and such others effects, if both the causes and effects be indifferent to us. Where the objects themselves do not affect us, their connection can never give them any influence; and it is plain, that as reason is nothing but the discovery of this connection, it cannot be by its means that the objects are able to affect us.

Since reason alone can never produce any action, or give rise to volition, I infer, that the same faculty is as incapable of preventing volition, or of disputing the preference with any passion or emotion. This consequence is necessary. It is impossible reason could have the latter effect of pre-venting volition, but by giving an impulse in a contrary direction to our passion; and that impulse, had it operated alone, would have been able to produce volition. Nothing can oppose or retard the impulse of passion, but a contrary impulse; and if this contrary impulse ever arises from reason, that latter faculty must have an original influence on the will, and must be able to cause, as well as hinder any act of volition. But if reason has no original influence, it is impos-sible it can withstand any principle, which has such an efficacy, or ever keep the mind in suspense a moment.

Thus it appears, that the principle, which opposes our passion, cannot be the same with reason, and is only called so in an improper sense. We speak not strictly and philosophically when we talk of the combat of passion and of reason. Reason is, and ought only to be the slave of the passions, and can I never pretend to any other office than to serve obey them. As this opinion may appear somewhat extraordinary, it may not be improper to confirm it by some other considerations.

A passion is an original existence, or, if you will, modi-fication of existence, and contains not any representative quality, which renders it a copy of any other existence or modification. When I am angry, I am actually possessed with the passion, and in that emotion have no more a reference to any other object, than when I am thirsty, or sick, or more than five foot high. It is impossible, therefore, that this passion can be opposed by, or be contradictory to truth and reason; since this contradiction consists in the disagreement of ideas, considered as copies, with those objects, which they represent.

What may at first occur on this head, is, that as nothing can be contrary to truth or reason, except what has a reference to it, and as the judgments of our understanding only have this reference, it must follow, that passions can be contrary to reason only so far as they are *accompanied* with some judgment or opinion. According to this principle, which is so obvious and natural, it is only in two senses, that any affection can be called unreasonable. First, when a passion as hope or fear, grief or joy, despair or security, founded on the supposition of the existence of objects, which really do not exist. Secondly, when in exerting any passion in action, we choose means insufficient for the designed end, and deceive ourselves in our judgment of causes and effects. Where a passion is neither founded on false sup-positions, nor chooses means insufficient for the end, the understanding can neither justify nor condemn it. It is not contrary to reason to prefer the destruction of the whole world to the scratching of my finger. It is not contrary to reason for me to choose my total ruin, to prevent the least uneasiness of an *Indian* or person wholly unknown to me. It is as little contrary to reason to prefer even my own acknow-ledged lesser good to my greater, and have a more ardent affection for the former than the latter. A trivial good may, from certain circumstances, produce a desire superior to what ' arises from the greatest and most valuable enjoyment; nor is there anything more extraordinary in this, than in mechanics to see one pound weight raise up a hundred by the advantage of its situation. In short, a passion must be accompanied with some false judgment, in order to its being unreasonable; and even then it is not the passion, properly speaking, which is unreasonable, but the judgment.

The consequences are evident. Since a passion can never, in any sense, be called unreasonable, but when founded on a false supposition, or when it chooses means insufficient for the designed end, it is impossible, that reason and passion can ever oppose each other, or dispute for the government of the will and actions. The moment we perceive the falsehood objects with a strict philosophic eye, to imagine, that those actions of the mind are entirely the same, which produce not a different sensation, and are not immediately distinguishable to the feeling and perception. Reason, for instance, exerts itself without producing any sensible emotion; and except in the more sublime disquisitions of philosophy, or in the frivolous subtleties of the schools, scarce ever conveys any pleasure or uneasiness. Hence it proceeds, that every action of the mind, which operates with the same calmness and tranquility, is confounded with reason by all those, who judge of things from the first view and appearance. Now it is certain, there are certain calm desires and tendencies, which, though they be real passions, produce little emotion in the mind, and are more known by their effects than by the immediate feeling or sensation. These desires are of two kinds; either certain instincts originally implanted in our natures, such as bene-volence and resentment, the love of life, and kindness to children; or the general appetite to good, and aversion to evil, considered merely as such. When any of these passions are calm, and cause no disorder in the soul, they are very readily taken for the determination of reason, and are supposed to proceed from the same faculty, with that, which judges of truth and falsehood. Their nature and principles have been supposed the same, because their sensations are not evidently different.

Beside these calm passions, which often determine the will, there are certain violent emotions of the same kind, which have likewise a great influence on that faculty. When I receive any injury from another, I often feel a violent passion of resentment, which makes me desire his evil and punishment, independent of all considerations of pleasure and. advantage to myself. When I am immediately threatened with any grievous ill, my fears, apprehensions, and aversions rise to a great height, and produce a sensible emotion.

The common error of metaphysicians has lain in ascribing the direction of the will entirely to one of these principles, and supposing the other to have no influence. Men often act knowingly against their interest; for which reason the view of the greatest possible good does not always influence them. Men often counteract a violent passion in prosecution of their interests and designs· it is not therefore the present uneasiness alone, which determines them. In general we may observe, that both these principles operate on the will; and where they are contrary, that either of them prevails, according to the *general* character or *present* disposition of the person. What we call strength of mind, implies the prevalence of the calm passions above the violent; though we may easily observe, there is no man so constantly possessed of this virtue, as never on any occasion to yield to the solici-tations of passion and desire. From these variations of temper proceeds the great difficulty of deciding concerning the actions and resolutions of men, where there is any contrajrtety of motives and passions.

(From *A Treatise of Human Nature* by David Hume.)

Justice

I have already hinted, that our sense of every kind of virtue is not natural; but that there are some virtues, that produce pleasure and approbation by means of an artifice or contrivance, which arises from the circumstances and necessity of mankind. Of this kind I assert *justice* to be; and shall endeavour to defend this opinion by a short, and, I hope, convincing argument, before I examine the nature of the artifice, from which the sense of that virtue is derived.

Tis evident, that when we praise any actions, we regard only the motives that produced them, and consider the actions as signs or indications of certain principles in the mind and temper. The external performance has no merit. We must look within to find the moral quality. This we cannot do directly; and therefore fix our attention on actions, as on external signs. But these actions are still considered as signs; and the ultimate object of our praise and approbation is the motive, that produced them.

After the same manner, when we require any action, or blame a person for not performing it, we always suppose, that one in that situation shou'd be influenc'd by the proper motive of that action, and we esteem it vicious in him to be regardless of it. If we find, upon enquiry, that the virtuous motive was still powerful over his breast, tho' check'd in its operation by some circumstances unknown to us, we retract our blame, and have the same esteem for him, as if he ahd actually perform'd the action, which we require of him.

It appears, therefore, that all virtuous actions derive their merit only from virtuous motives, nd are consider'd merely as signs of those motives. From this principle I conclude, that the first virtuous motive, which bestows a merit on any action, can never be a regard to the virtue of that action, but must be some other natural motive or principle. To suppose, that the mere regard to the virtue of the action, may be the first motive, which produc'd the action, and render'd it virtuous, is to reason in a circle. Before we can have such a regard, the action must be really virtuous; and this virtue must be derive'd from some virtuous motive: And consequently the virtuous motive must be different from the regard to the virtue of the action. A virtuous motive is requisite to render an action virtuous. An action must be virtuous, before we can have a regard to its virtue. Some virtuous motive, therefore, must be antecedent to that regard.

Nor is this merely a metaphysical subtilty; but enters into all our reasonings in common life, tho' perhaps we may not be able to place it in such distinct philosophical terms. We blame a father for neglecting his child. Why? because it shews a want of natural affection, which is the duty of every plant. Were not natural affection a duty, the care of children cou'd not be a duty; and 'twere impossible we cou'd have the duty in our eye in the attention we gives to our offspring. In this case, therefore, all men suppose a motive to the action distinct from a sense of duty.

Here is a man, that does many benevolent actions; relieves the distress'd comforts the afflicted, and extends his bounty even to the greatest strangers. No character can be more amiable and virtuous. We regard these actions as proofs of the greatest humanity. This humanity bestows a merit on the actions. A regard to this merit is, therefore, a secondary consideration, and deriv'd from the antecedent principle of humanity, which is meritorious and laudable.

In short, it may be establish'd as an undoubted maxim, *that no action can be virtuous, or morally good, unless be in human nature some motive to produce it, distinct from the sense of its morality.*

But may not the sense of morality or duty produce an action, without any other motive? I answer, It may: But this is no objection to the present doctrine. When any virtuous motive or principle is common in human nature, a person, who feels his heart devoid of that motive, may hate himself upon that account, and may perform the action without the motive, from a certain sense of duty, in order to acquire by practice, that virtuous principle, or at least, to disguise to himself, as much as possible, his want of it. A man that really feels no gratitude in his temper, is still pleas'd to perform grateful actions, and thinks he has, by that means, fulfill'd his duty. Actions are at least only consider'd as signs of motives: But 'tis usual, in this case, as in all others, to fix our attention on the signs, and neglect, in some measure, the thing signify'd. But tho', on some occasions, a person may perform an action merely out of regard to its moral obligation, yet still this supposes in human nature some distinct principles, which are capable of producing the action, and whose moral beauty renders the action meritorious.

Now to apply all this to the present case; I suppose a person to have lent me a sum of money, on condition that it be restor'd in a few days; and also suppose, that after the expiration of the term agreed on, he demands the sum: I ask, *What reason or motive have I restore the money?* It will, perhaps, be said, that may regard to justice, and abhorrence of villainy and knavery, are sufficient reasons for me, if I have the least grain of honesty, or sense of duty and obligation. And this answer, no doubt, is just and satisfactory to man in his civiliz'd state, and when trian'd up according to a certain discipline and education. But in his rude and more natural condition, if you are pleas'd to call such a condition natural, this answer wou'd be rejected as perfectly unintelligible and sophistical. For one in that situation wou'd immediately ask you, *Wherein consists this honesty and justice, which you find in restoring a loan, and abstaining from the property of others*? It does not surely lie in the eternal action. It must, therefore, be plac'd in the motive, from which the external action is deriv'd. This motive can never be a regard to the honesty of the action. For 'tis a plain fallacy to say, that a virtuous motive is requisite to render an action honest, and at the same time that a regard to the honesty is the motive of the action. We can never have a regard to the virtue of an action, unless the action be antecedently virtuous. No action can be virtuous, but so far as it proceeds from a virtuous motive. A virtuous motive, therefore, must precede the regard to the virtue; and 'tis impossible, that the virtuous motive and the regard to the virtue can be the same.

Tis requisite, then, to find some motive to acts of justice and honesty, distinct from our regard to the honesty; and in this lies the great difficulty. For shou'd we say, that a concern for our private interest or reputation is the legitimate motive to all honest actions; it wou'd follow, that wherever that concern ceases, honesty can no longer have place. But 'tis certain, that self-love, when it acts as its liberty, instead of engaging us to honest actions, is the source of all injustice and violence; nor can a man ever correct those vices, without correcting and restraining and natural movements of that appetite.

But shou'd it be affirm'd, that the reason or motive of such actions is the regard to tublick interest, to which nothing is more contrary than examples of injustice and dishonesty: shou'd this be said, I wou'd propose the three following considerations, as worthy of our attention. *First,* public interest is not naturally attach'd to the observation of the rules of justice; but is only connected with it, after an artificial convention for the establishment of these rules, as shall be shewn more at large hereafter. *Secondly,* if we suppose, that the loan was secret, and that it is necessary for the interest of the person, that the money be restor'd in the same manner (as when the lender wou'd conceal his riches) in that case the example ceases, and the public is no longer interested in the actions o the borrower; tho' I suppose there is no moralist, who will affirm, that the duty and obligation ceases. *Thirdly,* experience sufficiently proves, that men, in the ordinary conduct of life, look not so far as the public interest, when they pay their creditors, perform their promises, and abstain from theft, and robbery and robbery and injustice of every kind. That is a motive too remote and too sublime to affect the generality of mankind, and operate with any force in actions so contrary to private interest as are frequently those of justice and common honesty.

In general, it may be affirm'd, that there is no such passion in human minds, as the love of mankind, merely as such, independent of personal qualities, of services, or of relation to ourself. 'Tis true, there is no human, and indeed no sensible, creature, whose happiness or misery does not, in some measure, affect us, when brought near to us, and represented in lively colours: But this proceeds merely from sympathy, and is no proof of such an universal affection to mankind, since this concern extends itself beyond our own species. An affection betwixt the sexes is a passion evidently implanted in human nature; and this passion not only appears in its peculiar symptoms, but also in inflaming every other principle of affection, and raising a stronger love from beauty, wit, kindness, than what wou'd appear after the same manner. Any degree of a good quality wou'd cause a stronger affection than the same degree of a bad quality wou'd cause hatred; contrary to what we find by experience. Men's tempers are different, and some have a propensity to the tender, and others to the rougher, affections: But in the main, we may affirm, that man in general, or human nature, is nothing but the object both of love and hatred, and requires some other cause, which by a double relation of impression and ideas, may excite these passions. In vain wou'd we endeavour to elude this hypothesis. There are no phenomena that point out any such kind affection to men, independent of their merit, and every other circumstance. We love company in general; but 'tis as we love any other amusement. An *Englishmen* in Italy is a friend: A *European in China;* and perhaps a man wou'd be belov'd as such, were we to meet him in the moon. But this proceeds only from the relation to ourselves; which in these cases gathers force by being confined to a few persons.

If public benevolence, therefore, or a regard to the interests of mankind, cannot be the original motive to justice, much less can *private benevolence, or a regard to the interests of the party concernd,* be this motive. For what if he be my enemy, and has given me just cause to hate him? What if he be a vicious man, and deserves the hatred of all mankind? What if he be a miser, and can make no use of what I wou'd deprive him of? What if he be a profligate debauchee, and wou'd rather receive harm than benefit from large possessions? What if I be in necessity, and have urgent motives to acquire something to my family? In all these cases, the original motive to justice wou'd fail; and consequently the justice itself and along with it all property, right, and obligation.

A rich man lies under a moral obligation to communicate to those in necessity a share of his superfluities. Were private benevolence the original motive to justice, a man wou'd not be oblig'd to leave others in the possession of more than he is oblig'd to give them. At least the difference wou'd be very inconsiderable. Men generally fix their affections more on what they are possess'd of, than on what they never enjoy'd: For this reactions, it wou'd be greater cruelty to dispossess a man of any thing, than not to give it him. But who will assert, that this is the only foundation of justice?

Besides, we must consider, that the chief reason, why men attach themselves so much to their possessions is, that they consider them as their property, and as secur'd to them inviolably by the laws of society. But this is a secondary consideration, and dependent on the preceding notions of justice and property.

A man's property is suppos'd to be fenc'd against every moral, in every possible case. But private benevolence is, and ought to be, weaker in some persons, than in others: And in many, or indeed in most persons, must absolutely fail. Private benevolence, therefore, is not the original motive of justice.

From all this it follows, that we have no real or universal motive for observing the laws of equity, but the very equity and merit of that observance; and so no action can be equitable or meritorious, where it cannot arise from some separate motive, there is here an evident sophistry and reasoning in a circle. Unless, therefore, we will allow, that nature has establish'd a sophistry, and render'd it necessary and unavoidable, we must allow, that the sense of justice is not deriv'd from nature, but arises artificially, tho' necessarily from education, and human conventions.

I shall add, as a corollary to this reasoning, that since no action can be laudable or blameable, without some motives or impelling passions, distinct from the sense of morals, these distinct passions must have a great influence on that sense. 'Tis according to their general force in human nature, that we blame or praise. In judging of the beauty of animal bodies, we always carry in our eye the economy of a certain species, we pronounce them handsome and beautiful. In like manner we always consider the natural and usual force of the passions, when we determine concerning vice and virtue; and if the passions depart very much from the common measures on either side, they are always disaaprov'd as vicious. A man naturally loves his children better than his nephews, his nephews better than his cousins, his cousins better than strangers, where everything else is equal. Hence arise our common measures of duty, in preferring the one to the other. Our sense of duty always follows the common and natural course of our passions.

(From *A Treatise of Human Nature*, by David Hume, Tontana, 1972).

12

Edmund Burke

Edmund Burke (1729-1797) was born in Dublin, Ireland in 1729 to a Roman Catholic mother and a Protestant father. By all accounts, the family was not wealthy but was comfortable enough to allow Burke to attend Trinity College, Dublin where he took a first class honours degree in classics. He then displayed an inclination to follow his father's profession and commenced legal studies in London in 1750. These studies, however, were never completed and by the middle of the 1750s, Burke had seemingly settled upon a literary career. In 1757, he manifested the religious tolerance of his upbringing and married the daughter of an Irish, Roman Catholic physician. Burke's literary endeavours were soon coupled with an increasing interest and involvement in political affairs, which were to persist until his death in 1797. His formal political career commenced in 1765 when he was appointed secretary to the Marques of Rockingham. Britain in the eighteenth century possessed only an embryonic political party system. Lords and Commons were divided into Whigs and Tories. Party lines were never clearly drawn but the prominent, contentious issue was the relationship between king and parliament. Here the Whigs were the radicals wishing to curb the prerogative powers of the monarch and establish the constitutional dominance of parliament. Factions within the two 'parties' were usually centred around a prominent member of a traditional noble family. Lord Rockingham headed a liberal group within the Whigs to which Burke attached himself.

In 1774, at the age of forty-five, Burke entered the House of Commons as the member for Bristol, but he forfeited the seat at the elections of 1780. Through the grace and favour of Rockingham, he was then shifted to the constituency of Melton, which, unlike Bristol, was a 'rotten' or 'pocket' borough, requiring little but noble patronage to win and retain. He sat for Melton continuously until his retirement in 1794. Burke's twenty years of parliamentary experience placed him amongst that very small group of political thinkers who were also practising politicians. While he held governmental office for only two brief periods, Burke was an active and influential parliamentarian who was to be found at the centre of all the major political controversies of the later eighteenth century. Surprising as it may appear at first, Burke's political ideas and activities marked him as a progressive and, to some, even a radical.

Space does not permit a full account of Burke's political activities, but a brief summary of some of them is necessary better to understand his political beliefs. Burke was an admirer of the so-called Glorious Revolution of 1688–89 and sought regularly to defend and advance its achievements. These, he believed, involved the establishment in England of a balanced constitutional, monarchy and the defeat of the tyrannical pretensions of despots such as James II. Burke has rightly been criticized for an excessive servility, and even sycophancy towards those he perceived as his superiors; yet, at the same time, he could be courageous in his championship of unpopular and even dangerous causes. He never forsook his heritage and was a regular critic of British policy in Ireland; even to the extent of questioning the wisdom of establishing the English church there. Another of his famous parliamentary crusades concerned the impeachment moves against Warren Hastings, who had been Governor General of Bengal (1772–1785), on the grounds that his application of British colonial policy usurped the traditional rights of the Indian inhabitants. His pursuit of Hastings, who was acquitted on all charges, was not totally altruistic since personal animosity and the desire to assist the dubious financial schemes of two relatives seem also to have been motivating factors.

Burke's opposition to the slave trade was, however, genuine and probably contributed to his electoral defeat in the slave port of Bristol in 1780. Similarly, he was a consistent and articulate advocate for the North American colonists in their disputes with the administration of George III. Burke believed them to be suffering genuine and serious grievances at the hands of an autocracy, which was contemptuous of their rights. His preferred solution was to extend to the colonists the privileges and responsibilities of the British constitution. When the government displayed little inclination to do so, Burke supported the revolution of 1776.

Society is indeed a contract. Subordinate contracts for objects of mere occasional interest may be dissolved at pleasure—but the state ought not to be considered as nothing better than a partnership agreement in a trade of pepper and coffee, calico or tobacco, or some other such low concern, to be taken up for a little temporary interest, and to be dissolved by the fancy of the parties. It is to be looked on with other reverence; because it is not a partnership in things subservient only to the gross animal existence of a temporary and perishable nature. It is a partnership in all science; a partnership in every virtue and all perfection. As the ends of such a partnership can not be obtained in many generations, it becomes a partnership not only between those who are living, but between those who are living, those who are dead, and those who are to be born.

It has been rightly noted that the materials of Burke's thought never reappear in the same form in which he obtained them. They have been smelted and recoined. They have come under the drill and inspiration of a great constructive mind, have caught life and taken structure from it. Burke's is a master in the use of the greatt style. Every sentence, too, is steeped in the colors of his extraordinary imagination. The movement takes one's breath and quickens his pulses. The glow and power of the matter rejuvenate one's faculties. What makes Burke stand out so splendidly among politicians is that he treats politics with his thought and imagination; therefore "whether one agrees with him or not, he always interests you, stimulates you, and does you good."

—Editor

Change and Innovation

A spirit of innovation is generally the result of a selfish temper and confined views. People will not look forward to posterity, who never look backward to their ancestors. Besides, the people of England well know that the idea of inheritance furnishes a sure principle of conservation, and a sure principle of transmission, without at all excluding a principle of improvement. It leaves acquisition free; but it secures what it acquires. Whatever advantages are obtained by a state proceeding on these maxims are locked fast as in a sort of family settlement, grasped as in a kind of mortmain forever. By a constitutional policy working after the pattern of Nature, we receive, we hold, we transmit our government and our privileges, in the same manner in which we enjoy and transmit our property and our lives. The institutions of policy, the goods of fortune, the gifts of Providence, are handed down to us, and from us, in the same course and order. Our political system is placed in a just correspondence and symmetry with the order of the world, and with the mode of existence decreed to a permanent body composed of transitory parts, - wherein, by the disposition of a stupendous wisdom, moulding together the great mysterious incorporation of the human race, the whole, at one time, is never old or middle-aged or young, but, in a condition of unchangeable constancy, moves on through the varied tenor of perpetual decay, fall, renovation, and progression. Thus, by preserving the method of Nature in the conduct of the state, in what we improve we are never wholly new, in what we retain we are never wholly obsolete. By adhering in this manner and on those principles to our forefathers, we arc guided, not by the superstition of antiquarians, but by the spirit of philosophic analogy. In this choice of inheritance have given to our frame of polity the image of a relation in blood: binding up the Constitution of our country with dearest domestic ties; adopting our fundamental laws, the bosom of our family affections; keeping inseparable, cherishing with the warmth of all their combined and mutually reflected charities, our state, our hearths, our sepulchers and our altars.

Through the same plan of a conformity to Nature in our artificial institutions, and by calling in the aid of her unerring and powerful instincts to fortify the fallible and feeble contrivances of our reason, we have derived several other, and those no small benefits, from considering our liberties in the light of an inheritance. Always acting as if in the presence of canonized forefathers, the spirit of freedom, leading in itself to misrule and excess, is tempered with an awful gravity. This idea of a liberal descent inspires us with a sense of habitual native dignity, which prevents that upstart insolence almost inevitably adhering t" and disgracing those who are the first acquirers of any distinction. By this means our liberty becomes a noble freedom. It carries an imposing and majestic aspect. It has a pedigree and illustrating ancestors. It has its bearings and its ensigns armorial. It has its gallery of portraits, its monumental inscriptions, its records, evidences, and titles. We procure reverence to our civil institutions on the principle upon which Nature teaches us to revere individual men: on account of their age, and on account of those from whom they are descended. All your sophisters cannot produce anything better adapted to preserve a rational and manly freedom than the course that we have pursued, who have chosen our nature rather than our speculations, our breasts rather than our inventions, for the great conservatories and magazines of our rights and privileges.

You might, if you pleased, have profited of our example, and have given to your recovered freedom a correspondent dignity. Your privileges, though discontinued, were not lost to memory. Your Constitution, it is true, whilst you were out of possession, suffered waste and dilapidation; but you possessed in some parts the walls, and in all the foundations, of a noble and venerable castle. You might have repaired those walls; you might have built on those old foundations. Your Constitution was suspended before it was perfected; but you had the elements of a Constitution very nearly as good as could be wished. In your old states1 you possessed that variety of parts corresponding with the various descriptions of which your community was happily composed; you had all that combination and all that opposition of interests, you had that action and counteraction, which, in the natural and in the political world, from the reciprocal struggle of discordant powers draws out the harmony of the universe. These opposed and conflicting interests, which you considered as so great a blemish in your old and in our present Constitution, interpose a salutary check to all precipitate resolutions. They render—— deliberation a matter, not of choice, but of necessity; they make all change a subject of compromise, which naturally begets moderation; they produce temperaments, preventing the sore evil of harsh, crude, unqualified reformations, and rendering all the headlong exertions of arbitrary power, in the few or in the many, forever impracticable. Through that diversity of members and interests, general liberty had as many securities as there were separate views in the several orders; whilst by pressing down the whole by the weight of a real monarchy, the separate parts would have been prevented from warping and starting from their allotted places.

You had all these advantages in your ancient states; but you chose to act as if you had never been moulded into civil society, and had everything to begin anew. You began ill, because you began by despising everything that belonged to you. You set up your trade without a capital. If the last generations of your country appealed without much in your eyes, you might have passed them by, and your claims from a more early race of ancestors. Under a pious predilection for those ancestors, your imaginations would have realized in them a standard of virtue and wisdom beyond the vulgar practice of the hour; and you would have risen with the example to whose imitation you aspired. Respecting your forefathers, you would have been taught to respect yourselves. You would not have chosen to consider the French as a people of yesterday, as a nation of low-born, servile wretches until the emancipating year of 1789. In order to furnish, at the expense of your honor, an excuse to your apologists here for several enormities of yours, you would not have been content to be represented as a gang of Maroon slaves, suddenly broke loose from the house of bondage, and therefore to be pardoned for your abuse of the liberty to which you were not accustomed, and were ill fitted. Would it not, my worthy friend, have been wiser to have you thought, what I for one always thought you, a generous and gallant nation, long misled to your disadvantage by your high and romantic sentiments of fidelity, honour, and loyalty; that events had been unfavorable to you, but that you were not enslaved through any illiberal or servile disposition; that, in your most devoted submission, you were actuated by a principle of public spirit; and that it was your country you worshipped, in the person of your king? Had you made it to be understood, that, in the delusion of this amiable error, you had gone further than your wise ancestors, that you were resolved to resume your ancient privileges, whilst you preserved the spirit of your ancient and your recent loyalty and honor; or if, diffident of yourselves, and not clearly discerning the almost obliterated Constitution of your ancestors, you had looked to your neighbors in this land, who had kept alive the ancient principles and models of the old common law of Europe, meliorated and adapted to its present state, by following wise examples you would have given new examples of wisdom to the world. You would have rendered the cause of liberty venerable -in the eyes of every worthy mind in every nation. You would have shamed despotism from the earth, by showing that freedom was not only reconcilable, but, as, when well disciplined, it is, auxiliary to law. You would have had an unoppressive, but a productive revenue. You would have had a flourishing commerce to feed it. You would have had a free Constitution, a potent monarchy a disciplined army, a reformed and venerated clergy, - a mitigated, but spirited nobility, to lead your virtue, not to overlay it; you would have had a liberal order of commons, to emulate and to recruit that nobility; you would have had a protected, satisfied, laborious, and obedient people, taught to seek and to recognize the happiness that is to be found by virtue in all conditions, - in which consists the true moral equality of mankind, and not in that monstrous fiction which, by inspiring false ideas and vain expectations into men destined to travel in the obscure walk of laborious life, serves only to aggravate and embitter that real inequality which it never can remove, and which the order of civil life establishes as much for the benefit of those whom it must leave in an humble state as those whom it is able to exalt to a condition more splendid, but not more happy. You had a smooth and easy career of felicity and glory laid open to you, beyond anything recorded in the history of the world; but you have shown that difficulty is good for man.

Compute your gains; see what is got by those extravagant and presumptuous speculations which have taught your leaders to despise all their predecessors, and all their contemporaries, and even to despise themselves, until the moment in which may became truly despicable. By following those false lights, France has bought undisguised calamities at a higher price than any nation has purchased the most unequivocal blessings. France has bought poverty by crime. France has not sacrificed her virtue to her interest; but she has abandoned her interest, that she might prostitute her virtue. All other nations have begun the fabric of a new government, or the reformation of an old, by establishing originally, or by enforcing with greater exactness, some rites or other of religion. All other people have laid the foundations of civil freedom in severer manners, and a system of a more austere and masculine morality. France, when she let loose the reins of regal authority, doubled the license of a ferocious dissoluteness in manners, and of an insolent irreligion in opinions and practices, - and has extended through all ranks of life, as if she were communicating some privilege, or laying open some secluded benefit, all the unhappy corruptions that usually were the disease of wealth and power. This is one of the new principles of equality in France.

France, by the perfidy of her leaders, has utterly disgraced the tone of lenient council in the cabinets of princes, and disarmed it of its most potent topics. She has sanctified the dark, suspicious maxims of tyrannous distrust, and taught kings to tremble at (what will hereafter be called) the delusive plausibilities of moral politicians. Sovereigns will consider those who advise them to place an unlimited confidence in their people as subverters of their thrones, - as traitors who aim at their destruction, by leading their easy good-nature, under specious pretences, to admit combinations of bold and faithless men into a participation of their power. This alone (if there were nothing else) is an irreparable calamity to you and to mankind. Remember that your Parliament of Paris told your king, that, in calling the states together, he had nothing to fear but the prodigal excess of their zeal in providing for the support of the throne. It is right that these men should hide their heads. It is right that they should bear their art in the ruin which their counsel has brought on their sovereign and their country. Such sanguine declarations tend to lull authority asleep, — to encourage it rashly to engage in perilous adventures of untried policy, - to neglect those provisions, preparations, and precautions which distinguish benevolence from imbecility, and without which no man can answer for the salutary effect of any abstract plan of government or of freedom. For want of these, they have seen the medicine of the state corrupted into its poison. They have seen the French rebel against a mild and lawful monarch, with more fury, outrage, and insult than ever any people has been known to rise against the most illegal usurper or the most sanguinary tyrant. Their resistance was made to concession; their revolt was from protection; their blow was aimed at a hand holding out graces, favors, and immunities.

This was unnatural. The rest is in order. They have found their punishment in their success. Laws overturned; tribunals 'subverted; industry without vigor; commerce expiring; the revenue unpaid, yet the people impoverished; a church 'pillaged, and a state not relieved; civil and military anarchy made the constitution of the kingdom; everything human and divine sacrificed to the idol of public credit, and national bankruptcy the consequence; and, to crown all, the paper securities of new, precarious, tottering power, the discredited paper securities of impoverished fraud and beggared rapine, held out as a currency for the support of an empire, in lieu of the two great recognized species that represent the lasting, conventional credit of mankind, which disappeared and hid themselves in the earth from whence they came, when the principle of property, whose creatures and representatives they arc, was systematically subverted.

Were all these dreadful things necessary? Were they the inevitable results of the desperate struggle of determined patriots, compelled to wade through blood and tumult to the quiet shore of a tranquil and prosperous liberty? No nothing like it. The fresh ruins of France, which shock our feelings wherever we can turn our eyes, are not the devastation of civil war: they are the sad, but instructive monuments of rash and ignorant counsel in time of profound peace. They are the display of inconsiderate and presumptuous, because unresisted and irresistible authority. The persons who have thus squandered away the precious treasure of their crimes, the persons who have made this prodigal and wild waste of public evils (the last stake reserved for the ultimate ransom of the state), have met in their progress with little of rather with no opposition at all. Their whole march was more like a triumphal procession than the progress of a war. Their pioneers have gone before them, and demolished and laid everything level at their fee. Not one drop of their blood have they shed in the cause of the country they have ruined. They have made no sacrifices to their projects of greater consequence than their shoe-buckles, whilst they were imprisoning their king, murdering their fellow-citizens, and bathing in tears and plunging in poverty and distress thousands of worthy men and worthy families. Their cruelty has not even been the base result of fear. It has been the effect of their sense of perfect safety, in authorizing treasons, robberies, rapes, assassinations, slaughters, and burnings, throughout their harassed land. But the cause of al) was plain from the beginning.

If civil society be made for the advantage of man, all the advantages for which it is made become his right. It is an institution of beneficence; and law itself is only beneficence acting by a rule. Men have a right to live by that rule; they have a right to justice, as between their fellows, whether their fellows are in politic function or in ordinary occupation. They have a right to the fruits of their industry, and to the means of making their industry fruitful. They have a right to the acquisitions of their parents, to the nourishment and improvement of their offspring, to instruction in life and to consolation in death. Whatever each man can separately do, without trespassing upon others, he has a right to do for himself; and he has a right to a fair portion of all which society, with all its combinations of skill and force, can do in his favor. In this partnership all men have equal rights; but not to equal things. He that has but five shillings in the partnership has as good a right to it as he that has five hundred pounds has to his larger proportion; but he has not a right to an equal dividend in the product of the joint stock. And as to the share of power, authority, and direction which each individual ought to have in the management of the state, that I must deny to be amongst the direct original rights of man in civil society; for I have in my contemplation the civil social man, and no other. It is a thing to be settled by convention.

If civil society be the offspring of convention, that convention must be its law. That convention must limit and modify all the descriptions of constitution which are formed under it. Every sort of legislative, judicial, or executory power are its creatures. They can have no being in any other state of things; and how can any man claim, under the conventions of civil society, rights which do not so much as suppose its existence rights which are absolutely repugnant to it? One of the first motives to civil society, and which becomes one of its fundamental rules, is, that no man should be judge in his own cause. By this each person has at once divested himself of the first fundamental right of uncovenanted man that is, to judge for himself, and to assert his own cause. He abdicates all right toy be his own governor. He inclusively, in a great measure, abandons the right of self-defence, the first law of Nature. Men cannot enjoy the rights of an uncivil and of a civil state together. That he may obtain justice, he gives up his right of determining what it is in points the most essential to him. That he may secure some liberty, he makes a surrender in trust of the whole of it.

Government is not made in virtue of natural rights, which may and do exist in total independence of it - and exist in much greater clearness, and in a much greater degree of abstract perfection: but their abstract perfection is their practical defect. By having a right to everything they want everything. Government is a contrivance of human wisdom to provide for human wants. Men have a right that these wants should be provided for by this wisdom. Among these wants is to be reckoned the want, out of civil society, of a sufficient restraint upon their passions. Society requires not only that the passions of individuals should be subjected, but that even in the mass and body, as well as in the individuals, the inclinations of men should frequently be thwarted, their will controlled, and their passions brought into subjection. This can only be done by a power out of themselves, and not, in the exercise of its function, subject to that will and to those passions which it is its office to bridle and subdue. In this sense the restraints on men, as well as their liberties, are to be reckoned among their rights. But as the liberties and the restrictions vary with times and circumstances, and admit of infinite modifications, they cannot be settled upon any abstract rule; and nothing is so foolish as to discuss them upon that principle.

The moment you abate anything from the full rights of men each to govern himself, and suffer any artificial, positive limitation upon those rights, from that moment the whole organization of government becomes a consideration of convenience. This it is which makes the constitution of a state, and the due distribution of its powers, a matter of the most delicate and complicated skill. It requires a deep knowledge of human nature and human necessities, and of the things which facilitate or obstruct the various ends which are to be pursued by the mechanism of civil institutions. The state is to have recruits to its strength and remedies to its distempers. What is the use of discussing a man's abstract right to food or medicine? The question is upon the method of procuring and administering them. In that deliberation I shall always advise to call in the aid of the farmer and the physician, rather than the professor of metaphysics.

The science of constructing a commonwealth, or renovating it, or reforming it, is like every other experimental science, not to be taught a priori. Nor is it a short experience that can instruct us in that practical science; because the real effects of moral causes are not always immediate, but that which in the first instance is prejudicial may be excellent in its remoter operation, and its excellence may arise even from the ill effects it produces in the beginning. The reverse also happens; and very plausible schemes, with very pleasing commence ments, have often shameful and lamentable conclusions. In states there are often some obscure and almost latent causes, things which appear at first view of little moment, on which a very great part of its prosperity or adversity may most essentially depend. The science of government being, therefore, so practical in itself, and intended for such practical purposes, matter which requires experience, and even more experience than any person can gain in his whole life, however sagacious and observing he nay be, it is with infinite caution that man ought to venture upon pulling down an edifice which has answered in any tolerable degree for ages the common purposes of society, or on building it up again without having models and patterns of approved utility before his eyes.

These metaphysic rights entering into common life, like rays of light which pierce into a dense medium, are, by the laws of Nature, refracted from their straight line. Indeed, in the gross and complicated mass of human passions and concerns, the primitive rights of men undergo such a variety of refractions and reflections that it becomes absurd to talk of them as if they continued in the simplicity of their original direction. The nature of man is intricate the objects of society are of the greatest possible complexity and therefore no simple disposition of direction of power can be suitable either to man's nature or to the quality of his affairs. When I hear the simplicity of contrivance aimed at and boasted of in any new political constitutions, I am at no loss to decide that the artificers are grossly ignorant of their trade or totally negligent of their duty. The simple governments are fundamentally defective, to say no worse of them. If you were to contemplate society in but one point of view all these simple modes of polity are infinitely captivating. In effect each would answer its single end much more perfectly than the more complex is able to attain all its complex purposes. But it is better that the whole should be imperfectly and anomalously answered than that while some parts are provided for with great exactness, others might be totally neglected, or perhaps materially injured, by the over-care of a favorite member.

The pretended rights of these theorists are all extremes; and in proportion as they are metaphysically true, they are morally and politically false. The rights of men are in a sort of middle, incapable of definition, but not impossible to be discerned. The rights of men in governments are their advantages; and these are often in balances between differences of good - in compromises sometimes between good and evil, and sometimes between evil and evil. Political reason is a computing principle: adding, subtracting, multiplying, and dividing, morally, and not metaphysically or mathematically, true moral denominations.

(From "Reflections on the Revolution in France" in Edmund Burke – *On Government, Politics and Society* edited by B.W.Hill, The Harvester Press, UK 1975)

Representation

I am sorry I cannot conclude without saying a word on a topic touched upon by my worthy colleague. I wish that topic had been passed by at a time when I have so little leisure to discuss it. But since he has thought proper to throw it out, I owe you a clear explanation, of my poor sentiments on that subject.

He tells you that 'the topic of instructions has occasioned much altercation and uneasiness in this city'; and he expresses himself (if I understand him rightly) in favor of the coercive authority of such instructions.

Certainly, Gentlemen, it ought to be the happiness and glory of a representative to live in the strictest union, the closest correspondence, and the most unreserved communication with his constituents. Their wishes ought to have great weight with him; their 'opinions high' respect; their business unremitted attention. It is his duty to sacrifice his repose, his. pleasure his satisfactions, to theirs, and above all, ever, and in all cases, to prefer their interest to his own.

But his unbiased opinion, his mature judgment, his enlightened conscience, he ought not to sacrifice to you to any man, or to any set of men living. These he does not derive from your pleasure, no, nor from the law and the Constitution. They are a trust from Providence, for the abuse of which he is deeply answerable. Your representative, owes you, not his industry only, but his judgment,' and he betrays, instead of serving you, if he sacrifices it to your opinion :

My worthy colleague says, his will ought to be subservient to yours. If that be all, the thing is innocent. If government were a matter of will upon any side, yours, without question, ought' to be superior. But government and legislation are matters of reason and judgment, and not of inclination; and what sort of reason is that iii which the determination precedes the discussion, in which one set of men deliberate and another: decide, and where those who form the conclusion are perhaps three hundred miles distant from, those who hear the arguments?

To deliver an opinion is the right of all men; that of constituents is a weighty and respectable opinion, which a representative ought always tip rejoice to hear, and which he ought always most seriously to consider. But authoritative instructions, mandates issued, which the member is bound blindly and implicitly to obey, to vote, and to argue for though contrary to the clearest conviction of his judgment and conscience, these are things utterly unknown to the laws of this land, and which arise from a fundamental mistake of the whole order and tenor of our Constitution.

Parliament is not a congress of ambassadors from different and hostile interests, which interests each must maintain, as agent and advocate, against other agents arid advocates; but Parliament is a deliberative assembly of one nation, with one interest, that of the whole where not local prejudices, ought to guide, not local prejudices, ought to guide, but the general good, resulting from the general reason of the whole. You choose a member, indeed; but when you have chosen him, he is not member of Bristol, but he is a member of Parliament. If the local constituent should have an interest or should form an hasty opinion evidently opposite to the real good of the rest of the community, the member for that place ought to be the far as any other from any endeavor to give it effect. I beg pardon for saying so much on this subject; I have been unwillingly drawn into it; but I shall ever use a respectful frankness of communication with you. Your faithful friend, your devoted servant, I shall be to the end of my life: a flatter you do not wish for. On this point of instructions, however, I think it scarcely possible we ever can have any sort of difference. Perhaps I may give you too much, rather than too little trouble.

(From a "Speech to the Electors of Bristol," on his being declared by the Sheriffs duly elected (3 November 1774).

Political Party

The Wings those days believed that the only proper method of rising into power was through hard essays of practised friendship and experimented fidelity. At that time it was not imagined, that patriotism was a. bloody idol, which required the sacrifice or children arid parents, or dearest connections in private life, and of all the virtues that rise from those relations. They were not of that ingenious paradoxical morality, to imagine that a spirit of moderation was properly shown in patiently bearing the sufferings of your friends; or that disinterestedness was clearly manifested at the expense of other people's fortune. They believed that no men could act with effect, who did not act in concert; that no men could act in concert, who did not act with confidence; that no men could act with confidence, who were not bound together by common opinions, common affections, and common interests.

These wise men for such I must call Lord Sunderland, Lord Godolphin, Lord Somers, and Lord Marlborough, were too well principled in these maxims upon which the whole fabric of public strength is built, to be blown off their ground by the breath of every childish talker. They were not afraid that they should be called an ambitious junto; or that their resolution to stand for all together should, by placemen, be interpreted into a scuffle for places.

Party is a body of men united for promoting by their joint endeavors the national interest upon some particular principle in which they are all agreed. For my part, I find it impossible to conceive, that any one believes in his own politics, or thinks them to be of any weight, who refuses to adopt the means of having them reduced into practice. It is the business of the speculative philosopher to mark the proper ends of government. It is the business of the politician, who is the philosopher in action, to find out proper means towards those ends, and to employ them with effect. Therefore every honorable connection will avow it is their first purpose, to pursue every just method to put the men who hold their opinions into such a condition as may enable them to carry their common plans into execution, with all the power and authority of the state. As this power is attached to certain situations, it is their duty to contend for these situations. Without a proscription of others, they are bound to give to their own party the preference in all things; and by no means, for private considerations, to accept any offers of power in which the whole body is not included; nor to suffer themselves to be led, or to be controlled, or to be overbalanced, in office or in council, by those who contradict the very fundamental principles on which their party is formed, and even those upon which every fair connection must stand. Such a generous contention for power, on such manly and honorable maxims, will easily be distinguished from the mean and interested struggle for place and emolument. The very style of such persons will serve to discriminate them from those numberless impostors, who have deluded the ignorant with professions /incompatible with human practice, and have afterwards incensed them by practices below the level of vulgar rectitude.

It is an advantage to all narrow wisdom and narrow morals, that their maxims have a plausible air and, on a cursory view, appear equal to first principles. They are light and portable. They are as current as copper coin; and about as valuable. They serve equally the first capacities and the lowest; and they are, at least, as useful to the worst men as to the best. Of this stamp is the cant of Not men, but measures; a sort of charm by which many people get loose from every honorable engagement. When I see a man acting this desultory and disconnected part, with as much detriment to his own fortune as prejudice to the cause of any party, I am not persuaded that he is right; but I am ready to believe he is in earnest. I respect virtue in all its situations; even when it is found in the unsuitable company of weakness. I lament to see qualities, rare and valuable, squandered away without any public utility. But when a gentleman with great visible emoluments abandons the party in which he has long acted, and tells you, it is because he proceeds upon his own judgment; that he acts on the merits' of the several measures as they arise; and that he is obliged to follow his own conscience, and not that of others; he gives reasons which it is impossible to controvert, and discovers a character which it is impossible to mistake. What shall think of him who never differed from a certain get of men the moment they lost their power, and who never agreed with them in a single instance afterwards? Would not such; a coincidence of interested opinion be rather fortunate? Would it not be an extraordinary cast upon the dice, that a man's connections should degenerate into faction, precisely at the critical moment when they lose their power, or he accepts a place? When people desert their connections, the desertion is a manifest fact, upon which a direct simple issue lies, triable by plain men. Whether a measure of government be right or wrong, is no matter of fact, but a mere affair of opinion, on which men may, as they do, dispute arid wrangle without end. But whether the individual thinks the measure right or wrong, is a point at still a greater distance from the reach of all human decision. It is therefore very convenient to politicians, not to put the judgment of their conduct on overt acts, cognizable in any ordinary court, but upon such matter as can be triable only in that secret tribunal, where they are sure of being heard with favor, or where at worst the sentence will be only private whipping.

I believe the reader would wish to find no substance in a doctrine which has a tendency to destroy all test of character as deduced from conduct. He will therefore excuse my adding something more, towards the further clearing up a point, which the great convenience of obscurity to dishonesty has been able to cover with some degree of darkness and doubt.

In order to throw an odium on political connection, these politicians suppose it a necessary incident to it, that you are blindly to follow the opinions of your party, when in direct opposition to your own clear ideas; a degree of servitude that no worthy man could bear the thought of submitting to; and such as, I believe, no connections (except some court factions) ever could be so senselessly tyrannical as to impose. Men thinking freely, will, in particular instances, think differently. But still as the greater part of the measures which ariso in tin-course of public business are related to, or dependent on, some great, leading, general principles in government, a man must be peculiarly unfortunate in the choice of his political company, if he does not agree with them at least nine times in ten. If he does not concur in these general principles upon which the party is founded, and which necessarily draw on a concurrence in their application, he ought from the beginning to have chosen some other, more conformable to his opinions. When the question is in its nature doubtful, or not very material, the modesty which becomes an individual, and (in spite of our court moralists), that partiality which becomes a well-chosen friendship, will frequently bring on an acquiescence in the general sentiment. Thus the disagreement will naturally be rare; it will be only enough to indulge freedom, without violating concord, or disturbing arrangement. And this is all that ever was required for a character of the greatest uniformity and steadiness in connection.

How men can proceed without any connection at all, is to me utterly incomprehensible. Of what sort of materials must that man be made, how must he be tempered and put together, who can sit whole years in Parliament, with five hundred and fifty of his fellow-citizens, amidst the storm of such tempestuous passions, in the sharp conflict of so many wits, and tempers, and characters, in the agitation of such mighty questions, in the discussion of such vast and ponderous interests, without /seeing any one sort of men, whose character, conduct, or of disposition, would lead him to associate himself with them, to and be aided, in any one system of public utility? I remember an old scholastic aphorism, which says, 'that the man who lives wholly detached from others, must be either an angel or a devil. When I see in any of these detached gentlemen of our times the angelic purity, power, and beneficence, I shall admit them to be angels. In the mean time we are born only to be men. We shall do enough if we form ourselves to be good ones. It is therefore our business carefully to cultivate in our minds, to rear to the most perfect vigor and maturity, every sort of generous and honest feeling, that belongs to our nature. To bring the dispositions that are lovely in private life into the service and conduct of the common wealth; so to be patriots, as not to forget we are gentlemen. To cultivate friendships, and to incur enmities. To have both strong, but both selected: in the one, to be placable; in the other immovable. To model our principles to our duties and our situation. To be fully persuaded, that all virtue which is impracticable is spurious; and rather to run the risk of falling into faults in a course which leads us to act with effect and energy, than to loiter out our days without blame, and without 'use. Public life is a situation of power and energy; he trespasses against his duty who sleeps upon his watch, as well as he that goes over to the enemy.

There is, however, a time for all things. It is not every conjuncture which calls with equal force upon the activity of honest men; but critical exigencies now and then arise; and I am mistaken, if this be not one of them. Men will see the necessity of honest combination; but they may see it when it is too late. They may embody, when it will be ruinous to themselves, and of no advantage to the country; when, for want of such a timely union as may enable them to oppose in favor of the laws, with the laws on their side, they may at length find themselves under the necessity of conspiring, instead of consulting. The law, for which they stand, may become a weapon in the hands of its bitterest enemies; and they will be cast, at length, into that miserable alternative between slavery and civil confusion, which no good man can look upon without horror; an alternative in which it is impossible he should take either part, with a conscience perfectly at repose. To keep that situation of guilt and remorse at the utmost distance is, there fore, our first obligation. Early activity may prevent late and fruitless violence. As yet we work in the light. The scheme of the enemies of public tranquility has disarranged, it has not destroyed us.

If the reader believes that there really exists such a faction as I have described; a faction ruling by the private inclinations of a court, against the general sense of the people; and that this faction, whilst it pursues a scheme for undermining all the foundations of our freedom, weakens (for the present at least) all the powers of executory government, rendering us abroad contemptible, and at home distracted; he will believe also, that nothing but a firm combination of public men against this body, and that, too, supported by the hearty concurrence of the people at large, can possibly get the better of it. The people will see the necessity of restoring public men to an attention to the public opinion, and of restoring the constitution to its original principles. Above all, they will endeavor to keep the House of Commons from assuming a character which does not belong to it. They will endeavor to keep that House, for its existence, for its powers, and its privileges, as independent of every other, and as dependent upon themselves, as possible. This servitude is to a House of Commons (like obedience to the Divine law) 'perfect freedom.' For if they once quit this natural, rational, and liberal obedience, having deserted the only proper foundation of their power, they must seek a support in an abject and unnatural dependence somewhere else. When, through the medium of this just connection with their constituents, the genuine dignity of the House of Commons is restored, it will begin to think of casting from it, with scorn, as badges of servility, all the false ornaments of illegal power, with which it has been, for some time, disgraced. It will begin to think of its old office of control. It will not suffer that last of evils to predominate in the country men without popular confidence, public opinion, natural connection, or mutual trust, invested with all the powers of government.

(From "On the Present Discontents" in *Edmund Burke – On Government Politics and Society* edited by B.W. Hill, The Harvester Press, UK 1975.)

13

Mary Wollstonecraft

Mary Wollstonecraft (1759-1798) was a moral and political theorist whose analysis of the condition of women in modern society retains much of its original radicalism. One of the reasons her pronouncements on the subject remain challenging is that her reflections on the status of the female sex were part of an attempt to come to a comprehensive understanding of human relations within a civilization increasingly governed by acquisitiveness. Her first publication was on the education of daughters; she went on to write about politics, history and various aspects of philosophy in a number of different genres that included critical reviews, translations, pamphlets, and novels. Best known for her *Vindication of the Rights of Women* (1792), her influence went beyond the substantial contribution to feminism.

The second of seven children, Mary Wollstonecraft was born in Spitalfields, London, on 27 April, 1759. Her paternal grandfather was a successful master weaver who left a sizeable legacy, but her father, Edward John, mismanaged his share of the inheritance. He tried to establish himself as a gentleman farmer in Epping. This was the first of the family's several moves, each of which marked its financial and social decline. Only Mary's brother, Edward was to receive a formal education; he became a lawyer. He had also inherited directly from his grandfather a substantial part of the latter's legacy.

Wollstonecraft's own somewhat haphazard education was, however, not entirely unusual for someone of her sex and position. Her published writings show her to have acquired a true command of the Bible, a good knowledge of the works of several of the most famous Ancients and of the writings of Shakespeare and Milton. The nature and extent of her reading was partly owed to the friendship shown to her in her youth by a retired elergyman and his wife. In relatively rapid succession, she was to enter the most likely occupations for someone of her sex and circumstances: a lady's companion, a schoolteacher, and a governess. In 1778, she was engaged as a companion to a Mrs. Dawson and lived at Bath. She returned home to nurse her ailing mother in the latter part of 1781. After her mother's death, in the spring of 1782, Wollstonecraft lived with family of her dearest friend, Fanny. In the winter of 1783, Mary left them in order to attend to her sister Eliz and her newly born daughter.

By February of that year, two sisters had already been planning to establish a school with Fanny. Mary's other sister, Everina, joined in the project a little latter. They first set their sights on Islington, then moved to Newington Green, where Mary met the moral and political thinker, Richard Price. This was a crucial encounter for Mary. Several years later, she came to his defense in a *Vindication of the Rights of Men* (1790), and it was through her connections to Price that she was to gain an introduction to her future publisher, friend, and one might even say, patron, Joseph Johnson.

In November 1785, Wollstonecraft went on a trip to Lisbon, where her friend Fanny, who had married that February, was expecting her first child. On board the ship, Mary met a man suffering from consumption; she nursed him for a fortnight, the length of the journey. This experience is related in her first novel, *Mary, a Fiction* (1778). She gained a very unfavorable opinion of Portuguese life and society, which seemed to her ruled by irrationality and superstitions. Mary's brief stay in Portugal was, furthermore, to be a profoundly unhappy one, for both Fanny and her baby died shortly after the delivery. On her return to England, Wollstonecraft found her school in a dire state. Far from providing her with a reliable income and some stability, it was to be a source of endless worries and a financial drain.

Edmund Burke's attack on Price in Reflections led Wollstonecraft, persuaded by her publisher, Johnson, to take up her pen in the aged Price's defence. A Vindication of the Rights of Men (1790) was almost certainly the first of many responses Burke's *Reflections* elicited. Initially published anonymously at the end of November, the second edition that quickly followed in mid-December bore its author's name and marked a turning point in her career; it established her political writer. In September 1791, Wollstonecraft began *A Vindication of the Rights of Woman:* which elaborated a number of points made in the previous *Vindication*, namely, that in most cases, marriage was nothing but a property relation, and that the education women received ensured that they could not meet the expectations society had of them and almost certainly guaranteed them an unhappy life.

Following the publication of her second *Vindication*, Wollstonecraft was introduced to the French statesman and diplomat, Charles Talleyrand, on his mission to London on the part of the Constituent Assembly in February 1792. She dedicated the second edition of the A Vindication of the Rights of Women to him. In December 1792, she travelled to France where she met Gilbert Imlay, an American merchant. As British subjects were increasingly at risk under the Terror, Wollstonecraft passed as Imlay's wife so as to benefit from the security enjoyed at the time by American citizens. They never married. Imlay was probably the source of Wollstonecraft's greatest unhappiness, first through his lack of ardour for her, then because of his infidelity, and finally because of his complete rejection of her. Most of all, her love of Imlay brought Wollstonecraft to the realization that the passions are not so easily brought to heel by reason.

Wollstonecraft had a girl by Imlay. She was born at Le Havre in May 1794 and named Fanny, A year after Fanny's birth, Wollstonecraft twice attempted suicide, She broke with Imlay finally in March 1796. In April of the same year, she renewed her acquaintance with William Godwin and they became lovers that summer. They were to marryied at St Pancras church in March 1797. On the 30th August, Mary Wollstonecraft Godwin, future author of Frankenstein and future wife of English poet Shelley, was born.

Wollstonecraft's early writings were of a pedagogical nature. These reveal the profound influence John Locke had on Wollstonecraft's thought, and several of the arguments of his *Some Thoughts Concerning Education* (1693) are echoed in Wollstonecraft's conception of morality and the best manner to inculcate it in individuals at the earliest possible age. When Wollstonecraft began to engage in political commentary in reviewing Price's *A Discourse on the Love of our Country*, she praised him for his account of true patriotism as 'the result of reason, not the undirected impulse of nature, ever tending to selfish extremes' as well as his defence of Christianity's prescription of universal benevolence against those who argued such sentiment to be incompatible with the love of one's country. She endorsed his view of liberty of conscience as a sacred right and wrote sympathetically about his plea for the repeal of the Test and Corporation Acts, which imposed civil disabilities on Dissenters. She also seemed to support his claim that the political Settlement of 1689 was wanting in that it did not make for full representation of the people and hence made only for partial liberty. Finally, Wollstonecraft reproduced the passage in which Price linked the American and French revolutions and clamoured for the end of despotism throughout Europe.

Of the many disagreements between Price and Wollstonecraft, on the one hand, and Burke, on the other, one of the deepest was over their respective view of the nature of civil society and of political power in general. The two friends believed that government, the rule of law, and all human relations could be simplified, explicated, and rendered transparent, and both were convinced that this was the task ahead for all lovers of liberty. For Burke, on the contrary, civil society consisted of countless ineffable links between individuals. The latter's relationship to authority was for the most part no less ineffable; moreover, he believed sound political judgement to be the product of experience, and he cautioned prudence. To sweep away established practices and institutions and think of politics as a mere matter of administrating in accordance with a set of abstract rules or rights uninformed by the customs and culture, and hence the national character, of a people was, in his view, to demonstrate a crass disregard for the most obvious facts of human nature and history. Burke's argument led him to dwell on France's financial position in some detail, and he defended its royal family and its Church; he insisted, moreover, that it was already benefiting from a policy of gradual reform. The over-all effect he sought to achieve was to depict his opponent as theoretically confused, politically naive, generally misinformed, and, most damnable of all, his sermon on the *Love of our Country* with all its affirmation of feelings for humanity proved him to be unpatriotic.

Wollstonecraft's first *Vindication* was the first of many replies. It is an interesting and rhetorically powerful work in its own right as well as a necessary introduction to the *Vindication of the Rights of Woman*. It consists mostly of a sustained attack on Burke rather than a defence of the rights of man. This is partly because Wollstonecraft took for granted a Lockean conception of God-given rights discoverable by reason, except when the latter was warped by self-love. Wollstonecraft further believed that God made all things right and that the cause of all evil was man. In her view, Burke's *Reflections* showed its author to be blind to man-made poverty and injustice; this she attributed to his infatuation with rank, Queen Marie-Antoinette, and the English Constitution. Demonstrating her familiarity with Burke's other works and speeches, she also argued that Burke was inconsistent, because of the impossibility, of reconciling his sympathy for the American cause with his reaction to events in France. In this, Wollstonecraft was far from alone and many who had followed Burke's parliamentary career and heard his Speeches to the House of Commons were astonished by what they thought was a radical and inexplicable change of position.

Woll stone craft's first *Vindication* was written in response to Edmumd Burke's attack on the French Revolution in his *Reflections on the Revolution in France*. In that book, Burke blames the excesses of the revolution on the abandonment of tradition and the embrace of reason and abstract political rights. In denouncing the revolution and the government instituted afterward, Burke emotionally evokes female bodily and sexual metaphors, describing the revolution as 'an orgy" and the new government as a "diseased prostitute".

As she was to do in her next and more famous second *Vindication*, Wollstonecraft did not simply clamour for rights, but emphasized that these entail duties; but she also insisted that none could be expected to perform duties whose natural rights were not respected. Furthermore she used David Hume's *History of England* to contend that England's laws were the product of historical contingency and insisted that only those institutions that could withstand the scrutiny of reason and be shown to be in conformity with natural rights and God's justice merited respect and obedience. There was no question of blanket reverence for the past and its juridical legacy. As for civilization, she thought its progress very uneven and dismissed the culture of politeness and polish as nothing but a screen behind which hypocrisy, egotism and greed festered unchecked. Finally, opposing nature and reason to artifice and politeness, she made herself the true patriot and Burke the fickle Francophile. She was the clear-headed independent thinker, he the emotive creature of a system of patronage. She exhibited manly virtues, his effeminacy.

She condemned marriages of convenience together with late marriages: both fostered immorality in her view. Indeed, from her perspective, nearly every aspect of the prevailing culture had that consequence, for, in bringing girls up to be nothing but empty headed play-things, parents for a morally bankrupt society. Such beings could never make dutiful mothers, as they took the horizon to be the eyes of the men they flirted with. The moral depravity of a society devoted to the acquisition of property and its conspicuous display rather than to the pursuit of reason and the protection of natural rights found the means of its reproduction in the family, she contended. Here her dispute was not just with Burke, but implicitly also with Price. In his sermon, Price had deplored the sexual depravity of the times that he saw embodied even in those he considered patriots. But to seek only to vindicate the rights of men, as Price had done, was insufficient and misconceived. If one sought a truly moral society, the family had to be changed and this, in turn, required a complete change in the nature of the relationship between men and women before, and within, marriage. Only a sound upbringing of both the sexes could secure that. This was the nub of her attack on political theorists and educationalists alike.

When Wollstonecraft came to write *The Vindication of the Rights of Woman,* the moral rejuvenation of society and the happiness of individual women were woven together. Women were ill-prepared for their duties as social beings and imprisoned in a web of false expectations that would inevitably make them miserable. She wanted women to be transformed into rational and independent beings whose sense of worth came, not from their appearance, but from their inner perception of self-command and knowledge. Women had to be educated; their minds and bodies had to be trained. This would make them good companions, wives, mothers and citizens. Above all it would make them fully human, beings ruled by reason and characterized by self-command. Besides criticisms of existing pedagogical practices and theories, most notably Rousseau's *Emile* (1762), the *Vindication* contains many social and political proposals which range from a detailed outline of necessary changes in school curriculum to the suggestion that women be granted not only civil and political rights, but have elected representatives of their own. It argues that women should be taught skills so as to be able to support themselves and their children in widowhood, and never have to marry or remarry out of financial necessity. It seeks to reclaim midwifery for women, against the encroachment of men into this profession, and contends that women could be physicians just as well as nurses. It urges women to extend their interests to encompass politics and the concerns of the whole of humanity. It also contains advice on how to make marriages last. In Wollstonecraft's view, marriages ought to have friendship rather than physical attraction as their basis. Husbands and wives ought not, moreover, to be overly intimate and should maintain a degree of reserve toward's each other.

Wollstonecraft wanted women to aspire to full citizenship, to be worthy of it, and this necessitated the development of reason. Rational women would perceive their real duties. They would forgo the world of mere appearances, the world of insatiable needs on which eighteenth-century society was based, as Adam Smith had explained more lucidly than anyone, and of which France was the embodiment, in Wollstonecraft's conception.

That she embraced the social and economic consequences of her vision of happy marriages, based on friendship in her subsequent work, *An Historical and Moral View of the Origin and Progress of the French Revolution;* (1794). In that work, she endeavored, amongst other things, to assess the merits and demerits of the progress of humanity and establish the causes of French despotism. The picture she drew of *ancient regime* France was of a country ruled by superstition, and morally and politically degenerates. Borrowing from Adam Smith, *Theory of Moral Sentiments* (1759) and *Wealth of Nations* (1776) she had drawn on previously, she sketched a possible future society in which the division of labor would be kept to a minimum and the sexes would be not only educated together but encouraged to work in family units. Single sex institutions and, for instance, all-male workshops encouraged lasciviousness in her view. She thus looked forward to a society in which small businesses and farms would provide basic, instead of superfluous, needs.

Mary Wollstonecraft is a Janus-faced in political theory. Writing in the midst of a tradition of political theory dominated by men, she employs many of their techniques, assumptions, and arguments regarding human nature and government, yet her conclusions define a new role for woman in society-that of equals to men. Thus her political philosophy both looks backward in its borrowing of traditional tools of analysis and looks forward in her innovative use of these tools to serve new ends that challenged the gender-roles beliefs that were embedded in, and supported by the writings of Hobbes, Locke and Rousseau.

Mary Wollstonecraft took many of the arguments of modern politics and science and applied them to women. Her second, *A Vindication* was widely read during her time and often commented upon by both her contemporaries and later feminists, who described it as the origin and touchstone of modern feminism.

Mary Wollstonecraft turned much of then-contemporary political theory on its head. The tools of reason that the political writings of thinkers such as Machiavelli, Hobbes, Locke and Rousseau had employed to challenge the authority of the church, faith, and absolute monarchy were instead directed at the views they had on women. Wollstonecraft joined her male theorists in attacking the religious and familial metaphors that supported all three of these institutions, but she extended their arguments to question the conventional assumptions about the nature of men and women. Thus while she shared much with these thinkers, she also broke new ground.

For philosophers such as Locke and Hobbes, in place of earlier appeals to God and the Bible to sustain authority, novel concepts articulated a new vision of politics. These concepts included appeals to social contracts constructed by individuals and contractual analogies as the basis of a political order that had to ultimately rest upon a rational foundation if it were to be considered legitimate. Hence ultimate political power resided in the individual who, outside of political society, created and defined the scope and authority of the polity. But the development of modern political assumptions and ideas was primarily undertaken by men. Although the use of reason and the new assumptions challenged many traditional assertions about politics, views on the family and the role of women in both the family and politics were generally left undisturbed. Social contract logic redefined political society as a voluntary and artificial community constructed by humans, not by God. But it was a contract by and among men that appeared to exclude women from participation. Thus women were still relegated to a secondary status.

The emergence of social contract thinking posed many challenges to the traditional role of women, however. First, modern social contract thinking assumed that the construction of political society was an act of reason or rationality. Hobbes, Locke, and Rousseau employed various conceptions of reason to challenge old political truths en route to showing how men, equipped with deliberative capacity, could create a new type of political order premised on consent. But the reason they defined, as universal, was really something found only among men, especially those who had been educated to control or eliminate the biases and passions that clouded the human understanding. Men had rational capacity, and women a more emotional, passionate, of affective personality, meaning that there were contrasting roles for men and women due to their contrasting natures. Rousseau wrote in *Emile* that men and women have different capacities, and therefore Emile and Sophie should be educated differently in order to assume their respective roles as citizen-man and wife.

In emphasizing that political society is voluntary and premised on individual consent, writers such as Hobbes and Locke had to contend with defining how women consented to their roles. For premodern thinkers, justifying the subordination of women through consent was not problem because appeals to religion, tradition, and nature, not reason or personal consent, were invoked to defend it. But among the moderns, recasting society in terms of secular, rational, and consensual arguments meant that these same arguments could be applied to family and gender roles. Despite attempts to apply some of their political assumptions and tools of analysis to the family, for the most part modern philosophers exempted the private realm of women and family from the logic of their own arguments. The problem for Hobbes and Locke, as well as for other political philosophers, was how to argue that women are free and rational enough to consent to a voluntary political order and at the same time argue that women are not free or rational and are therefore properly subordinate to men. These writers were trying to contend with a contradictory vision of human nature: that men, when educated or civilized, achieve their real rational nature, but that women are naturally passionate or irrational and that education does not change this. One way out of these dilemmas was not to challenge the stereotypes at all, to just live with the contradictions. This meant the continued use of patriarchal and familial assumptions that date back to Aristotle, appropriated to serve new ends. As political society was redefined, so was the family. Yet the traditional-family model was never severed from the assumption that it was natural. It was redefined so that the patriarchal underpinnings continued to support it. Reason failed to challenge the structures of the family and women's roles, a redefined political order continued to support them, and a social contract among men presupposed a sexual contract that subordinated women.

In *A Vindication of the Rights of Woman*, Wollstonecraft argued against the proposition that women are naturally emotional or intellectually inferior: Her contention is that the lack of intellectual development in women is due to the differences in educational opportunities between the two sexes. While men receive an intellectual education, women are left to be educated by society, which results in cultivation of emotional and feminine traits. Wollstonecraft agreed in large part with Rousseau that manners are artificial, simply the product of society and education. But while Rousseau argues that the traits of men in society are artificial and those of women natural, Wollstonecraft extends Rousseau's arguments by asserting that feminine traits are the products of social convention and opinion as much as masculine ones are. *A Vindication of the Rights of Women* is in many ways as much a response to Rousseau and his discussion of Emile, Sophie, and gender roles in *Emile*, Wollstonecraft appropriates many of Rousseau's assumptions regarding men in civilization and addresses them to the circumstances facing women. She thus questions the differences in social roles, education, and expectations between men and women in Rousseau's works and argues for similar educationall opportunities for both. For Wollstonecraft, the character of women is artificial, a consequence of the roles society defines for them. Women are fond of dress and gossip; are helpless, emotional, and weak; and act like children not because it is their nature but because they are educated or trained to be this way. The primary focus of Mary Wollstonecraft's arguments was directed toward the liberation of women from conventional societal views. Paralleling but diverging from Rousseau, her primary concern is reformation of the educational system. Change the way people are educated, and one will create a new and more equal society. But much like Locke, reformation of the family appears to be key to political reform. If John Locke rethought the relationship of the family to civil society in an effort to reject the patriarchialism of Filmer, Wollstonecraft takes Locke's arguments to their logical conclusion, making marriage a voluntary union of equals. Such a marriage is the model for political society. Thus she does not advocate abandoning marriage as a cornerstone for civil society; instead Wollstonecraft reinvents it to serve her political vision.

Mary Wollstonecraft did not ignore the need for other political reforms, and she addresses them throughout her writings. Yet her political reforms are dual edged. On the one hand she called for radical change – equal respect and treatment of men and women-but she seemed to believe that this equalization of gender roles an occur within the institutions called for by many other of the reformers of the day. Like John Locke and Thomas Paine, she called for the abolition of monarchy and aristocratic privilege, and she appeared to endorse a republican form of government that protects both liberty and virtue. In fact, she endorsed a vision of an ideal or good government very much in language reminiscent of Locke, in that the "end of all political association is the preservation of the natural and imprescriptible rights of man which rights are-liberty, property, security, and the resistance of opposition.

Wollstonecraft also attacked as corrupt both elections and parliamentary representation. She advocated that women should have their own representatives while rejecting representation in general because it fosters despotism. Moreover, in joining perhaps some of the more radical reformers of the day who saw society as pervaded by inequalities of all types, she contended that "the end of government ought to be, to destroy this inequality by protecting the weak. Wollstonecraft's conception of the state, then, is more activist or interventionist than might be expected , in that tending to the improvement of the virtue of the people ought to be a duty of the government. This, of course, would primarily be accomplished through her education reforms."

Finally, Wollstonecraft also demanded an end to primogeniture and reform of marriage property laws. She called for abolition of the death penalty, public executions, slavery, and standing armies. She also demands religious toleration. Other reformers of the day advocated similar positions. However, in her last book, *The Wrongs of Women*, she parted company form her male contemporaries and presses the case for divorce. While radical in its time, perhaps the right to divorce was a logical application of Locke's right to political revolution, only in this case applied to marriage. If both civil societies and marriages are the product of voluntary consent to secure certain ends, the parties to both should equally have the right to end both of these institutions. Mary Wollstonecraft is an early modern theorist sharing many ideas with other moderns such as Locke and Rousseau. She adopts the language of reason and the Enlightenment used by men to question political and parental authority and the structure of the family. By doing so, she seeks to extend the revolution of reason and liberalism to the status of women in the state as well as the family.

Although woll stone craft was very much encouraged by her publisher, Joseph Johnson, she received little support from fellow intellectuals in her lifetime. Even Godwin did not take her seriously on their first meeting. Very few of the foremost women writers gave Wollstonecraft their wholehearted support in the eighteenth century. Many mocked her, but only very rarely were her ideas genuinely assessed in the way they have come to be in the last few decades. By the end of the 1790s and for most of the nineteenth century, Wollstonecraft was derided by many, because of what her scandalous personal life. There were, to be sure, important exceptions, especially in America. Such praise as she did receive on both sides of the Atlantic came, however, from only the most superficial acquaintance with her ideas or her intellectual persona.

In the twentieth century, and especially following the growth of feminism in the Anglo-Saxon world in the 1960s, scholars disregarded the vicissitudes of Wollstonecraft's private life and honored her as the first English feminist. She came to be read principally within the context of the history of the women's movement. In the last two decades of the twentieth century, however, a growing number of commentators have looked at *A Vindication of the Rights of Women* in its historical and intellectual context rather than in isolation or in relation to subsequent feminist theories. Wollstonecraft is thus no longer seen as just a scandalous literary figure, nor the embodiment of a nascent feminism which only reached maturity two hundred years later, but as an Enlightenment moral and political thinker whose works present a self-contained argument about the kind of change society would need to undergo for men and women to be virtuous in both the private and the public sphere and thereby secure the chance of a measure of happiness.

Wollstonecraft's political legacy is significant yet ambiguous. Her writings influenced later feminists such as Susan B. Anthony and Elizabeth Cady Stanton. Emma Golden and Suzanne Lafollette, both famous in the early twentieth century, saw wall stone craft's legacy as declaration of independence for woman. However, Harriet Martineau, an important nineteenth- century British writer, stated that Wollstonecraft was "not a successful champion of woman and her Rights" because she was a "poor victim of passion, with no control over her own peace. " To Martineau, Wollstonecraft's personal life and unhappiness made the claims in her book too personal to address the broader needs and concerns of woman. For others, depending on their viewpoint, Wollstonecraft's advocacy of universal morality and same set of duties for men and women, and her appeal for women to be treated more like men, offer either the promise of equality or a denial of women's special insights, experiences, and feeling that distinguish them from men.

Mary Wollstonecraft's assertions that men and women are alike in all essential characteristics, except for those produced as a result of education, anticipate later feminists arguments over the biological versus the social; that is, which factors account for differences between the two, while others have contended that, except for the anatomical differences, the only important distinctions to emerge so far are those that are the result of education or political socialization.

Yet one wonders if the changes Wollstonecraft wanted could occur as she hoped. She seemed to believe that men and women could achieve equality within the existing political and familial institutions, but could these institutions really permit the equality she wanted? Contemporary feminists, such as Catherine MacKinnon, argue that the law and society's political institutions are based on male assumptions such that women can never achieve equality within them. A wholesale reform of society is needed – if women are to achieve parity. The debate over whether women can become equals within the existing institutions, or whether the emancipation of women could only take place within the context of more radical reform, remains a question to this day.

Vindication offers either the right prescription for women's emancipation by challenging family authority and contrasting gender roles, or it yet again limits women by preserving the family structure, maintaining traditional roles, and denying the distinct sphere of experience all women share. Whatever the final consensus on her legacy, Mary Wollstonecraft represents an important voice in the history of political thought. By extending the arguments of seventeenth and eighteenth century philosophers beyond religion and the political community to the family, she launched important challenges to the way tradition, politics, reason, and gender interacted.

—Editor

Vindication of the Rights of Woman

Of the pernicious effects which arise from the unnatural distinctions established in society.

From the respect paid to property flow, as from a poisoned fountain, most of the evils and vices which render this world such a dreary scene to the contemplative mind. For it is in the most polished society that noisome reptiles and venomous serpents lurk under the rank herbage; and there is voluptuousness pampered by the still sultry air, which relaxes every good disposition before it ripens into virtue.

One class presses on another, for all are aiming to procure respect on account of their property; and property once gained will procure the respect due only to talents and virtue. Men neglect the duties incumbent on man, yet are treated like demigods. Religion is also separated from morality by a ceremonial veil, yet men wonder that the world is almost, literally speaking, a den of sharpers or oppressors.

There is a homely proverb, which speaks a shrewd truth, that whoever the devil finds idle he will employ. And what but habitual idleness can hereditary wealth and titles produce? For man is so constituted that he can only attain a proper use of his faculties by sing them, and will not exercising them unless necessity of some kind first set the wheels in motion. Virtue likewise can only be acquired by the discharge of relative duties; but the importance of these sacred duties will scarcely be felt by the being who is cajoled out of his humanity by the flattery of sycophants. There must be more equality established in society, or morality will never gain ground, and this virtuous equality will not rest firmly even when founded on a rock, if one-half of mankind be chained to its bottom by fate, for they will be continually undermining it through ignorance or pride.

It is vain to expect virtue from women till they are in some degree independent of if nay, it is vain to expect the strength of natural affection which would make them good wives and mothers. Whilst they are absolutely dependent on their husbands they will be cunning, mean, and selfish; and the men who can be gratified by the fawning fondness of spaniel-like affection have not much delicacy, for love is not to be bought; in any sense of the words, its silken wings are instantly shrivelled up when anything beside a return in kind is sought. Yet whilst wealth enervates men, and women live, as it were, by their personal charms, how can we expect them to discharge those ennobling dudes which equally require exertion and self-denial? Hereditary property sophisticates the mind, and the unfortunate victims to it—if I may so express myself—swathed from their birth, seldom exert the locomotive faculty or body of mind, and thus viewing everything through one medium, and that a false one, they are unable to discern in what true merit and happiness consist. False, indeed, must be the light when the drapery of situation hides the man, and makes him stalk in masquerade, dragging from one scene of dissipation to another the nerveless limbs that hang with stupid listlessness, and rolling round the vacant eye, which plainly tells us that there is no mind at home.

I mean therefore to infer that the society is not properly organized which does not compel men and women to discharge their respective duties by making it the only way to acquire that countenance from their fellow-creatures, which every human being wishes some way to attain. The respect consequently which is paid to wealth and mere personal charms is a true north-east blast that blights the tender blossoms of affection and virtue. Nature has wisely attached affections to duties to sweeten toil, and to give that vigour to the exertions of reason which only the heart can give. But the affections which is put on merely because it is die appropriated insignia of a certain character, when its duties are not fulfilled, is one of the empty compliments which vice and folly are obliged to pay to virtue and the real nature of things.

To illustrate my opinion, I need only observe that when a woman is admired for her beauty, and suffers herself to be so far intoxicated by the admiration she receives as to neglect to discharge the indispensable duty of a mother, she sins against herself by neglecting to cultivate an affection that would equally tend to make her useful and happy. True happiness—I mean all the contentment and virtuous satisfaction that can be snatched in this imperfect state—must arise from well-regulated affections, and an affection includes a duty. Men are not aware of the misery they cause, and the vicious weakness cherish, by only inciting women to render themselves pleasing; they do not consider that they thus make natural and artificial duties clash by sacrificing the comfort and responsibility of a woman's life to voluptuous notions of beauty when in nature they all harmonize.

Cold would be the heart of a husband, were he not rendered unnatural by early debauchery, who did not feel more delight at seeing his child suckled by its mother than the most artful wanton tricks could ever raise, yet this natural way of cementing matrimonial tie, and twisting esteem with fonder recollections, wealth leads women to spurn. To preserve their beauty, and wear the flowery crown of the day, which gives them a kind of right to reign for a short time over the. sex, they neglect to stamp impressions on their husbands' hearts that would be remembered with more tenderness when the snow on the head began to chill the bosom than even their virgin charms. The maternal a reasonable affectionate woman is very interesting, and the chastened dignity with which a mother returns the caresses that she and her child receive from a father who has been fulfilling the serious duties of his station is not only a respectable, but a beautiful sight. So singular, indeed, are my feelings—and I have endeavoured not to catch factitious ones—that after having been fatigued with the sight of insipid grandeur and the slavish ceremonies that with cumbrous pomp supplied the place of domestic affections, I have turned to some other scene to relieve my eye by resting it on the refreshing green everywhere scattered by Nature. I have then viewed with pleasure a woman nursing her children, and discharging the duties of her station with perhaps merely a servant-maid to take off her hands the servile part of the household business. I have seen her prepare herself and children, with only the luxury of cleanliness, to receive her husband, who, returning weary home in the evening, found smiling babes and a clean hearth. My heart has loitered in the midst of the group, and has even throbbed with sympathetic emotion when the scraping of the well-known foot has raised a pleasing tumult.

Whilst my benevolence has been gratified by contemplating this artless picture, I have thought that a couple of this description, equally necessary and independent of each other, because each fulfilled the respective dudes of their station, possessed all that life could give. Raised sufficiently above abject poverty not to be obliged to weigh the consequence of every farthing they spend, and having sufficient to prevent their attending to a frigid system of economy which narrows both heart and mind, I declare, so vulgar are my conceptions, that I know not what is wanted to render this the happiest as well as the most respectable situation in the world, but a taste for literature, to throw a little variety and interest into social converse, and some superfluous money to give to the needy and to buy books. For it is not pleasant when the heart is opened by compassion, and the head active in arranging plans of usefulness, to have a prim urchin continually twitching back the elbow to prevent the hand from drawing out an almost empty purse, whispering at the same time some prudential maxim about the priority of justice.

Destructive, however, as riches and inherited honours are to the human character, women are more debased and cramped, if possible, by them than men, because men may still in some degree unfold their faculties by becoming soldiers and statesmen.

As soldiers, I grant they can now only gather for the most part vain-glorious laurels, whilst they adjust to a hair the European balance, taking especial care that no bleak northern nook or sound incline the beam. But the days of true heroism are over, when a citizen fought for his country like a Fabricius or a Washington, and then returned to his farm to let his virtuous fervour run in a more placid, but not a less salutary, stream. No, our British heroes are oftener sent from the gaming-table than from the plough; and their passions have been rather inflamed by hanging with dumb suspense on the turn of a die, than sublimated by panting after the adventurous march of virtue in the historic page.

The statesman, it is true, might with more propriety quit the faro bank, or card-table, to guide the helm, for he has still but to shuffle and trick—the whole system of British politics, if system it may courteously be called, consisting in multiplying dependents and contriving taxes which grind the poor to pamper the rich. Thus a war, or any wild-goose chase, is, as the vulgar use the phrase, a lucky turn-up' of patronage for the minister, whose chief merit is the art of keeping himself in place. It is not necessary then that he should have bowels for the poor, so he can secure for his family the odd trick. Or should some show of respect, for what is termed with ignorant ostentation an Englishman's birthright, be expedient to bubble the gruff mastiff that he has to lead by the nose, he can make an empty show, very safely, by giving his single voice, and suffering his light squadron to file off to the other side. And when a question of humanity is agitated, he may dip a sop in the milk of human kindness to silence Cerberus, and talk of the interest which his heart takes in an attempt to make the earth no longer cry for vengeance as it sucks in its children's blood, though his cold hand may at the very moment rivet their chains, by sanctioning the abominable traffic. A minister is no longer a minister, than while he can carry a point, which he is determined to carry. Yet it is not necessary that a minister should feel like a man, when a bold push might shake his seat.

But, to have done with these episodical observations, let me return to the more specious slavery which chains the very soul of woman, keeping her for ever under the bondage of ignorance.

The preposterous distinctions of rank, which render civilization a curse, by dividing the world between voluptuous tyrants and cunning envious dependents, corrupt, almost equally, every class of people, because respectability is not attached to the discharge of the relative duties of life, but to the station, and when the duties are not fulfilled the affections cannot gain sufficient strength to fortify the virtue of which they are the natural reward. Still there are some loop-holes out of which a man may creep, and dare tolhinkandact for himself; but for a woman it is an Herculean task, because she has difficulties peculiar to her sex to overcome, which re-quire almost superhuman powers.

A truly benevolent legislator always endeavours lo make it the interest of each individual to be virtuous; and thus private virtue becoming the cement of public happiness, an orderly whole is consolidated by the tendency of all the parts towards a common centre. But the private or public virtue of woman is very problematical, for Rousseau, and a numerous list of male writers, insist that she should all her life be subjected to a severe restraint, that of propriety. Why subject her lo propriety—blind propriety—if she be capable of acting from a nobler spring, if she be an heir of immortality? Is sxigar always to be produced by vital blood? Is one half of the human species, like the poor African slaves, to be subjected to prejudices that brutalize them, when principles would be a surer guard, only to sweeten the cup of man? Is not this indirectly to deny woman reason for a gift is a mockery, if it be unfit for use.

Women are, in common with men, rendered weak and luxurious by the relaxing pleasures which wealth procures; but added to this they are made slaves to their person arid must render them alluring that man may lend them his reason to guide their tottering steps aright Or should they be ambitious, they must govern their tyrants by sinister tricks, for without rights there cannot be any incumbent duties. The laws respecting woman, which I mean to discuss in a future part, make an absurd unit of a man and his wife; and then, by the easy transition of only considering him as responsible, she is reduced to a mere cipher.

The being who discharges the duties of its station is independent; and, speaking of women at large, their first duty is to themselves as rational creatures, and the next, in point of importance, as citizens, is that, which includes so many, of a mother. The in life which dispenses with their fulfilling this duty, necessarily degrades them by making them mere dolls. Or should they turn to something more important than merely fitting drapery upon a smooth block, their minds are only occupied by some soft platonic attachment; or the actual management of an intrigue may keep their thoughts in motion; for when they neglect domestic duties, they have it not in their power to take the field and march and counter-march like soldiers, or wrangle in the senate to keep their faculties from rusting.

I know that, as a proof of the inferiority of the sex, Rousseau has exultingly exclaimed, How can they leave the nursery for the camp! And the camp has by some moralists been proved the school of the most heroic virtues; though I think it would puzzle a keen casuist to prove the reasonableness of the greater number of wars that have dubbed heroes. I do not mean to consider this question critically; because, having frequently viewed these freaks of ambition as the first natural mode of civilization, when die ground must be torn up, and the woods cleared by fire and sword, I do not choose to call them pests; but surely the present system of war has little connection with virtue of any denomination, being rather the school of finesse and effeminacy than of fortitude.

Yet, if defensive war, the only justifiable war, in the present advanced state of society, where virtue can show its face and ripen amidst the rigours which purify the air on the mountain's top, were alone to be adopted as just and glorious, the true heroism of antiquity might again animate female bosoms. But fair and softly, gentle reader, male or female, do not alarm thyself, for though I have compared the character of a modern soldier with that of a civilized woman, I am not going to advise them to turn their distaff into a musket, though I sincerely wish to see the bayonet converted into a pruning-hook. I only re-created an imagination, fatigued by contemplating the vices and follies which all proceed from a feculent stream of wealth that has muddied the pure rills of natural affection, by supposing that society will some time or other be so constituted, that man must necessarily fulfil the duties of a citizen, or be despised, and that while he was employed in any of the departments of civil life, his wife, also an active citizen, should be equally intent to manage her family, educate her children, and assist her neighbours.

But to render her really virtuous and useful, she must not, if she discharge her civil duties, want individually the protection of civil laws; she must not be dependent on her husband's bounty for her subsistence during his life, or support after his death; for how can a being be generous who has nothing of its own? or virtuous who is not free? The wife, in the present state of things, who is faithful to her husband, and neither suckles not educates her children, scarcely deserves the name of a wife, and has no right to that of a citizen. But take away natural rights, and duties become null.

Women then must be considered as only the wanton solace of men, when they become so weak in mind and body that they cannot exert themselves unless to pursue some frivolous pleasure, or to invent some frivolous fashion. What can be a more melancholy sight to a thinking mind, than to look into the numerous carriages that drive helter-skelter about this metropolis in a morning full of pale-faced creatures who are flying from themselves! I have often wished, with Dr Johnson, to place some of them in a little shop with half a dozen children looking up to their languid countenances for support I am much mistaken, if some latent vigour would not soon give health and spirit to their eyes, and some lines drawn by the exercise of reason on the blank cheeks, which before were only undulated by dimples, might restore lost dignity to the character, or rather enable it to attain the true dignity of its nature. Virtue is not to be acquired even by speculation, much less by the negative supineness that wealth naturally generates.

Besides, when poverty is more disgraceful than even vice, is not morality cut to the quick? Still to avoid misconstruction, though I consider that women in the common walks of life are called to fulfil the dudes of wives and mothers, by religion and reason, I cannot help lamenting that women of a superior cast have not a road open by which they can pursue more extensive plans of usefulness and independence. I may excite laughter, by dropping a hint, which I mean to pursue, some future time, for I really think that women ought to have representatives, instead of being arbitrarily governed without having any direct share allowed them in the deliberations of government.

But, as the whole system of representation is now, in this country, only a convenient handle for despotism, they need not complain, for they are as well represented as a numerous class of hard-working mechanics, who pay for the support of royalty when they can scarcely stop their children's mouths with bread. How are they represented whose very sweat supports the splendid stud of an heir-apparent, or varnishes the chariot of some female favourite who looks down on shame? Taxes on the very necessaries of life, enable an endless tribe of idle princes and princesses to pass with stupid pomp before a gaping crowd, who almost worship the very parade which costs them so dear. This is mere gothic grandeur, something like the barbarous useless parade of having sentinels on horseback at Whitehall, which I could never view without a mixture of contempt and indignation.

How strangely must the mind be sophisticated when this sort of state impresses it! But, till these monuments of folly are levelled by virtue, similar follies will leaven the whole mass. For the same character, in some degree, will prevail in the aggregate of society; and the refinements of luxury, or the vicious repinings of envious poverty, will equally banish virtue from society, considered as the characteristic of that society, or only allow it to appear as one of the stripes of the harlequin coat, worn by the civilized man.

In the superior ranks of life, every duty is done by deputies, as if duties could ever! be waived, and the vain pleasures which consequent idleness forces the rich to pursue, I appear so enticing to the next rank, that the numerous scramblers for wealth sacrifice everything to tread on their heels. The most sacred trusts are then considered as sinecures, because they were procured by interest, and only sought to enable a man to keep good company. Women, in particular, all want to be ladies. Which is simply to have nothing to do, but listlessly to go they scarcely care where, for they cannot tell what.

But what have women to do in society? I may be asked, but to loiter with easy surely you would not condemn them all to suckle fools and chronicle small beer! No. Women might certainly study the art of healing and be physicians as well as nurses. And | midwifery, decency seems to allot to them though I am afraid the word midwife, in our dictionaries, will soon give place to accoucheur, and one proof of the former delicacy the sex be effaced from the language.

They might also study politics, and settle their benevolence on the broadest basis; for the reading of history will scarcely be more useful than the perusal of romances if read as mere biography; if the character of the times, the political improvements, etc., be not observed. In short, if it be not considered as the history of man; and not of particular men, who filled a niche in the temple of fame, and dropped into the black rolling stream of time, that silently sweeps all before it into the shapeless void called— eternity.—For shape, can it be called, "that shape hath none"?

Business of various kinds, they might likewise pursue, if they were educated in a more orderly manner, which might save many from common and legal prostitution. Women would not then marry for a support, as men accept of places under Government, and neglect the implied duties; nor would an attempt to earn their own subsistence, a most laudable one sink them almost to the level of those poor abandoned creatures who live by prostitution. For are not milliners and mantua-makers reckoned the next class? The few employments open to women, so far, from being liberal, are menial; and when a superior education enables them to take charge of the education of children as governesses, they are not treated like the tutors of sons, though even clerical tutors are not always treated in a manner calculated to render them respectable in the eyes of their pupils, to say nothing of the private comfort of the individual. But as women educated like gentlewomen, are never designed for the humiliating situation which necessity sometimes forces them to fill; these situations are considered in the light of a degradation; and they know little of the human heart, who need to be told, that nothing so painfully sharpens sensibility as such a fall in life.

Some of these women might be restrained from marrying by a proper spirit of delicacy, and others may not have had it in their power to escape in this pitiful way from servitude; is not that Government then very defective, and very unmindful of the happiness of one-half of its members, that does not provide for honest, independent women, by encouraging them to fill respectable stations? But in order to render their private virtue a public benefit, they must have a civil existence in the State, married or single; else we shall continually see some worthy woman, whose sensibility has been rendered painfully acute by undeserved contempt, droop like "the lily broken down by a plowshare."

It is a melancholy truth; yet such is the blessed effect of civilization! the most respectable women are the most oppressed; and, unless they have understandings far superior to the common run of understandings, taking in both sexes, they must, from being treated like contemptible beings, become contemptible. How many women thus waste life away the prey of discontent, who might have practised as physicians, regulated a farm, managed a shop, and stood erect, supported by their own industry, instead of hanging their heads surcharged with the dew of sensibility, that consumes the beauty to which it at first gave lustre; nay, I doubt whether pity and love are so near akin as poets feign, for I have seldom seen much compassion excited by the helplessness of females, unless they were fair; then, perhaps, pity was the soft handmaid of love, or the harbinger of lust.

How much more respectable is the woman who earns her own bread by fulfilling any duty, than the most accomplished beauty!—beauty did I say!—so sensible am I of the beauty of moral loveliness, or the harmonious propriety that attunes the passions of a well-regulated mind, that I blush at making the comparison; yet I sigh to think how few women aim at attaining this respectability by withdrawing from the giddy whirl of pleasure, or the indolent calm that, stupefies the good sort of women it sucks in.

Proud of their weakness, however, they must always be protected, guarded from care, and all the rough toils that dignify the mind. If this be the fiat of fate, if they will make themselves insignificant and contemptible, sweetly to waste "life away," let them not expect to be valued when their beauty fades, for it is the fate of the fairest flowers to be admired and pulled to pieces by the careless hand that plucked them. In how many ways do I wish, from the purest benevolence, to impress this truth on my sex; yet fear that they will not listen to a truth that dear bought experience has brought home to many an agitated bosom, nor willingly resign the privileges of rank and sex for the privileges of humanity, to which those have no claim who do not discharge its duties.

Those writers are particularly useful, in my opinion, who make man feel for man, independent of the station he fills, or the drapery of factitious sentiments. I then would fain convince reasonable men of the importance of some of my remarks; and prevail on them to weigh dispassionately the whole 'tenor of my observations. I appeal to their understandings; and, as a fellow-creature, claim, in the name of my sex, some interest in their hearts. I entreat them to assist to emancipate their companion, to make her a helpmeet for them.

Would men but generously snap our chains, and be content with rational fellowship instead of slavish obedience, they would find us more observant daughters, more affectionate sisters, more faithful wives, more reasonable mothers—in a word, better citizens. We should then love them with true affection, because we should learn to respect ourselves; and the peace of mind of a worthy man would not be interrupted by the idle vanity of his wife, nor the babes sent to nestle in a strange bosom, having never found a home in their mother's.

Feminist philosophy as an academic discipfineold not emerge until the seventies in the United States,Europe, and Australia. But this doesn't mean there were no feminist philosophers until then—far from it!There have been women philosophers since the eighteenth century, and they have made significant contributions to feminist philosophy today.

An important thing to remember aljiiofcrtbis-dsfag.gtar is that there is really no such thing as feminism; instead, there are feminisms. This is because feminism has developed out of different issues and goals in different countries, cul-

Iures, and circumstances. Feminists do not always agree on what the agenda should be, but what they do all share is a deep commitment that women and men should be treated equalSy. Beyond that, complexities have evolved.

As feminist theory has mushroomed in the field of women's studies, new inter-disciplinary bases have formed, and each of these contributes to the proliferation of feminisms. *Svralarly, feminist philosophy* must now be considered a loose term for the many varieties of feminist philosophical discourse: liberal, Marxist/ socialist, radical/ anarchical, ecological, phenomenological, postmodern, and postfeminist.

Traditional philosophy has developed around some major categories of ques-tions and issues—the ontologicai concerns of subjectivity and the nature of reality; thr epistemological concerns of truth and knowledge; the ethical concerns of morality and the good; the political concerns of rights and responsibilities—so we can see that philosophy as an intellectual discipline has provided us with the grounding to understand ordinary life as we live it. It has historically presented itself as a neutral, disinterested set of discourses, and therein lies the problem as feminist philosophers view it. Traditional philosophy is viewed by feminists as a masculine body of theoretical concepts through its sexism, its underlying patriar-chal constructs, and its social misogyny: it is a phallocentric (male-centered) dis-cursive strategy. Traditional philosophy, feminist thinkers claim, has defined women in negative ways, has misrepresented them, and has rendered them sub-servient or even invisible.

Feminist philosophy has evolved in response to these systematic injustices and demands that the fundamental questions of philosophy be reconceived before they can be reconsidered. Feminist philosophy is thus both a reconstruction of the philosophical canon and a revisionist approach to those philosophical claims that misrepresent women. The challenge of feminist philosophy is to transform the ideas of traditional philosophy by producing new ideas that include women and women's issues and ideas, particularly in the world of the other and the constitu-tion of the self. The oppositions between body and mind and between emotion and reason are gendered oppositions as viewed by feminist philosophers. The tension of these opposing alterities and the accompanying social identities that compose the field of feminist philosophy.

Feminist thought in general is often divided into categories known as first wave, second wave, postfeminism, and third wave. Note that these distinctions do have approximate timelines, but the borders are somewhat merged because femi-nists do not all agree to be categorized and have independent ideas that may carry over from one wave to another. As Marilyn Frye points out, "Thought is universal, but philosophy is local—temporally, culturally, and historically specific."

One of the grandmothers of feminist thought was Mary Wollstonecraft (1759-1797). She was a precursor of the first-wave feminist movement, which did not begin in any organized way until the 1850s and lasted to the early part of the twentieth century. Some scholars regard her as the founder of what is now the fem-inist movement. Wollstonecraft was particularly interested in the education of women, opposing Rousseau's view that women's role was to please men and be useful to them in various solicitous ways. Wollstonecraft argued that educating women to be the ornaments and playthings of men would have negative conse-quences for society in the long run as well as for the women themselves. She argued that women are as capable as men of the "masculine" virtues of wisdom and rationality if they are permitted to cultivate them. She published several important pamphlets and books, including what has now become a classic of fern.

(From *A Vindication of the Rights of Woman* by Mary Wollstonecraft, Oxfor University Press, Oxford 1993)

14

Immanuel Kant

Immanuel Kant, (1724-1804) writing at the end of the eighteenth century, is still widely considered the thinker who, more than any other, addresses the philosophical concerns of modernity. His attempt to build philosophy on a scientific basis in order to secure for it objective knowledge remains one of the dominant projects of modern philosophy.

Kant was born in Konigsberg then in Prussia but part now of Russia in 1724 and died there in 1804. The paucity of the accounts of Kant's life tells much about the manner in which he lived. Kant avoided all external change in his life. In a letter to his friend Herz, he wrote, "All changes make me anxious." This attitude led him to turn down a professorship at Hale, one of the foremost Protestant universities in Germany. Kant never married, and it is said that although he contemplated marriage once or twice, he lost the opportunity while reflecting on the matter. Kant's life was ordered according to a rigid schedule that precluded any spontaneity or disruptions. He would rise at five o'clock and work for two or three hours. He held lectures from seven or eight until nine or ten and would continue work until one o'clock. Then he would dine with one or two friends and occasionally with as many as five. Kant would then walk for an hour, spend the rest of the day in reading and meditation, and retire at ten o'clock. This rational control of his life was exemplified in his abhorrence of emotional expressiveness. All emotions of a "soft-hearted kind," as he himself called them, were alien to his nature. Schiller once said of Kant that had he been able to feel love, he would have been one of the greatest phenomena of mankind; but since he could not, there was something defective in his nature. The only emotion that Kant recognized as valid was the ethical emotion, the universal respect for the freedom of the moral person.

Kant lived a celibate life. His sexual abstinence was indicative of his general indifference to the role of pleasure in life. In the *Critique of Judgment,* he wrote that the value of life is "less than nothing" when it is measured according to the sum of pleasure. The asceticism that pervaded Kant's outlook on the world and the conduct of his life reflects the Protestant adherence to monastic discipline in everyday life. Kant was deeply influenced by the Protestantism of the world in which he lived. Although he explicitly rejected elements of his pietist upbringing, the dominant currents of ascetic Protestantism remained decisive for both his life and thought.

Kant's personal history brought him in close contact with the Pietist sect of the Reformation. Pietism was a form of Protestantism that intensified the ascetic tendencies of the Reformation, emerging in Germany as a reaction against the orthodoxy of the Lutheran church. However there is an uneasy tension in German Pietism between both Lutheran and Calvinist elements. Because of the emotional nature of Pietism, its asceticism was perhaps weaker than that made possible by the thoroughly rational nature of Calvinism. But it was certainly more deceptive to ascetic tendencies than was Orthodox Lutheranism. Kant's pietist religious and educational training exposed him to both the Lutheran and Calvinist elements of Protestantism. His parents, particularly his mother, were religious people.

Although Kant later rejected many aspects of pietism, he maintained a high respect for certain aspects of it. He wrote, "Even though the religious ideas of that time and the concepts of what they called virtue and piety were anything but clear and adequate, still they really got hold of the basic thing. You can say what you want about pietism— the people who were serious about it were outstanding in a praiseworthy respect. They possess the highest thing men can possess, that calm, that serenity, that inner peace undisturbed by any passion." On entering the university of Kenigsborg, Kant began his studies in the philosophy faculty, which included the study of mathematics and science.

In some respects, Kant sought to distance himself from the religious influences of his youth. German pietism attempted to recover Luther's early teaching regarding the importance of faith rather than dogma. Thus pietism led at times to an excess of emotionalism, an obsession with the internal dimensions of religious faith. Kant's criticism of pietism was directed against this emphasis on internal feelings and the conception of piety as based on a personal relation to God.

Despite Kant's rejection of pietist practice, certain fundamental elements of Protestantism remained decisive for his thought. Paulsen regards Kant as the "finisher of what Luther had begun." Luther had revolted against the confusion of religion and science in scholastic philosophy and attempted to free faith from knowledge and faith epitomizes this Protestant position. In the preface to the *Critique of Pure Reason*, Kant writes, "I have therefore found it necessary to deny knowledge, in order to make room for faith." Moreover, Kant's treatment of practical reason, which emphasizes the individual relation to the moral law as opposed to the dominance of church authority, echoes the Protestant turn toward the inner man.

Kant distanced himself from the formal practice of Christianity and toward the end of his life his writings on religion brought him into conflict with the religious enthusiasts in the government. Yet his moral philosophy can be seen as the "translation of this Christianity from the religious language to the language of reflection: in place of God we have pure reason, instead of the Ten Commandments the moral law, and in place of heaven the intelligible world." In Paulsen's view, Kant reflects the "true spirit" of Christianity. He writes, "Its depreciation of the world and its pumps and glories, its insistence on the equality of all men before God—these are all characteristic of Kant's view of life."

Kant's denial of the value of pleasure reflects the ascetic discipline that so strongly characterized Calvinist strains of Protestantism. But his transposition of these religious tenets into a rational morality did not leave these values untouched. Kant's basic disagreement with the pietism of his youth was its unbridled emotionalism and personalism. Insofar as Lutheranism originally led in the direction of an emotional faith, Kant distanced himself from it. But Kant's inner man distinguishes between acting according to inclination and acting according to duty. Obedience to the rational law, not the inner felt emotion, provides the inner bond of Kantian morality. Consequently, it is not the natural endowment of sensibility that forms the basis of original sin in Kant's philosophy of religion. Instead, he attributes the evil in human nature to an impurity of disposition that shows itself in the failure to make the law the only determining ground of the will.

The effect of these religious elements in Kant's thought extends beyond his moral theory into his discussion of knowledge. Paulsen's suggestion that Kant completed the work of Luther by separating faith from reason is misleading if it implies that Kant's treatment of reason is free of ascetic tendencies. Kant's treatment of knowledge cannot be divorced from the practices that shaped his own orientation toward life. His theory of knowledge, morality, and beauty must be examined in the context of this ascetic ideology.

His early works (known as the pre-critical' writings) were followed by a period of silence (1770-1781) and then by the first of the three great Critiques-the *Critique of Pure Reason* (1781,). Conversed with a systematic way with the entire field of epistemology and metaphysics; it was followed by the *Critique of Practical Reason* (1788), concerned with ethics, and the *Critique of Judgment* (1790), concerned largely with aesthetics. Among Kant's other works, the most important are the *Prolegomena to any Future Metaphysics* (1783) and *The Foundation of the Metaphysic of Morals* (1785).

Of diminutive stature and austere habits, Kant was nevertheless a gregarious man, a brilliant talker, and a loved and respected member of social and literary circles. He was a founding spirit of the German Romantic movement, which was to change the consciousness of Europe, and the father of nineteenth- century idealism. He was the greatest philosopher since Aristotle, and his most important book — the *Critique of Pure Reason*—is of an intellectual depth and grandeur that defy description.

Kant's early philosophical inspiration had been the system of Leibniz. But despite this influence, which is everywhere apparent in the *Critique of Pure Reason*—Kant's philosophy is unique, both in its methods and in its aims. In order to understand those aims we must again consider the impact, during the seventeenth and eighteenth centuries, of the rise of science. Science presented itself as a universal discipline, the premises of which were certain, and the methods of which were disputable only by the adoption of a stance of philosophical skepticism. No one could engage in science without accepting both the established results of his predecessors, and the empirical methods that led to their discovery. Science presented a picture of unanimity and objectivity, which no system of metaphysics could rival. Forced by this fact into unnatural self-consciousness, philosophy found itself with no results that it could offer as its own peculiar contribution to the fund of human knowledge. The very possibility of metaphysics was thrown in doubt, and this doubt was only exacerbated by Hume's radical skepticism-a skepticism, which, according to Kant, aroused him from his 'dogmatic slumbers'. All philosophy, then for Kant, must begin from the question 'How is metaphysics possible?

In answer to that question, Kant attempted a systematic critique of human thought and reason. He tried to explore not just scientific beliefs, but all beliefs, in order to establish exactly what is presupposed in the act of belief as such. He wished to describe the nature and limits of knowledge, not just in respect of scientific discovery, but absolutely: his metaphysics was designed, not as a postscript to physics, but as the very foundation of discursive thought.

According to Kant, scientific knowledge is a posteriori: it arises from, and is based in actual experience. Science, therefore, deals not with necessary truths but with matters of contingent fact, however, it rests upon certain universal axioms and principles, Because their truth is presupposed at the start of any thoughts it seems both vulnerable to philosophical skepticism and at the same time basic to our conception of ourselves. Once again, Kant considered himself to be responding to the challenge of Hume's skepticism.

Hume formulated the fundamental premises of this skepticism in two succinct but complex thoughts. First, there is no derivation of an 'ought' from an 'is' which is to say that moral judgments, since they do not describe how things are, gain no justification from natural science. Secondly, since the sole motive to action is desire, and reason itself is no motive, the only rational justification that can be offered for any action lies in showing that it contributes to the satisfaction of an agent's wishes. All reasoning is reasoning about means, and has no authority beyond that of the desire, which compels it. There is no innate power of reason to overrule desire, and hence no power of reason to determine action objectively.

The first great insight contained in Kant's moral philosophy was the realization that Hume's first source of skepticism was of no real significance. Suppose that the 'is—ought' problem were solved, so that moral judgments could be determined with the objectivity of a natural science. That would not refute skepticism. For to refute skepticism we must also show how such judgments provide reasons for acting. In other words, Hume's second objection would still be sufficient to refute the objectivity of morals. On the other hand, if we can show that there are objective reasons for acting, then the 'is—ought' problem becomes insignificant. It no longer matters that we can or cannot derive an ought' from an is' for morality will gain its rational basis independently. It seemed to Kant therefore that the ancient distinction between theoretical and practical reason should be revived, and the foundations of the second explored with the same discipline that he had devoted to the exposition of the first. This reintroduction and elaboration of the concept of practical reason was among one of the most influential of Kant's achievements and provided the grounds not only for his own partial repudiation of the metaphysics of the first Critique but also for many of the insights of later German idealists.

Theoretical reason guides belief, and practical reason guides action; the first therefore aims at truth, the second at rightness. The first, when employed legitimately, Kant called understanding; when illegitimately, pure reason. Reason can, however, also be employed legitimately, but it must then be subjected to those determinations which transform it into practical reason. Understanding issues in judgments, practical reason issues in imperatives, which may be acted on, but which cannot be called true. Practical reason consists, therefore, in the justification of imperatives. And the problem is to define and validate a concept of objectivity, which will both apply to such to imperatives and generate a recognizable system of morality.

Kant disagrees entirely with Hume's discounting of the possibility that reason can settle whether an act is morally right. In Kant's opinion, reason and reason alone can settle this. Kant argued that scientific inquiry can never reveal to us principles that we know hold without exception. Scientific inquiry is based on experience, and in the final analysis experience can show only how things have been to this point, not how they must be. For example, science reveals to us physical "laws" that hold true of the universe as it is now, but it cannot provide absolutely conclusive guarantees that these laws wiil forever hold true.

Kant further mintained that moral principles, however, hold without exception. For example, if it is wrong to torture helpless animals, then it would be wrong for anyone, at any time, to do so.Thus, from these two premises—that moral principles hold without exception and that scientific investigations cannot reveal what holds without exception—it follows that moral principles cannot be revealed through scientific investigation. Because Kant believed that any principle that holds without exception is knowable only through reason, he maintained that reason alone can ascertain principles of morality.

Further, according to Kant, because a moral rule is something that holds without exception—that is, holds universally—one should act only on principles that could hold universally. For example, if you think you must then the principle on which you would act (if you were to steal) would be this: To become rich it is acceptable to steal. But now consider: If this principle were a universal law, then to become rich would be meaningless right? And in that case the principle itself would be meaningless. In short, the principle logically could not hold universally, and because his property may be stolen by someone. It would be irrational for anyone to want it to hold universally.Now, if it would be irrational for you to want the principle on which you act to be a universal law, then that principle is morally improper, and the act should not be done. Thus, for Kant, the supreme prescription of morality, which he calls the supreme categorical imperative, is to act always in such a way that you could, rationally, will the principle on which you act to be a universal law. In Kant's words, "Act only on that maxim whereby you can at the same time will that it should become a universal law." Because, in Kant's view, a universal law would in effect be a sort of law of nature, he offers a second formulation of the categorical imperative: "Act as if the maxim of your action were to become by your will a Universal Law of Nature." Moral principles, Kant observed, may always be expressed in the imperative form: Do not steal! Be kind to others! Further, because moral imperatives must hold without exception, they are different from hypothetical imperatives, which state, in effect, that one ought to do something if such-and-such an end is desired.

For example, the imperatives "If you wish to be healthy, then live moderately!" and "If you wish to secure your own survival, then surrender your rights to a sovereign power!" are both hypothetical imperatives. Neither is a moral imperatives for a moral imperative holds unconditionally, or categorically. This means that a moral imperative commands obedience for the sake of no other end than its own rightness. Thus, for Kant, what 1 should do, I should do because it is right. Doing something for any other purpose—for the sake of happiness or the welfare of humankind, for example—is not to act morally. It is to act under the command of a hypothetical imperative, which is not unconditional, as a moral imperative must be. According to Kant, you should do your moral duty simply because it is your moral duty. You should be aware that duty-based ethical systems, like Kant's, are known as deontological ethical systems.Furthermore, according to Kant, it's not the effects or consequences of your act that determine whether your act is good, for these are not totally within your control. What is within your control is the intent with which you act. Thus, what determines whether your act is good or bad is the intent with which it is undertaken. He wrote, "Nothing can possibly be conceived in the world, or even out of it, which can be called good, without qualification, except a good will." And because a morally good will is one that acts solely for the sake of doing what is right, it follows, in Kant's opinion, that there is no moral worth in, say, helping others because you are sympathetic or inclined to do so. Moral worth lies only in helping others for the sake of doing the right thing.

—Editor

What is Enlightenment?

Enlightenment is man's emergence from his self-incurred immaturity. Immaturity is the inability to use one's own understanding without the guidance of another. This immaturity is self-incurred if its cause is not lack of understanding, but lack of resolution and courage to use it without the guidance of another. The motto of enlightenment is therefore: Sapere aude![1] Have courage to use your own understanding!

Laziness and cowardice are the reasons why such a large proportion of men, even when nature has long emancipated them from alien guidance nevertheless gladly remain immature for life. For the same reasons, it is all too easy for others to set themselves up as their guardians. It is so convenient to be immature! If I have a book to have understanding in place of me, a spiritual adviser to have a conscience for me, a doctor to judge my diet for me, and so on, I need not make any efforts at all. I need not think, so long as I can pay; o thers will soon enough take the tiresome job over for me. The guardians who have kindly taken upon themselves the work of supervision will soon see to it that by far the largest part of mankind (including the entire fair sex) should consider the step forward to maturity not only as difficult but also as highly dangerous. Having first infatuated their domesticated animals, and carefully prevented the docile creatures from daring to take a single step without the leading-strings to which they are tied, they next show them the danger which threatens them if they try to walk unaided. Now this danger is not in fact so very great, for they would certainly learn to walk eventually after a few falls. But an example of this kind is intimidating, and usually frightens them off from further attempts.

Thus it is difficult for each separate individual to work his way out of the immaturity which has become almost second nature to him. He has even grown fond of it and is really incapable for the time being of using his own understanding, because he was never allowed to make the attempt. Dogmas and formulas, those mechanical instruments for rational use (or rather misuse) of his natural endowments, are the ball and chain of his permanent immaturity. And if anyone did throw them off, he would still be uncertain about jumping over even the narrowest of trenches, for he would be unaccustomed to free movement of this kind. Thus only a few, by cultivating their own minds, have succeeded in freeing themselves from immaturity and in continuing boldly on their way.

There is more chance of an entire public enlightening itself. This is indeed almost inevitable, if only the public concerned is left in freedom. For there will always be a few who think for themselves, even among those appointed as guardians of the common mass. Such guardians, once they have themselves thrown off the yoke of immaturity, will disseminate the spirit of rational respect for personal value and for the duty of all men to think for themselves. The remarkable thing about this is that if the public, which was previously put under this yoke by the guardians, is suitably stirred up by some of the latter who are incapable of enlighten-ment, it may subsequently compel the guardians themselves to remain under the yoke. For it is very harmful to propagate prejudices, because they finally avenge themselves on the very people who first encouraged them (or whose predecessors did so), Thus a public can only achieve enlightenment slowly. A revolution may well put an end to autocratic despotism and to rapacious or power-seeking oppression, but it will never produce a true reform in ways of thinking. Instead, new prejudices, like the ones they replaced, will serve as a leash to control the great unthinking mass.

For enlightenment of this kind, all that is needed is freedom. And the freedom in question is the most innocuous form of all—freedom to make *public use* of one's reason in all matters. But I hear on all sides the cry: Don't argue! The officer says: Don't argue, get on parade! The tax-official: Don't argue, pay! The clergyman: Don't argue, believe! (Only one ruler in the world says: Argue as much as you like and about whatever you like, but obey!) All this means restrictions on freedom everywhere. But which sort of restriction prevents enlightenment, and which, instead of hindering it, can actually promote it ? I reply: The public use of man's reason must always be free, and it alone can bring about enlightenment among men; the private use of reason may quite often be very narrowly restricted, however, without undue hindrance to the progress of enlighten-ment. But by the public use of one's own reason I mean that use which anyone may make of it as a man of learning addressing the entire reading public. What I term the private use of reason is that which a person may make of it in a particular *civil* post or office with which he is entrusted. Now in some affairs which affect the interests of the commonwealth, we require a certain mechanism whereby some members of the common-wealth must behave purely passively, so that they may, by an artificial common agreement, be employed by the government for public ends (or at least deterred from vitiating them). It is, of course, impermissible to argue in such cases; obedience is imperative. But in so far as this or that individual who acts as part of the machine also considers himself as a member of a complete commonwealth or even of cosmopolitan society, and thence as a man of learning who may through his writings address a public in the truest sense of the word, he may indeed argue without harming the affairs in which he is employed for some of the time in a passive capacity.

Thus it would be very harmful if an officer receiving an order from his superiors were to quibble openly, while on duty, about the appropriateness or usefulness of the order in question. He must simply obey. But he cannot reasonably be banned from making observations as a man of learning on the errors in the military service, and from submit-ting these to his public for judgement. The citizen cannot refuse to pay the taxes imposed upon him; presumptuous criticisms of such taxes, where someone is called upon to pay them, may be punished as an outrage which could lead to general insubordination. Nonetheless, the same citizen does not contravene his civil obligations if, as a learned individual, he publicly voices his thoughts on the impropriety or even injustice of such fiscal measures. In the same way, a clergyman is bound to instruct his pupils and his congregation in accordance with the doctrines of the church he serves, for he was employed'by it on that condition. But as a scholar, he is completely free as well as obliged to impart to the public all his carefully considered, well-intentioned thoughts on the mistaken aspects of those doctrines, and to offer suggestions for a better arrange-ment of religious and ecclesiastical affairs. And there is nothing in this which need trouble the conscience. For what he teaches in pursuit of his duties as an active servant of the church is presented by him as something which he is not empowered to teach at his own discretion, but which he is employed to expound in a prescribed manner and in someone else's name. He will say: Our church teaches this or that, and these are the arguments it uses. He then extracts as much practical value as possible for his congregation from precepts to which he would not himself sub-scribe with full conviction, but which he can nevertheless undertake to expound, since it is not in fact wholly impossible that they may contain truth. At all events, nothing opposed to the essence of religion is present in such doctrines. For if the clergyman thought he could find anything of this sort in them, he would not be able to carry out hi official duties in good conscience, and would have to resign. Thus the use which someone employed as a teacher makes of his reason in the presence of his congregation is purely private, since a congregation, however large it is, is never any more than a domestic gathering. In view of this, he is not and cannot be free as a priest, since he is acting on a commission imposed from outside. Conversely, as a scholar addressing the real public {i.e. the world at large) through his writings, the clergyman making public use of his reason enjoys unlimited freedom to use his own reason and to speak in his own person. For to maintain that the guardians of the people in spiritual matters should themselves be immature, is an absurdity which amounts to making absurdities permanent.

But should not a society of clergymen, for example an ecclesiastical synod or a venerable presbytery (as the Dutch call it), be entitled to commit itself by oath to a certain unalterable set of doctrines, in order to secure for all time a constant guardianship over each of its members, and through them over the people? I reply that this is quite impossible. A contract of this kind, concluded with a view to preventing all further enlightenment of mankind for ever, is absolutely null and void, even if it is ratified by the supreme power, by Imperial Diets and the most solemn peace treaties. One age cannot enter into an alliance on oath to put the next age in a position where it would be impossible for it to extend and correct its knowledge, particularly on such important matters, or to make any pro-gress whatsoever in enlightenment. This would be a crime against human nature, whose original destiny lies precisely in such progress. Later generations are thus perfectly entitled to dismiss these agreements as unauthorised and criminal. To test whether any particular measure can be agreed upon as a law for a people, we need only ask whether a people could well impose such a law upon itself. This might well be possible for a specified short period as a means of introducing a certain order, pending, as it were, a better solution. This would also mean that each citizen, particularly the clergyman, would be given a free hand as a scholar to comment publicly, i.e. in his writings, on the inadequacies of current institutions. Meanwhile, the newly established order would continue to exist, until public insight into the nature of such matters had progressed and proved itself to the point where, by general consent (if not unanimously), a proposal could be submitted to the crown. This would seek to protect the congregations who had, for instance, agreed to alter their religious establishment in accordance with their own notions of what higher insight is, but it would not try to obstruct those who wanted to let things remain as before. But it is absolutely impermissible to agree, even for a single lifetime, to a permanent religious constitution which no-one might publicly question. For this would virtually nullify a phase in man's upward progress, thus making it fruitless and even detrimental to subsequent generations.

A man may for his own person, and even then only for a limited period, postpone enlightening himself in matters he ought to know about. But to renounce such enlightenment completely, whether for his own person or even more so for later generations, means violating and trampling underfoot the sacred rights of mankind. But something which a people may not even impose upon itself can still less be imposed on it by a monarch; for his legislative authority depends precisely upon his uniting the collective will of the people in his own. So long as he sees to it that all true or imagined improvements are compatible with the civil order, he can otherwise leave his subjects to do whatever they find necessary for their salvation, which is none of his business. But it is his business to stop anyone forcibly hindering others from working as best they can to define and promote their salvation. It indeed detracts from his majesty If he interferes in these affairs by subjecting the writings in which his subjects attempt to clarify their religious ideas to governmental super-vision. This applies if he does so acting upon his own exalted opinions— in which case he exposes himself to the reproach: *Caesar non est supra Grammaticos**—but much more so if he demeans his high authority so far as to support the spiritual despotism of a few tyrants within his state against the rest of his subjects.

If it is now asked whether we at present live in an enlightened age, the answer is: No, but we do live in an age of enlightenment. As things are at present, we still have a long way to go before men as a whole can be in a position {or can even be put into a position) of using their own under-standing confidently and well in religious matters, without outside guid-ance. But we do have distinct indications that the way is now being cleared for them to work freely in this direction, and that the obstacles to universal enlightenment, to man's emergence from his self-incurred immaturity, are gradually becoming fewer. In this respect our age is the age of enlightenment, the century of Frederick.

A prince who does not regard it as beneath him to say that he considers it his duty, m religious matters, not to prescribe anything to his people, but to allow them complete freedom, a prince who thus even declines to accept the presumptuous tide *of tolerant,* is himself enlightened. He deserves to be praised by a grateful present and posterity as the man who first liberated mankind from immaturity (as far as government is concerned), and who left all men free to use their own reason in all matters of conscience. Under his rule, ecclesiastical dignitaries, notwithstanding - their official duties, may in their capacity as scholars freely and publicly submit to the judgement of the world their verdicts and opinions, even if these deviate here and there from orthodox doctrine. This applies even more to all others who are not restricted by any official duties. This spirit of freedom is also spreading abroad, even where it has to struggle with outward obstacles imposed by governments which misunderstand their own function. For such governments can now witness a shining example of how freedom may exist without in the least jeopardising public concord and the unity of the commonwealth. Men will of their own accord gradually work their way out of barbarism so long as artificial measures are not deliberately adopted to keep them in it.

I have portrayed matters of religion as the focal point of enlightenment, i.e. of man's emergence from his self-incurred immaturity. This is firstly because our rulers have no interest in assuming the role of guardians over their subjects so far as the arts and sciences are concerned, and secondly, because religious immaturity is the most pernicious and dishonourable variety of all. But the attitude of mind of a head of state who favours freedom in the arts and sciences extends even further, for he realises that there is no danger even to his legislation if he allows his subjects to make public use of their own reason and to put before the public their thoughts on better ways of drawing up laws, even if this entails forthright criticism of the current legislation. We have before us a brilliant example of this kind, in which no monarch has yet surpassed the one to whom we now pay tribute.

But only a ruler who is himself enlightened and has no fear of phantoms, yet who likewise has at hand a well-disciplined and numerous army to guarantee public security, may say what no republic would dare to say: Argue as much as you like and about whatever you like, but obey! This reveals to us a strange and unexpected pattern in human affairs (such as we shall always find if we consider them in the widest sense, in which nearly everything is paradoxical). A high degree of civil freedom seems advantageous to a people's intellectual freedom, yet it also sets up insuperable barriers to it. Conversely, a lesser degree of civil freedom gives intellectual freedom enough room to expand to its fullest extent. Thus once the germ on which nature has lavished most care—man's inclination and vocation to think freely—has developed within this hard shell, it gradually reacts upon the mentality of the people, who thus gradually become increasingly able to act freely. Eventually, it even influences the principles of governments, which find that they can themselves profit by treating man, who is more than a machine? in a manner appropriate to his dignity.

(From *Kant: Political Writing* ed. Hans Reiss trans. H.B. Nisbet, Cambride Urivensity Prees, Cambridge, 1991)

Categorical Imaperatives

Imperatives as formulated above – namely, the imperative enjoining conformity of actions to universal law on the analogy of a natural order and that enjoining the universal supremacy of rational beings in themselves as ends-did, by the mere fact that they were represented as categorical, exclude from their sovereign authority every admixture of interest as a motive. They were, however, merely assumed to be categorical because we were bound to make this assumption if we wished to explain the concept of duty. That there were practical propositions which commanded categorically could not itself be proved, any more than it can be proved in this chapter generally; but one thing could have been done – namely, to show that in willing for the sake of duty renunciation of all interest, as the specific mark distinguishing a categorical from a hypothetical imperative, was expressed in the very imperative itself by means of some determination inherent in it. This is what is done in the present third formulation of the principle – namely, in the idea of the will of every rational being as *a will which makes universal law.*

Once we conceive a will of this kind, it becomes clear that while a will which is subject to law may be bound to this law by some interest, nevertheless a will which is itself a supreme lawgiver cannot possibly as such depend on any interest; for a will which is dependent in this way would itself require yet a further law in order to restrict the interest of self-love to the condition that this interest should itself be valid as a universal law.

Thus the principle that every human will is a will which by all its maxims enacts universal law – provided only that it were right in other ways – would be well suited to be a categorical imperative in this respect: that precisely because of the Idea of making universal law, it is based on no interest and consequently can alone among all possible imperatives be unconditioned. Or better still – to convert the proposition – if there is a categorical imperative (that is, a law for the will of every rational being), it can command us only to act always on the maxim of such a will in us as can at the same time look upon itself as making universal law; for only then is the practical principle and the imperative which we obey unconditioned, since it is wholly impossible for it to be based on any interest.

We need not now wonder, when we look back upon all the previous efforts that have been made to discover the principle of morality, why they have one and all been bound to fail. Their authors saw man as tied to laws by his duty, but it never occurred to them that he is subject only to laws which are made by himself and yet are universal, and that he is bound only to act in conformity with a will which is his own but has as nature's purpose for it the function of making universal law. For when they thought of man merely as subject to a law (whatever it might be), the law had to carry with it some interest in order to attract or compel, because it did not spring as a law from his own will: in order to conform with the law, his will had to be necessitated by something else to act in a certain way. This absolutely inevitable conclusion meant that all the labour spent in trying to find a supreme principle of duty was lost beyond recall; for what they discovered was never duty, but only the necessity of acting from a certain interest. This interest might be one's own or another's; but on such a view the imperative was bound to be always a conditioned one and could not possibly swerve as a moral law. I will therefore call my principle the principle of the Autonomy of the will no contrast with all others, which I consequently class under *Heteronomy.*

[The Formula of the Kingdom of Ends]

The concept of every rational being as one who must regard himself as making universal law by, all the maxims of his will, and must seek to judge himself and his actions from this point of view, leads to a closely connected and very fruitful concept – namely, that of a *kingdom of ends.*

I understand by a 'kingdom' a systematic union of different rational beings under common laws. Now since laws determine ends as regards their universal validity, we shall be able – if we abstract from the personal differences between rational beings, and also from all the content of their private ends – to conceive a whole of all ends in systematic conjunction (a whole both of rational beings as ends in themselves and also of the personal ends which each may set before himself); that is, we shall be able to conceive a kingdom of ends which is possible in accordance with the above principles.

For rational beings all stand under the law that each of them should treat himself and all others, *never merely as a means,* but always *at the same time as an end in himself.* But by so doing there arises a systematic union of rational beings under common objective laws – that is, a kingdom. Since these laws are directed precisely to the relation of such beings to one another as ends and means, this kingdom can be called a kingdom of ends (which is admittedly only an Ideal).

A rational being belongs to the kingdom of ends as a member, when, although he makes its universal laws, he is also himself subject to these laws. He belongs to it as its head, when as the maker of laws, he is himself subject to the will of no other.

A rational being must always regard himself as making laws in a kingdom of ends which is possible through freedom of the will – whether it be as member or as head. The position f the later he can maintain, not in virtue of the maxim of his will alone, but only if he is a completely independent being, without needs and with an unlimited power adequate to his will.

Thus, morality consists in the relation of all action to the making of laws whereby alone a kingdom of ends is possible. This making of laws must be found in every rational being himself and must be able to spring from his will. The principle of his will is therefore never to perform an action except on a maxim such as can also be a universal law, and consequently such *that the will can regard itself as at the same time making universal law by means of its maxim*. Where maxims are not already by their very nature in harmony with this objective principle of rational being as makers of universal law, the necessity of acting on this principle is practical necessitation – that is duty. Duty does not apply to the head in a kingdom of ends, but it does apply to every member and to all members in equal measure.

The practical necessity of acting on this principles—that is, duty –is in no way based on feelings, impulses, and inclinations, but only on the relation of rational beings to one another, a relation in which the will of a rational being must always be regarded as making universal law, because otherwise he could not be conceived as an end in himself. Reason thus relates every maxim of the will, considered as making universal law, to every other will and also to every action towards oneself: it does so, not because of any further motive or future advantage, but from the Idea of the dignity of a rational being who obeys no law other than that which he at the same time enacts himself.

There is, therefore, only one categorical imperative. It is: Act only according to that maxim by which you can at the same time will that it should become a universal law.Now if all imperatives of duty can be derived from this one imperative as a principle, we can at least show what we understand by the concept of duty and what it means, even though it remains undecided whether that which is called duty is an empty concept or not.The universality of law according to which effects are produced constitutes what is properly called nature in the most general sense (as to form), i.e., the existence of things so far as it is determined by universal laws. [By analogy], then, the universal imperative of duty can be expressed as follows: Act as though the maxim of your action were by your will to become a universal law of nature.

We shall now enumerate some duties, adopting the usual division of them into duties to ourselves

1. A man who is reduced to despair by a series of evils feels a weariness with life but is still in possession of his reason . . . sufficientiy to ask whether it '.vould not be contrary to his duty to himself to take his own life. Now he asks whether the maxim of his action could become a universal law of nature. His maxim, however, is: For love of myself, I make it my principle to shorten my life when by a longer duration it threatens more evil than satisfaction. But it is questionable whether this principle of self-love could become a universal law of nature. One immediately sees a contradiction in a system of nature whose law would be to destroy life by the feeling whose special office is to impel the improvement of life. In this case it would not exist as nature; hence that maxim cannot obtain as a law of nature, and thus it wholly contradicts the supreme principle of all duty.

2. Another man finds himself forced by need to borrow money. He well knows that he will not be able to repay it, but he also sees that nothing will be loaned him if he does not firmly promise to repay it at a certain time. He desires to make such a promise, but he has enough conscience to ask himself whether it is not improper and opposed to duty to relieve his distress in such a way. Now, assuming he does decide to do so, the maxim of his action would be as follows: When I believe myself to be in need of money, I will borrow money and promise to repay it, although I know I shall never do so. Now this principle of self-love or of his own benefit may very well be compatible with his whole future welfare, but the question is whether it is right. He changes the pretension of

self-love into a universal law and then puts the question: How would it be if my maxim became a universal law? He immediately sees that it could never hold as a universal law of nature and be consistent with itself; rather, it must necessarily contradict itself. For the universality of a law which says that anyone who bebeves himself to be in need could promise what he pleased the intension of not ful filling it would make the promise itself.

3. A third finds in himself a talent which could, by means of some cultivation, make him in many respects a useful man. But he finds himself in comfortable circumstances and prefers indulgence in pleasure to troubling himself with broadening and improving his fortunate natural gifts. Now, however, let him ask whether his maxim of neglecting his gifts, besides agreeing with his propensity to idle amusement, agrees also with what is called duty. He sees that a system of nature could indeed exist in accordance with such a law, even though man (like the inhabitants of the South Sea Islands) should let his talents rust and resolve to devote his life merely to idleness, indulgence, and propagation—in a word, to pleasure. But he cannot possibly will that this should become a universal law of nature or that it should be implanted in us by a natural instinct. For, as a rational being, he necessarily wills that all his faculties should be developed, inasmuch as they are given to him for all sorts of possible purposes.

4. A fourth man, for whom things are going well, sees that others (whom he could help) have to struggle with great hardships, and he asks, "What concern of mine is it? Let each one be as happy as heaven wills, or as he can make himself; I will thinking were a universal law of nature, certainly the human race could exist, and without doubt even better than in a state where everyone talks of sympathy and good will, or even exerts himself occasionally to practice them while, on the other hand, he cheats when he can and betrays or otherwise violates the rights of man. Now although it is possible that a universal law of nature according to that maxim could exist, it is nevertheless impossible to will that such a principle should hold everywhere as a law of nature. For a will which resolved this would conflict with itself, since instances can often arise in which he would need the love and sympathy of others, and in which he would have robbed himself, by such a law of nature springing from his own will, of all hope of the aid he desires. The

foregoing are a few of the many actual duties, or at least of duties we hold to be actual, whose derivation from the one stated principle is clear. We must be able to will that a maxiin of our action become a universal law; this is the canon of the moral estimation of our action generally. Some actions are of such a nature that their maxim cannot even be thought as a universal law of nature without contradiction, far from it being possible that one could will that it should be such. In others this internal impossibility is not found, though it is still impossible to will that their maxim should be raised to the universality of a law of nature, because such a will would contradict itself. We easily see that the former maxim conflicts with the stricter or narrower (imprescriptible) duty, the latter with broader (meritorious) duty. Thus all duties, so far as the kind of obligation (not the object of their action) is concerned, have been completely exhibited by these examples in their dependence on the one principle.

(From *Foundations of the Metaphysics of Morals by* Emmanuel Kant, Trans. by Tewis While Back Pearson Education, 1990).

World Peace

This natural condition is a state of war in which the right of the stronger prevails; and although it may not in fact be always found as real state of actual war and incessant hostility, and although no wrong is done to any one therein, yet the condition is wrong in itself in the highest degree, and the nations which form states contiguous to each other are bound mutually to pass out of it.

Hence the perpetual peace, which is the ultimate end of all the right of nations, becomes in fad an impracticable idea. The political principles, however, which aim at such an end, and which enjoin the form at ton of such unions among the states as may promote a continuous approximation to a perpetual peace, art; not impracticable; they are as practicable as this approximation itself, which is a practical problem involving a duty, and founded upon the right of individual men and states.

Now, as a matter of fad, the morally practical reason utters within us its irrevocable veto;" There shall be no war." So there ought to be no war. Hence the question no longer is as to whether perpetual peace is a real thing or not a real thing, or as to whether we may not be deceiving ourselves when we adopt the former alternative, but we must act on the supposition of its being real. We must work for what may perhaps not be realized, and establish that constitution which yet seems best adapted to bring it about. And thus we may put n end to the evil of wars. And although the realization of is purpose may always remain but a pious wish, yet we do certainly not deceive ourselves in adopting the maxim of action that walleyed us in working incessantly for it; for it is a duty to do this. To suppose that the moral law within us is itself deceptive, would be sufficient to excite the horrible wish rather to be deprived of all re; son than to live under such deception, and even to see oneself, according to such principles, degraded like the lower anvils to t level of the mechanical play of nature. (The Philosophy Law)

Nature has accordingly again used the unsociable ness of men, and even of great societies and political bodies, her creatures of this kind, as a means to work out through their mutual antagonism a condition of rest and security. She works through wars, through the strain of never relaxed preparation for them, and through the necessity which every state is at last compelled to feel within itself, even in the midst of peace, to begin some imperfect efforts to carry out her purpose. And, at last, after many devastations, overthrows, and even complete internal exhaustion of their powers, the nations are driven forward to the goal which reason might have, well impressed upon them, even without so much said experience. This is none other than the advance out of the lawless state of savages and (the entering into a federation of nations. However visionary his idea may appear to be, it is nevertheless the inevitable issue if the necessity in which men involve one another. For this necessity must compel the nations to the very resolution —however hard t may appear—to which the savage in his uncivilised state, was so in willingly compelled, when he had to surrender his brutal liberty and seek rest and security in a constitution regulated by law.

A state of peace among men living together is not the same as the state of nature, which is rather a state of war. For even if it does not involve active hostilities, it involves a constant threat of their breaking out. Thus the state of peace must be formally instituted, for a suspension of hostilities is not in itself a guarantee of peace. And unless one neighbour gives guarantee to the other at his request (which can happen only in a lawful state), the latter may treat him as an enemy,

A republican constitution is founded upon three principles: firstly, the principle of freedom for all members of a society as men; secondly, the principle of the dependence of everyone upon a single common legislation as subjects and thirdly, the principle of legal equality for everyone as citizens. It is the only constitution which can be derived from the idea of an original contract, upon which all rightful legislation of a people must be founded. Thus as far as right is concerned, republicanism is in itself the original basis of every kind of civil constitution, and it only remains to ask whether it is the only constitution which can lead to a perpetual peace.

The republican constitution is not only pure in its origin (since it springs from the pure concept of right); it also offers a prospect of attaining the desired result, i.e. a perpetual peace, and the reasons for this is as follows. If, as is inevitably the case under this constitution, the consent of the citizens is required to decide whether or not war is to be declared, it is very natural that they will have great hesitation in embarking on .so dangerous art enterprise. For this would mean calling down on themselves all the miseries of war, such as doing the fighting themselves, supplying the costs of the war from their own resources, painfully making good the ensuing devastation, and, as the crowning evil, having to take upon themselves a burden of debt which will embitter peace itself and which can never be paid off on account of the constant threat of new wars. But under a constitution where the subject is not a citizen, and which is therefore not republican, it is the simplest thing in the world to go to war. For the head of state is not a fellow citizen, but the owner of the state, and a war will not force him to make the slightest sacrifice so far as his banquets, hunts, pleasure palaces and court festivals are concerned. He can thus decide on war, without any significant reason, as a kind of amusement, and unconcernedly leave it to the diplomatic corps (who are always ready for such purposes) to justify the war for the sake of propriety.

Peoples who have grouped themselves into nation states may be judged in the same way as individual men living in a state of nature, independent of external laws; for they are a standing offence to one another by the very fact that they are neighbours. Each nation, for the sake of its own security, cart and ought to demand of the others that they should enter along with it into a constitution, similar to the civil one, within which the rights of each could be secured. This would mean establishing a federation of peoples. But a federation of this sort would not be the same thing as an international state. For the idea of an international state is contradictory, since every state involves a relationship between a superior (the legislator) and an inferior (the people obeying the laws), whereas a number of nations forming one state would constitute a single nation. And this contradicts our initial assumption, as we are here considering the right of nations in relation to one another in so far as they are a group of separate states which are not to be welded together as a unit.

We look with profound contempt upon the way in which savages cling to their lawless freedom. They would rather engage in incessant strife than submit to a legal constraint which they might impose upon themselves, for they prefer the freedom of folly to the freedom of reason. We regard this as barbarism, coarseness, and brutish debasement of humanity. We might thus expect that civilised peoples, each united within itself as a state, would hasten to abandon so degrading a condition as soon as possible. But instead of doing so, each slate sees its own majesty (for it would be absurd to speak of the majesty of a people) precisely in not having to submit to any external legal constraint, and the glory of its ruler consists in his power to order thousands of people to immolate themselves for a cause which does not truly concern them, while he need not himself incur any danger whatsoever. And the main difference between the savage nations of Europe and those of America is that while some American tribes have been entirely eaten up by their enemies, the Europeans know how to make better use of those they have defeated than merely by making a meal of them. They would rather use them to increase the number of their own subjects, thereby augmenting their stock of instruments for conducting even more extensive wars.

The idea of international right presupposes the separate existence of many independent adjoining states. And such a state of affairs is essentially a state of war, unless there is a federal union to prevent hostilities breaking out. But in the light of the idea of reason, this state is still to be preferred to an amalgamation of the separate nations under a single power which has overruled the rest and created a universal monarchy. For the laws progressively lose their impact as the government increases its range, and a soulless despotism, after crushing the germs of goodness, will finally lapse into anarchy. It is nonetheless the desire of every state or its ruler to achieve lasting peace by thus dominating the whole world, if at all possible. But nature wills it otherwise, and uses two means to separate the nations and prevent them from intermingling—linguistic and religious differences. These may certainly occasion mutual hatred and provide pretexts for wars, but as culture grows and men gradually move towards greater agreement over their principles, they lead to mutual understanding and peace. And unlike that universal despotism which saps all man's energies and ends in the graveyard of freedom, this peace is created and guaranteed by an equilibrium of forces and a most vigorous rivalry.

Thus nature wisely separates the nations, although the will of each individual state, even basing its arguments on international right, would gladly unite them under its own sway by force or by cunning. On the other hand, nature also unites nations which the concept of cosmopolitan right would not have protected from violence and war, and does so by means of their mutual self-interest. For the spirit of commerce sooner or later takes hold of every people, and it cannot exist side by side with war. And of all the powers (or means at the disposal of the power of the state, financial power can probably be relied on most. Thus states find themselves compelled to promote the noble cause of peace, though not exactly from motives of morality. And wherever in the world there is a threat of war breaking out, they will try to prevent it by mediation, just as if they had entered into a permanent league for this purpose for by the very nature of things, large military alliances can only rarely be formed, and will even more rarely he successful.

In this way, nature guarantees perpetual peace by the actual mechanism of human inclinations. And while the likelihood of its being attained is not sufficient to enable us to prophesy the future theoretically, it is enough for practical purposes. It makes it our duty to work our way towards this goal, which is more than an empty chimera.

(From 'Perpetual Peace,' in *Kant: Political Wittings*, ed. Hans Reiss, trans H.B. Nisbet, Cambridge University Press, Cambridge. 1991.)

15

G.W.F. Hegel

G.W.F. Hegel (1770-1831) led a very unexciting life for a thinker who was such an inspiration to his contemporaries and successors. Nineteenth-and twentieth-century social and political thought are unthinkable without Hegel, yet Hegel's own life did not come into much contact with the great events he lived through and commented on. The one exception is the famous occasion when Hegel saw Napoleon-the world soul on horseback at Jena in 1806. Prussia's defeat at the battle of Jena established French hegemony in Germany. That hegemony only lasted a few years. Nevertheless, it was Jena and its aftermath that made Germany one of the key players in world history in Hegel's sense.

Nearly all of Hegel's life was spent as a teacher and a scholar. He was brought up a Protestant in the relatively liberal south German atmosphere of Wurttemberg, and he was a student at Tubingen (1788-93) when the Bastille fell. From then on, Hegel's own life can be seen as a paradigm of the responses and reactions to the French Revolution—the initial enthusiasm for Reason and Liberty; the doubts beginning with the establishment of the French republic and then quickening with the execution of the king and queen; the hostility to the wars of conquest, and then the full nationalist reaction when Napoleon conquered nearly the whole of Europe.

While all this was going on, Hegel was quietly climbing the academic ladder. He spent some years as a tutor, then was appointed at the University of Jena (1801) where he completed *The Phenomenology of Mind* (1807), thus setting the agenda for the study of the history of culture for a very long time to come. After that he spent eight years as a rector of a Gymnasium (1808-16) at Nuremberg; he got married and finished his great work on *Logic*. There followed a chair of philosophy at Heidelberg and later (1818-31) at Berlin. We are told that as a lecturer he mumbled, which is odd, considering that some of his works were put together posthumously from lecture notes taken by high-minded students who were members of the Prussian officer corps. His great work, *The Philosophy of Right*, appeared in1821.

Hegel's Christianity was always eccentric, and it is hard to pin down. Some argue that Hegel's theology is the way into his politics, while others argue the reverse. Hegel was taken in his own day to be a conservative and it is true that he was appainted to his chair in Berlin University to combat dangerously liberal tendencies among its teachers and students. Hegel has the reputation of being a 'difficult' thinker in the English-speaking world, and it is easy to see why. Hegel speaks the language of German idealist philosophy, which is at the same time technical and slippery in translation. Nobody denies the influence of Hegelianism on the development of Marxism, though there are disputes about the extent to which Hegelianism can still be detected in Marxism as a finished product. This question of how influential Hegel was on Marx has had the unfortunate tendency, happily now beginning to be reversed, of making people think that Hegel is only interesting to the extent that he influenced Marxism. Hegel's political theory, it is sometimes said, was seen and seen through by Marx in his *Critique of Hegel's Philosophy of Right*, and this in its turn has led to the view that Hegel on his own isn't up to much. Hegel is in fact a much tougher thinker than this view would have us suppose.

As a philosopher, Hegel was interested in how the thinking mind actually views the world. Philosophy is about mind, Hegel calls 'the thinking view of things', and so he is interested in the history of human consciousness. The mind is there for understanding the world outside the self, while that self is still part of the world which the mind seeks to understand. Hegel thinks the mind really does try to grasp the world outside the self. Mind is active. It does not wait for sense impressions queuing up at the fingers' ends or at the eyeball to ask politely for admission to the mind. The mind reaches out to make the world coherent. And Hegel means the world as a whole. Hegel is an idealist; he thinks that an idea of the world presents itself to mind, or created by mind as a whole. Thinking mind are full of impressions from the outside, and the more a mind is a thinking mind the more it will go after those impressions, but mind's real job is to organise these impressions into a coherent whole. In a sense, we have a view of the whole before we have a view of the parts of the world because the mind which reaches out to understand the world is a whole mind already.

Writing a quarter of a century after the publication of Kant's revolutionary first *Critique,* whose ideas were now as established as the slogans of the great political revolution in France,. Hegel without Kant's timidity, pursued to the limits the ideas of transcendental idealism, and the significance of the insight that it is we who give structure to our own experience. From Fichte he borrowed the now transformed notion of 'the Absolute', the rejection of the world 'in itself, and the alternative 'forms of consciousness' and forms of life. From Schelling he borrowed the idea of dialectic of such forms, developing through time and history with ourselves as the authors, and becoming increasingly more adequate and encompassing. According to Hegel, every form of consciousness has its truth, in a certain context and from a certain perspective. But a larger context and broader perspective will show that some forms are more satisfactory, more complete, more 'true' than others.

With the exception of the *Logic,* Hegel's works are all concerned with the necessity of a social conception of humanity. This seems obvious until one glances back at the history of philosophy. Of course philosophers treat people as social creatures when they are discussing politics but when they are discussing the nature of knowledge, consciousness, the self, or religion, they almost always treat the matter as a relationship between the individual and reason, or God. The idea that what we know, think, feel, and worship is circumscribed by, much less is a product of, our relations with other people is treated with disdain as popular superstition, as 'heteronomy'. The Enlightenment since Descartes honoured autonomy above all else, and romanticism valued inward feelings and intuitions just because these were untainted by social conditioning and corruption. Rousseau more than anyone else celebrated this sense of the isolated individual in touch with himself and nature, and out of touch with society. True, he developed the most persuasive theory of the social contract, but he did so against a background of a state of nature in which individuals were 'born free and happy' and were 'indifferent' to one another. The idea that there are no individuals in nature, that knowledge, self, and everything else human is a product not of nature but of culture, is an idea that comes quite new to philosophy and it comes mainly with Hegel.

Hegel's ethical theory is too often seen as subservient to his political views—though the latter are more often understood through their unforeseen consequences in modern German history than through Hegel's own rather moderate opinions. But ethics is, in an important sense, the heart of Hegel's philosophy. His early work on religion tries—following Kant—to understand religious belief and ritual wholly within the secular framework of an ethical theory, to see religion as a vehicle of morality. The *Phenomenology* has as its largest part a series of explorations of various ethical systems and models.

Hegel does not accept the Kantian conception of morality. In his early essays, despite the Kantian flavour and his devotion to Kant's philosophy of religion, he had attacked Kant's view of morality—as did Schiller—as overly abstract, cold, and alienating. He argued that the formality of Kant's categorical imperative made it very difficult to apply it to any concrete ethical situation, at least without sneaking in personal evaluations, which it was the very point of the moral law to preclude. He particularly objected to the exclusion of feeling and all inclination from moral consideration, recognizing with imagined world might be as real as any other. The dialectic is not so much a method as it is the central idea of Hegel's philosophy, and its purpose, in each of his works, is to demonstrate the ultimate necessity of an all-encompassing acceptance of the self as absolute — which Hegel calls 'Spirit'.

One of the dialectical devices Hegel uses to show how such a movement takes place is to interpose the story of Antigone between his account of custom and his discussion of the ethical norms of civil society. He takes Antigone to represent the divine law of the family, of mutual affection and loyalty. When her brother is killed in an abortive attempt at a coup Antigone's duty is to bury him in accordance with religious law. But as a traitor her brother is denied burial by the king he sought to depose, and she faces a fatal conflict between her divine family duty and the human law of society. She opts for her duty, and is killed by the State in return, but the point of the play for Hegel is nothing less than the nature of the dialectic as such. Life, history and philosophy are defined by such crisis points. For the individual who is caught in the crisis there may well be no 'happy ending', but it is on the basis of such tragedies and sacrifices that the dialectic and human history moves forward. So understood, Kant's view of morality is an extremely sophisticated version of that forward-reaching tendency, but because it is also too narrow and limited it must be moved beyond as well.

Where does the dialectic go from here? In the *Phenomenology*, it moves to the dialectic of religion, which Hegel sees not as the superimposition of Christianity on morals but rather as the reintegration of custom and more abstract conceptions of morality and society. In *The Philosophy of Right* and the *Lectures on the Philosophy of History* it moves to a new and enlarged sense of internationalism, a vision of the Self, or Spirit that embraces us all, finally recognizing itself in all of us, and ending the conflicts that drive us apart. It is not only the culmination of the transcendental pretence; it is 'the end of history', according to Hegel. But this hyperinflation of the self marks the beginning of a new era of European history, a reaction in which the premises and basic ideals of the Enlightenment will come under fire.

—Editor

Civil Society and State

The concrete person, who is himself the object of r his as a totality of wants and a mixture of caprice and physical necessity, one principle of civil society. But the particular person is essentially so related to other particular persons that each establishes himself and finds satisfaction by means of the others, and at the same time purely and simply by means of the form of universality, the second principle here.

In the course of the actual attainment of selfish ends—an attainment conditioned in this way by universality—there is formed a system of complete interdependence, wherein the livelihood, happiness, and legal status of one man is interwoven with the livelihood, happiness, and rights of all. On this system, individual happiness, depend, and only in this connected system are they actualized and secured. This system may be prima facie regarded as the external state, the state based on need, the state as the Understanding envisages it.

The Idea in this its stage of division imparts to each of its moments a characteristic embodiment; to particularity it gives the right to develop and launch forth in all directions; and to universality the right to prove itself not only the ground and necessary form of particularity, but also the authority standing over it and its final end It is the system of the ethical order, split into its extremes and lost, which constitutes the Idea's abstract moment, its moment of reality. Here the Idea is present only as a relative totality and as the inner necessity behind this outward appearance.

Particularity by itself, given free rein in every direction to satisfy its needs, accidental caprices, and subjective desires, destroys itself and its substantive concept in this process of gratification. At the same time, the satisfaction of need, necessary and accidental alike, is accidental because it breeds new desires without end, is in thoroughgoing dependence on caprice and external accident, and is held in check by the power of universality. In these contrasts and their complexity, civil society affords a spectacle of extravagance and want as well as of the physical and ethical degeneration common to them both.

The development of particularity to self-subsistence is the moment which appeared in the ancient world as an invasion of ethical corruption and as the ultimate cause of that world's downfall. Some of these ancient states were built on the patriarchal and religious principle, others on the principle of an ethical order which was more explicitly intellectual, though still comparatively simple; in either case they rested on primitive unsophisticated intuition. Hence they could not withstand the disruption of this state or mind when self-consciousness was infinitely reflected into itself; when this reflection began to emerge, they succumbed to it, first in spirit and then in substance, because the simple principle underlying diem lacked the truly infinite power to be found only in that unity which allows both sides of the antithesis of reason to develop themselves separately in all their strength and which has so overcome the antithesis that it maintains itself in it and integrates it in itself.

In his Republic, Plato displays the substance of ethical life in its ideal beauty and truth; but he could only cope with the principle of self-subsistent particularity, which in his day had forced its way into Greek ethical life, by setting up in opposition to it his purely substantial state. He absolutely excluded it from his state, even in its very beginnings in private property and the family, as well as in its more mature form as the subjective will, the choice of a social position, and so forth. It is this defect which is responsible body for the misunderstanding of the deep, and substantial truth of Plato's state and also for the usual view— of it as a dream of abstract thinking, as what is often called a 'mere ideal'. The principle of the self-subsistent inherently infinite personality of the individual, the principal of subjective freedom, is denied its right in the purely substantial form which Plato gave to mind in its actuality. This principle dawned in an inward form in the Christian religion and in an external form (and therefore in one linked with abstract universality) in the Roman world. It is historically subsequent to the Greek world, and the philosophic reflection which descends to its depth is likewise subsequent to the substantial Idea of Greek philosophy.

But in developing itself independently to totality, the principle of particularity passes over into universality, and only there does it attain its truth and the right to which its positive actuality is entitled. This unity is not the identity which the ethical order requires, because at this level, that of division, both principles are self-subsistent. It follows that this unity is present here not as freedom but as necessity, since it is by compulsion that the particular rises to the form of universality and seeks and gains its stability in that form.

Individuals in their capacity as burghers in this state are private persons whose end is their own interest. This end is mediated through the universal which thus appears as a means to its realization. Consequently, individuals can attain their ends only in so far as they themselves determine their knowing, willing, and acting in a universal way and make themselves links in this chain of social connexions. In these circumstances, the interest of the Idea—an interest of which these members of civil society are as such unconscious—lies in the process whereby their singularity and their natural condition are raised, as a result of the necessities imposed and their natural as well as of arbitrary needs, to formal freedom and formal universality of knowing and willing—the process whereby their particularity is educated up to subjectivity.

Civil society Contains Three Moments:

(A) The mediation of need and one mans satisfaction through his work and the satisfaction of the needs of all others—the System of Needs.

(B) The actuality of the universal principle of freedom therein contained— the protection of property through the Administration of Justice.

(C) Provision against contingencies still lurking in systems (A) and (B), and care for particular interest, by means of the Police and the Corporation.

The State is the realization of the ethical idea. It is the ethical spirit as revealed, self-conscious, substantial will. It is the will which thinks and knows itself, and carries out what it knows, and in so far as it knows. The unreflected existence of the State rests on custom, and its reflected existence on the self-consciousness of the individual, on his knowledge and activity. The individual, in return, has his substantial freedom in the State, as the essence, purpose, and product of his activity.

The true State is the ethical whole and the realization of freedom. It is the absolute purpose of reason that freedom should be realized. The State is the spirit, which lives in the world and there realizes itself consciously; while in nature it is actual only as its own other or as dormant spirit. Only as present in consciousness, knowing itself as an existing object, is it the State. The State is the march of God through the world, its ground is the power of reason realizing itself as will. The idea of the State should not denote any particular State, or particular institution; one must rather consider the Idea only, this actual God, by itself. Because it is more easy to find defects than to grasp the positive meaning, one readily falls into the mistake of emphasizing so much the particular nature of the State as to overlook its inner organic essence. The State is no work of art. It exists in the world, and thus is the realm of caprice, accident, and error. Evil behavior toward it may disfigure it on many sides. But the ugliest man, the criminal, the invalid, and the cripple, are still living human beings. The affirmative, life, persists in spite of defects, and it is this affirmative which alone is here in question.

In the State, everything depends upon me unity of the universal and the particular. In the ancient States the subjective purpose was absolutely one with the will of the State In modern rimes, on the contrary, we demand an individual opinion, an individual will and conscience. The ancients had none of these in the modern sense; the final thing for them was the will of the State. While in Asiatic despotisms .the individual had no inner self and no self-justification, in the modern world man demands to be honored for the sake of his subjective individuality.

The union of duty and right, has the twofold aspect that what the State demands as duty should directly be the right of the individual, since the State is nothing but the organization of the concede of freedom. The determinations of "the individual will are given by the State objectively, and it is through the State alone that they attain truth and realization. The State is the sole condition of the attainment of the particular end and good.

Political disposition, called patriotism—the assurance resting in truth and the will which has become a custom—is simply the result of the institutions subsisting in the State, institutions in which reason is actually present.

Under patriotism one frequently understands a mere willingness to perform extraordinary acts and sacrifice. But patriotism is essentially the sentiment of regarding, in the ordinary circumstances and ways of life, the weal of the community as the substantial basis and the final end. It is upon this consciousness, present in the ordinary course of life and under all circumstances, that the disposition to heroic effort is founded. But as people are often rather magnanimous than just, they easily persuade themselves chat they possess the heroic kind of patriotism, in order to save themselves the trouble of having the truly patriotic sentiment, or to excuse the lack of it.

Political sentiment, as appearance, must be distinguished from what people truly will. What they at bottom will is the real cause, but they cling to particular interests and delight in the vain contemplation of improvements. The conviction of the necessary stability of the State in which alone the particular interests can be realized people indeed possess, bar custom makes invisible that upon which our whole existence rests; it does not occur to any one, when he safely passes through the streets at night, that :: could be otherwise. The habit or safety has become a second nature, and we c: not reflect that it is the result or me activity of special institutions. It is through force—this is frequently the superficial opinion—that the State coheres, but what alone holds it together is the fundamental sense of order, which is possessed by all.

The state is an organism or the development of the idea into its differences. These different sides are the different powers or the State with their functions and activities, by means of which the universal is constantly and necessarily producing itself, and, being presupposed in its own productive function, it is thus always actively present. This organism is the political constitution. It eternally springs from the State, just as the State in turn maintains itself through the constitution. If these two things fall asunder, if both different sides become independent of each other, then the unity' which the constitution produces is no longer operative; the fable of the stomach and the other organs may be applied to it. It is the nature of an organism that all its parts-must constitute a certain unity; if one part asserts its independence the other parts must go to destruction. No predicates, principles, and the like suffice to express the nature of the State; it must be comprehended as an organism.

The State is real, and its reality consists in the interest of the whole being realized in particular ends. Actuality is always the unity of universality and particularity, and the differentiation of the universal into particular ends. These particular ends seem independent, though they arc borne and sustained by the whole only. In so far as this unity is absent, no thing is real, though it may exist. A bad State is one which merely exists. A sick body also exists, but it has no true reality. A hand, which is cut off, still looks like a hand and exists, but it has no reality. True reality is necessity. What is real is eternally necessary.

To the complete State belongs, essentially, consciousness and thought. The State knows thus what it wills, and it knows it under the form of thought.

The essential difference between the State and religion consists in that the commands of the State have the form of legal duty, irrespective of the feelings accompanying their performance; the sphere of religion, on the other hand, is in the inner life. Just as the State, were it to frame its commands as religion does, would endanger the right of the inner life, so the church, if it acts as a State and imposes punishment, degenerates into o a tyrannical religion.

In the State one must want nothing which is not an expression of rationality. The State is the world which me spirit has made for itself; it has therefore a determinate and self-conscious course. One often speaks of the wisdom of God in nature, but one must not believe that the physical world of nature is higher than the world of spirit. Just as spin: is superior to nature, so is the State superior to the physical life. We must therefore worship the State as the manifestation of the divine on earth, and consider that, if it is difficult to comprehend nature, it is infinitely harder to grasp the essence of the State. It is an important fact that we, in modern times, have attained definite insight into the State in general and are much engaged in discussing and making constitutions; but that does not advance the problem much. It is necessary to treat a rational matter in the light of reason, in order to learn its essential nature and to know that the obvious does not always constitute the essential.

When we speak of the different functions of the powers of the State, we must not fall into the enormous error of supposing each power to have an abstract, independent existence, since the powers are rather to he differentiated as elements in the conception of the State. Were the powers to be in abstract independence, however, it is clear that two independent things could never constitute a unity, but must produce war, and the result would be destruction of the whole or restoration of unity by force. Thus, in the French Revolution, at one time the legislative power had swallowed up the executive, at another time the executive had usurped the legislative power.

(From *Philosophy of Right* by G.W.F. Hegel translated by T.H. Knox, Oxford University Press, 1942)

16

John Stuart Mill

John Stuart Mill (1806-1873) was born in London in 1806. A child of precocious intelligence, he was systematically educated by his father, Many years ago, one of the authors came across a table of projected IQ scores for various historic "geniuses" in a psychology text. (Who knows how the scores were calculated?) At the top list, with some incredible score, was John Stuart Mill. James Mill, to follow in his footsteps as champion of the utilitarian philosophy. By the age of twenty he had achieved this aim: he was leader of the younger philosophical radicals, achieve as a propagandist in their intellectual and reforming pursuits. In 1826, however, he endured his first period of mental crisis and found he no longer believed in many aspects of the Benthamite creed. He then began a systematic examination of the alternative positions offered by Coleridge, Carlyle, the St. Simonians, Comte and Tocqueville. While keeping his links with the utilitarian circle and contributing to their journal, the *London and Westminster Review.*

By the 1804s Mill was able to put forward a mature reinterpretation of his philosophical position; his *System of Logic* (1843) and the *Principles of Political Economy* (1848) formed the basis for his dominant position in Victorian intellectual life. During the years 1859-65 he wrote the other works for which he is now famous. *On Liberty, Representative Government, Utilitarianism, Auguste Comte and Positivism* and *The Subjection of Women.*

After working for thirty-five years in the East India Company, Mill was a Member of Parliament from 1865 to 1868, voting with the Radical party and strongly advocating women's stuff age. He was also concerned with such issues as the Irish land question, slavery and the American Civil War, income and property taxation, tenure reform, and trade unionism. He ded at Avignon in 1873, having finished his *Autobiography* in the same year.

Mill began reading Greek at three and Latin at eight; by adolescence he had completed an extensive study of Greek and Latin literature as well as history, mathematics, and logic. Mill's education was administered by his father, who subjected young John to a rigorous regimen.

At fifteen Mill settled on his lifelong objective, to work for social and political reform and it is as a reformer and an ethical and political philosopher that he is most remembered. Mill championed individual rights and personal freedom and advocated emancipation of women and proportional representation. His most famous work, On Liberty (1859), is thought by many to be the definitive defense of freedom of thought and discussion.

In ethics Mill was a utilitarian. He published *Utilitarianism* in 1863. Mill's interests also ranged over a broad variety of topics in epistemology, metaphysics, and logic. His *System of Logic* (1843), which was actually read at the time by the person in the street, represented an empiricist approach to logic, abstraction, psychology, sociology, and morality. Mill's methods of induction are still standard fare in university courses in beginning logic.

When Mill was twenty-five, he met Harriet Taylor, a merchant's wife, and this was the beginning of one of the most celebrated love affairs of all time. Twenty years later, and three years after her husband died, Mrs. Taylor married Mill, on whose thought she had a profound influence. *On Liberty* was perhaps jointly written with her and, in any case, was dedicated to her. Harriet Taylor died in 1858. Mill spent his remaining years in Avignon, France, where she had died, to be near her grave. Mill's *Autobiography*, widely read, appeared in the year of his death. Mill still is the most celebrated English philosopher of his country.

Like many women philosophers, Harriet Taylor (1807-1858) has been known to the public primarily through her association with a male philosopher; in Taylor's case the male philosopher was John Stuart Mill. Taylor and Mill shared a long personal and professional intimacy, and each shaped and influenced the ideas of the other. However, Taylor was a published author of poetry before she even met Mill in 1831. Recently, a draft of an essay on toleration of nonconformity was discovered in Taylor's handwriting; it appears to have been written in 1832. She was a regular contributor, and eventually Taylor and Mill began writing together. However, their writings were published under Mill's name, partly because a man's name gave the work more legitimacy within a sexist culture but also because Taylor's husband was unhappy with the idea of his wife's gaining notoriety. Nevertheless, from the evidence of their manuscripts and their personal correspondence, it is possible to piece together ideas of which works were primarily Taylor's and which were Mill's; she was a profound thinker in her own right.

Taylor was interested both in sweeping transformations of society and in specific legal reforms. One of her greatest concerns was the tendency of English society to stifle individuality, originality, and radical political and religious views. English society, in her opinion, was intolerant of opinions that failed to conform to the mainstream. She considered the intolerance of nonconformity to be morally wrong and ultimately dangerous to human progress. Taylor's essay on such intolerance is a stirring statement of the theory that "the opinion of society – majority opinion – is the root of all intolerance." Her defense of minority viewpoints and individuality predated by twenty-seven years Mill's famous treatise *on Liberty* .

Like Locke and Rousseau, John Stuart Mill was much concerned with liberty. Mill was a utilitarian. He believed that happiness not only is the good, the ultimate end of all action and desire. "Actions are right in proportion as they tend to promote happiness, wrong as they tend to produce the reverse of happiness," he wrote. But remember that utilitarian's are not egoists, and Mill believed that it is not one's own happiness that one should seek but instead the greatest amount of happiness altogether – that is, the general happiness. Unlike Rousseau, Mill does not view a community, a society, a people, or a state as an organic entity separate and distinct from the sum of the people in it. When Mill says that one should seek the general happiness, he is not referring to the happiness of the community as some kind of organic whole. For Mill, the general happiness is just the total happiness of the individuals in the group.

Now, Mill, following Jeremy Bentham and Hume and like Rousseau, rejected Locke's theory that people have God-given natural rights. But he maintained that the general happiness requires that all individuals enjoy personal liberty to the fullest extent consistent with the liberties of others. "The only part of the conduct of anyone, for which he is amenable to society, is that which concerns others. In the part which merely concerns himself, his independence is...absolute." Mill regarded personal liberty, including freedom of thought and speech, as essential to the general happiness. It is essential, he argued, because truth and the development of the individual's character and abilities are essential to the general happiness, and only if there is personal liberty can truth be ascertained and each individual's capacities developed. It therefore follows that an individual should enjoy unrestrained personal liberty up to the point where his or her activities may harm others.

Of course, it is difficult to identify when an action may be said to harm others. Liberalism places the burden of proof on the person who claims that harm to others will be done. The best form of government, according to Mill, is that which, among all realistic and practical alternatives, produces the greatest benefit. The form of government best suited to do this, he maintained, is representative democracy. But Mill was especially sensitive to the threat to liberty posed in democracies by the tyranny of public opinion as well as by the suppression by the majority of minority points of view. For this reason he emphasized the importance of safeguards such as proportional representation, universal suffrage, and enforcement of education by the state.

Now, promoting the general happiness would seem sometimes to justify restrictions on personal liberty. Zoning ordinances, antitrust laws, and motorcycle helmet laws, to take modern examples, are arguably, restrictions of this sort. Mill recognized the dilemma that potentially confronts anyone who wishes both to promote the general happiness and to protect personal liberty. His general position is this: The government should not do anything that could be done more effectively by private individuals themselves; and even if something could be done more effectively by the government, if the government's doing it would deprive individuals of an opportunity for development or education, the government should not do it. In short, Mill was opposed to enlarging the power of the government unnecessarily.

John Stuart Mill, who claimed to have discovered in Bentham's ethical theory what he needed to give purpose to his own life, was also concerned with providing a philosophical justification for the utilitarian doctrine that it is the general happiness that one should aim to promote. The justification, according to Mill, lies in the fact that a moral principle by its very nature singles out no one for preferential treatment. Thus, Mill wrote, "as between his own happiness and that of others," the utilitarian is required "to be as strictly impartial as a disinterested and benevolent spectator." Probably the most important difference between Mill and Bentham is that Mill believed that some pleasures are inherently better than others and are to be preferred even over a greater amount of pleasure of an inferior grade.

That some pleasures are better than others can be seen, Mill argued, in the fact that few people would be willing to trade places with an animal or even with a more ignorant person than themselves, even if the exchange guaranteed their having the fullest measure of an animal's or an ignoramus's pleasure. Here is what he meant. Would you trade places with a pig or a lunkhead? Would you do it even if you knew that as a pig or a lunkhead you would have more pig or lunkhead pleasures than you now have pleasure as an intelligent human being?

Thus, for Mill, in determining the pleasure for which we should strive, we must consider the quality of the pleasure as well as the quantity: Choose the pleasure of the highest quality. In Mill's words, it is better a socrates satisfied, than a fool satisfied. Now, this is all very well, but what settles which of two pleasures is of higher quality? Mill's answer is quite simple: Of two pleasures, if there is one to which most have experienced both give a decided preference, that is the more desirable pleasure. Notice what this answer seems to entail. It seems to entail that the pleasures preferred by the intellectual will be found to be of superior quality, for non-intellectuals "only know their own side of the question. The other party to the comparison knows both sides," said Mill.

According to Mill, then, it is not simply the quantity of pleasure an act produces that determines its moral worth; the quality of the pleasure produced must also be taken into account. Mill is thus said to have recognized implicitly a factor other than pleasure by which the moral worth of actions should be compared: the factor of quality. In other words, he is said to have proposed, in effect, a standard of moral worth other than pleasure, a standard of "quality" by means of which pleasure itself is to be evaluated. So he sometimes is said not to be a pure utilitarian one who believes that the pleasure an act produces is the only standard of good. It is not unusual, therefore, to find philosophers who think of Bentham's philosophy as more consistently utilitarian than Mill's, through everyone refers to both Mill and Bentham as the utilitarians.

—Editor

Utilitarianism

The creed which accepts as the foundation of morals "utility" or the "greatest happiness princi-ple" holds that actions are right in proportion as they lend to promote happiness; wrong as they tend to produce the reverse of happiness. By happiness is intended pleasure and, tile-absence of pain; by unhappiness, pain and the privation of pleasure. To give a clear view of the moral standard set up by the theory, much more requires to be said; in particular, what things it includes in the ideas of pain and plea-sure, and to what extent this is left an open ques-tion. But these supplementary explanations do not affect the theory of life on which this theory of morality is grounded—namely, that pleasure and freedom from pain are the only things desirable as ends; and that all desirable things (which are as numerous in the utilitarian as in any other scheme) are desirable either for pleasure inherent in them-selves or as means to the promotion of pleasure and the prevention of pain.

Now such a theory of life excites in many minds, and among them in some of the most estimable in feeling and purpose, inveterate dislike. To suppose that life has (as they express it) no higher end than pleasure—no better and nobler object of desire and pursuit—they designate as utterly mean and grov-as a doctrine worthy only of swine, to whom the followers of Epicurus were, at a very early period, contemptuously likened; and modern hold-ers of the doctrine are occasionally made the sub-ject of equally polite comparisons by its German, French, and English assailants.

When thus attacked, the Epicureans have always answered that it is not they, but their accusers, who represent human nature in a degrading light, since the accusation supposes human beings to be capa-ble of no pleasures except those of which swine are capable.... It is quite compatible with the principle of utility to recognize the fact that some kinds of pleasure are more desirable and more valuable than others. It would be absurd that, while in estimating all other things quality is considered as well as quantity, the estimation of pleasure should be sup-posed to depend on quantity alone.

If I am asked what I mean by difference of quality in pleasures, or what makes one pleasure more valu-able than another, merely as a pleasure, except its being greater in amount, there is but one possible an-swer. Of two pleasures, if there be one to which all or almost all of who have experience of both give a de-cided preference, irrespective of any feeling of moral obligation to prefer it, that is the more desirable plea-sure. If one of the two is, by those who are compe-tently acquainted with both, placed so far above the other that they prefer it, even though knowing it to be attended with a greater amount of discontent, and would not resign it for ny quantity of the other plea-sure which their nature is capable of, we are justified in ascribing to the preferred enjoyment a superiority in quality so far outweighing quantity as to render it, in comparison, of small amount, Now it is an unquestionable fact that those who are equally acquainted with and equally capable of appreciating and enjoying both do give a most marked preference to the manner of existence which employs their higher faculties. Few human creatures would consent to be changed into any of the lower animals for a promise of the fullest allowance of a beast's pleasures; no intelligent human being would consent to be a fool, no instructed person would be an ignoramus, no person of feeling and conscience would be selfish and base, even though they should be persuaded that the fool, the dunce, or the rascal is better satisfied with his lot than they are with theirs. They would not resign what they possess more than he for the most complete satisfaction of all the desires which they have in common with him. If they ever fancy they would, it is only in cases of unhappiness so extreme that to escape from it they would exchange their lot for almost any other, however un-desirable in dieir own eyes. A being of higher faculties requires more to make him happy, is capable probably of more acute suffering, and certainly accessible to it at more points, than one of an inferior type; but in spite of these liabilities, he can never really wish to sink into what he feels to be a lower grade of existence. ... It is indisputable that the being whose capacities of enjoyment are low has the greatest chance of having them fully satisfied; and a highly endowed being will always feel that any happiness which he can look for, as the world is constituted, is imperfect. But he can learn to bear its imperfections, if they are at all bearable; and they will not make him envy the being who is indeed unconscious of the imperfections, but only because he feels not at all the good which those imperfections qualify. It is better to be a human being dissatisfied than a pig satisfied; better to be Socrates dissatisfied than a fool satisfied. And if the fool, or the pig, are of a different opinion, it is because they only know their own side of the question. The other party to the comparison knows both sides.

It may be objected that many who are capable of the higher pleasures occasionally, under the in-fluence of temptation, postpone them to the lower. But this is quite compatible with a full appreciation of the intrinsic superiority of the higher. Men often, from infirmity of character, make their election for the nearer good, though they know it to be the less valuable; and this is no less when the choice is between two bodiiy pleasures than when it is between bodily and mental. They pursue sensual indulgences to the injury of health, though perfectly aware that health is the greater good. It may be further objected that many who begin with youthful enthusiasm for everything noble, as they advance in years, sink into indolence and selfishness. But I do not believe that those who undergo this very common change voluntarily choose the lower description of pleasures in preference to the higher. I believe that, before they devote themselves exclusively to the one, they have already become incapable of the other. Capacity for the nobler feelings is in most natures a very tender plant, easily killed, not only by hostile influences, but by mere want of sustenance; and in the majority of young persons it speedily dies away if the occupations to which their position in life has devoted them, and the society into which it has thrown them, are not favorable to keeping that higher capacity in exercise. Men lose their high aspirations as they lose their intellectual tastes, because they have not the time or opportunity for indulging them; and they addict themselves to inferior pleasures, not because they deliberately prefer them, but because they are either the only ones to which they have access or the only ones which they are any longer capable of enjoying. It may be questioned whether anyone who has remained equally susceptible to both classes of pleasures ever knowingly and calmly preferred the lower, though many, in all ages, have broken down in an ineffectual attempt to combine both.

From this verdict of the only competent judges, I apprehend there can be no appeal. On a question which is the best worth having of two pleasures, or which of two modes of existence is the most grateful to the feelings, apart from its moral attributes and from its consequences, the judgment of those who are qualified by knowledge of both, or, if they differ, that of the majority among them, must be admitted as final. And there needs to be the less hesitation to accept this judgment respecting the quality of pleasures, since there is no other tribunal to be referred to even on the question of quantity. What means are there of determining which is the acutest of two pains, or the intensest of two pleasurable sensations, except the general suffrage of those who are familiar with both? Neither pains nor pleasures are homogeneous, and pain is always heterogeneous with pleasure. What is there to decide whether a particular pleasure is worth purchasing at the cost of a particular pain, except the feelings and judgment of the experienced? When, therefore, those feelings and judgment declare the pleasures derived from the higher faculties to be preferable m *kind,* apart from the question of intensity, to those of which the animal nature, disjoined from the higher faculties, is susceptible, they are enti-tled on this subject to the same regard,

I have dwelt on this point as being a necessary part of a perfectly just conception of utility or happiness considered as the directive rule of human conduct. But it is by no means an indispensable condition to the acceptance of the utilitarian standard; for that standard is not the agent's own greatest happiness, but the greatest amount of happiness altogether; and if it may possibly be doubted whether a noble character is always the happier for its nobleness, there can be no doubt that it makes other people happier, and that the world in general is immensely a gainer by it. Utilitarianism, therefore, could only attain its end by the general cultivation of nobleness of character, even if each individual were only benefited by the nobleness of other and his own, so far as happiness is concerned, were a sheer deduction from the benefit. But the bare enunciation of such an absurdity as this last renders refutation superfluous.

According to the greatest happiness principle, as above explained, the ultimate end, with reference to and for the sake of which all other things are desirable—whether we are considering our own good or that of other people—is an existence exempt as far as possible from pain, and as rich as possible in enjoyments, both in point of quantity and quality; the test of quality and the rule for measuring it against quantity being the preference felt by those who, in their opportunities of experience, to which must be added their habits of self-consciousness and self-observation, are best furnished with the means of comparison. This, being according to the utilitarian opinion the end of human action, is necessarily also the standard of morality, which may accordingly be denned "the rules and precepts for human conduct," by the observance of which an existence such as has been described might be, to the greatest extent possible, secured to all mankind; and not to them only, but, so far as the nature of things admits, to the whole sentient creation.

... The utilitarian morality does recognize in human beings the power of sacrificing their own greatest good for the good of others. It only refuses to admit that the sacrifice itself is a good. A sacrifice which does not increase or tend to increase the sum total of happiness, it considers as wasted. The only self-renunciation which it applauds is devotion to the happiness, or to some of the means of happi-ness, of others, either of mankind collectively or of individuals within the limits imposed by the collec-tive interests of mankind.

I must again repeat what the assailants of utilitar-ianism seldom have the justice to acknowledge, that the happiness which forms the utilitarian standard of what is right in conduct is not the agent's own happiness but that of all concerned. As between his own happiness and that of others, utilitarianism re-quires him to be as strictly impartial as a disinter-ested and benevolent spectator. In the golden rule of Jesus of Nazareth, we read the complete spirit of the ethics of utility. "To do as you would be done by," and "to love your neighbor as yourself," constitute the ideal perfection of utilitarian morality.

[From *Utilitarianism* by J.S. Mill]

Liberty

The object of this essay is to assert one very simple principle, as entitled to govern absolutely the dealings of society with the individual in the way of compulsion and control, whether the means used by physical force in the form of legal penalties or the moral coercion of public opinion. That principle is that the sole end for which mankind are warranted, individually or collectively, in interfering with the liberty of action of any of their number is self-protection. That the only purpose for which power can be rightfully exercised over any member of a civilized community, against his will, is to prevent harm to others. His own good, either physical or moral, is not a sufficient warrant. He cannot rightfully be compelled to do or forbear because it will be better or him to do so, because it will make him happier, because, in the opinions of others, to do so would be wise or even right. These are good reasons for remonstrating with him, or reasoning with him, or persuading him, or entreating him, but not for compelling him or visiting him with any evil in case he do otherwise. To justify that, the conduct from which it is desired to deter him must be calculated to produce evil to someone else. The only part of the conduct of anyone for which he is amenable to society is that which concerns others. In the part which merely concerns himself, his independence is, of right, absolute. Over himself, over his own body and mind, the individual is sovereign.

It is, perhaps, hardly necessary to say that this doctrine is meant to apply only to human beings in the maturity of their faculties. We are not speaking of children or of young persons below the age which he law may fix as that of manhood or womanhood. Those who are still in a state to require being taken care of by others must be protected against their own actions as well as against external injury. For the same reason we may leave out of consideration those backward states of society in which the race itself may be considered as in its nonage. The early difficulties in the way of spontaneous progress are so great that there is seldom any choice of means for overcoming them; and a ruler full of the spirit of improvement is warranted in the use of any expedients that will attain an end perhaps otherwise unattainable. Despotism is a legitimate mode of government in dealing with barbarians, provided the end be their improvement and the means justified by actually effecting that end. Liberty, as a principle, has no application to any state of things anterior to the time when mankind have become capable of being improved by free and equal discussion. Until then, there is nothing for them but implicit obedience to an Akbar or a Chrlemgne, if they are so fortunate as to find one. But as soon as mankind have attained the capacity of being guided to their own improvement by conviction or persuasion (a period long since reached in all nations with whom we need here concern ourselves), compulsion, either in the direct form or in that of pains and penalties for noncompliance, is no longer admissible as a mean other joint work necessary to the interest of the society of which he enjoys the protection and to perform certain acts of individual beneficence, such as saving a fellow creature's life or interposing to protect the defence-less against ill usage – things which whenever it is obviously a man's duty to do he may rightfully be made responsible to society for not doing. A person may cause evil to others not only by his actions but by his inaction, and in either case he is justly accountable to them for the injury. The latter case, it is true, requires a much more cautious exercise of compulsion than the former. To make anyone answerable for doing evil to others is the rule; to make him answerable for not preventing evil is, comparatively speaking, the exception. Yet there are many cases clear enough and grave enough to justify that exception. In all things which regard the external relations of the individual, he id de jure amenable to those whose interests are concerned, and, if need be, to society as their protector. There are often good reasons for not holding him to the responsibility; but these reasons must arise from the special expediencies of the case: either because it is a kind of case in which he is on the whole likely to act better when left to hie own discretion that when controlled in any way in which society have it in their power to control him; or because the attempt to exercise control would produce other evils, greater than those which it would prevent. When such reasons as these preclude the enforcement of responsibility, the conscience of the agent himself should step into the vacant judgment scat and protect those interests of others which have no external protection; judging himself all the more rigidly, because the case does not admit of his being made accountable to the judgment of his fellow creatures.

But there is a sphere of action in which society, as distinguished from the individual, has, if any, only an indirect interest: comprehending all that portion of a person's life and conduct which effects only himself or, if it also effects others, only with their free, voluntary, and undeceived consent and participation. When I say only himself, I mean directly and in the first instance; for whatever affects himself may affect others through himself; and the objection which may be grounded on this contingency will receive consideration in the sequel. This, then, is the appropriate region of human liberty. It comprises, first, the inward domain of consciousness, demanding liberty of conscience in the most comprehensive sense, liberty of thought and feeling, absolute freedom of opinion and sentiment on all subjects, practical or speculative, scientific, moral, or theological. The liberty of expressing and publishing opinions may seem to fall under a different principle, since it belongs to that part of the conduct of an individual which concerns other people, but being almost of as much importance as the liberty of thought itself and resting in great part on the same reasons, is practically inseparable from it. Secondly, the principle requires liberty of tastes and pursuits, of framing the plan of our life to suit our own character, of doing as we like, subject to such consequences as may follow, without impediment from our fellow creatures, so long as what we do does not harm them, even though they should think our conduct foolish, perverse, or wrong. Thirdly, from this liberty of each individual follows the liberty, within the same limits, of combination among individuals; freedom to unite for any purpose not involving harm to others: the persons combining being supposed to be of full age and not forced or deceived.

No society in which these liberties are not, on the whole, respected is free, whatever may be its form of government; and none is completely free in which they do not exist absolute and unqualified. The only freedom which deserves the name is that of pursuing our own good in our own way, so long as we do not attempt to deprive others of theirs or impede their efforts to obtain it. Each is the proper guardian of his own health, whether bodily or mental and spiritual. Mankind are greater gainers by suffering each others to live as seems good to themselves than by compelling each to live as seems good to the rest.

Though his doctrine is anything but new and, to some persons, may have the air of a truism, there is no doctrine which stands more directly opposed to the general tendency of existing opinion and practice. Society has expended fully as much effort in the attempt (according to its lights) to compel people to conform to its notions of personal as of social excellence. The ancient commonwealths thought themselves entitled to practice, and the ancient philosophers countenanced, the regulation of every part of private conduct by public authority, on the ground that the State had a deep interest in the whole bodily and mental discipline of every one of its citizens – a mode of thinking which may have been admissible in small republics surrounded by powerful enemies, in constant peril of being subverted by foreign attack or internal commotion, and to which even a short interval of relaxed energy and self-command might so easily be fatal that they could not afford to wait for the salutary permanent effects of freedom. In the modern world, the greater size of political communities and, above all, the separation between spiritual and temporal authority (which placed the direction of men's consciences in other hands than those which controlled their worldly affairs) prevented so great an interference by law in the details of private life; but the engines of moral repression have been wielded more strenuously against divergence from the reigning opinion in self-regarding than even in social matters; religion, the most powerful of the elements which have entered into the formation of moral feeling, having almost always been governed either by the ambition of a hierarchy seeking control over every department of human conduct, or by the spirit of Puritanism. And some of those modern reformers who have placed themselves in strongest opposition to the religions of the past have been noway behind either churches or sects in their assertion of the right of spiritual domination: M. Comte, in particular, whose social system, as unfolded in his *Systeme de Politique Positive,* aims at establishing (though by moral more than by legal appliances) a despotism of society over the individual surpassing anything contemplated in the political ideal of the most rigid disciplinarian among the ancient philosophers.

Apart from the peculiar tenets of individual thinkers, there is also in the world at large an increasing inclination to stretch unduly the powers of society over the individual both by the force of opinion and even by that of legislation; and as the tendency of all changes taking place in the world is to strengthen society and diminish the power of the individual, this encroachment is not one of the evils which tend spontaneously to disappear, but, on the contrary, to grow more and more formidable. The disposition of mankind, whether as rulers or as fellows citizens, to impose their own opinions and inclinations as a rule of conduct on others is so energetically supported by some of the best and by some of the worst feelings incident to human nature that it is hardly ever kept under restraint by anything but want of power; and as the power is not declining, but growing, unless a strong barrier of moral conviction can be raised the mischief, we must expect, in the present circumstances of the world, to see it *increase.*

(From *On Liberty and the Subjection of Women* by J.S. Mill, with an Introduction by Jone O' Grady, wordsworth Classis, 1996).

17

Karl Marx

Karl Marx (1818-1883) is arguably the most controversial figure in the long history of political philosophy. Intellectual and activist, journalist, pamphleteer, revolutionary organizer and essayist, public figure and fugitive, he was author or coauthor of some fifty volumes of both scholarly and political writings. He was an opponent of much of the past, even while appreciating how that past served as a foundation of a more desirable future. A complex thinker, sharp-tempered, and an articulate speaker, debater, and critic of various contemporaries, he clashed with many people during his life.

In addition to the immeasurable effects of his work on world events, Marx profoundly affected a number of scholarly disciplines beyond political philosophy, most importantly economics and sociology but also art and literature. Because of the wide reach of his theories and their many implications, it is hard to imagine an important aspect of study or life that has been immune to his influence. All the points to the multiple ways that thinking (and dogmatic) individuals have understood the tremendous output of this literary giant. Entering into the field of Marx studies is like embarking on an intellectual adventure relatively few other authors or books can offer. The questions he raised, the insights he had, and the solutions he proposed deal with the most significant issues facing humanity. Interpreters have found in Marx worthwhile ideas that they believe can be applied to such concerns as poverty, peace, feminism, discrimination, ecology, and , ultimately, human survival. Given his vast output, and that of commentators on his work, there are many paths one can use to approach his writings. Any single route has its supporters and no one choice fully satisfies every critic.

Einstein, Freud, Jesus, and Karl Marx have been listed as the most important figures in history. Of course, the followers of Marx probably outnumber even the followers of Jesus. Some people, moreover, regard themselves as both Marxists and Christians. Marx was the son of a Jewish lawyer who converted to Lutheranism despite having descended from generations of rabbis; Marx was thus raised as a Protestant. He studied at German universities in Bonn, Berlin, and Jena, first in law and then in philosophy. His PhD at Jena (received when he was only twenty-three) was based on a completely ordinary dissertation on Democritus and Epicurus. While in Berlin, Marx had come under the sway of Hegelianism and a group of radical Hegelians. But later, strongly influenced by the philosophy of Ludwig Feuerbach, he rejected idealism for materialism and his own theory of history as the outworking of economic factors.

Marx's radical views prevented him from occupying an academic post. In 1842 he became editor of a Cologne newspaper that during his tenure became much too radical for the authorities and was suppressed. The twenty-five-year-old Marx then went to Paris, where he mingled with many famous radicals and established another radical periodical. In Paris he also met his future collaborator, Friedrich Engels. In about a year Marx was expelled from Paris, and from 1845 to 1848 he lived in Brussels. While there, he helped form a worker's union that, together with other similar groups, became known as the Communist League. It was for this organization that he and Engles wrote their famous and stirring *Communist Manifesto* (1848). Marx spent a brief period again in Paris and then in Cologne, participating in both the French and the German revolutions of 1848. He was, however, expelled once again from both countries. In 1849 he went to London and stayed there for the rest of his life.

In London, Marx required financial help from Engels, for just as some are addicted to gambling, Marx was addicted to reading and writing, and these activities did not produce much of an income. Despite Engels help and the small amount of money he received for articles he wrote for the New York *Tribune*, he lived in poverty, illness, and – when his children and wife died one by one – immense sadness.

During this period Marx wrote the *Critique of Political Economy* (1859) and, more important, the work destined to become the primary document of international communism, *capital* (vol. 1, 1867; vols. 2 and 3, edited by Enegls, 1885 and 1894). In 1864 he helped create the International Working-men's Association (the so-called First International), which he later led. A famous clash between Marx and the anarchist Mikhail Bakunin, however, led to its dissolution within about ten years. Marx died of pleurisy in London when he was sixty-five.

The utilitarians pursed social and political reform. Karl Marx went even further. Marx wanted not merely to reform society but to transform it. Marx, who is famous for his remark that philosophers have tried only to interpret the world, whereas the real point is to change it, did not regard his work as philosophy. Marx offers a description and analysis of the human social and political condition, but he did not himself present this understanding as the absolute and final truth. For Marx the ideal society has no economic classes, no wages, no money, no private property, and no exploitation. Each person will not only be provided a fully adequate material existence but will also be given the opportunity to develop freely and completely all physical and mental faculties. The alienation of the individual from the surroundings world will be minimal.

Humans, Marx believed, are social animals with physical needs, needs that are satisfied when we develop the means to satisfy them. These means of producing the satisfaction of needs are called the means or forces of production. The utilization of any one set of means of production leads to fresh needs and therefore to further means of production. For example, the invention of iron tools (a new means of production) for the cultivation of needed crops leads to still a newer need – for iron – and therewith to the means for satisfying this newer need. Thus, human history consists of successive stages of development of various means of production. Furthermore, the utilization of any given means of production, whether it is a simple iron tool or a complex machine, necessarily involves certain social relationships, especially those involving property. These social relationships (institutions or practices) are called the productive relations. Thus, the social relationships (the productive relations) depend on the stage of evolution of the forces of production.

The forces of production at a given stage, however, develop to the point where they come into conflict with the existing social relationships, which are then destroyed and replaced by new social relationships. For example, the need at the end of the Middle Ages to supply the new markets in the Far East and the colonies in the New World required new methods of manufacture and commerce, which brought with their development societal changes incompatible with the feudal social structure of the Middle Ages.

The new social relationships then endure until new needs arise and a new stage is reached in the evolution of the forces of production. This dialectical process repeats itself over and over again and is the history of people, economics, and society. To put this another way, history is the result of productive activity in interplay with social relationships. According to Marx, this interplay accounts not only for all socio economic – political situations but also for morality, law, religion, and, to a greater or lesser extent, even philosophy and art. According to Marx the critical social relationships involve property. With the advent of private property, society became divided into two classes: those with property and those without.

Hostility between the two classes was, and is, inevitable, Marx said. Those with property, of course, are the dominant class, and government and morality are always the instruments of the dominant class. When the forces of production create conflict with the existing social relationships, class struggle becomes acute, revolution results, and a new dominant class seizes control of the organs of state and imposes its ethic. The dialectical process repeats itself until private property and the division of society into opposed classes disappears In modern capitalist societies, what has happened, according to Marx, is that the means of production are primarily concentrated in large factories and workshops in which a group of individual workers cooperatively produces a product. They collectively "mix their labor with the product", as Locke would say. But the product they mix their labor with is not owned by them. Rather, it is appropriated by the owners of the factories, who thus in effect also own the workers. Out of this circumstance comes the fundamental conflict of capitalist society: production is socialized, but ownership is not. Furthermore, Marx argued, capitalists obviously must sell what their workers produce for more than they pay the workers to make it. The laborers thus produce goods that are worth more than their wages. This exploitation of the workers is inevitable as long as the conflict between socialized means of production and non-socialized ownerships continues. It is a necessary part of the capitalist system and is not a result of wickedness or inhumanity on the part of the capitalist.

There are two further unavoidable consequences of continuing capitalism, in Marx's opinion. First, the longer the capitalist system continues, the smaller and wealthier the possessing class becomes. This is simply the result of the fact that the surplus value of products – that is, the value of a product less its "true" cost, which is the cost of the labor put into it- continues to accrue to the capitalists. Further, as smaller capitalists cannot compete, and as a result fail in their enterprise and sink into the ranks of the workers, society's wealth becomes increasingly concentrated: fewer and fewer people control more and more of it.

The second consequence of continued capitalism, according to Marx, is the increasing alienation of the workers. The more wealth the workers produce, the poorer they become, relatively speaking, for it is not they who retain this wealth. So the result of increased productivity for the workers is; paradoxically but inevitably, their devaluation in their own eyes and in fact. They have become mere commodities.

In addition because workers produce through their labor what does not belong to others, the worker's labor nor are the products they make their own. Both labor and products are as alien things that dominate them. Thus, workers feel at home with themselves only during their leisure time and in eating, drinking, and having sex. Worker's presence at work is not voluntary but imposed and, whenever possible, avoided. Because they have put their lives into what belongs to others, workers are abject, debased, physically exhausted, and overcome with malaise. And because the relation of people to themselves in first realized and expressed in the relationship between each person and another, workers are alienated from their fellows.

The situation Marx describes is, in his view, self-liquidating. The capitalist system of property ownership is incompatible with the socialized conditions of production and ultimately destined to failure. Inevitable overproduction will result in economic crises, a falling rate of profit, and increased exploitation of the working class, which will increasingly become conscious of itself and its own intolerable condition, the inadequacy of capitalism, and the inevitability of history. The revolution of the proletariat (working class), leading to a dictatorship of the proletariat, will follow. In this instance, however, the overturning of the existing social order will eventually result in the classless society just described, for property, as well as the means of production, will have become socialized. The disappearance of classes will mark the end of class struggle and also, therefore, the end of political power because the sole function of political power is the suppression of one class at the expense of another.

By the end of the nineteenth century, most European socialist parties were committed to Marxism, but a split developed between the revolutions, those who believed that a violent revolution was necessary to set in the place the collective ownership of the means of production and distribution of goods, and the revisionists or evolutionary socialists, those who thought that these ends could be achieved through peaceful and piecemeal reform.

Although evolutionary socialism became strong in Great Britain and survives in the socialist parties of many nations to the present day, the revolution gained ascendancy in the Second International, the successor to Marx's International Workingmen's Association, or the First International. Under the leadership of Lenin, the revolutionist

Bolsheviks came to control the Russian Social Democratic Labor Party and seized control of Russia itself in the Revolution of 1917, becoming in 1918 the Communist Party of the USSR.

Although the Russian Communists withdrew from the Second International and founded Third International or Comintern in 1919 to gain leadership of the world socialist movement, most European Socialist parties disassociated themselves from the Communists. The term Communism, with a capital C, today still denotes the Marxist-Leninist ideology of the parties founded under the banner of the Comintern and is to be distinguished from lowercase-*c* communism, which denotes any form of society in which property or other important goods are held in common by the community.

—Editor

Money, the Universal Whore

Money, inasmuch as it possesses the property of being able to buy everything and appropriate all objects, is the object most worth possessing. The universality of this property is the basis of money's omnipotence; hence it is regarded as an omnipotent being. .. Money is the pimp between need and object, between life and man's means of life. But that which mediates my life also mediate the existence of other men for me. It is for me the other person.

What, man confound it, hands and feet And head and backside, all are yours! And what we take while life is sweet, Is that to be declared nut ours? Six stallions, say, I can afford, Is not their strength my property? I tear along, a sporting lord As if their legs belonged to me. (Goethe, Fazssi—Mephistopheles) Shakespeare—in Timon of Athens'.

Gold? Yellow, glittering, precious gold? No. gods, I am no idle votanst: roots, you clear heavens! Thus much of this will make black while; foul, fair; Wrong, right; base, noble; old, young coward, valiant.

Why, this Will lug your priests and servants from your sides, Pluck stout men's pillows from below their heads; This yellow slave Will knit and break religions; bless the accurse; Make the hoar leprosy adored; place thieves. And give them title, knee, and approbation, With senators on the bench: this is it That makes the wrapper's widow wed again; She whom the spinal-house and ulcerous sores Would cast the gorge at, this embalms and spices

To the April day again. Come, damned earth, Thou common whore of mankind, that putty's odds Among the rout of nations, I will make thee, Do they right nature.

And later on; O thou sweet king-killer, and dear divorce Twit natural son and sire! Thou bright defiler Of Hymen's purest bed Thou valiant Mars Thou ever young fresh, loved and delicate wxx3r, Whose blush doth thaw the consecrated snow That lies on Dian's lap! Thou viable gin, that solder's close And mark's them kiss! That sneak's with every tongue. To every purpose! O thou touch of hearts Think, thy slave man rebels; and by thy virtue Set them into confounding odds, that beasts May have the world in empire Shakespeare paints a brilliant picture of the nature of money. To understand him let us begin by expounding the passage from Goethe.

That which exists for me through the medium of money, that which I can pay for, i.e. which money can buy, that am!, the possessor of the money. The stronger the power of my money, the stronger am /, The properties of money are my, the possessor's, properties and essential powers. Therefore what I am and what I can do is by no means determined by my individuality. I am ugly, but I can buy the most beautiful woman. Which means to say that I am not ugly, for the effect of ugliness, its repelling power, is destroyed by money. As an individual, I am lame, but money procures me twenty-four legs. Consequently. I am not lame. I am a wicked, dishonest, unscrupulous and stupid individual, but money is respected, and also is its owner. Money is the highest good, and consequently its owner is also good. Moreover, money spares me the trouble of being dishonest, and I am therefore presumed to be honest. I am mindless, hut if money is the trite mind of all things, how can its owner he mindless? What is more, he can buy clever people for himself, and is not he who has power over clever people cleverer than them? Through money I can have anything the human heart desires. Do I not therefore possess all human abilities? Does not money therefore transform all my incapacities into their opposite?

If money is the bond which ties me to human life and society tome, which links me to nature and to man, is money not the bond of all bonds'! Can it not bind and loose all bonds? Is it therefore not the universal means of separation? It is the true agent of separation and the true cementing agent, it is the chemical power of society. Shakespeare brings out two properties of money in particular:

(1) It is the visible divinity, the transformation of all human and natural qualities into their opposites, the universal confusion and inversion

of things; it brings together impossibilities.

(2) It is the universal whore, the universal pimp of men and peoples.

The inversion and confusion of all human and natural qualities, the bringing together of impossibilities, the divine power of money lies in its mealier as the estranged and alienating species-essence of man which alienates itself by selling itself. It is the alienated capacity of mankind.

What I as a man cannot do, i.e. what all my individual powers cannot do, can do with the help of money. Money therefore transforms each of these essential powers into something which it is not, into its opposite. If I desire a meal or want to take the mail coach because I am not strong enough to make the journey on foot, money can procure me both the meal and the mail coach, i.e. it transfers my wishes from the realm of imagination, it translates them from their existence as thought, imagination and desires into their sensuous, real existence, from imagination into life, and from imagined being into real being. In this mediating role money is the truly creative power.

Demand also exists bar those who have no money, but their demand is simply a figment of the imagination. For me or for any other third party it has no effect, no existence. For me it therefore remains unreal and without an object. The difference between effective demand based on money and ineffective demand based on my need, my passion, my desire, etc., is the difference between being and thinking, between a representation which merely exists within me and one which exists outside me as a real object.

(From *Marx: Early Writings translated* by Rodway living stone, Penguin Books, England, 1975)

Thesis on Feuerbach

Thesis 1

Hence, in opposition to materialism, the active side was developed in abstract fashion by idealism which naturally does not know of real, sensible activity as such. Feuerbach appeals to sensible objects-ones really distinct from thought objects: but he does not conceive human activity itself as activity which belongs the objective world. Hence in the 'Essence of Christianity' he considers only the theoretical stance as the genuinely human one, whilst practice is conceived and set off only in its grubby Jewish form. Hence he does not grasp the meaning of 'revolutionary', of 'practical-critical' activity."

Thesis 2

The question whether truth about the objective world is attained by human thinking is not a question of theory, but a practical question. In practice must man prove the truth, that is reality and power, this-worldliness of his thinking. The dispute over the reality on non-reality of thinking - that is isolated from practice- is a purely scholastic question.

Thesis 3

The materialist doctrine about change of circumstances and education forgets that circumstances are hanged by men and the educator himself must be educated. Hence it must sunder society into two parts of which one is superior to society. The coincidence of the changing of circumstances and of human activity or self- change can be conceived and rationally understood only as icvolittionaiy practice?

Thesis 4

Feuerbach starts from the fact of religious elf-estrangement, of the duplication of the world into a religious and a secular one. His work consists in resolving the religious would into its secular basis. But that the secular basis takes off from itself and establishes itself as realm m the doubts can only be explained in terms of the inwardly even and inwardly contradictory character of this secular basis.

Therefore this itself must both be understood in its contradiction and revolutionized in practice. Thus once for example the earthly family is revealed as the secret of the holy family, the former must itself be destroyed in theory and in practice.

Thesis 5

Feuerbach, not satisfied with abstract thinking, appeals to observation; but he does not conceive the sensible world as practical human activity involving the senses."

What is said here is substantially only a reprise of part of what has already been said in Thesis and one may therefore pass on immediately to the next thesis, which resumes the critique of Feuerbach on religion initiated in Thesis 4.

Thesis 6

Feuerbach resolves the essence of religion into the essence of man. Hut the essence of man is no abstraction indwelling in each separate individual. In its reality it is the ensemble of social relations.

Feuerhach, who does not enter into the critique of this real essence, is hence obliged:

(1) to abstract from the course of history and to set off the religious I attitude as something self-contained, and to assume an abstract-isolated- human individual.

(2) Hence the essence can be conceived only as 'genus', as an inner, mute, universal character uniting the many individuals in a natural way.

Thesis 7

Hence Feuerbach does not sec that the 'religious attitude' itself is a social product and that the abstract individual which he analyzes belongs to a definite form of society.'

The first clause of this thesis only sums up what has just gone before. The second clause makes explicit an implication of the doctrines just outlined and in effect poses a question (precisely what form of society?) which is in fact answered in Theses 9 and 10. Hut before this answer is presented Marx generalizes the insight illustrated in the preceding criticism of Feuerbach's traditional materialist view of religion.

Thesis 8

All social life is essentially practical. All mysteries that turn theory towards mysticism find their rational solution in human practice and in the comprehension of this practice.

Thesis 9

The highest point attained by materialism based on observation, that is materialism which docs not comprehend the sensible world as practical activity, is the observation of separate individuals and of civil society."

Thesis 10

The standpoint of the old materialism is civil society, the standpoint of the new, human society or social humanity.

Thesis 11

The philosophers have only interpreted the world in different ways, the point is to change it.

(*Marx*: *Early Writings* Translated by Rodway Living Stone and Gregar Barlon, Penguin Books, England, 1975).

Productive and Unproductive Labour

A philosopher produces ideas, a poet poems, a clergyman sermons, a professor compendia and so on. A criminal produces crimes. If we look a little closer at the connection between this latter branch of production and society as a whole, we shall rid ourselves of many prejudices. The criminal produces not only crimes but also criminal law, and with this also the professor who gives lectures on criminal law and in addition to this the inevitable compendium in which this same professor throws his lectures onto the general market as "commodities". This brings with it augmentation of national wealth, quite apart from the personal enjoyment which - as a competent witness, Heir Professor Roscher, [tells] us - the manuscript of the compendium brings to its originator himself.

The criminal moreover produces the whole of the police and of criminal justice, constables, judges, hangmen, juries, etc.; and all these different lines of business, which form equally many categories of the social division of labour, develop different capacities of the human spirit, create new needs and new ways of satisfying them. Torture alone has given rise to the most ingenious mechanical inventions, and employed many honourable craftsmen in the production of instruments.

The criminal produces an impression, partly moral and partly tragic, as the case may be, and in this way renders a "service" by arousing the moral and aesthetic feelings of the public. He produces not only compendia on Criminal Law, not only penal codes and along with them legislators in this field, but also art, belles-letters, novels, and even tragedies, as not only Mullner's Schuld and Schiller's Rauber show, but also *Oedipus and Richard the Third.* The criminal breaks the monotony and everyday security of bourgeois life. In this way he keeps it from stagnation, and gives rise to that uneasy tension and agility without which even the spur of competition would get blunted. Thus he gives a stimulus to the productive forces. While crime takes a part of the superfluous population of the labour market and thus reduces competition among the labourers - up to a certain point preventing wages from falling below the minimum -the struggle against crime absorbs another part of his population. Thus the criminal conies in as one of those natural "counterweights" which bring about a correct balance and open up a whole perspective of "useful" occupations.

The effects of the criminal on the development of productive power can be shown in detail. Would locks ever have reached their present degree of excellence had there been no thieves? Would the making of bank-notes have reached its present perfection had there been no forgers? Would the microscope have found its way into the sphere of ordinary commerce (see Babbage) but for trading frauds? Doesn't practical chemistry owe just as much to adulteration of commodities and the efforts to show it up as to the honest zeal for production? Crime, through its constantly new methods of attack on property, constantly calls into being new methods of defence, and so is as productive as strikes for the invention of machines. And if one leaves the sphere of private crime: would the world-market ever have come into being but for national crime? Indeed, would even the nations have arisen? And hasn't the Tree of Sin been at the same time the Tree of Knowledge ever since the-time of Adam?

In his *Fable of the Bees* (1705) Mandevillė had already shown that every possible kind of occupation is productive, and had given expression to the line of this whole argument:

That what we call Evil in this World, Moral as well as Natural, is the grand Principle that makes us Sociable Creatures, the solid Basis, the *Life and Support of all Trades and Employments* without exception [...] there we must look for the true origin of all Arts and Sciences; and [.,.] the moment, Evil ceases, the Society must be spoil'd if not totally dissolved. Only Mandeville was of course infinitely bolder and more honest than the philistine apologists of bourgeoisie society.

(From *Selected Works*, Karl Marx and F. Engels, Progress Publishers, Moscow, 19973)

The Communist Manifesto

A spectre is haunting Europe - the spectre of Communism. All the Powers of old Europe have entered into a holy alliance to exorcise this spectre: Pope and Czar, Metternich and Guizot, French Radicals and German police-spies.

Communism is already acknowledged by all European Powers to be itself a Power. It is high time that Communists should openly, in the face of the whole world, publish their views, their aims, their tendencies, and meet this nursery tale of the Spectre of Communism with a Manifesto of the party itself.

The history of all hitherto existing society is the history of class struggles. Freeman and slave, patrician and plebian, lord and serf, guide-master and journeyman, in a word, oppressor and oppressed, stood in constant opposition to one another, carried on an uninterrupted, now hidden, now open flight, a flight that each time ended, either in a revolutionary re-constitution of society at large, or in the common ruin of the contending classes.

In the earlier epochs of history, we find almost everywhere a complicated arrangement of society into various orders, a manifold gradation of social rank. In ancient Rome we have patricians, knights, plebeians, slaves; in the Middle Ages, feudal lords, vassals, guild-masters, journeyman, apprentices, serfs; in almost of these classes, again, subordinate gradations. The modern bourgeois society that has sprouted from the ruins of feudal society has not done away with class antagonisms. It has but established new classes, new conditions of oppression, new forms of struggle in place of the old ones. Our epoch, the epoch of the bourgeoisie, possesses, however, this distinctive feature: it has simplified the class antagonisms. Society as a whole is more and more splitting up into great hostile camps, into two great classes directly facing each other. Bourgeoisie and Proletariat.

Modern's industry has established the world market, for which the discovery of America paved the way. This market has given an immense development to commerce, to navigation, to communication by land. This development has, in its turn, reacted on the extension of industry; and in proportion as industry, commerce, navigation, railway extended, in the same proportion the bourgeoisie developed, increased its capital, and pushed into the background every class handed down from the Middle Ages.

We see, therefore, how the modern bourgeoisie is itself the product of a long course of development, of a series of revolutions in the modes of production and of exchange. The bourgeoisie has at last, since the establishment of Modern Industry and of the world market, conquered for itself, in the modern representative State, exclusive political sway. The executive of the modem State is but a committee for managing the common affairs of the whole bourgeoisie.

The bourgeoisie, historically, has played a most revolutionary part. The bourgeoisie, wherever it has got the upper hand, has put an end to all feudal, patriarchal, idyllic relations. It has pitilessly torn asunder the motley feudal ties that bound man to his "natural superiors", and has left remaining no other nexus between man and man than naked self-interest, than callous "cash payment". It has drowned the most heavenly ecstasies of religious fervour , of chivalrous enthusiasm, of philistine sentimentalism, in the icy water of egotistical calculation. It has resolved personal worth into exchange value, and in place of the numberless indefeasible chartered freedoms, has set up that single, unconscionable freedom - Free Trade. In one word, for exploitation, veiled by religious and political illusions, it has substituted naked, shameless, direct, brutal exploitation.

The bourgeoisie has stripped of its halo every occupation hitherto honoured and looked up to with reverent awe. It has converted the physician, the lawyer, the priest, the poet, the man of science, into its paid wage-labourers.

The bourgeoisie has torn away from the family its sentimental veil, and has reduced the family relation to a mere money relation. The bourgeoisie has disclosed how it came to pass that the brutal display of vigour in the Middle Ages, which Reactionists so much admire, found its fitting complement in the most slothful indolence. It has been the first to show what men's activity can bring about.

The bourgeoisie cannot exist without constantly revolutionizing the instruments of production, and thereby the relations of production, and with them the whole relations of society. Conservation of the old modes of production in unaltered form, was, on the contrary, the first condition of existence for all earlier industrial classes. Constant revolutionizing of production, uninterrupted disturbance of all social conditions, everlasting uncertainty and agitation distinguish the bourgeois epoch from all earlier ones. All fixed, fast-frozen relations, with their tram of ancient and venerable prejudices and opinions, are swept away, all new-formed ones become antiquated before they can ossify. All that is solid melts into air, all that is holy is profaned and man is at last compelled to face with sober senses, his real conditions of life, and his relations with his kind.

The need of a constantly expanding market for its products chases the bourgeoisie over the whole surface of the globe. It must nestle everywhere, establish connexions everywhere.

We see then: the means or production and of exchange, on whose foundation the bourgeoisie built itself up, were generated in feudal society. At a certain stage in the development of these means of production and of exchange, the conditions under which feudal society produced and exchanged, the feudal organization of agriculture and manufacturing industry, in one word, the feudal relations of property became no longer compatible with the already developed productive forces; they became so many fetters. They had to be burst asunder; they were burst asunder.

Into their place stepped free competition, accompanied by a social and political constitution adapted to it, and by the economical and political sway of the bourgeois class.

A similar movement is going on before our own eyes. Modern bourgeois society that has conjured up such gigantic means of production and of exchange, is like the sorcerer, who is no longer able to control the powers of the nether world whom he has called up by his spells. For many a decade past the history of industry and commerce is but the history of revolt of modem productive forces against modern conditions of production, against the property relations that are the conditions for the existence of the bourgeoisie and of its rule. It is enough to mention that commercial crises that by their periodical return put on its trial, each time more threateningly, the existence of the entire bourgeois society. In these crises a great part not only of the existing products, but also of the previously created productive forces, are periodically destroyed.

The weapons with which the bourgeoisie felled feudalism to the ground are now turned against the bourgeoisie itself. But not only has the bourgeoisie forged the weapons that bring death to itself; it has also called into existence the men who are to wield those weapons - the modem working class-the proletarians. In proportion as the bourgeoisie, i.e., capital, is developed, in the same proportion is the proletariat, the modern working class, developed - a class of labourers, who live only so long as they find capital. These labourers, who must sell themselves piecemeal, are a commodity, like every other article of commerce, and are consequently exposed to all the vicissitudes of competition to all the fluctuations of the market.

Owing to the extensive use of machinery and to division of labour, the work of the proletarians has lost all individual character, and, consequently, all charm for the workman. He becomes as appendage of the machine, and it is only the most simple, most monotonous, and most easily acquired knack, that is required of him. hence, the cost of production of a workman is restricted, almost entirely, to the means of subsistence that he requires for his maintenance, and for the propagation of his race. But the price of a commodity, and therefore also of labour, is equal to its cost of production, hi proportion, therefore, as the repulsiveness of the work increases, the wage decreases. Nay more, in proportion as the use of machinery and division of labour increases, in the same proportion the burden of toil also increases, whether by prolongation of the working hours, by increase of the work exacted in a given time or by increased speed of the machinery, etc.

The proletariat goes through various stages of development. With its birth begins its struggle with the bourgeoisie. At first the contest is carried on by individual labourers, then by the workpeople ef a factory, then by the operatives of one trade, in one locality, against the individual bourgeois who directly exploits them. They direct their attacks not against the bourgeois conditions of production, but imported wares that compete with their labour, they smash to pieces machinery, they set factories ablaze, they seek to restore by force the vanished status of the workman of the Middle Ages.

But with the development of industry the proletariat not only increases in number; it becomes concentrated in greater masses, its strength grows, and it feels that strength more. The various interests and conditions of life within the ranks of the proletariat are more and more equalished, in proportion as machinery obliterates all distinctions of labour, and nearly everywhere reduces wages to the same low level, The growing competition among the bourgeois, and the resulting commercial crises, make the wages of the workers ever more fluctuating the unceasing improvement of machinery, ever more rapidly developing, makes their livelihood more and more precautions; the collisions between individual workmen and individual.

Now and then workers are victorious, but only for a time. The real fruit of their battles lies, not in the immediate result, but in the ever-expanding union of the workers. This union is helped on by the improved means of communication that are created by modern industry and that place the workers of different localities in contact with one another. It was just this contact that was needed to centralize the numerous local struggles between classes. But every class struggle is a political struggle. And that union, to attain which the burghers of the Middle Ages, with their miserable highways, required centuries, the modern proletarians, thanks to railways, achieve in a few years.

This organization of the proletarians into a class, and consequently into a political party, is continually being upset again by the competition between the workers themselves. But it ever rises up again, stronger, firmer, mightier. It compels legislative recognition of particular interests of the workers, by taking advantage of the divisions among the bourgeoisie itself. Thus the ten-hours' bill in England was carried.

Finally, in times when the class struggle nears the decisive hour, the process of dissolution going on within the ruling class, in fact within the whole range of old society, assumes such a violent, glaring character, that a small section of the ruling class cuts itself adrift, and joins the revolutionary class, the class that holds the future in its hands. Just as, therefore, at an earlier period, a section of the nobility went over to the bourgeoisie, so now a portion of the bourgeoisie goes over to the proletariat, and in particular, a portion of the bourgeois ideologists, who have raised themselves to the level of comprehending theoretically the historical movement as a whole.

Of all the classes that stand face to face with the bourgeoisie today, the proletariat alone is a really revolutionary class. The other classes decay and finally disappear in the face of Modern Industry; the proletariat is its special and essential product.

All previous historical movements were movements of minorities, or in the interest of minorities. The proletarian movement is the self-conscious, independent movement of the immense majority, in the interest of the immense majority. The proletariat, the lowest stratum of our present society, cannot stir, cannot raise itself up, without the whole superincumbent strata of official society being sprung into the air.

Hitherto, every form of society has been based on the antagonism of oppressing and oppressed classes. But in order to oppress a class, certain conditions must be assured to it under which it can, at least, continue its slavish existence. The serf, in the period of serfdom, raised himself to membership in the commune, just as the petty bourgeois, under the yoke of feudal absolutism, managed to develop into a bourgeois. The modern labourer, on the contrary, instead of rising with the progress of industry, sinks deeper and deeper below the conditions of existence of his own class. He becomes a pauper, and pauperism develops more rapidly than population and wealth. And here it becomes evident, that the bourgeoisie is unfit any longer to be the ruling class in society, and to impose its conditions of existence upon society as an over-riding law. It is unfit to rule because it is incompetent to assure an existence to its slave within his slavery, because it cannot helps letting him sink into such a state, that it has to feed him, instead of being fed by him. Society can no longer compatible with society.

The essential condition for the existence, and for the sway of the bourgeois class, is the formation and augmentation of capital; the condition for capital is wage-labour. Wage-labour rests exclusively on competition between the labourers. The advance of industry, whose involuntary promoter is the bourgeoisie, replaces the isolation of the labourers, due to competition, by their revolutionary combination, due to association. The development of Modem Industry, therefore, cuts from under its feet the very foundation on which the bourgeoisie produces and appropriates products. What the bourgeoisie, therefore, produces, above all, is its own grave-diggers. Its fall and the victory of the proletariat are equally inevitable.

(From *The Communist Manifesto* by Karl Marx, Progress Publishers, Moscow, 1975)

18

Friedrich Nietzsche

Friedrich Nietzsche (1844-1900), a German philosopher and classical scholar, spent most of his life in Switzerland, where he taught at the university in Bern. He is a major Western philosopher whose ideas are often misunderstood. Although he has been described as an inspiration for Nazi Germany, careful reading of his works shows that his ideas are not the basis of fascist thought; the Nazis used his writings to suit their own purposes. In addition, he has been described as a nihilist and relativist, but Nietzsche himself dismissed such labels.

Nietzsche, like Freud, is very pessimistic about civilization. He agrees with Freud that bourgeois culture frustrates true human nature. But unlike Freud, who viewed all forms of culture as inhibiting, Nietzsche sees Christianity and early modern values as the triumph of social decadence over human nature and the victory of a slave morality over a master morality. Nietzsche sees clear limits to the ability of reason and modern philosophy and politics to secure firm foundations for moral and political values. Modernity, if anything, undermines itself, producing nihilism, or belief in nothing, and the urge to destroy.

Friderich Nietzsche was son of a Lutheran minister. His father died of insanity when Nietzsche was four, and Nietzsche was raised until he was fourteen in a household of women, consisting of his mother, sister, grandmother, and two maiden aunts. After studying at the universities of Bonn and Leipzig, Nietzsche, whose genius was evident from the beginning was appointed associate professor of classical philology at the University of Basel at the unheard-of young age of twenty-four without even having written a doctoral thesis. Within two years he had became a full professor. In 1879, however, he was forced by ill health to resign his chair, and by 1889, he, like his father earlier, had became irretrievably insane. Nietzsche's insanity, however, may have been caused by medication.

Two of the principal intellectual influences on Nietzsche's life were the writings of Schopenhauer and the music of Richard Wagner, which Nietzsche compared to hashish in its ability to relieve mental pressure. For a period Nietzsche and Wagner – one of the century's most brilliant philosophers and one of its most brilliant composers – were friends, though this friendship did not last.

Nietzsche's writings have been enormously influential in Continental philosophy. Nietzsche saw himself as an active nihilist whose role was to tear down the old "slave morality" of Christian civilization. He looked to the *Superman* , whose will-to-power would set him beyond conventional standards of morality, a line of thought that later was seized upon, misinterpreted, and misused by defenders of Nazism. Nietzsche's widespread popularity outside philosophical circles owes much to the power of thought expressed in numerous infamous quotations, "Which is it," Nietzsche asked in one of these, "is man one of God's blunders or is God one of man's"?

Nietzsche read Arthur Schopenhauer and became convinced that the world is driven by cosmic will, not by reason. Nietzsche rejected Hegel's idealism and all similar rationalist metaphysics. However, he disagreed with Schopenhauer as to the nature of the cosmic will. For Nietzsche, the world is driven and determined by the "will to power". However, according to Nietzsche, Western society had become increasingly decadent. People had come to lead lives largely devoid of joy and grandeur. They were enslaved by a morality that says "no" to life and to all that affirms it. They had become part of herd, part of a mass that is only too willing to do what it is told. The herd animal, he held, is cowardly, reactionary, he believed, was a reflection of these qualities. Only the rare isolated individual, the Superman, - a famous concept in Nietzsche's philosophy – can escape the triviality of society. The Superman, according to Nietzsche, embraces the will-to-power and overthrows the submissive and mediocre "slave" mentality that permeates society and dominates religion. In his embrace of the will-to-power, the Superman not only lives a full and exciting life but creates a new, life-affirming morality as well. He creates rather than discovers values. God, whom the meek and compassionate worship as the source of values, is just simply "dead".

Nietzsche also believed we have no access to absolute truths – such things as Plato's Forms and Kant's priori principles of knowing. Indeed, he believed there are no facts, only interpretations. Metaphysics is difficult for those who believe there are no facts, and Nietzsche's philosophy is consciously antimetaphysical. Nevertheless,

Nietzsche did subscribe to one metaphysical concept, "the eternal recurrence of the same". This is the theory that what happens recurs, exactly the same, again and again. Those with the slave mentality despise their lives and have a deep resentment for most everything that happens. They long to escape this life and hope that some afterlife will provide a modicum of happiness and fulfillment. They would look with horror and regret on the idea that what happens recurs again and again. The Superman by contrast, affirms, and celebrates life and bends it to his will. Having no regrets, he would relish the idea that life would happen again and again in exactly the same way.

In Nietzsche's view, moralities are social institutions, and basically there are just two moralities: master morality and slave morality – the morality of the masses. Slave morality – for Nietzsche, epitomized by Christian ethics – emphasizes such virtues as compassion, humility, patience, warm-heartedness, and turning the other cheek. These "virtues" glorify weakness. Master morality, by contrast, is the morality of noble individuals, who are egoistic, hard, intolerant, but bound by a code of honor to their peers. Noble individuals define harm entirely in terms of what is harmful to themselves and despise altruism and humility.

According to Nietzsche, the enhancement of the species is always the result of aristocratic societies, which, he held, are the ultimate justification of human social existence. The primal life force, for Nietzsche, is the will-to-power, whose essence is the overpowering and suppression of what is alien and weaker and which finds its highest expression in the noble man, "Superman". He is the source of ethical truth.

Nietzsche followed the ancient Greek philosopher Heraclitus in holding that life is quintessentially strife or warfare. It is only within the dark eye of battle that human energies are truly stretched and fruit-bearing actions become possible. Battles make heroes, he thought; peace renders us weak and ineffectual. One of Nietzsche's most famous proverbs was, "What doesn't kill us makes us stronger".

The ultimate battle, Nietzsche thought, take place within the human frame and is the battle between two forces, the Apollonian and the Dionysian. The Greek god Apollo represents the force of measure, order, and harmony. The Greek god Dionysius represents the counterforce of excess, destruction, and creative power, the ecstatic rush and rave of the original, formless will. In the human soul, these two forces contest each other for ascendancy. While both are necessary if one is to be fully and creatively alive, the creative Dionysian force has been lost almost entirely in the slave mentality, with its emphasis on humility, meekness, mediocrity, and the denial of life.

"God is dead", said Nietzsche. By this infamous remark, he did not mean that God once existed and now no longer does. He meant that all people with an ounce of intelligence would now perceive that there is no intelligence plan to the universe or rational order in it: they would now understand that there is no reason why things happen one way and not another and that the harmony and order we imagine to exist in the universe is merely pasted on by the human mind. Nietzsche, however, would have regarded very few people as having this required ounce of intelligence, and he in fact had a way of denigrating everyone in sight. For the mass of people, Nietzsche thought, God certainly is not dead. But these people, in Nietzsche's opinion, are pathetic wretches governed by a worldview inculcated by religion, science, and philosophy, a worldview that in Nietzsche's opinion makes them feeble losers who are motivated mainly by resentment. They view the world as a rational, law-governed place and adhere to a slave morality that praises the man who serves his fellow creatures with meekness and self-sacrifice.

In Nietzsche's opinion, the negative morality of these pitiful slaves – the mass of humankind, ordinary people – must be revaluated and replaced by life-affirming values. The new morality will be based on the development of a new kind of human being, whom Nietzsche calls the "Over man" or "Superman". Such a one not only accepts life in all its facets, including all its pain, but also makes living into an art. Among the forerunners of the Overman, Nietzsche cites Alexander the Great and Napoleon.

Nietzsche's thesis that one is no God and its apparent corollary, that there are no absolute and necessary criteria of right and wrong, were accepted by such twentieth-century existentialist philosophers as Albert Camus and Jean-Paul Sartre. For these thinkers, the fundamental problem of philosophy is how to live one's life, given the absence of absolutely valid standards by which to evaluate one's choices and decisions. Nietzsche, Kierkegaard, and some existentialists would all have agreed that the various rational discussions about God's existence are meaningless. Religion is an exercise in mass delusion and serves mainly to keep people in a state of psychological infantilism. Religion is wish-fulfillment; it offers up the "figure of an enormously exalted father" who reassures us as our own fathers did. The infallible and omnipotent father in heaven assures us that there is meaning and purpose in life and that all will be well in the end. However, although religion enables us to retain our status as children throughout our lives, it is a dangerous illusion. Religion intimidates intelligence with its demands for unconditional submission to inscrutable laws and keeps us from distinguishing between fact and wishful thinking. It does this even when philosophers and theologians try to salvage the illusion by redefining God as an "impersonal, shadowy and abstract principle". Sometimes belief in religion is fostered by the psychological feeling of the oneness of everything. Such "oceanic feelings", according to Freud, are just a recurrence of the limitless narcissism typical of early childhood. Freud thought human beings would be happier if they retained a modicum of reality in their thinking and cultivated their own gardens, as Voltaire had suggested.

—Editor

Genealogy of Morals

Now the first argument that comes ready to my hand is that the real home-stead of the concept "good" is sought and located in the wrong place: the judgment "good" did not originate among those to whom goodness was shown. Much rather has it been the good themselves, that is, the aristocratic, the powerful, the high-stationed, the high-minded, who have felt that they themselves were good, and that their actions were good, that is to say of the first order, in contradistinction to all the low, the low-minded, the vulgar, and the plebeian. It was out of this pathos of distance that they first arrogated die right to create values for their own profit, and to coin the names of such values: what had they to do with utility? The standpoint of utility is as alien and as inapplicable as it could possibly be, when we have to deal with so volcanic an effervescence of supreme values, creating and demarcating as they do a hierarchy within themselves: it is at this juncture that one arrives at an appreciation of the contrast to that tepid temperature, which is the presupposition on which every combination of worldly wisdom and every calculation of practical expediency is always based—and not for one occasional, not for one exceptional instance, but chronically. The pathos of nobility and distance, as I have said, the chronic and despotic esprit de corps and fundamental instinct of a higher dominant race coming into association with a meaner race, an "under race," this is the origin of the antithesis of good and bad.

The masters' right of giving names goes so far that it is permissible to look upon language itself as the expression of the power of the masters: they say "this is that, and that," they seal finally every object and every event with a sound, and thereby at the same rime take possession of it. It is because of this origin that the word "good" is far from having any necessary connection with altruistic acts, in accordance with the superstitious belief of these moral philosophers.

On the contrary, it is on the occasion of the decay of aristocratic values, that the antitheses between "egoistic" and "altruistic" press more and more heavily on the human conscience — it is, to use my own language, the herd instinct which finds in this antithesis an expression in many ways. And even then it takes a considerable time for this instinct to become sufficiently dominant, for the valuation to be inextricably dependent on this antithesis (as is the case in contemporary Europe); for today the prejudice is predominant, which, acting even now with all the intensity of an obsession and brain disease, holds that "moral," "altruistic," and " desinteresse" are concepts of equal value.

The guide-post which first put me on the right track was this question — what is the true etymological significance of the various symbols for the idea "good" which have been coined in the various languages? I then found that they all led back to the same evolution of the same idea — that everywhere "aristocrat," "noble" (in the social sense), is the root idea, out of which have necessarily developed "good" in the sense of "with aristocratic soul," "noble," in the sense of "with a soul of high calibre," "with a privileged soul" — a development which invariably runs parallel with that other evolution by which "vulgar," "plebeian," "low," are made to change finally into "bad."....

The reader will have already surmised with what ease the priestly mode of valuation can branch oft from the knightly aristocratic mode, and then develop into the very antithesis of the latter: special impetus is given to this opposition, by every occasion when the castes of the priests and warriors confront each other with mutual jealousy and cannot agree over the prize. The knightly-aristocratic "values" are based on a careful cult of the physical, on a flowering, rich, and even effervescing healthiness, that goes considerably beyond what is necessary for maintaining life, on war, adventure, the chase, the dance, the tourney—on everything, in fact, which is contained in strong, free, and joyous action. The priestly-aristocratic mode of valuation is—we have seen—based on other hypotheses: it is bad enough for this class when it is question of war! Yet the priests are, as is notorious, the worst enemies—why? Because they are the weakest. Their weakness causes their hate to expand into a monstrous and sinister shape, a shape which is most crafty and most poisonous. The really great haters in the history of the world have always been priests, who are also the cleverest haters—in comparison with the cleverness of priestly revenge, every other piece of cleverness is practically negligible. Human history would be too fatuous for anything were it not for the cleverness imported into it by the weak—take at once the most important instance. All the world's efforts against the "aristocrats," the "mighty," the "masters," the "holders of power," are negligible by comparison with what has been accomplished against those classes by the Jews— the Jews, that priestly nation which eventually realised that the one method of effecting satisfaction on its enemies and tyrants was by means of a radical trans-valuation of values, which was at the same time an act of the cleverest revenge. Yet the method was only appropriate to a nation of priests, to a nation of the most jealously nursed priestly revengefulness. It was the Jews who, in opposition to the aristocratic equation (good = aristocratic = beautiful = happy = loved by the gods), dared with a terrifying logic to suggest the contrary equation, and indeed to maintain with the teeth of the most profound hatred (the hatred of weakness) this contrary equation, namely, "the wretched are alone the good; the poor, the weak, the lowly, are alone the good; the suffering, the needy, the sick, the loathsome, are the only ones who are pious, the only ones who are blessed, for them alone is salvation—but you, on the other hand, you aristocrats, you men of power, you are to all eternity the evil, the horrible, the covetous, the insatiate, the godless; eternally also shall you be the unblessed, the cursed, the damned!" We know who it was who reaped the heritage of this Jewish transvaluation. In the context of the monstrous and inordinately fateful initiative which the Jews have exhibited in connection with this most fundamental of all declarations of war, I remember the passage which came to my pen on another occasion (Beyond Good and Evil, Aph. 195)—that it was, in fact, with the Jews that the revolt of the slaves begins in the sphere of morals; that revolt which has behind it a history of two millennia, and which at the present day has only moved out of our sight, because it—has achieved victory.

The revolt of the slaves in morals begins in the very principle of resentment becoming creative and giving birth to values—a resentment experienced by creatures who, deprived as they are of the proper outlet of action, are forced to find their compensation in an imaginary revenge. While ever)' aristocratic morality springs from a triumphant affirmation of its own demands, the slave morality says "no" from the very outset to what is "outside itself," "different from itself," and "not itself": and this "no" is its creative deed. This volte-face of the valuing standpoint — this inevitable gravitation to the objective instead of back to die subjective — is typical of "resentment": the slave-morality requires as the condition of its existence an external and objective world, to employ physiological terminology, it requires objective stimuli to be capable of action at all — its action is fundamentally a reaction. The contrary is the case when we come to the aristocrat's system of values: it acts and grows spontaneously, it merely seeks its antithesis in order to pronounce a more grateful and exultant "yes" to its own self; — its negative conception, "low," "vulgar," "bad," is merely a pale late-born foil in comparison with its positive and fundamental conception (saturated as it is with life and passion), of "we aristocrats, we good ones, we beautiful ones, we happy ones."....

While the aristocratic man lived in confidence and openness with himself...., the resentful man, on the other hand, is neither sincere not honest nor honest and candid with himself. His soul squints; his mind loves hidden crannies, tortuous paths and backdoors, everything secret appeals to him, am safety, his balm; he is past master in silence, in not forgetting, in wailing, in provisional self-depreciation and self-abasement. A race of such resentful men will of necessity eventually prove more prudent than any aristocratic race, it will honour prudence on quite a distinct scale, as, in fact, a paramount condition of existence, while prudence among aristocratic men is apt to be tinged with a delicate flavour of luxury and refinement; so among them it plays nothing like so integral a part as that complete certainty of function of the governing unconscious instincts, or as indeed a certain lack of prudence, such as a vehement and valiant charge, whether against danger or the enemy, or as those ecstatic bursts of rage, love, reverence, gratitude, by which at all times noble souls have recognised each other. When the resentment of the aristocratic man manifests itself, it fulfils and exhausts itself in an immediate reaction, and consequently instills no venom: on the other hand, it never manifests itself at all in countless instances, when in the case of the feeble and weak it would be inevitable. An inability to take seriously for any length of time their enemies, their disasters, their misdeeds — that is the sign of the full strong natures who possess a superfluity of moulding plastic force, that heals completely and produces forgetfulness: a good example of this in the modern world is Mirabeau, who had no memory for any insults and meannesses which were practised on him, and who wa1: only incapable of forgiving because he forgot. Such a man indeed shakes off with a shrug many a worm which would have buried itself in another; it is only in characters like these that we see the possibility (supposing, of course, that there is such a possibility in the world) of the real "love of one's enemies." What respect for his enemies is found, forsooth, in an aristocratic man—and such a reverence is already a bridge to love! He insists on having his enemy to himself as his distinction. He tolerates no other enemy but a man in whose character there is nothing to despise and much to honour! On die other hand, imagine the "enemy" as the resentful man conceives him—and it is here exactly that we see his work, his creativeness; he has conceived "the evil enemy," the "evil one," and indeed that is the root idea from which he now evolves as a contrasting and corresponding figure a "good one," himself—his very self.

... What wonder, if the suppressed and stealthily simmering passions of revenge and hatred exploit for their own advantage their belief, and indeed hold no belief with a more steadfast enthusiasm than this—"that the strong has the option of being weak, and the bird of prey of being a lamb." Thereby do they win for themselves the right of attributing to the birds of prey the responsibility for being birds of prey: when the oppressed, downtrodden, and over powered say to themselves with the vindictive guile of weakness, "Let us be otherwise than the evil, namely, good! and good is every one who does not oppress, who hurts no one, who does not attack, who does not pay back, who hands over revenge to God, who holds himself, as we do, in hiding; who goes out of the way of evil, and demands, in short, little from life; like ourselves the patient, the meek, die just,"—yet all this, in its cold and unprejudiced interpretation, means nothing more than "once for all, the weak are weak; it is good to do nothing for which we are not strong enough"; but this dismal state of affairs, this prudence of the lowest order, which even insects possess (which in a great danger are fain to sham death so as to avoid doing "too much"), has, thanks to the counterfeiting and self-deception of weakness, come to masquerade in the pomp of an ascetic, mute, and expectant virtue, just as though the very weakness of the weak—that is, forsooth, its being, its working, its whole unique inevitable inseparable reality—were a voluntary result, something wished, chosen, a deed, an act of merit. This kind of man finds die belief in a neutral, free-choosing "subject" necessary.

(From *On The Genealogy of Morals*, by Friedrich Nietzsche, Random House, 1967)

God is Dead

The greatest recent event—that "God is dead," that the belief in the Christian god has become unbelievable—is already beginning to cast its shadows over Europe. For the few at least, whose eye—the *suspicion* in whose eyes is strong and subtle enough for this spectacle, some sun seem to have set and some ancient and profound trust has been turned into doubt; to them our old world - must appear daily more like evening, more mistrustful, stranger, "older." But in the main one may say: The event itself is far too great, too distant, too remote from the multitude's capacity for comprehension even for the tidings of it to be thought of as having *arrived* as yet. Much less may one suppose that many people know as yet *what* this event really means—and how much must collapse now that this faith has been undermined because it was built upon this faith, propped by it, grown into it; for example, the whole of our European morality. This long plenitude and sequence of breakdown, destruction, ruin, and cataclysm that is now impending—who could guess enough of it today to be compelled to play the teacher and advance proclaimer of this monstrous logic of ter-ror, the prophet of a gloom and an eclipse of the sun whose like has probably never yet occurred on earth?

Even we born gucssers of riddles who are, as it L were, waiting on the mountains, posted between I today and tomorrow, stretched in the contradiction between today and tomorrow, we firstlings and pre-mature births of the coming century, to whom the shadows that must soon envelop Europe really *should* have appeared by now—why,.is it that even we look forward to the approaching gloom without any real sense of involvement and above all without any worry and fear for *ourselves* ? Are we perhaps still too much under the impression of the *initial consequences* of this event—and these initial consequences, the consequences for *ourselves,* are quite the opposite of what one might perhaps expect: They are not at all sad and gloomy but rather like a new and scarcely describable kind of light, happiness, relief, exhilara-tion, encouragement, dawn.

Indeed, we philosophers and "free spirits" feel, when we hear the news that "the old god is dead," as if a new dawn shone on us; our heart overflows with gratitude, amazement, premonitions, expectation. At long last the horizon appears free to us again, even if it should not be bright; at long last our ships may venture out again, venture out to face any danger; all the daring of the lover of knowledge is permitted again; the sea, *our sea,* lies open again; perhaps there has never yet been such an "open sea."

(From *The Gay Science* by Friedrich Nietzsche, translated by Walter Kaufmann, Random House, Inc. 1967)

19

Herbert Marcuse

Herbert Marcuse (1898-1979) was a noted philosopher of revolution and the most widely known member of the Frankfurt School. A leading theorist of the New Left and outspoken opponent of the Vietnam War, he became the mentor of the worldwide student movement. Studied German literature and philosophy in Berlin and Freiburg, did his Ph.D. on "The German Artist Novel" (1922), and became assistant to Martin Heidegger at the University of Freiburg in 1928. He was member of the Frankfurt Institute for Social Research since 1931. He emigrated with the Institute to Geneva 1933, and New York 1934. He worked for the American State Department 1942-50. He professor of political science at Brandels University 1954-65, he was appointed professor of philosophy at the University of California at San Diego, 1965, and visiting professor Berkeley, Berlin, Paris, publications: include *Reason and Revolution* (1941), *Eros and Civilization* (1955), *Soviet Marxism: A Critical Analysis (1961), The One-Dimensional Man (1964), Repressive Tolerance (1965), An Essay on Liberation (1969), Counter Revolution an0d Revolt (1972), The Aesthetic Dimension (1978), Technology, War, and Fascism (1998).*

He was the most influential thinker worldwide of the Frankfurt School Herbert Marcuse of whom Martin Heidegger, his former teacher, once said: "one of my best students, unfortunately corrupted by Freud." Marcuse, co-founder of Critical Theory, hoped for a new sensibility with whose help modern technology could develop into an unfettered art of living. A visionary philosopher of technology and thinker of the revolution of consciousness, he combined Marx with Freud, inner and external liberation. A native Berliner and Jewish antifascist, Marcuse declared the power of negation to be the basis of an aesthetics of freedom. As the intellectual father of the international student movement, he was more a phenomenologically rather than ideologically oriented student of Marx, and in the 1960s he became known through such cult books as *Eros and Civilization* and *One-Dimensional Man*. The counterculture hailed Marcuse's insistence that Eros should not be repressed nor should culture be built on sublimation. But the political philosopher who had rescued Marx's *Economic Philosophical Manuscripts* from oblivion strove to complement his hedonism with uncompromising social criticism. With his review of Hegel he argued that Reason and Revolution are not mutually exclusive. And his *One-Dimensional Man*, an astute forecast of the triumphal advance of the capitalistic system, became the bible of leftist critics of civilization. Since every protest is assimilated by capitalism and transformed into a product of consumption, Marcuse urged us to follow the example of authentic art and its "Great Refusal". The romantic realist could not be won for the class struggle. But he believed in the idealistic students capable of bonding together in solidarity with the exploited, the ostracized, and the incapacitated out of disgust with the obscene affluent society. Not in the repressive tolerance of a society out only for a good time, which cheats us out of our autonomy, but in an aesthetic revolution did Marcuse see our chance of liberated consciousness and a radical change in our senses. Works of art cannot take the place of revolutions, but the permanence of art is brought about through its ceaseless rebellion against society. The philosopher emphasized early on the subversive role played here by pop culture.

But Marcuse was not cut out for the part of guru for the believers in the revolution, he knew the classics of philosophical literature all to well for that. Marcuse came from a well-to-do-family and studied in Berlin and Freiburg, his strongest formative influence coming from the Freiburg phenomenologis Husserl and Heidegger. After completing his dissertation on the German artist novel, Marcuse sought unsuccessfully to win Hedigger's support for his habilitation. He became interested in psychoanalysis, developed an enthusiasm for the early Marx, and established close ties with Adorno and Horkheimer, who, like Marcuse, incorporated phenomenology and historical materialism into a critical theory. When the Frankfurt Institute for Social Research was forced to flee Hitler, Marcuse also went into exile, first to Paris, then arriving in New York in 1934. He became an American citizen in 1940, and in 1954 accepted an appointment to Brandeis University. One of the sharpest critics of the Vietnam War, Marcuse was dismissed from his post, but in 1965 he was offered a professorship in San Diego. He had gained fame by then, staunchly supporting the insurgent students as well as scorning fossilized communism, and began a series of extended lecture tours.

In Berkeley, Berlin and Paris, Marcuse encouraged the New Left to uphold the right to liberation in defiance of the doctrine of nonviolence, but without falling into terrorism. Marcuse died in July 1979 during a stay at a sanatorium in Starnberg, near Munich. The two decades since his death have seen postmodernism easily overcome the Oedipus complex that had created false authorities. But from Marcuse's viewpoint this liberation must be judged as half-hearted, lacking as it is in the life-enhancing solidarity of a socially fulfilled life.

In the late 1960s, the most famous philosopher in the United States was Herbert Marcuse. This was the era of tumultuous social and political unrest, the era of the New Left, Vietnam War protest, "people power", militant black and feminist disaffection, hippies, acid, four-letter words, and Woodstock. Marcuse was in.

In 1968, however, it was reported in the national media that Marcuse had invited "Red Rudi" Dutschke, a notorious West German student radical, to visit him in San Diego. After this, the local populace quickly informed police about Marcuse. The outcry against any possible Dutschke visit and against the perceived radicalism of Marcuse in that conservative naval community was vigorous and strident. In thundering editorials, the *San Diego Union* denounced Marcuse and called for his ouster. Thirty-two American Legion posts in San Diego County demanded termination of his contract and offered the regents of the University of California the money to buy it out. Marcuse began receiving death threats and hate mail, and his student followers armed themselves with guns to protect him.

When the appointment neared its end in 1969, the question of reappointment arose and attracted nationwide attention. With the strong support of the faculty but in the face of strenuous opposition from the Union, the Legion, and other powerful groups, university chancellor John McGill decided to offer Marcuse a one-year contract of reappointment. When the regents of the University of California met to discuss McGill's decision, they had to do so under the protection of the San Francisco Police Department's Tactical Force. Though a substantial number strongly dissented, the majority supported McGill. Marcuse was reappointed. By the expiration of the reappointment contract, Marcuse had passed the age of mandatory retirement. Nevertheless, he was permitted to keep his office and to teach informally.

Marcuse's reputation on the street arose from his book *One-Dimensional Man* (1964), a Marxist-oriented appraisal of contemporary industrial society. For the New Left, the book was a clear statement of deficiencies in American society. The thought of Karl Marx has been interpreted, expanded, and amended by his many followers, conspicuously so, of course, by the Communist Party. Today, Marxism, like Christianity is a family of doctrines continually being renewed and revised. Herbert Marcuse is one of the leading interpreters of Marxism.

It is a Marxist doctrine that a disenfranchised working class is the inevitable instrument of social change. But according to Marcuse, the working class has been integrated into advanced capitalist society. Indeed, it has been integrated so well that it "can actually be characterized as a pillar of the establishment", he said. This integration has been affected, he believed, through the overwhelming efficiency of technology in improving the standard of living. Because today's workers share so largely in the comforts of consumer society, they are far less critical of the status quo because they had been indoctrinated through propaganda or even brainwashed. In fact, Marcuse said, today's workers do not merely share these comforts, they actually recognize themselves in their commodities. They find their soul in their automobile, hi-fi set, split-level home, kitchen equipment. Their needs have been determined by what are, in effect, new forms of social control, such as advertising, consumerism, the mass media, and the entertainment industry, all of which produce and enforce conformity in what people desire, think, and do.

Thus, according to Marcuse, in the West, with its advanced capitalist societies, the workers have lost their individual autonomy, their capacity to choose and act for themselves, to refuse and to dissent and to create. Yes, needs are satisfied, but the price the workers pay for satisfaction of need is loss of ability to think for themselves. Further, the perceived needs that are satisfied, in Marcuse's opinion, are "false" needs, needs stimulated artificially by producers.

Marcuse emphasized that the integration of the working class into the advanced capitalist society by the satisfaction of false needs created by advertising, television, movies, music, and other forms of consumerism does not mean that society has become classless. Despite the fact that their "needs" are satisfied, members of the working class are still slaves, in effect, because they remain mere instruments of production that capitalists use for their own purposes. Further, he wrote in *One Dimensional Man* that if the worker and his boss enjoy the same television program and visit the same resorts, if the typist is as attractively made up as the daughter of her employer...if they all read the same newspaper, then this assimilation indicates not the disappearance of classes, but the extent to which the needs and satisfactions that serve the preservation of the Establishment are shared by the underlying population. The working class has become willing slaves. Thus, the working class in advanced capitalist societies, according to Marcuse, has been transformed from a force for radical change into a force for conservatism and the status quo.

The neutralizing of possible sources of radical social change through the integration of the working class into a one-dimensional society is visible everywhere. In the political sphere, the onne-dimensionalization of society is apparent in the unification of labor and capital against communism in a "welfare and warfare state", in which the cold war and the arms race unite all against the Communist threat while simultaneously stimulating the economy through the production of weapons.

Likewise, Marcuse said, a one-dimensional quality pervades contemporary art, language, philosophy, science, and all of contemporary culture. Thus, for example, art has lost its power to criticize, challenge, and transcend society and has been integrated as mere entertainment mass-produced in paperbacks, records, and television shows. As such, art now serves to promote conformity in thought, aspiration, and deed. The same is true of philosophy and science, he believed. The elite classes can tolerate free speech simply because such conformity of thought in art, philosophy, science, and politics is present.

Thus, as Marcuse saw it, advanced capitalist society, has managed to assimilate and integrate into itself the forces that oppose it and to defeat or refute all protest in the name of the historical prospects of freedom from toil and domination. Still, at the very end of *One-Dimensional Man*, Marcuse acknowledged that there is a slim chance of revolutionary change at the hands of a substratum of the outcasts of society, such as persecuted ethnic minorities and the unemployed and unemployable.

In his later thought, moreover, Marcuse perceived a weakening of the integration of the working classes into society and a growing awareness on the part of workers, students, and the middle class that consumer prosperity has been purchased a too high a price and that a society without war, exploitation, repression, poverty, or waste is possible. The revolution that will produce this society, Marcuse said – and only through revolution can it be created, he maintained – will be born not of privation but of "disgust at the waste excess of the so-called consumer society".

Herbert Marcuse kept denouncing as the evils of our age: the blind struggle for existence, relentless competition, wasteful productivity, deceitful repression, false virility and cynical brutality. Whenever he felt that he should speak as a teacher and philosopher he encouraged the negation of the performance principle, of possessive individualism, of alienation in labor – as well as love relations. But the negation of suffering was for him only a start. No doubt, Herbert Marcuse claimed negation to be the very essence of thinking – as did Adorno and Horkheimer; but the driving force of criticism, of contradiction and contest carried him well beyond the limits of an accusation of unnecessary mischief. Marcuse moved further ahead. He did not hesitate to advocate, in an affirmative mood, the fulfillment of human needs, of the need for undeserved happiness, of the need for beauty, of the need for peace, calm, and privacy. Although, certainly, Marcuse was not affirmative thinker, he was nevertheless the most affirmative among those who praised negativity. With him negative thinking retained the dialectical trust in determinate negation, in the disclosure of positive alternatives. Marcuse did not, in contrast to Adorno, only encircle the ineffable; he made appeals to future alternatives.

At a first glance, this consideration is nothing but a translation, of what the dialectic of instrumental reason means, into Freudian language. On a careful reading, the difference however comes to the force – the difference is in the move to keep separate the internal or instinctual from the external or social forces of domination. If the psychic as compared with the socio-historic thermidor gains a dynamic of its own, it is no longer social theory alone, but the theory of instincts which also provides the key. The question, whether the psychic thermidor must be repeated again and again, gains an almost existentialist dignity, since the answer to this question no longer depends on whether or not late capitalism, as an economic and a political system, can contain its inner conflicts.

From the metahistory of instincts Marcuse defends two related propositions. (1) There is no final opposition between Eros and Thanatos; in the spite of their antagonism both are conservative in nature, both strive for pacification, and both are unproductive and similarly directed against a relentless struggle for existence. (2) As soon as the progress of civilization, which is based on the repressive modification of the instincts, increases the existence of a surplus product not leading to individual gratification provokes a reaction from both Eros and Thanatos. Once instinctual repression loses its function for necessary self-preservation, the two conservative powers behind the scenes of civilization form a coalition and demand the recalling of energies from alienated labor.

Moreover, Marcuse was one of the few philosophers who were severely and chronically rebuked for the seriousness of their philosophical attitude. In summer 1967, at the Free University, Marcuse was exposed to a situation where he knew that any single word could have irrevocable consequences. He was invited to talk about the use of violence, and he had just declared the unity of moral, sexual, and political rebellion, when he found himself confronted with questions about the doubtful nature of moral justifications. Some of the questions indicated a then-widespread inclination, on the sides of the students, to free political activism from the painful hesitations of moral-practical reasoning. One student complained about difficulties he had experienced in discussions with a worker: "What does this worker care about the terror in Vietnam? Humanitarian arguments wouldn't do, since humanity itself gave rise to terror". The student apparently referred, although in an elliptic and misleading form, to the core of the analysis of the eclipse of reason. But Marcuse was not irritated at all. "As to your suspicion about humanitarian arguments . . . We must finally relearn what we forgot during the fascist period, or what you, who were not even born . . . have not fully become conscious of : that humanitarian and moral arguments are not merely deceitful ideology. Rather, they can and must become central social forces," Another student countered this straight answer with a moral skepticism which often reveals the strong influence of Carl Schmitt even on the left: "On the right of resistance: in your essay on tolerance you put this right in quotation marks, but now you have interpreted it as an ancient principle. What is this right based on? Is it a romantic relic of natural law, or is it a self-posited right and, if so, how can the opposition invoke a right which it must first generate?"

In this moment, Marcuse decided to be inconsistent rather than irresponsible. He swept aside his own doubts on a corrupted practical reason which supposedly had been absorbed into a totality of instrumental reason. His answer was clear, without the slightest ambiguity: . . . "appealing to the right of resistance is an appeal to a higher law, which has universal validity, that is, which goes beyond the self-defined right and privilege of a particular group. And there really is a close connection between the right of resistance and natural law. Now you will say that such a universal higher law simply does not exist. I believe that it does exist. Today we no longer call it Natural Law . . . If we appeal to humanity's right to peace, to the right to abolish exploitation and oppression, we are not talking about self-defined, special, group interests, but rather and, in fact, interests demonstrable as universal rights".

Before his eighths birthday, and in preparation for an interview on that occasion, Marcuse and Habermas had a long discussion on how they could and should explain the normative base of Critical Theory.

Habermas when saw him for the first time since that discussion, Marcuse was under intensive care in a hospital in Frankfurt, all types of controlling apparatuses on his left and on his right. None of us knew that this was the beginning of the end. On this occasion, Marcuse told Habermas, "Look, I know wherein our most basic value judgments are rooted – in compassion, in our sense for the suffering of others."

—Editor

The New Forms of Control

To the degree to which freedom from want, the concrete substance of all freedom, is becoming a real possibility, the liberties which pertain to a state of lower productivity are losing their former content. Independence of thought, autonomy, and the right to political opposition are being deprived of their basic critical function in a society which seems increasingly capable of satisfying the needs of the individuals through the way in which it is organized. Such a society may justly demand acceptance of its principles and institutions, and reduce the opposition to the discussion and promotion of alternative policies within the status quo. In this respect, it seems to make little difference whether the increasing satisfaction of needs is accomplished by an authoritarian or a nonauthoritarian system. Under the conditions of a rising standard of living, nonconformity with the system itself appears to be socially useless, and the more so when it entails tangible economic and political disadvantages and threatens the smooth operation of the whole. Indeed, at least in so far as the necessities of life are involved, there seems to be no reason why the production and distribution of goods and services should proceed through the competitive concurrence of individual liberties.

Freedom of enterprise was from the beginning not altogether a blessing. As the liberty to work or to starve, it spelled toil, insecurity, and fear for the vast majority of the population. If the individual were no longer compelled to prove himself on the market, as a free economic subject, the disappearance of this kind of freedom would be one of the greatest achievements of civilization. The technological processes of mechanization and standardization might release individual energy into a yet uncharted realm of freedom beyond necessity. The very structure of human existence would be altered; the individual would be liberated from the work world's imposing upon him alien needs and alien possibilities. The individual would be free to exert autonomy over a life that would be his own. If the productive apparatus could be organized and directed toward the satisfaction of the vital needs, its control might well be centralized such control would not prevent individual autonomy, but render it possible..

This is a goal within the capabilities of advanced industrial civilization, the "end" of technological rationality. In actual fact, however, the contrary trend operates: the apparatus imposes its economic and political requirements for defense and expansion on labor time and free time, on the material and intellectual culture. By virtue of the way it has organized its technological base, contemporary industrial society tends to be totalitarian. For "totalitarian" is not only a terroristic political coordination of society, but also a nonterroristic economictechnical coordination which operates through the manipulation of needs by vested interests. It thus precludes the emergence of an effective opposition against the whole. Not only a specific form of government or party rule makes for totalitarianism, but also a specific system of production and distribution which may well be compatible with a "pluralism" of parties, newspapers, "countervailing powers," etc.

Today political power asserts itself through its power over the machine process and over the technical organization of the apparatus. The government of advanced and advancing industrial societies can maintain and secure itself only when it succeeds in mobilizing, organizing, and exploiting the technical, scientific, and mechanical productivity available to industrial civilization. And this productivity mobilizes society as a whole, above and beyond any particular individual or group interests. The brute fact that the machine's physical power surpasses that of the individual, and of any particular group of individuals, makes the machine the most effective political instrument in any society whose basic organization is that of the machine process. But the political trend may be reversed; essentially the power of the machine is only the storedup and projected power of man. To the extent to which the work world is conceived of as a machine and mechanized accordingly, it becomes the potential basis of a new freedom for man.

Contemporary industrial civilization demonstrates that it has reached the state at which "the free society" can no longer be adequately defined in the traditional terms of economic, political, and intellectual liberties, not because these liberties have become insignificant, but because they are too significant to be confined within the traditional forms. New modes of realization are needed, corresponding to the new capabilities of society.

Such new modes can be indicated only in negative terms because they would amount to the negation of the prevailing modes. Thus economic freedom would mean freedom from the economy—from being controlled by economic forces and relationships; freedom from the daily struggle for existence, from earning a living. Political freedom would mean liberation of the individuals/from politics over which they have no effective control. Similarly, intellectual freedom would mean the restoration of individual thought now absorbed by mass communication and indoctrination, abolition of "public opinion" together with its makers. The unrealistic sound of these propositions is indicative, not of their Utopian character, but of the strength of the forces which prevent their realization. The most effective and enduring form of warfare against liberation is the implanting of material and intellectual needs that perpetuate obsolete forms of the struggle for existence.

The intensity, the satisfaction and even the character of human needs, beyond the biological level, have always been preconditioned. Whether or not the possibility of doing or leaving, enjoying or destroying, possessing or rejecting something is seized as a need depends on whether or not it can be seen as desirable and necessary for the prevailing societal institutions and interests. In this sense, human needs are historical needs and, to the extent to which the society demands the repressive development of the individual, his needs themselves and their claim for satisfaction are subject to overriding critical standards.

We may distinguish both true and false needs. "False" are those which are superimposed upon the individual by particular social interests in his repression: the needs which perpetuate toil, aggressiveness, misery, and injustice. Their satisfaction might be most gratifying to the individual, but this happiness is not a condition which has to be maintained and protected if it serves to arrest the development of the ability (his own and others) to recognize the disease of the whole and grasp the chances of curing the disease.

The result then is euphoria in unhappiness. Most of the prevailing needs to relax, to have fun, to behave and consume in accordance with the advertisements, to love and hate what other love and hate, belong to this category of false needs.

Such needs have a societal content and function which are determined by external powers over which the individual has no control; the development and satisfaction of these needs is heteronomous. No matter how much such needs may have become the individual's own, reproduced and fortified by the conditions of his existence; no matter how much he identifies himself with them and finds himself in their satisfaction, they continue to be what they were from the beginning—products of a society whose dominant interest demands repression.

The prevalence of repressive needs is an accomplished fact, accepted in ignorance and defeat, but a fact that must be undone in the interest of the happy individual as well as all those whose misery is the price of his satisfaction. The only needs that have an unqualified claim for satisfaction are the vital ones—nourishment, clothing, lodging at the attainable level of culture. The satisfaction of these needs is the prerequisite for the realization of all needs, of the unsublimated as well as the sublimated ones.

For any consciousness and conscience, for any experience which does not accept the prevailing societal interest as the supreme law of thought and behavior, the established universe of needs and satisfactions is a fact to be questioned—questioned in terms of truth and falsehood. These terms are historical throughout, and their objectivity is historical. The judgment of needs and their satisfaction, under the given conditions, involves standards or priority—standards which refer to the optimal development of the individual, of all individuals, under the optimal utilization of the material and intellectual resources available to man. The resources are calculable. "Truth" and "falsehood" of needs designate objective conditions to the extent to which the universal satisfaction of vital needs, and beyond it, the progressive alleviation of toil and poverty, are universally valid standards. But as historical standards, they do not only vary according to area and stage of development, they also can be defined only in (greater or lesser) contradiction to the prevailing ones. What tribunal can possibly claim the authority of decision?

In the last analysis, the question of what are true and false needs must be answered by the individuals themselves, but only in the last analysis; that is, if and when they are free to give their own answer. As long as they are kept incapable of being autonomous, as long as they are indoctrinated and manipulated (down to their very instincts), their answer to this question cannot be taken as their own. By the same token, however, no tribunal can justly arrogate to itself the right to decide which needs should be developed and satisfied. Any such tribunal is reprehensible, although our revulsion does not do away with the question: how can the people who have been the object of effective and productive domination by themselves create the conditions of freedom?

The more rational, productive, technical, and total the repressive administration of society becomes, the more unimaginable the means and ways by which the administered individuals might break their servitude and seize their own liberation. To be sure, to impose Reason upon an entire society is a paradoxical and scandalous idea—although one might dispute the righteousness of a society which ridicules this idea while making its own population into objects of total administration. All liberation depends on the consciousness of servitude, and the emergence of this consciousness is always hampered by the predominance of needs and satisfactions which, to a great extent, have become the individual's own. The process always replaces one system of preconditioning by another; the optimal goal is the replacement of false needs by true ones, the abandonment of repressive satisfaction.

The distinguishing features of advanced industrial society is its effective suffocation of those needs which demand liberation—liberation also from that which is tolerable and rewarding and comfortable—while it sustains and absolves the destructive power and repressive function of the affluent society. Here, the social controls exact the overwhelming need for the production and consumption of waste; the need for stupefying work where it is no longer a real necessity; the need for modes of relaxation which soothe and prolong this stupefication; the need for maintaining such deceptive liberties as free competition at administered prices, a free press which censors itself, free choice between brands and gadgets.

Under the rule of a repressive whole, liberty can be made into a powerful instrument of domination. The range of choice open to the individual is not the decisive factor in determining the degree of human freedom, but what can be chosen and what is chosen by the individual. The criterion for free choice can never be an absolute one, but neither is it entirely relative. Free election of masters does not abolish the masters or the slaves. Free choice among a wide variety of goods and services does at signify freedom if these goods and services sustain social controls over a life of toil and fear—that is, if they sustain alienation. And the spontaneous reproduction of superimposed needs by the individual does not establish autonomy; it only testifies to the efficacy of the controls.

Our insistence on the depth and efficacy of these controls is open to the objection that we overrate greatly the indoctrinating power of the "media", and that by themselves the people would feel and satisfy the needs which are now imposed upon them. The objection misses the point. The preconditioning does not start with the mass production of radio and television and with the centralization of their control. The people enter this stage as preconditioned receptacles of long standing; the decisive difference is in the flattening out of the contrast (or conflict) between the given and the possible, between the satisfied and the unsatisfied needs. Here, the so-called equalization of class distinctions reveals its ideological function. If the worker and his boss enjoy the same television program and visit the same resort places, if the typist is as attractively made up as the daughter of her employer, if the Negro owns a Cadillac, if they all read the same newspaper, then this assimilation indicates not the disappearance of classes, but the extent to which the needs and satisfactions that serve the preservation of the Establishment are shared by the underlying population.

Indeed, in the most highly developed areas of contemporary society, the transplantation of social into individual needs is so effective that the difference between them seems to be purely theoretical. Can one really distinguish between the mass media as instruments of information and entertainment, and as agents of manipulation and indoctrination? Between the automobile as nuisance and as convenience? Between the horrors and the comforts of functional architecture? Between the work for national defense and the work for corporate gain? Between the private pleasure and the commercial and political utility involved in increasing the birth rate?

We are again confronted with one of the most vexing aspects of advanced industrial civilization: the rational character of its irrationality. Its productivity and efficiency, its capacity to increase and spread comforts, to turn waste into need, and destruction into construction, the extent to which this civilization transforms the object world into an extension of man's mind and body makes the very notion of alienation questionable. The people recognize themselves in their commodities; they find their soul in their automobile, hi-fi set, split-level home, kitchen equipment. The very mechanism which the individual to his society has changed, and social control is anchored in the new needs which it has produced.

The prevailing forms of social control are technological in a new sense. To be sure, the technical structure and efficacy of the productive and destructive apparatus has been a major instrumentality for subjecting the population to the established social division of labor throughout the modern period. Moreover, such integration has always been accompanied by more obvious forms of compulsion: loss of livelihood, the administration of justice, the police, the armed forces. It still is. But in the contemporary period, the technological controls appear to be the very embodiment of Reason for the benefit of all social groups and interests—to such an extent that all contradiction seems irrational and all counteraction impossible.

No wonder then that, in the most advanced areas of this civilization, the social controls have been introjected to the point where even individual protest is affected at its roots. The intellectual and emotional refusal "to go along" appears neurotic and impotent. This is the socio-psychological aspect of the political event that marks the contemporary period: the passing of the historical forces which, at the preceding stage of industrial society, seemed to represent the possibility of new forms of existence.

But the term "introjection" perhaps no longer describes the way in which the individual by himself reproduces and perpetuates the external controls exercised by his society. Introjection suggests a variety of relatively spontaneous processes by which a Self (Ego) transposes the "outer" into the "inner". Thus introjection implies the existence of an inner dimension distinguished from and even antagonistic to the external exigencies—an individual consciousness and an individual unconscious apart from public opinion and behavior. The idea of "inner freedom" here has its reality: it designates the private space in which man may become and remain "himself".

Today this private space has been invaded and whittled down by technological reality. Mass production and mass distribution claim the entire individual, and industrial psychology has long since ceased to be confined to the factory. The manifold processes of introjection seem to be ossified in almost mechanical reactions. The result is, not adjustment but mimesis: an immediate identification of the individual with his society and, through it, with the society as a whole.

This immediate, automatic identification (which may have been characteristic of primitive forms of association) reappears in high industrial civilization; its new "immediacy", however, is the product of a sophisticated, scientific management and organization. In this process, the "inner" dimension of the mind in which opposition to the status quo can take root is whittled down. The loss of this dimension, in which the power of negative thinking—the criticaTpower of Reason—is at home, is the ideological counterpart to the very material process in which advanced industrial society silences and reconciles the opposition. The impact of progress turns Reason into submission to the facts of life, and to the dynamic capability of producing more and bigger facts of the same sort of life. The efficiency of the system blunts the individuals' recognition that it contains no facts which do not communicate the repressive power of the whole. If the individuals find themselves in the things which shape their life, they do so, not by giving, but by accepting the law of things—not the law of physics but the law of their society.

I have just suggested that the concept of alienation seems to become questionable when the individuals identify themselves with the existence which is imposed upon them and have in it their own development and satisfaction. This identification is not illusion but reality. However, the reality constitutes a more progressive stage of alienation. The latter has become entirely objective; the subject which is alienated is swallowed up by its alienated existence. There is only one dimension, and it is everywhere and in all forms. The achievements of progress defy ideological indictment as well as justification; before their tribunal, the "false consciousness" of their rationality becomes the true consciousness.

This absorption of ideology into reality does not, however, signify the "end of ideology". On the contrary, in a specific sense advanced industrial culture is more ideological than its predecessor, inasmuch as today the ideology is in the process of production itself. In a provocative form, this proposition reveals the political aspects of the prevailing technological rationality. The productive apparatus and the goods and services which 4t produces "sejrj' or impose the social system as a whole. The means of mass transportation and communication, the commodities of lodging, food, and clothing, the irresistible output of the entertainment and information industry carry with them prescribed attitudes and habits, certain intellectual and emotional reactions which bind the consumers more or less pleasantly to the producers and, through the latter, to the whole. The products indoctrinate and manipulate; they promote a false consciousness which is immune against its falsehood. And as these beneficial products become available to more individuals in more social classes, the indoctrination they carry ceases to be publicity; it becomes a way of life. It is a good way of life—much better than before—and as a good way of life, it militates against qualitative change. Thus emerges a pattern of one dimensional thought and behavior in which ideas, aspirations, and objectives that, by their content, transcend the established universe of discourse and action are either repelled or reduced to terms of this universe. They are redefined by the rationality of the given system and of its quantitative extension.

The trend may be related to a development in scientific method: operationalism in the physical, behaviorism in the social sciences. The common feature is a total empiricism in the treatment of concepts; their meaning is restricted to the representation of particular operations and behavior. The operational point of view is well illustrated by

Outside the academic establishment, the "far-reaching change in all our habits of thought" is more serious. It serves to coordinate ideas and goals with those exacted by the prevailing system, to enclose them in the system, and to repel those which are irreconcilable with the .system. The reign of such a one dimensional reality does not mean that materialism rules, and that the spiritual, metaphysical, and bohemian occupations are petering out. On the contrary, there is a great deal of "Worship together this week," "Why not try God," Zen, existentialism, and beat ways of life, etc. But such modes of protest and transcendence are no longer contradictory to the status quo and no longer negative. They are rather the ceremonial part of practical behaviorism, its harmless negation, and are quickly digested by the status quo of its healthy diet.

One dimensional thought is systematically promoted by the makers of politics and their purveyors of mass information. Their universe of discourse is populated by self-validating hypotheses which, incessantly and monopolistically repeated, become hypnotic definitions or dictations. For example, "free" are the institutions which operate (and are operated on) in the countries of the Free World; other transcending modes of freedom are by definition either anarchism, communism, or propaganda. "Socialistic" are all encroachments on private enterprises not undertaken by private enterprises itself (or by government contracts), such as universal and comprehensive health insurance, or the protection of nature from all too sweeping commercialization, or the establishment of public services which may hurt private profit. This totalitarian logic of accomplished facts has its Eastern counterpart. There, freedom is the way of life instituted by a communist regime, and all other transcending modes of freedom are either capitalistic, or revisionist, or leftist sectarianism. In both camps, non-operational ideas are non-behavioral and subversive. The movement of thought is stopped at barriers which appear as the limits of Reason itself.

Such limitation of thought is certainly not new. Ascending modern rationalism, in 1 its speculative as well as empirical form, shows a striking contrast between extreme critical radicalism in scientific and philosophic method on the one hand, and uncritical quietism in the attitude towards established and functioning social institutions. Thus Descartes' ego conditions was to leave the "great public bodes" untouched and Hobbes held that "the present ought always to be preferred, maintained, and accounted best." Kant agreed with Locke in justifying revolution if and when it ha succeeded in organizing the whole and in preventing subversion.

However, these accommodating concepts of Reason were always contradicted by the evident misery and injustice of the "great public bodies" and the effective, more or less conscious rebellion against them. Societal conditions existed which provoked | and permitted real dissociation from the established state of affairs; a private as well as political dimension was present in which dissociation could develop into effective | opposition, testing its strength and the validity of its objectives.

With the gradual closing of this dimension by the society, the self-limitation of thought assumes a larger significance. The interrelation between scientific-philosophical and societal processes, between theoretical and practical Reason, asserts itself "behind the back" of the scientists and philosophers. The society bars a whole type of oppositional operations and behavior; consequently, the concepts pertaining to them are rendered illusory or meaningless. Historical transcendence appears as metaphysical transcendence, not acceptable to science and scientific thought. The operational and behavioral point of view, practiced as a "habit of thought" at large, becomes the view of the established universe of discourse and action, needs and aspi1 rations. The "cunning of Reason" works, as it so often did, in the interest of the powers that be. The insistence on operational and Behavioral concepts turn against the; efforts to free thought and behavior from the given reality and for the suppressed« alternatives. Theoretical and practical Reason, academic and social behaviorism meet on common ground: that of an advanced society which makes scientific and technical progress into an instrument of domination.

"Progress" is not a neutral term; it moves toward specific ends, and these ends are defined by the possibilities of ameliorating the human condition. Advanced industrial, society is approaching the stage where continued progress would demand the radical subversion of the prevailing direction and organization of progress. This stage would be reached when material production (including the necessary services) becomes automated to the extent that all vital needs can be satisfied while necessary labor time is reduced to marginal time. From this point on, technical progress would transcend the realm of necessity, where it served as the instrument of domination and exploitation which thereby limited its rationality; technology would become subject to the free play of faculties in the struggle for the pacification of nature and of society.

Such a state is envisioned in Marx's notion of the "abolition of labor." The term "pacification of existence" seems better suited to designate the historical alternative of a world which—through an international conflict which transforms and suspends the contradictions within the established societies—advances on the brink of a global war. "Pacification of existence" means the development of man's struggle with man and with nature, under conditions where the competing needs, desires, and aspirations are no longer organized by vested interests in domination and scarcity—an organization which perpetuates the destructive forms of this struggle.

Today's fight against this historical alternative finds a firm basis in the underlying population, and finds its ideology in the rigid orientation of thought and behavior to the given universe of facts. Validated by the accomplishments of science and technology, justified by its growing productivity, the status quo defies all transcendence. Faced with the possibility of pacification on the grounds of its technical and intellectual achievements, the mature industrial society closes itself against this alternative. Operationalism, in theory and practice, becomes the theory and practice of containment. Underneath its obvious dynamics, this society is a thoroughly static system of life: selfpropelling in its oppressive productivity and in its beneficial coordination. Containment of technical progress goes hand in hand with its growth in the established direction. In spite of the political fetters imposed by the status quo, the more technology appears capable of creating the conditions for pacification, the more are the minds and bodies of man organized against this alternative.

The most advanced areas of industrial society exhibit throughout these two features: a trend toward consummation of technological rationality, and intensive efforts to contain this trend within the established institutions. Here is the internal contradiction of this civilization: the irrational element in its rationality. It is the token of its achievements. The industrial society which makes technology and science its own is organized for the ever more effective domination man and nature, for the ever more effective utilization of its resources. It becomes irrational when the success of these efforts opens new dimensions of human realization. Organization for peace is different from organization for war; the institutions which served the struggle for existence cannot serve the pacification of existence. Life as an end is qualitatively different from life as a means.

Such a. qualitatively new mode of existence can never be envisaged as the mere byproduct of economic and political changes, as the more or less spontaneous effect of the new institutions which constitute the necessary prerequisite. Qualitative change also involves a change in the technical basis on which this society rests—one which sustains the economic and political institutions through which the "second nature" of man as an aggressive object of administration is stabilized. The techniques of industrialization are political techniques; as such, they prejudge the possibilities of Reason and Freedom.

To be sure, labor must precede the reduction of labor, and industrialization must precede the development of human needs and satisfactions. But as all freedom depends on the conquest of alien necessity, the realization of freedom depends on the techniques of this conquest. The highest productivity of labor can be used for the perpetuation of labor, and the most efficient industrialization can serve the restriction and manipulation of needs.

When this point is reached, domination—in the guise of affluence and liberty— extends to all spheres of private and public existence, integrates all authentic opposition, absorbs all alternatives. Technological rationality reveals its political character as it becomes the great vehicle of better domination, creating a truly totalitarian universe in which society and nature, mind and body are kept in a state of permanent mobilization for the defense of this universe.

(From *One Dimensional Man* by Herbert Marcuse, Beacon Press, Boston, 1964)

20

Michel Foucault

Michel Foucault is undoubtedly among our greater thinkers of modern "power", and virtually no contemporary academic discussion of the concept can proceed without positioning itself somehow in the orbits of Foucault's analyses. One consequence of Foucault's centrality has been the development of a kind of normative consensus concerning Foucault's theory of power. The bare bones of the critical consensus might go something like this: Foucaultian power is not something held but something practiced; power is not imposed from "above" a system or socius, but consists of a series of relations within such a system or socius; there is no "outside" of power, no place untouched by power; conversely, there is no place of liberation of absolute freedom from power; in the end, power produces desires, formulation, objects of knowledge, and discourses, rather than primarily repressing, controlling, or capalizing the powers already held by preexisting subjects, knowledge, or formulations. Resistance, then, doesn't primarily function "against" power, trying to eradicate it altogether; rather, resistance attempts to harness power otherwise, in the production of different effects. This consensus is well grounded in Foucault's texts and interviews, and it is well presented in the voluminous secondarily literature.

Born in Poitiers, France, on October 15, 1926, Foucault was the firstborn son of a surgeon. He was a professor of the College de France from 1970, Foucault's major works include *Madness and Civilization: The Birth of the Clinic:, Discipline and Punish: The Birth of the Prison* (1977), *The Order of Things: An Archaeology of the Human Sciences* (1970), and *The History of Sexuality* (3 volumes, of translation 1978-1986).

Foucault told a group of American philosophers in Berkeley, California, in April 1983 that when Jurgen Habermas visited him in Paris, Foucault "was quite struck by his observation of the extent to which the problem of Heidegger and of the political implications of Heidegger's thought was quite a pressing and important one for him". Habermas interpreted Heidegger as a German neoconservative and Heidegger's Nazism as somehow connected with Heidegger's own philosophical positions. Foucault told the interviewers that he believed there was a very tenuous analytic link between a philosophical conception and the concrete political attitude of someone who is appealing to it; the best theories do not constitute a very effective protection against disastrous political choices." But, Foucault added, "I don't conclude from this that one may say just anything within the order of theory, but, on the contrary, that a demanding, prudent, 'experimental' attitude is necessary; at every moment, step by step, one must confront what one is thinking and saying with what one is doing, with what one is."

Before he died on June 25, 1984, as a result of AIDS, Foucault was engaged during most of his academic career in a project that attempted to chart the power relations by which societies exclude, lock up, or institutionalize the insane, the prisoner, the homosexual – those persons society defines as "other." Unlike Habermas, Foucault denied that societies could ever free themselves from such exclusionary forces; no "ideal speech situation" was possible. Foucault himself was something of a scandal to polite French society. One biographer writes of the philosopher's sadomasochistic erotic practices, his appearance in public wearing leather clothes, his open affection for men, and his fondness of the gay bathhouses of San Francisco.

Foucault was intensely suspicious of philosophic or scientific truth claims, especially claims by the human sciences (such as psychology and sociology) to have discovered something true – that is, objectively true- about the human being. At first, Foucault thought of himself as an archaeologist, digging through historical strata to lay bare the discourses that shaped societies. Discourse here is a word that describes how people talk, the shape they give to the multitude of interactions within a society, and how they act as a result. It is Foucault's point that a study of such discourse reveals not the steady march of science in its smashing of superstition but rather the substation of one invented reality for another, neither more nor less true.

For example, the old view of disease as an outside "evil power" that attempted to kill the body was replaced in the eighteenth century by the discourse of professionalized medicine, in which disease was spoken of as internal to the body. The proper role of medicine was not to cast out invading evil spirits but physically to cut out diseased flesh. But the success of such surgery has come at the price of turning ourselves into mere objects in need of fixing up. Medical technology can sustain the human body for a long time if in our discourse it is seen as some complex machine, but the image of a machine, which permeates our thinking, effectively reduces the human being to a mere mechanism, an object. The meaning this image gives to human existence is not truer than the ancient view, just other. The dominant view of death or insanity, or criminality is part of a discourse that – finds a never-ending parade of sick people, the insane, the criminal.

In his "archaeological" period, Foucault's work seemed to owe something to the structuralist movement in France, although he would disavow any connection. Foucault claimed to have found in his archaeological method a series of discontinuous created realities, or epistemes, that serve in each era as the ground of the true and false. But since these epistemes are a social given, there can be no appeal to any absolute truth of things such a concept is merely a construct of social discourse. Though the nature of the epistemes cannot be spelled out here, suffice it to say that Foucault program is decidedly anti-Hegelian. Where Hegel saw the working out of history as the Absolute Reason becoming self-conscious, Foucault saw history as a series of discontinuities, one following the next but with no hint or true progress.

Yet Foucault's own project was brought into question by the implications of the archaeological method. It assumes a kind of objectivity on the part of the researcher and his finding, but such objectivity, Foucault came to believe, was mere illusion. After all, if Foucault was himself working from within a particular episteme, no objective history of other epistemes would even be possible. Rather than abandon his relativistic stance, Foucault abandoned archaeology. Instead, beginning in the 1970s, he devoted himself to what Friedrich Nietzsche had earlier called genealogy.

For Foucault, genealogy did not commit one to a universal theory or to a particular view of the human subject. The emphasis in genealogy was not knowledge but power. In his later books Foucault was less concerned with his language – worlds created by various societies than with the micropractises of the body within a given society. This is not simply the physical body but lived body, an embodied consciousness. For example, one of the features of the embodied person is ability to dominate others; therefore, it is possible to trace the development (the genealogy) of various laws against assault. A court sets up its own rules and acts on them and calls it justice; the practice of the court is just what justice is, but justice is really an illusion for a reordering of power relationships. Genealogy does not provide any theories to explain what is going on; it simply evokes the small practices and social habits that constitute you and us, illuminating how such practices express the working of the power of the body. Genealogy is not prescriptive but descriptive.

Michel Foucault wrote extensively about historical reconfigurations of knowledge in what would now be called the human sciences. During the 1970s, however he argued most notably in *Discipline and Punish* and the first volume of *The History of Sexuality* that these reorganizations of knowledge were also intertwined with new forms of power and domination. Foucault's works from this period have often yielded contradictory responses from readers. His detailed historical remarks on the emergence of disciplinary and regulatory biopower have been widely influential. Yet these detailed studies are connected to a moral general conception of power, and of the epistemic and political positioning of the criticism of power, which many critics have found less satisfactory. Foucault's discussions of the relation between truth and power have similarly provoked concerns about their reflexive implications for his own analysis.

Many critics have treed to offer a sympathetic interpretation of the understanding of power and of knowledge that informs Foucault's historical studies of prisons and of the construction of a scientific discourse about sexuality. Since Foucault discussed power in this period rather more thematically than he did on knowledge, discussion of knowledge have been built extensively upon his remarks about power. Foucault has offeredan account of the interconnected emergence of new forms of power and knowledge in the eighteenth and nineteenth centuries. Secondly Foucault reflections upon the concepts of "power" and "knowledge" has emerged with a critical discussion of political and epistemic sovereignty. Foucault framed his investigations as an alternative to the preoccupation of political thought with questions about sovereignty and legitimacy. Many of his readers have found this critical concern troubling because they worry that it undercuts any possible stance from which Foucault might be able to criticize the modern forms of knowledge and power that he has described. But this worry is plausible only if one ignores Foucault understanding of both power and knowledge as dynamic. Foucault explicitly sketched a dynamics of power. I dynamic interpretation of knowledge. In both cases, Foucault's account provides ample possibilities for reasoned critical response.

However, the Foucault of the 1980s is substantially different from the Foucault of today. Along with the massive sea changes in the world at large since Foucault's death in 1984 (the HIV/AIDS pandemic, the end of the cold war, the neoliberal revolution and the waning of the welfare state, the rise of identity politics, the Internet, globalization, the so-called War on Terror), the dominant critical picture of Foucault's work has also morphed considerably. In the mid-1980s, Foucault's name was virtually synonymous with power, and more specifically with his analysis of disciplinary power in 1975's *Discipline and Punish*. Since his death, however, Foucault's midcareer work on power has been eclipsed in the academic conceptual imaginary by his "late" work on the ethico-aesthetics of subjectivity. Foucault in short, is today primarily referenced as a thinker of subjectivity, rather than as a thinker of power. Foucault himself lays down the bass line for this critical refrain in his late essay. "The Subject and Power", he writes, "it is not power, but the subject, that is the general theme of my research".

Since September 2001, however, we've seen the nation-state, and its investments in disciplinary power and panoptic surveillance, come roaring back, indeed intensifying beyond our wildest dreams or nightmares. We live in a world where outright torture of detainees and constant government surveillance of the citizenry are no longer projects that have to be carried out in secret: they've became official policy, at least in the United States. This historical (re)birth of discipline and panopticism is, one of the primary reasons for us today to reexamine Foucault's midcareer work on punitive power and its relations to his late work on the ethics and aesthetics of resistant subjectivity.

Foucault's work on power seem all too clear, even if they often go unstated. In short, critics seem to have agreed that Foucault's midcareer work constituted a dead-end, a totalizing cage, an omnipresent panopticon with no possibility for any subjective or collective resistance. In Fourcault's words:

"What we need . . . is a political philosophy that isn't erected around the problem of sovereignty or, therefore, around the problems of law and prohibition. We need to cut off the king's head. In political theory, that has still to be done."

However, there's at least one aspect of Foucault's work on power that's not so extensively commented upon: the question of power's historical mutations or the genealogical account of emergent, "new" modes of power. In short, how do dominant modes of power change over time, mutate from one form to another? Or, more specifically, how does Foucault account for those diachronic changes outside the historicism of progress, or without the teleological metaphorics of historical development? how does the disciplinary mode of power, for example, emege out of prior modes of "sovereign" and "social" power? In turn, how does contemporary "biopower" emerge out of the disciplinary regimes of the eighteenth and nineteenth centuries? And if these developments or mutations of power over time are not the teleological unfolding of power, then how are we to understand these changes?

In his 1975-76 lectures at the College de France delivered during the brief interval between the publication of *Discripline and Punish and The History of Sexuality*, volume I), Foucault explains that "biopower" constitutes a new technology of power, but this time it is not disciplinary. This technology of power does not exclude the former, does not exclude disciplinary technology, but it does dovetail into it, integrate it, modify it to some extent, and above all, use it by sort of infiltrating it, embedding itself in existing disciplinary techniques. This new technique does not simply do away with the disciplinary technique, because it exists on another level, on a different scale, and because it has a different bearing area, and makes use of very different instruments. Unlike discipline, which is addressed to bodies, the new nondisciplinary power is applied non to man-as-body but to the living man, to man-as-living-being. Unlike "discipline", whose work on bodies is primarily realized through institutional training and the exercise, "biopower" is an even more intense and saturated from of power that works throughout entire populations and takes on its target, "life", quite directly.

So, after all this, why or how is this rereading of Foucault's history of power important – outside simply being "right" about power's intense, mutative itinerary from sovereign power to biopower? What force does this genealogy deploy for us, in the present? One admittedly and deliberately indirect way at this question would be consider Franz Kafka's famous parable "Before the Law" in terms of the Foucaulatian genealogy of power. Read through the lens of power and its genealogical intensification, Kafka's text functions as a kind of instruction manual for demonstrating the costs of misdiagnosing various forms of power: the man from the country performs his relation to power on a sovereign model of law, which is to say he sees power as centralized, housed in a specific place or person. Hence, he wants an audience with power, finally to confront the hidden law which, "he thinks, should surely be accessible at all times to everyone; but as he now takes a closer look at the doorkeeper in his fur coat, with his big sharp nose and long, thin, tartar beard, he decides that it is better to wait until he gets permission to enter". The parable, however, shows us that biopower is already at work everywhere inside and outside the law. Unlike sovereign power, biopower is wholly immanent to the socius rather than organizing it from above, or from some central location that's hidden behind everyday social structures, "behind Kafka's series of doors". As the doorkeeper reminds the man from the country in the text's final lines, "No one else could ever be admitted here, since the gate was made only for you'.

Mistaking biopower for sovereign power is a matter of misdiagnosing a back-and-forth relation of force as the one-way street of sovereignty. As Foucault reminds us, "It is in this sphere of force relations that we must try to analyze the mechanisms of power. In this way we will escape from the system of Law-and-Sovereign that has captivated political thought for such a long time. And if it is true that Machiavelli was among the few who conceived the power of the Prince in terms of force relationships, perhaps we need to go one step further, do without the persona of the prince, and decipher power mechanisms on the basis of a strategy that is immanent in force relationships". In analyzing the force relationships of power, Foucault will in the late 1970s and early 1980s increasingly deploy the concept of "governmentality", which names this virtual mutation of power from law/sovergnity's investment in directly controlling individual bodies, toward power's increasing investment in regulating the relations among them: "Law and sovereignty were absolutely inseparable", Foucault writes. "On the contrary, with government it is a question of not imposing law on men but of disposing things: that is, employing tactics rather than laws, and even of using laws themselves as tactics".

And with a mutation in power's tactics or targets, the desired result or end of power relations then mutates as well: "We are at an important turning point here: whereas the end of sovereignty is internal to itself and possesses its own intrinsic instruments in the shape of its laws, the finality of government resides in the things it manages and in the pursuit of the perfection and intensification of the processes it directs". With the rise of governmentality, in the historical linkage between discipline and biopower, Foucaultian intensification becomes both the useful tool and the desired end of power relations. As power's targets and modes become more virtual, more disengaged from the actual surface of individual bodies, the strategies of regulating practice become more effective at governing those very bodies – precisely because of the Nietzschean truism that bodies or identities are nothing other than after-effects of actions. Power increasingly comes to target the economic relations among bodies, rather than the bodies themselves.

In the end, we might learn from a Foucaultian analysis of Kafka's parable that we needn't wait for the admittance to the law through a central portal. Rather, the entrances to the law of biopower are actually and virtually everywhere, as ubiquitous as the form of power itself.

Foucault's genealogy of power is simultaneously and importantly also a genealogy of resistance. In a sovereign mode, power is concentrated on the King, and thereby so is resistance. As power becomes increasingly more capillary, more invested in everyday matters and everyday lives, so too an immense new field of possibility for resistance is opened. "The everyday" in Foucault functions not as someplace untouched by power, but rather as a figure for the proliferation, saturation, and intensification of power. It's axiomatic that where power goes, there is resistance as well. With power's discovery of "everyday life", these dramas become infinitely more intense, more generalized, more ubiquitous: alongside power, resistance increasingly saturates the public sphere, the family and the job, and finally the subject's very relation to itself. And this increasing intensity is neither for celebration nor despair. In Foucault's work, it's first and foremost a descriptive claim: as power becomes increasingly more invested in the minute details of our lives, so too have our modes of resistance became increasingly subtle and intense.

In the end, continuing to insist on resistance's scarcity is both expensive and disenabling, a version of the condescending conventional wisdom that most people don't know what they're doing. Well, Foucault might answer, sure they do, maybe not around strictly speaking theoretical questions but people do tend to know their way around the questions of power and resistance in their own contexts. And even if they don't, the resistance tools that most people desire are diagnostics ones, precisely because the potted solutions and concepts of midcentury social theory have, "There are no machines of freedom, by definition", Foucault reminds us. Just as our dominant understandings of power are becoming anachronistic, Foucault shows us that many of our categories of resistance remain as holdovers from sovereign understandings of power. Which, again, isn't to say those strategies of direct confrontation against centralized power are not effective in certain circumstances. But, genealogically speaking, sovereignty is no longer the dominant mode of power, no longer the only game in town.

Perhaps this Foucaultian emphasis on irreducible experimental struggle, rather than a binary skeleton of power versus resistance, is merely to suggest that the diagnostic project of responding to power is ongoing, collective, and emerging at myriad discontinuous sites, as are the collective processes of constructing ways to hack the dangerous contemporary world of accelerated capitalism. However, in the service of that project, the theme of 'resistance' can often name a stopping point rather than a rallying cry – a moral condemnation or judgment rather than an ethical provocation or map. As Foucault insists, the critical project is not one where individual intellectuals judge problems, but a more collective procedure organized around naming and responding to the problems themselves.

In short, it seems that while Foucault has been gone for more than three decades now, his thought continues to present us with an unmet provocation or for a political theory of the present: work on contemporary culture must consistently be reinscribed outside the binary realm of resistance versus power. Resistance is not a rare attribute of certain heroic subjects, but an essential fact of everyone's everyday life out of the toolboxes of theory and practice, which is something we can only imagine would have pleased Foucault immensely.

—Editor

Power/Knowledge

A certain fragility been discovered in the very bedrock of existence—even, and perhaps above all, in those aspects of it that are most familiar, most solid and most intimately related to our bodies and to our everyday behaviour. But together with this sense of instability and this amazing efficacy, of discontinuous, particular and local criticism, one in fact also discovers something that perhaps was not initially foreseen, something one might describe as precisely the inhibiting effect of global, totalitarian theories. It is not that these global theories have not provided nor continue to provide in a fairly consistent fashion useful tools for local research: Marxism and psychoanalysis are proofs of this. But I believe these tools have only been provided on the condition that the theoretical unity of these discourses was in some sense put in abeyance, or at least curtailed, divided, overthrown, caricatured, the atricalised, or what you will. In each case, the attempt to think in terms of a totality has in fact proved a hindrance to research.

So, the main point to be gleaned from these events of the last fifteen years, their predominant feature, is the local character of criticism. That should not, I believe, be taken to mean that its qualities are those of an obtuse, naive or primitive empiricism; nor is it a soggy eclecticism, an opportunism that laps up any and every kind of theoretical approach nor does it mean a self-imposed ascetism which taken by itself would reduce to the worst kind of theoretical impoverishment. I believe that what this essentially local character of criticism indicates in reality is an autonomous, noncentralised kind of theoretical production, one that is to say whose validity is not dependent on the approval of the established regimes of thought.

It is here that we touch upon another feature of these events that has been manifest for some time now: it seems to me that this local criticism has proceeded by means of what one might term 'a return of knowledge'. What I mean by that phrase is this: it is a fact that we have repeatedly encountered, at least at a superficial level, in the course of most recent times, an entire thematic to the effect that it is not theory but life that matters, not knowledge but reality, not books but money etc.; but it also seems to me that over and above, and arising out of this thematic, there is something else to which we are witness, and which we might describe as an insurrection of subjugated knowledges. By subjugated knowledges I mean two things: on the one hand, I am referring to the historical contents that have been buried and disguised in a functionalist coherence or formal systemisation. Concretely, it is not a semiology of the life of the asylum, it is not even a sociology of delinquency, that has made it possible to produce an effective criticism of the asylum and likewise of the prison, but rather the immediate emergence of historical contents. And this is simply because only the historical contents allow us to rediscover the ruptural effects of conflict and struggle that the order imposed by functionalist or systematising thought is designed to mask. Subjugated knowledges are thus those blocs of historical knowledge which were present but disguised within the body of functionalist and systematising theory and which criticism—which obviously draws upon scholarship—has been able to reveal.

On the other hand, I believe that by subjugated knowledges one should understand something else, something which in a sense is altogether different, namely, a whole set of knowledges that have been disqualified as inadequate to their task or insufficiently elaborated: naive knowledges, located low down on the hierarchy, beneath the required level of cognition or scientificity. I also believe that it is through the reemergence of these low-ranking knowledges, these unqualified, even directly disqualified knowledges (such as that of the psychiatric patient, of the ill person, of the nurse, of the doctor—parallel and marginal as they are to the knowledge of medicine—that of the delinquent etc.), and which involve what I would call a popular knowledge (lesavoir des gens) though it is far from being a general commonsense knowledge, but is on the contrary a particular, local, regional knowledge, a differential knowledge incapable of unanimity and which owes its force only to the harshness with which it is opposed by everything surrounding it—that it is through the reappearance of this knowledge, of these local popular knowledges, these disqualified knowledges, that criticism performs its work.

However, there is a strange kind of paradox in the desire to assign to this same category of subjugated knowledges what are on the one hand the products of meticulous, erudite, exact historical knowledge, and on the other hand local and specific knowledges which have no common meaning and which are in some fashion allowed to fall into disuse whenever they are not effectively and explicitly maintained in themselves. Well it seems to me that our critical discourses of the last fifteen years have in effect discovered their essential force in this association between the buried knowledges of erudition and those disqualified from the hierarchy of knowledges and sciences.

In the, two cases—in the case of the erudite as in that of the disqualified knowledges— with what in fact were these buried, subjugated knowledges really concerned? They were concerned with a historical knowledge of struggles. In the specialised areas of erudition as in the disqualified, popular knowledge there, lay the memory of hostile encounters which even up to this day have been confined to the margins of knowledge.

What emerges out of this is something one might call a genealogy, or rather a multiplicity of genealogical researches, a painstaking rediscovery of struggles together with the rude memory of their conflicts. And these genealogies, that are the combined product of an erudite knowledge and a popular knowledge, were not possible and could not even have been attempted except on one condition, namely that the tyranny of globalising discourses with their hierarchy and all their privileges of a theoretical avant-garde was eliminated.

Let us give the term genealogy to the union of erudite knowledge and local memories which allows us to establish a historical knowledge of struggles and to make use of this knowledge tactically today. This then will be a provisional definition of the genealogies which I have attempted to compile with you over the last few years.

You are well aware that this research activity, which one can thus call genealogical, has nothing at all to do with an opposition between the abstract unity of theory and the concrete multiplicity of facts. It has nothing at all to do with a disqualification of the speculative dimension which opposes to it, in the name of some kind of scientism, the rigour of well established knowledges. It is not therefore via an empiricism that the genealogical project unfolds, nor even via a positivism in the ordinary sense of that term. What it really does is to entertain the claims to attention of local, discontinuous, disqualified, illegitimate knowledges against the claims of a unitary body of theory which would filter, hierarchisc and order them in the name of some true knowledge and some arbitrary idea of what constitutes a science and its objects. Genealogies are therefore not positiyistic returns to a more careful or exact form of science. They are precisely anti-sciences. Not that they vindicate a lyrical right to ignorance or non-knowledge: it is not that they are concerned to deny knowledge or that they esteem the virtues of direct cognition and base their practice upon an immediate experience that escapes encapsulation in knowledge. It is not that with which we are concerned. We are concerned, rather, with the insurrection of knowledges that are opposed primarily not to the contents, methods or concepts of a science, but to the effects of the centralising powers which are linked to the institution and functioning of an organised scientific discourse within a society such as ours. Nor does it basically matter all that much that this institutionalisation of scientific discourse is embodied in a university, or, more generally, in an educational apparatus, in a theoreticalcommercial institution such as psychoanalysis or within the framework of reference that is provided by a political system such as Marxism; for it is really against the effects of the power of a discourse that is considered to be scientific that the genealogy must wage its struggle.

To be more precise, I would remind you how numerous have been those who for many years now, probably for more than half a century, have questioned whether Marxism was, or was not, a.

science. One might say that the same issue has been posed, and continues to be posed, in the case of psychoanalysis, or even worse, in that of the semiology of literary texts. But to all these demands of: 'Is it or is it not a science?', the genealogies or the genealogists would reply: 'If you really want to know, the fault lies in your very determination to make a science out of Marxism or psychoanalysis or this or that study". If we have any objection against Marxism, it lies in the fact that it could effectively be a science. In more detailed terms, I would say that even before we can know the extent to which something such as Marxism or psychoanalysis can be compared to a scientific practice in its everyday functioning, its rules of construction, its working concepts, that even before we can pose the question of a formal and structural analogy between Marxist or psychoanalytic discourse, it is surely necessary to question ourselves about our aspirations to the kind of power that is presumed to accompany such a science. It is surely the following kinds of question that would need to be posed: What types of knowledge do you want to disqualify in the very instant of your demand: 'Is it a science'? Which speaking, discoursing subjects—which subjects of experience and knowledge—do you then want to 'diminish' when you say: T who conduct this discourse am conducting a scientific discourse, 'and lam a scientist'? Which theoretical political avant-garde do you want to enthrone in order to isolate it from all the discontinuous forms of knowledge that circulate about it? When I see you straining to establish the scientificity of Marxism I do not really think that you are demonstrating once and for all that Marxism has a rational structure and that therefore its propositions are the outcome of verifiable procedures; for me you are doing something altogether different, you are investing Marxist discourses and those who uphold them with the effects of, a power which the West since Medieval times has attributed to science and has reserved for those engaged in scientific discourse.

By comparison, then, and in contrast to the various projects which aim to inscribe knowledges in the hierarchical order of power associated with science, a genealogy should be seen as a kind of attempt to emancipate historical knowledges from that subjection, to render them, that is, capable of opposition and of struggle against the coercion of a theoretical, unitary, formal and scientific discourse. It is based on a reactivation of local knowledges—of minor knowledges, as Deleuze might call them—in opposition to the scientific hierarchisation of knowledges and the effects intrinsic to their power: this, then, is the project of these disordered and fragmentary genealogies. If we were to characterise it in two terms, then 'archaeology' would be the appropriate methodology of this analysis of local discursivities, and 'genealogy' would be the tactics whereby, on the basis of the descriptions of these local discursivities, the subjected knowledges which were thus released would he brought into play.

So, it is the rules of right, the mechanisms of power, the effects of truth or if you like, the rules of power and the powers of true discourses, that can be said more or less to have formed the general terrain of my concern, even if, as I know full well, I have traversed it only partially and in a very zigzag fashion. I should like to speak briefly about this course of research, about what I have considered as being its guiding principle and about the methodological imperatives and precautions which I have sought to adopt. As regards the general principle involved in a study of the relations between right and power, it seems to me that in Western societies since Medieval times it has been royal power that has provided the essential focus around which legal thought has been elaborated. It is in response to the demands of royal power, for its profit and to serve as its instrument or justification, that the juridical edifice of our own society has been developed. Right in the West is the King's right. Naturally everyone is familiar with the famous, celebrated, repeatedly emphasised role of the jurists in the organisation of royal power. We must not forget that the revitalisation of Roman Law in the twelfth century was the major event around which, and on whose basis, the juridical edifice which had collapsed after the" fall of the Roman Empire was reconstructed. This resurrection of Roman Law had in effect a technical and constitutive role to play in the establishment of the authoritarian, administrative, and, in the final analysis, absolute power of the monarchy. And when this legal edifice escapes in later centuries from the control of the monarch, when, more accurately, it is turned against that control, it is always the limits of this sovereign power that are put in question, its prerogatives that are challenged. In other words, I believe that the King remains the central personage in the whole legal edifice of the West. When it comes to the general organisation of the legal system in the West, it is essentially with the King, his rights, his power and its eventual limitations, that one is dealing. Whether the jurists were the King's henchmen or his adversaries, it is of royal power that we are speaking in every case when we speak of these grandiose edifices of legal thought and knowledge.

There are two ways in which we do so speak. Either we do so in order to show the nature of the juridical armoury that invested royal power, to reveal the monarch as the effective embodiment of sovereignty, to demonstrate that his power, for all that it was absolute, was exactly that which befitted his fundamental right. Or, by contrast, we do so in order to show the necessity of imposing limits upon this sovereign power, of submitting it to certain rules of right, within whose confines it had to be exercised in order for it to remain legitimate. The essential role of the theory of right, from medieval times onwards, was to fix the legitimacy of power; that is the major problem ground which the whole theory of right and sovereignty is organised.

When we say that sovereignty is the central problem of right in Western societies, what we mean basically is that the essential function of the discourse and techniques of right has been to efface the domination intrinsic to power in order to present the latter at the level of appearance under two different aspects: on the one hand, as the legitimate rights of sovereignty, and on the other, as the legal obligation to obey it. The system of right is centred entirely upon the King, and it is therefore designed to eliminate the fact of domination and its consequences.

My general project over the past few years has been, in essence, to reverse the mode of analysis followed by the entire discourse of right from the time of the Middle Ages. My aim, therefore, was to invert it, to give due weight, that is, to the fact of domination, to expose both its latent nature and its brutality. I then wanted to show not only how right is, in a general way, the instrument of this domination—which scarcely needs saying—but also to show the extent to which, and the forms in which right (not simply the laws but the whole complex of apparatuses, institutions and regulations responsible for their application) transmits and puts in motion relations that are not relations of sovereignty, but of domination. Moreover, in speaking of domination I do not have in mind that solid and global kind of domination that one person exercises over others, or one group over another, but the manifold forms of domination that can be exercised within society. Not the domination of the King in his central position, therefore, but that of his subjects in their mutual relations: not the uniform edifice of sovereignty, but the multiple forms of subjugation that have a place and function within the social organism.

The system of right, the domain of the law, are permanent agents of these relations of domination, these polymorphous techniques of subjugation. Right should be viewed, I believe, not in terms of a legitimacy to be established, but in terms of the methods of subjugation that it instigates.

The problem for me is how to avoid this question, central to the theme of right, regarding sovereignty and the obedience of individual subjects in order that I may substitute the problem of domination and subjugation for that of sovereignty and obedience. Given that this was to be the general line of my analysis, there were a certain number of methodological precautions that seemed requisite to its pursuit. In the very first place, it seemed important to accept that the analysis in question should not concern itself with the regulated and legitimate forms of power in their central locations, with the general mechanisms through which they operate, and the continual effects of these. On the contrary, it should be concerned with power at its extremities, in its ultimate destinations, with those points where it becomes capillary, that is, in its more regional and local forms and institutions. Its paramount concern, in fact, should be with the point where power surmounts the rules of right which organise and delimit it and extends itself beyond them, invests itself in institutions, becomes embodied in techniques, and equips itself with instruments and eventually even violent means of material intervention. To give an example: rather than try to discover where and how the right of punishment is founded on sovereignty, how it is presented in the theory of monarchical right or in that of democratic right, I have tried to see in what ways punishment and the power of punishment ate effectively embodied in a certain number of local, regional, material institutions, which are concerned with torture or imprisonment, and to place these in the climate—at once institutional and physical, regulated and violent—of the effective apparatuses of punishment. In other words, one should try to locate power at the extreme points of its exercise, where it is always less legal in character.

A second methodological precaution urged that the analysis should not concern itself with power at the level of conscious intention or decision; that it should not attempt to consider power from its internal point of view and that it should refrain from posing the labyrinthine and unanswerable question: 'Who then has power and what has he in mind? What is the aim of someone who possesses power?' Instead, it is a case of studying power at the point where its intention, if it has one, is completely invested in its real and effective practices. What is needed is a study of power in its external visage, at the point where it is in direct and immediate relationship with that which we can provisionally call its object, its target, its field of application, there— that is to say—where it installs itself and produces its real effects.

Let us not, therefore, ask why certain people want to dominate, what they seek, what is their overall strategy. Let us ask, instead, how things work at the level of ongoing subjugation, at the level of those continuous and uninterrupted processes which subject our bodies, govern our gestures, dictate our behaviours etc. In other words, rather than ask ourselves how the sovereign appears to us in his lofty isolation, we should try to discover how it is that subjects are gradually, progressively, really and materially constituted through a multiplicity of organisms, forces, energies, materials, desires, thoughts etc. We should try to grasp subjection in its material instance as a constitution of subjects.

A third methodological precaution relates to the fact that power is not to be taken to be a phenomenon of 6rie"ihdividuars consolidated and homogeneous domination over others, or that of one group or class over others. What, by contrast, should always be kept in mind is that power, if we do not take too distant a view of it, is not that which makes the difference between those who exclusively possess and retain it, and those who do not have it and submit to it. Power must by analysed as something of which circulates, or rather as something which only functions in the form of a chain. It is never localised here of there, never in anybody's hands, never appropriated as a commodity or piece of wealth. Power is employed and exercised through a net like organisation. And not only do individuals circulate between its threads; they are always in the position of simultaneously undergoing and exercising this power. They are not only its inert or consenting target; they are always also the elements of its articulation. In other words, individuals are the vehicles of power, not its points of application.

The individual is not to be conceived as a sort of elementary nucleus, a primitive atom, a multiple and inert material on which power comes to fasten or against which it happens to strike, and in so doing subdues or crushes individuals. In fact, it is already one of the prime effects of power that certain bodies, certain gestures, certain discourses, certain desires, come to be identified and constituted as individuals. The individual, that is, is not the vis-a-vis of power; it is, I believe, one of its prime effects. The individual is an effect of power, and at the same time, or precisely to the extent to which it is that effect, it is the element of its articulation. The individual which power has constituted is at the same time its vehicle.

There is a fourth methodological precaution that follows from this: when I say that power establishes a network through which it freely circulates, this is true only up to a certain point. In much the same fashion we could say that therefore we all have a fascism in our heads, or, more profoundly, that we all have a power in our bodies. But I do not believe that one should conclude from that that power is the best distributed thing in the world, although in some sense that is indeed so. We are not dealing with a sort of democratic or anarchic distribution of power through bodies. That is to say, it seems to me—and this then would be the fourth methodological precaution—that the important thing is not to attempt sonie kind of deduction of power starting from its centre and aimed at the discovery of the extent to which it permeates into the base, of the degree to which it reproduces itself down to and including the most molecular elements of society One must rather conduct an ascending analysis of power, starting, that is, from its infinitesimal mechanisms, which each have their own history, their own trajectory, their own techniques and tactics, and then see how these mechanisms of power have been—and continue to be—invested, colonised, utilised, involuted, transformed, displaced, extended etc., by ever more general mechanisms and by forms of global domination. It is not that this global domination extends itself right to the base in a plurality of repercussions: I believe that the manner in which the phenomena, the techniques and the procedures of power enter into play at the most basic levels must be analysed, that the way in which these procedures are displaced, extended and altered must certainly be demonstrated; but above all what must be shown is the manner in which they are invested and annexed by more global phenomena and the subtle fashion in which more general powers or economic interests are able to engage with these technologies that are at once both relatively autonomous of power and act as its infinitesimal elements. In order to make this clearer, one might cite the example of madness. The descending type of analysis, the one of which I believe one ought to be wary, will say that the bourgeoisie has, since the sixteenth or seventeenth century, been the dominant class; from this premise, it will then set out to deduce the internment of the insane. One can always make this deduction, it is always easily done and that is precisely what I would hold against it. It is in fact a simple matter to show that since lunatics are precisely those persons who are useless to industrial production, one is obliged to dispense with them. One could argue similarly in regard to infantile sexuality—and several thinkers, including Wilhelm Reich have indeed sought to do so up to a certain point. Given the domination of the bourgeois class, how can one understand the repression of infantile sexuality? Well, very simply—given that the' human body had become esdtentially a force of production from the time of the seventeenth and eighteenth century, all the forms of its expenditure which did not lend themselves to the constitution of the productive forces—and were therefore exposed as redundant—were banned, excluded and repressed. These kinds of deduction are always possible. They are simultaneously correct and false. Above all they are too glib, because one can always do exactly the opposite and show, precisely by appeal to the principle of the dominance of the bourgeois class, that the forms of control of infantile sexuality could in no way have been predicted. On the contrary, it is equally plausible to suggest that what was needed was sexual training, the encouragement of a sexual precociousness, given that what was fundamentally at stake was the constitution of a labour force whose optimal state, as we well know, at least at the beginning of the nineteenth century, was to be infinite: the greater the labour force, the better able would the system of capitalist production have been to fulfil and improve its functions.

I believe that anything can be deduced from the general phenomenon of the domination of the bourgeois class. What needs to be done is something quite different. One needs to investigate historically, and beginning from the lowest level, how mechanisms of power have been able to function. In regard to the confinement of the insane, for example, or the repression and interdiction of sexuality, we need to see the manner in which, at the effective level of the family, of the immediate environment, of the cells and most basic units of society, these phenomena of repression or exclusion possessed their instruments and their logic, in response to a certain number of needs. We need to identify the agents responsible for them, their real agents (those which constituted the immediate social entourage, the family, parents, doctors etc.), and not be content to lump them under the formula of a generalised bourgeoisie. We need to see how these mechanisms of power, at a given moment, in a precise conjuncture and by means of a certain number of transformations, have begun to become economically advantageous and politically useful. I think that in this way one could easily manage to demonstrate that what the bourgeoisie needed, or that in which its system discovered its real interests, was not the exclusion of the mad or the surveillance and prohibition of infantile masturbation (for, to repeat, such a system can perfectly well tolerate quite opposite practices), but rather, the techniques and procedures themselves of such an exclusion. It is the mechanisms of that exclusion that are necessary, the apparatuses of surveillance, the medicalisation of sexuality, of madness, of delinquency, all the micromechanisms of power, that came, from a certain moment in time, to represent the interests of the bourgeoisie.

As for our fifth methodological precaution: it is quite possible that the major mechanisms of power have been accompanied by ideological productions. There has, for example, probably been an ideology of education, an ideology of the monarchy, an ideology of parliamentary democracy etc.; but basically I do not believe that what has taken place can be said to be ideological. It is both much more and much less than ideology. It is the production of effective instruments for the formation and accumulation of knowledge—methods of observation, techniques of registration, procedures for investigation and research, apparatuses of control. All this means that power, when it is exercised through these subtle mechanisms, cannot but evolve, organise and put into circulation a knowledge, or rather apparatuses of knowledge, which are not ideological constructs.

By way of summarising these five methodological precautions, I would say that we should direct our researches on the nature of power not towards the juridical edifice of sovereignty, the State apparatuses and the ideologies which accompany them, but towards domination and the material operators of power, towards forms of subjection and the inflections and utilisations of their localised systems, and towards strategic apparatuses. We must eschew the model of Leviathan in the study of power. We must escape from the limited field of juridical sovereignty and State institutions, and instead base our analysis of power on the study of the techniques and tactics of domination.

In short, what I have wanted to demonstrate in the course of the last few years is net the manner in which at the advance front of the exact sciences the uncertain, recalcitrant, confused dominion of human behaviour has little by little been annexed to science: it is not through some advancement in the rationality of the exact sciences that the human sciences are gradually constituted. I believe that the process which has really rendered the discourse of the human sciences possible is the juxtaposition, the encounter between two lines of approach, two mechanisms, two absolutely heterogeneous types of discourse: on the one hand there is the reorganisation of right that invests sovereignty, and on the other, the mechanics of the coercive forces whose exercise takes a disciplinary form. And I believe that in our own times power is exercised simultaneously through this right and these techniques and that these techniques and these discourses, to which the disciplines give rise invade the area of right so that the procedures of normalisation come to be ever more constantly engaged in the colonisation of those of law. I believe that all this can explain the global functioning of what I would call a society of normalisation. I mean, more precisely, that disciplinary normalisations come into ever greater conflict with the juridical systems of sovereignty: their incompatibility with each other is ever more acutely felt and apparent; some kind of arbitrating discourse is made ever more necessary, a type of power and of knowledge that the sanctity of science would render neutral. It is precisely in the extension of medicine that we see, in some sense, not so much the linking as the perpetual exchange or encounter of mechanisms of discipline with the principle of right. The developments of medicine, the general medicalisation of behaviours, conducts, discourses, desires etc., take place at the point of intersection between the two heterogeneous levels of discipline and sovereignty. For this reason, against these usurpations by the disciplinary mechanisms, against this ascent of a power that is tied to scientific knowledge, we find that there is no solid recourse available to us today, such being our situation, except that which lies precisely in the return to a theory of right organised around sovereignty and articulated upon its ancient principle. When today one wants to object in some way to the disciplines and all the effects of power and knowledge that are linked to them, what is it that one does, concretely, in real life, what do the Magistrates Union or other similar institutions do, if not precisely appeal to this canon of right, this famous, formal right, that is said to be bourgeois, and which in reality is the right of sovereignty? But I believe that we find ourselves here in a kind of blind alley: it is not through recourse to sovereignty against discipline that the effects of disciplinary power can be limited, because sovereignty and disciplinary mechanisms are two absolutely integral constituents of the general mechanism of power in our society.

If one wants to look for a nondisciplinary form of power, or rather, to struggle against disciplines and disciplinary power, it is not towards the ancient right of sovereignty that one should turn, but towards the possibility of a new form of right, one which must indeed be antidisciplinarian, but at the same time liberated from the principle of sovereignty. It is at this point that we once more come up against the notion of repression, whose use in this context I believe to be doubly unfortunate. On the one hand, it contains an obscure reference to a certain theory of sovereignty, the sovereignty of the sovereign rights of the individual, and on the other hand, its usage introduces a system of psychological reference points borrowed from the human sciences, that is to say, from discourses and practices that belong to the disciplinary realm. I believe that the notion of repression remains a juridical disciplinary notion whatever the critical use one would make of it. To this extent the critical application of the notion of repression is found to be vitiated and nullified from the outset by the twofold juridical and disciplinary reference it contains to sovereignty on the one hand and to normalisation on the other.

(From *Power/Knowledge* by Michel Joucault ed. Lolin Gordon, Pantheon, New York, 1980)

21

John Rawls

John Rawls's (1921-2002) *A Theory of Justice* is perhaps the single most influential publication in moral philosophy in the twentieth century. The work heralded a renewed concern in philosophy with justice; further, virtually every philosophical writer on justice subsequent to the publication of this work identified his or her position with reference to it. One recent commentator, Charles Larmore believes that Rawls is one of the three most important philosophers of the twentieth century, the other two being Wittgenstein and Heidegger.

Rawls writes from within the liberal tradition, but he had grown dissatisfied with the utilitarianism on which liberalism was often based. He was also dissatisfied with attempts merely to circumscribe utilitarianism with ad hoc "self-evident" principles about our dudes. Rawls said that in writing *A Theory of Justice* he wanted vo "carry to a higher order of abstraction the traditional doctrine of the social contract." The result was a lengthy and systematic attempt to establish, interpret, and illuminate the fundamental principles of justice; to apply them to various central issues in social ethics; to use them for appraising social, political, and economic institutions; and to examine their implications for duty and obligation.

According to Rawls, because society is typically characterized by a conflict as well as an identity of interests, it must have a set of principles for assigning basic rights and duties and for determining the appropriate distribution of the benefits and burdens of social cooperation. These are the principles of distributive or social justice. They specify the kinds of social cooperation that can be entered into and the forms of government that can be established. Rawls's theory of justice intersects with traditional philosophical questions about the ethically legitimate functions and organization of the state. For Rawls, a society or a state is not well ordered unless its members know and accept the same principles of social justice and the basic social institutions generally satisfy and are generally known to satisfy these principles.

If a society is to be well ordered, its members must determine by rational reflection what are to be their principles of justice, says Rawls. If the principles selected are to be reasonable and justifiable, they must be selected through a procedure that is fair.

Rauds in Rawls insists that, if the selection of principles of justice is to be fair, the possibility of bias operating in their selection must be removed. Ideally, therefore, in our selection of the principles, none of us should have insider's knowledge. We should all be ignorant of one another's—and our own—wealth, status, abilities, intelligence, inclinations, aspirations, and even beliefs about goodness. Of course, no group of people ever were or could be in such a state of ignorance. Therefore, says Rawls, we must select the principles as if we were behind a veil of ignorance. This is to ensure that nobody is advantaged or disadvantaged in the choice of principles by her or his own unique circumstances.

If from behind a veil of ignorance we were to deliberate on what principles of justice we would adopt, we would be in what Rawls calls the original position or sometimes the initial situation. Like Locke and Rousseau's state of nature, the original position is an entirely hypothetical condition. Because people never were and never could be in such a condition of ignorance. Rawls's concepts of a veil of ignorance and an original position are intended "simply to make vivid to ourselves the restrictions that it seems reasonable to impose on arguments for principles of justice, and therefore on these principles themselves." Determining our principles of justice by imagining ourselves in the original position simply ensures that we do not tailor our conception of justice to our own case. In short; according to Rawls, the basic principles of justice are those to which we will agree if we are thinking rationally and in our own self-interest and if we eliminate irrelevant considerations. Because the basic principles of justice are those to which we will agree, Rawls's theory of justice is said to be a contractarian theory, as were the theories of Hobbes, Locke, and Rousseau.

The principles we would select in the original position, if we are thinking rationally and attending to our own self-interest, are two, Rawls says. The first, which takes precedence over the second when questions of priority arise, requires that each person has an equal right to "the most extensive basic liberty compatible with a similar liberty for others."

The second requires that social and economic inequalities be arranged "so that they are both (a) reasonably expected to be to everyone's advantage and (b) attached to positions and offices open to all." These two principles, writes Rawls, are a special case of a more general conception of justice to the effect that all primary social goods (e.g., liberty, opportunity, income) are to be distributed equally unless an unequal distribution is to everyone's advantage.

We are led to this concept, Rawls writes, when we decide to find a concept of justice that nullifies the accidents of natural endowment and the contingencies of social circumstances as counters in quest for political and economic advantage. It follows from these principles, of course, that an unequal distribution of the various assets of society—wealth, for instance—can be just, as long as these inequalities are to everyone's benefit. For example, it may be to everyone's benefit that physicians are paid more than say, concrete workers.

It also follows from the priority of the first principle over the second that, contrary to what utilitarian theory seems to require, someone's personal liberty cannot be sacrificed for the sake of the common good. Does the pleasure of owning slaves bring more happiness to the slave owners than it brings unhappiness to the slaves? If so, then the total happiness of society may be greater with slavery than without it. Thus, slavery would be to the common good, and utilitarianism would require that it should be instituted. Of course, utilitarians may maintain that slavery or other restrictions of liberties will as a matter of fact diminish the sum total of happiness in a society and for this reason cannot be condoned, but they must nevertheless admit that, as a matter of principle, violations of liberty would be justified for the sake of the happiness of the many. According to Rawls's principles, such violations for the sake of the general happiness are not justified.

Although Rawls does not explicitly discuss the rights of individuals as a major topic, his theory obviously can be interpreted as securing such rights. Many have believed that, without God, talk of rights is pretty much nonsense; Rawls does not discuss God, and it seems plain that he does not need to do so to speak meaningfully of a person's rights. According to Rawls, a just society guarantees persons the right to pursue their own ends so long as they do not interfere with the right of others to pursue their own ends. It is not acceptable to restrict this right for some supposed higher good. Rawls, in effect, attempts to derive social ethics from a basis in rational self-interest rather than from God, natural law, human nature, utility, or other ground.

If Rawls's theory is correct, he has spelled out in plain language the fundamental requirements of the just society. Furthermore, if his theory is correct, these are the requirements that self-interested but rational people would, on reflection, accept. This means that Rawls's theory provides a strong answer to the person who asks of any provision entailed by one or the other of the two principles just stated, "Why should I accept this provision?"

The most important good, according to John Rawls, is self-respect. Thus, self-respect is essential for any activity at all. When we lack it, it seems pointless to do anything, Self-respect, says Rawls, has two aspects: first, a conviction that one's plans and aspirations are worthwhile, and second, confidence in one's ability to accomplish these objectives. Without self-respect, therefore, our plans have little or no value to us, and we cannot continue in we want to know what is wrong with enslaving another person. The answer is that the wrongfulness of slavery logically follows from the two principles of social justice. But why should you agree to those principles? The answer is that you would agree to them. Why? Because they are the principles that would be selected by self-interested but rational people playing on a level playing field—one, that is, on which no one has an unfair advantage. They are the principles that would be selected by self-interested but rational people if the procedure through which they were selected was unbiased by anyone having insider's knowledge of his or her or anyone else's unique circumstances. They are, in short, the principles that self-interested but rational people would select if the procedure by which they were selected was a fair one. So, then, the reason you should accept that slavery is wrongful is because you would accept the principles from which the wrongfulness of slavery logically follows.

Few philosophical works by analytic philosophers have received such wide-spread attention and acclaim outside the circles of professional philosophers as did Rawls's *A Theory of Justice.* Though uncompromisingly analytical, it dealt with current issues of undeniable importance and interest and did so in light of recent work in economics and die social sciences. The book was reviewed not merely in philosophical journals but also in the professional literature of other disciplines and very widely in the popular press and in magazines of opinion and social commentary. It also became the focal point of numerous conferences, many of them interdisciplinary.

In a later work, *Political Liberalism* (1993), Rawls considered more carefully how his conception of justice as fairness can be endorsed by the diverse array of incompatible religious and philosophical doctrines that exist over time in a modern democratic society like ours. To answer this question, he found that he must characterize justice more narrowly than he did earlier, as a freestanding political conception rather than as a comprehensive value system (like Christianity) that governs all aspects of one's life, both public and private. Political justice becomes the focus of an overlapping consensus of comprehensive value systems and thus can still be embraced by all in a pluralistic democratic society. This change in Rawls's theory marks a change in Rawls's own theoretical understanding of justice as fairness. As a practical matter, though, the two principles of justice mentioned earlier still. constitute the best conception of political cooperation required for stability in a democratic regime, in Rawls's view.

According to Rawls, in a just society individuals are guaranteed the right to pursue . their own ends to the extent that they do not interfere with the right of others to pursue their own ends. Compromising this basic right to individual liberty for the sake of any so-called higher good is not acceptable in the Rawlsian view, and any such "good" is not really a good thing at all.You could say that, for Rawls, the right to personal liberty is more basic or fundamental than goodness. This is a view widely held by liberals. However, some recent critics of Rawls say there exists a common good whose attainment has priority over individual liberty. Some of these critics are known as communitarians, for they hold that this common good is defined by one's society or community. Important communitarian critics of Rawls include Michael Sandel *(Liberalism and the Limits of Justice,* 1982), Michael Walzer *(Spheres of Justice,* 1983, and *Thick and Thin,* 1994), and Alasdair Maclntyre (*After Virtue*, 1984).

Sandel believes that the community is an intersubjective or collective self because self-understanding comprehends more than just an individual human being: it comprehends one's family or tribe or class or nation or people—in short, one's community, with its shared ends and common vocabulary and mutual understandings. Sandel insists that the Rawlsian principle of equal liberty is subordinate to the good of this social organism.

Walzer contrasts "thick" or particularist moral argument, which is internal to and framed within a specific political association or culture, with "thin" moral argument, which is abstract and general and philosophical. Political philosophers, according to Walzer, seek an abstract, universal thin point of view and are concerned with the appropriate structure of political association in general. But any full account of how social goods ought to be distributed, he says, will be thick; it "will be idiomatic in its language, particularist in its cultural reference, and historically detailed." For Walzer, a society is just if its way of life is faithful to the shared understanding of its members. There "are no eternal or universal principles" that can replace a "local account" of justice. All such principles are abstractions and simplifications but nevertheless still reflect particular cultural viewpoints.

—Editor

Justice as Fairness

My aim is to present a conception of justice which generalizes and carries to a higher level of abstraction the familiar theory of the social contract as found, say, in Locke, Rousseau, and Kant. In order to do this we are not to think of the original contract as one to enter a particular society or to set up a particular form of government. Rather, the guiding idea is that die principles of justice for the basic structure of society are the object of the original agreement. They are the principles that free and rational persons concerned to further their own interests would accept in an initial position of equality as defining the fundamental terms of their association.These principles are to regulate all further agreements; they specify the kinds of social cooperation that can be entered into and the forms of government that can be established.This way of regarding the principles of justice I shall call justice as fairness.

Thus we are to imagine that those who engage in social cooperation choose together, in one joint act, the principles which are to assign basic rights and duties and to determine the division of social benefits. Men are to decide in advance how they are to regulate their claims against one another and what is to be the foundation charter of their society. Just as each person must decide by rational reflection what constitutes his good, that is, the system of ends which it is rational for him to pursue, so a group of persons must decide once and for all what is to count among them as just and unjust. The choice which rational men would make in this hypothetical situation of equal liberty, assuming for the present that this choice problem has a solution, determines the principles of justice.

In justice as fairness the original position of equality corresponds to the state of nature in the traditional theory of the social contract.This original position is not, of course, thought of as an actual historical state of affairs, much less as a primitive condition of culture. It is understood as a purely hypothetical situation characterized so as to lead to a certain conception of justice. Among the essential features of this situation is that no one knows his place in society, his class position or social status, nor does any one know his fortune in the distribution of natural assets and abilities, his intelligence, strength, and the like. I shall even assume that the parties do not know their conceptions of the good or their special psychological propensities. The principles of justice are chosen behind a veil of ignorance. This ensures that no one is advantaged or disadvantaged in the choice of principles by the outcome of natural chance or the contingency of social circumstances. Since all are similarly situated and no one is able to design principles to favor his particular condition, the principles of justice are the result of a fair agreement or bargain. For given circumstances of the original position, the symmetry of everyone's relations to each other, this initial situation is fair between individuals as moral persons, that is, as rational beings with their own ends and capable, I shall assume, of a sense of justice. The original position is, one might say, the appropriate initial status quo, and thus the fundamental agreements reached in it are fair.

Justice as fairness begins, as I have said, with one of the most general of all choices which persons might make together, namely, with the choice of the first principles of a conception of justice which is to regulate all subsequent criticism and reform of institutions. Then, having chosen a conception of justice, we can suppose that they are to choose a constitution and a legislature to enact laws, and so on, all in accordance with the principles of justice initially agreed upon. Our social situation is just if it is such that by this sequence of hypothetical agreements we would have contracted into the general system of rules which defines it.

I shall maintain . . . that the persons in the initial situation would choose two rather different principles: the first requires equality in the assignment of basic rights and duties, while the second holds that social and economic inequalities, for example inequalities of wealth and authority, are just only if they result in compensating benefits for everyone, and in particular for the least advantaged members of society. These principles rule out justifying institutions on the grounds that the hardships of some are offset by a greater good in the aggregate. It may be expedient but it is not just that some should have less in order that others may prosper. But there is no injustice in the greater benefits earned by a few provided that the situation of persons not so fortunate is thereby improved. The intuitive idea is that since everyone's well-being depends upon a scheme of co-operation without which no one could have a satisfactory life, the division of advantages should be such as to draw forth the willing cooperation of everyone taking part in it, including those less well situated.Yet this can be expected only if reasonable terms are proposed. The two principles mentioned seem to be a fair agreement on the basis of which those better endowed, or more fortunate in their social position, neither of which we can be said to deserve, could expect the willing cooperation of others when some work-able scheme is a necessary condition of the welfare of all. Once we decide to look for a conception of justice that nullifies the accidents of natural endowment and the contingencies of social circumstance as counters in quest for political and economic advantage, we are led to these principles. They express the result of leaving aside those aspects of the social world that seem arbitrary from a moral point of view.

(From *A Theory of Justice by* John Rawls, Harvard University Press. Cambridge, Mass. 1971)

22

Robert Nozick

Robert Nozick (1938-2002) occupied a prominent place in libertarian tradition. If any other book by an analytic philosopher attracted as much attention as *A Theory of Justice*, it was *Anarchy, State, and Utopia*, published in 1974. By this time it was not unusual to find analytic philosophers speaking to "big" issues, and Nozick 'certainly did that.

The reaction to *Anarchy, State, and Utopia* was more mixed than' that to Rawls's book, and, though many reviewers acclaimed it enthusiastically, others condemned it, often vehemently. These negative reactions are easily understandable in view of Nozick's vigorous espousal of principles of political philosophy that are not very popular with many contemporary liberal political theorists. The basic question asked in *Anarchy, State, and Utopia* is, simply: Should there even be a political state and, if so, why? Nozick's answer was worked out in elaborate detail through the course of his book, but it consisted essentially of three claims; A minimal state, limited to the narrow functions of protection against forcej theft, fraud, breach of contracts, and so on, is justified. Any more extensive state will violate persons' rights not to be forced to do certain things and is unjustified. The minimal state is inspiring as well as right.

The first claim, that a minimal state is justified, will seem so obvious to many as hardly to require lengthy argument. The basic idea accepted by political theorists in the liberal political tradition, from John Locke through Mill and up to and including Rawls, is that the political state—as compared with a state of anarchy or "the state of nature"—"advances the good of those taking part of it". But does it? If, as Nozick believed, "individuals have rights, and there are things no person or group may do to them without violating their rights," then it may well be true, as anarchists believe, that "any state necessarily violates people's moral rights and hence is intrinsically immoral." In the first part of his book, Nozick considered carefully whether this anarchist belief is true. His conclusion was that it is not.To establish this conclusion, he attempted to show that a minimal state can arise by the mechanism of an "invisible hand" from a hypothetical state of nature without violating any natural rights.

Often an action intended for a certain purpose generate—though unforeseen indirect consequences. Adam Smith, people, in intending only their own gain, are "led by an invisible hand to promote an end" that was not part of their intention, namely, the general good. minimal state can arise without violating people's rights. Nozick, after Adam Smith, calls an invisible hand explanation one that explains the seemingly direct result of what someone has intended or to happen as not being brought about by such intentions or desires at all.

The main claim advanced by Nozick in the second part of his book, and by far the most controversial claim of the work as a whole, is that any state more powerful or extensive than the minimal night-watchman state that protects its citizens from force and fraud and like things impinges on the individual's natural rights to his or her holdings and therefore is not legitimate or justifiable. It is further a corollary to this claim that concepts of justice that mandate the distribution of assets in accordance with a formula (e.g., "to each according to his __") or in accordance with a goal or objective (e.g., to promote the general happiness) always require redistributing the goods of society and thus require taking from some individuals the goods that are rightfully theirs. Such concepts of justice are therefore illegitimate.

Nozick's own concept of justice rested on an idea that comes naturally to many people. The idea is that what is yours is yours: redistributing your income or goods against your wishes for the sake of the general happiness or to achieve any other objective is unjust. Nozick defended this idea. A person is entitled to what he or she has rightfully acquired, and justice consists in each person's retaining control over his or her rightful acquisitions. This is Nozick's entitlement concept of social justice.

Nozick did not clarify or attempt to defend his entitlement concept of social justice. He basically accepted a refined version of Locke's theory of property acquisition, according to which, you will remember, what is yours is what you mix your labor with. Instead, he mainly sought to show that alternative conceptions of social justice, conceptions that ignore what a person is entitled to by virtue of rightful acquisition, are defective. According to Nozick, social justice, that is, justice in the distribution of goods, is not achieved by redistributing these goods to achieve some objective but rather by permitting them to remain in the hands of those who have legitimately acquired them:Your being forced to contribute to another's welfare violates your rights, whereas someone else's not providing you with things you need greatly, including things essential to the protection of your rights, does not itself violate your rights, even though it avoids making it more difficult for someone else to violate them.

According to Nozick's view of social justice, taking from the rich without compensation and giving to the poor is never just assuming the rich did not become rich through force or fraud, etc. This would also be Locke's view. According to the strict utilitarian view, by contrast, doing so *is* just if it is to the greater good of the aggregate of people (as would be the case, for example, if through progressive taxation you removed from a rich person's income an amount that he or she would miss but little and used it to prevent ten people from starving). Finally, according to Rawls's view of justice, taking from the rich and giving to the poor is just if it is to the greater good of the aggregate, provided it does not compromise anyone's liberty.

In the opening sentence of his book, Nozick asserted that individuals have rights, and indeed his entire argument rested on that supposition, especially those many aspects that pertain to property rights. Unfortunately, Nozick's theoretical justification of the supposition was very obscure: it had something to do, evidently, with a presumed inviolability of individuals that prohibits their being used as means to ends and perhaps also with the necessary conditions for allowing them to give meaning to their lives. If Nozick didn't make his thought entirely clear in this area, he did set forth very plainly as he saw them. In addition, his work contained many interesting and provocative side discussions, including critical discussions of Marx's theory of exploitation.

—Editor

Justice as Entittement

A principle, suggested by Herbert Hart, which (following John Rawls) we shall call the *principle of fairness,* would be of service here if it were ade-quate. This principle holds that when a number of persons engage in a just, mutually advantageous, cooperative venture according to rules and thus restrain their liberty in ways necessary to yield advantages for all, those who have submitted to these restrictions have a right to similar acquies-cence on the part of those who have benefited from their submission. Acceptance of benefits (even when this is not a giving of express or tacit under-taking to cooperate) is enough, according to this principle, to bind one. . . ,

The principle of fairness, as we stated it following Hart and Rawls, is objectionable and un-acceptable. Suppose some of the people in your neighborhood (there are 364 other adults) have found a public address system and decide to insti-tute a system of public entertainment. They post a list of names, one for each day, yours among them. On his assigned day (one can easily switch days) a person is to run the public address system, play records over it, give news bulletins, tell amusing stories he has heard, and so on. After 138 days on which each person has done his part, your day arrives. Are you obligated to take your turn? You have benefited from it, occasionally opening your window to listen, enjoying some music or chuckling at someone's funny story. The other people *have* put themselves our. But must you answer me call when it is your turn to do so? As it stands, surely not. Though you benefit from the arrangement, you may know all along that 364 days of entertainment supplied by others will not be worth your giving up *one* day. You would rather not have any of it and not give up a day than have it all and spend one of your days at it. Given these preferences, how can it be that you are required to participate when your scheduled time comes? . . .

At the very least one wants to build into the principle of fairness the condition that the benefits to a person from the actions of the others are greater than the costs to him of doing his share....

If the principle of fairness were modified so as to contain this very strong condition, it still would be objectionable. The benefits might only barely be worth the costs to you of doing your share, yet others might benefit from this institution much more than you do; they all treasure listening to the public broad-casts. As the person least benefited by the practice, are you obligated to do an equal amount for it? ...

On the face of it, enforcing the principle of fairness is objectionable. You may not decide to give me something, for example a book, and then grab money from me to pay for it, even if I have nothing better to spend the money on. You have, if anything, even less reason to demand payment if your activity that gives me the book also benefits you; suppose that your best way of getting exercise is by throwing books into people's houses, or that some other activity of yours thrusts books into people's houses as an unavoidable side effect. Nor are things changed if your inability to collect money or payments for the books which unavoidably spill over into others' houses makes it inadvisable or too expensive for you to carry on the activity with this side effect. One cannot, whatever one's purposes, just act so as to give people benefits and then demand (or seize) payment. Nor can a group of persons do this. If you may not charge and collect for benefits you bestow without prior agreement, you certainly may not do so for benefits whose bestowal costs you nothing, and most certainly people need not repay you for cosdess to provide benefits which yet others provided them. So the fact that we partially are "social products" in that we benefit from current patterns and forms created by the multitudinous actions of a long string of long-forgotten people, forms which include institutions, ways of doing things, and language (whose social nature may involve our current use depending upon Wittgensteinian matching of the speech of others), does not create in us a general floating debt which the current society can collect and use as it will.

Perhaps a modified principle of fairness can be stated which would be free from these and similar difficulties. What seems certain is that any such principle, if possible, would be so complex and involuted that one could not combine it with a special principle legitimating *enforcement* within a state of nature of the obligations that have arisen under it. Hence, even if the principle could be formulated so that it was no longer open to objection, it would not serve to obviate the need for other persons' consenting to cooperate and limit their own activities.

(From *Anarchy, Scale, and Utopia* by Robert Nozick. Basic Books, inc. 1974)

23

Jurgen Habermas

Jurgen Habermas (1929-) was born in Dusseldorf, Germany. He was raised in Gummersbach, where his father was the director of a seminary. When World War II ended, he was sixteen years old. He studied at the University of Bonn and was especially interested in Hegel, Marx, and modern Marxist thinkers. After receiving his PhD in 1954, he became an assistant to Theodor Adorno at the University of Frankfurt. Adorno and Marx Horkheimer were the leading figures in the Frankfurt School, renowned for the attempts its followers made to integrate the disciplines of philosophy, psychoanalysis, social science, and literary criticism. Habermas would make his own substantial contribution to the school's thought. The subject matter of his books varies greatly, but his overall concern has been to free people from unnecessary and unhelpful rules, categories, and other constraints. He achieved widespread recognition relatively early on with books such as *Theory and Practice* (1962). *The Logic of the Social Sciences* (1967), *Toward a Rational Society* (1971), *Knowledge and Human Interest* (1981), and *Theory of Social Action* (1984).

Bridging continental and Anglo-American traditions of thought, Habermas has engaged in debates with thinkers as diverse as Gadamer and Putnam, Foucault and Rawls and Derrida. His extensive written work addresses topics stretching from social-political theory to aesthetics, epistemology and language to philosophy of religion, and his ideas have significantly influenced not only philosophy but also political-legal thought, sociology, communication studies, argumentation theory and rhetoric, developmental psychology and theology. Moreover, he has figured prominently in Germany as a public intellectual, commenting on controversial issues of the day in German newspapers.

Habermas's interest in the political subsequently led him to a series of philosophical studies and critical-social analyses that eventually appeared in English in his Toward a Rational Society (1970) and *Theory and Practice* (1973b). Whereas the latter consists primarily of reflections on the history of philosophy, the former represents an attempt to apply his emerging theory of rationality to the critical analysis of contemporary society, in particular the student protest movement and its institutional target, the authoritarian and technocratic structures that held sway in higher education and politics.

Habermas a professor at the University of Frankfurt, is one of many thinkers influenced by the critical approach of the Frankfurt School. In this context "critical" does not necessarily mean negative but rather reflective or thoughtful. This goes far beyond the reflection a physicist might bring to the results of a failed experiment. The kind of reflection critical theory emphasizes is reflection on the assumptions of science or philosophy. For instance, empirical science approaches the world with a view of finding law like regularities in the things it examines; the measure of knowledge thus becomes the predictive power of the experimental method. Underlying the practice of empirical science is the assumption that its findings are independent of the observer. When the experimental method is used on the human being, it is no surprise that what emerges is a picture of a thing (a human thing) that also follows law like regularities and for which more or less sophisticated predictions can be made.

The tendency in modern technocratic society, Habermas says, is for this description of experimental science to become definitional of all knowledge. Although logical positivism has been sharply criticized, its influence is still felt in the normal, ongoing scientific enterprise. But Habermas points out that "positivistic science" is only one way of looking at the world, and it is no surprise that such a perspective would claim to find "objective facts" that would make it possible for human beings to exert control over nature. Yet such a perspective, says Habermas, is inappropriate for the investigation of mutually shared meanings we experience in the everyday human world in which we live. Positivistic science treats human beings as objective things; what is needed is an approach to knowledge that treats the human being as a subject, one not isolated from other subjects but, on the contrary, interacting with them. This interaction takes place in a domain that allows the sharing of intersubjective experiences and that provides contexts of history, art, literature, and language itself that enable us to understand one another.

This practical interest each of us has in undertaking one another, Habermas says, is the realm of a science he calls historical/ hermeneutical. Hermeneutics deals with the principles of interpretation – of the Bible, of other texts, and of the language of human interactions. He emphasizes that in this practical science, the individual cannot be treated as an objective unit; on the contrary, my human identity is to a greater or lesser extent the creation of human language and of the society into which I am born. Through this society and language, I gain a "preunderstanding" of others in my quest for mutual self-understanding; that is, I cannot understand myself if I cannot understand the words and actions of others. The meanings of those words and actions give me a context for making sense of myself in the human world.

But, for Habermas, there is a second kind of knowledge that is also inappropriate for the positivistic sciences. Habermas calls this "emancipatory knowledge", and it is the concern of critical theory. It is the work of critical theory to make explicit the controlling ideology of a political or social order. Ideology misrepresents and distorts the truth about the existence and use of arbitrary power throughout a society. The roots of ideology go deep into the heart of what a society takes to knowledge. For example, a social order may be blind to its own fundamental belief that the method of positivistic science, which reduces the human being to the status of a thing for purposes of study, is the surest road to truth. In the realm of the practical, such a reductionistic ideology can be seen, say, in the treatment of a poem as a single object, independent of the society that produced that produced it, to be studied just for itself. Habermas would agree with Marx that ideology produces reification takes human acts or properties, objectifies them, and then treats them as independent of the human. In a capitalist society, for example, money is the reification of human labor and is the end used against the laborer. But Habermas is critical of Marx's own reduction of human art and literature – Marx called them the "superstructure" – to the "base" of strict materialism. Thus, Habermas's own critical theorizing is Marxian – in the critical spirit of Marx – but not Marxist.

For Habermas, critical theory can bring a kind of freedom or emancipation from the chains of ideology as those who practice the method come to reflect on their own most deeply held assumptions and come to see that they are false. Ultimately, such emancipation would change society and the way human beings communicate one with another. Habermas proposed a theory of communicative competence in which what he called the ideal speech situation supplies the basis for rational nonidealogical communication. The ideal speech situation, in which persons are free to speak their minds and listen to reason without fear of being blocked, is product of language itself, he said, and is presupposed in every discourse. The person who lies, for example, does so with the assumption that there is such a thing as speaking the truth otherwise, the concept of a lie would be meaningless. In a paper published in 1970, Habermas declared that "insofar as we master the means for the construction of an ideal speech situation, we can conceive the ideas of truth, freedom, and justice, which interpret each other – although of course only as ideas. On the strength of communicative competence alone, however,... we are quite unable to realize the ideal speech situation; we can only anticipate it". Recent work by Habermas has focused on the rise of countercultural groups, feminism, and various liberation movements and whether they constitute the beginnings of the kind of free society he envisions.

Habermas's critical reflection takes a nuanced approach to both sides of the social unrest that characterized the late sixties. Although sympathetic with students' demand for more democratic participation and hopeful that their activism harbored a potential for positive social transformation, he also did not hesitate to criticize its militant aspects, which he labeled self-delusory and pernicious. In his critique of technocracy—governance by scientific experts and bureaucracy—he relied on a philosophical framework that anticipates categories in his later thought, minus the philosophy of language he would work out in the 1970s. Specifically, Habermas sharply distinguished between two modes of action, "work" and "interaction," which correspond to enduring interests of the human species. The former includes modes of action based on the rational choice of efficient means, that is, forms of instrumental and strategic action, whereas the latter refers to forms of "communicative action" in which actors coordinate their behaviors on the basis of "consensual norms". Habermas's distinction in effect appropriates the classical Aristotelian contrast between *techne* and *praxis* for critical social theory. The result is a distinctively Habermasian critique of science and technology as ideology: by reducing practical questions about the good life to technical problems for experts, contemporary elites eliminate the need for public, democratic discussion of values, thereby depoliticizing the population. The legitimate human interest in technical control of nature thus functions as an ideology—a screen that masks the value-laden character of government decision-making in the service of the capitalist status quo. Unlike Herbert Marcuse, who regarded that interest as specific to capitalist society, Habermas affirmed the technical control of nature as a genuinely universal species-interest; the technical interest did not necessitate social domination.

Habermas defended this philosophical anthropology most fully in his *Knowledge and Human Interests,* the work that represents his first attempt to provide a systematic framework for an interdisciplinary critical social theory. As Habermas conceived his task, he had to establish critical social theory as a respectable, distinct form of knowledge, in large measure through a methodological critique of the then-dominant positivist philosophy of science and historicist hermeneutics. He thus develops a theory of "knowledge-constitutive interests" that are tied both to "the natural history of the human species" and to "the imperatives of the socio-cultural form of life," but are not reducible to them.

There are three knowledge-constitutive interests, each rooted in human existence and expressed in a particular type of scientific or scholarly inquiry technical interest, Practical interest and emancipatory interest. The first is the "technical interest," the "anthropologically deep-seated interest" we have in the prediction and control of the natural environment. This interest structures modes of inquiry and knowledge-production in the "empirical-analytic" sciences, that is, the natural sciences.

The second in the interpretive, or cultural-hermeneutic sciences, rest on that, equally deep-seated "practical interest" in securing and expanding possibilities of mutual and self-understanding in the conduct of life. These sciences presuppose and articulate modes of action-orienting interpersonal understanding that operates within socio-cultural forms of life and the grammar of ordinary language. Human societies depend on such understanding, and the interpretive competences that go with it, just as much as they depend on mastering the natural environment. The hermeneutic sciences, then, bring methodical discipline to features of everyday interaction, and in that sense are on a par with the empirical-analytic sciences, which elevate everyday instrumental action to experimental method. By making these first two cognitive interests explicit, Habermas seeks to go beyond positivist accounts of the natural and social sciences. On his view, those accounts tend to ignore the role that deep-seated human interests play in the constitution of possible objects of inquiry.

The third is emancipatory interests which engage in a kind of critical self-reflection, more precisely a methodological reflection that aims to free science from its positivist illusions. Such reflection exemplifies the cognitive interest, the emancipatory interest of reason in overcoming dogmatism, compulsion, and domination. For scientific expressions of this interest, he looked to Freudian psychology and a version of Marxist social theory. The status of the emancipatory interest, however, was problematic from the start, for it conflated two kinds of critical reflection. Whereas his critique of positivism and theory of cognitive interests involve reflective articulation of the formal structures of knowledge, Freudian and Marxist critique aim to unmask concrete cases of personal self-deception and social-political ideology. Nor was it clear that psychoanalysis provided an apt model of laboratory reflection in any case, as critics pointed out how the asymmetries between patient and analyst could not represent the proper intersubjective form for emancipation. These and other deficits of his analysis posed a challenge for Habermas that would guide a decade-long search for the normative and empirical basis of critique. Whatever the best path to the epistemic and normative basis for critique might be, it would have to pass a democratic test: that "in Enlightenment there are only participants". Habermas will not resolve this methodological issue until a series of transitional studies in the 1970s culminates in his mature systematic work, *The Theory of Communicative Action*.

As a theory of rationality and knowledge, his theory of knowledge-constitutive interests is both pragmatic and pluralistic: pragmatic, inasmuch as human interests constitute knowledge; pluralistic, in that different forms of inquiry and knowledge emerge from different core interests. In *Knowledge and Human Interests* we can thus see the beginnings of a methodologically pluralistic approach to critical social theory. The analysis was hampered by a framework that still relied on motifs from a "philosophy of consciousness" fixated on the constitution of objects of possible experience—an approach that cannot do justice to the discursive dimensions of inquiry. In the 1970s Habermas set about a fundamental overhaul of his framework for critical theory.

In the period between *Knowledge and Human Interests* and *The Theory of Communicative Action*, Habermas began to develop a distinctive method for elaborating the relationship between a theoretical social science of modern societies, on the one hand, and the normative and philosophical basis for critique, on the other. Following Horkheimer's definition of Critical Theory, Habermas pursued three aims in his attempt to combine social science and philosophical analysis: it must be at once explanatory, practical, and normative. This meant that philosophy could not, as it did for Kant, become the sole basis for normative reflection. Rather, Habermas argued, adequate critique requires a thoroughgoing cooperation between philosophy and social science. This sort of analysis is characteristic of *Legitimation Crisis* (1975); in which Habermas analyzes the modern state as subject to endemic crises, which arise from the fact that the state cannot simultaneously meet the demands for rational problem solving, democracy, and cultural identity. Here the social science to which Habermas appeals is more sociological and functional. Similarly, in this work and in *Communication and the Evolution of Society* (1979),

Habermas begins to develop a distinctive conception of rational reconstruction, which models societal development as a learning process. In these works, Habermas begins to incorporate the results of developmental psychology, which aligns stages of development with changes in the kinds of reasons that the maturing individual considers acceptable. Analogously, societies develop through similar changes in the rational basis of legitimacy on the collective level. At this point in his theorizing, Habermas's appropriation of the social sciences has become methodologically and theoretically pluralistic: on his view, a critical social theory is not distinctive in light of endorsing some particular theory or method but as uniting normative and empirical inquiry.

In this transitional phase from *Knowledge and Human Interests* to *The Theory of Communicative Action*, Habermas's basic philosophical endeavor was to develop a more modest, fallibilist, empirical account of the philosophical claim to universality and rationality. This more modest approach moves Critical Theory away from its strong transcendental framework, exemplified in the theory of cognitive interests with the unmistakably Kantian language of object-constitution. In setting that earlier project aside, Habermas adopts a more naturalistic, "post metaphysical" approach, characterized by the fallible hermeneutic explication or "reconstruction" of shared competences and normative presuppositions that allow actors to engage in familiar practices of communication, discourse, and inquiry. In articulating presuppositions of practice, reconstructive analysis remains weakly transcendental. But it also qualifies as a "weak naturalism" inasmuch as the practices it aims to articulate are consistent with the natural evolution of the species and located in the empirical world consequently, post metaphysical reconstruction links up with specific forms of social-scientific knowledge in analyzing general conditions of rationality manifested in various human capacities and powers.

Habermas's encounter with speech act theory proved to be particularly decisive for this project. In speech act theory, he finds the basis for a conception of communicative competence. Given this emphasis on language, Habermas is often said to have taken a kind of "linguistic turn" in this period. He framed his first essay on formal pragmatics as an alternative to Niklas Luhmann's systems theory. Habermas understands formal pragmatics as one of the "reconstructive sciences," which aim to render theoretically explicit the intuitive, pretheoretical know-how underlying such basic human competences as speaking and understanding, judging and acting. Unlike Kant's transcendental analysis of the conditions of rationality, reconstructive sciences yield knowledge that is not necessary but hypothetical, not a priori but empirical, not certain but fallible. They are nevertheless directed to invariant structures and conditions and raise universal, but defeasible claims to an account of practical reason. With the turn to language and reconstructive science, Habermas undermines both of the traditional Kantian roles for philosophy: philosophy as the sole judge in normative matters and as the methodological authority that assigns the various domains of inquiry to their proper questions. In Habermas's view, philosophy must engage in a fully cooperative relationship with the social sciences and the empirical disciplines in general.

Habermas's mature positions begin with his *Theory of Communicative Action* (*TCA*), a two-volume critical study of the theories of rationality that informed the classical sociologies of Weber, Durkheim, Parsons, and neo-Marxist critical theory (Lukács, Horkheimer, Adorno). In *TCA* we find Habermas's conception of the task of philosophy and its relation to the social sciences—a conception that still guides much of his work. While *TCA* defends the emphasis on normativity and the universalist ambitions found in the philosophical tradition, it does so within a framework that includes particular sorts of empirical social research, with which philosophy must interact. Philosophers, that is, must cooperate with social scientists if they are to understand normative claims within the current historical context, the context of a complex, modern society that is characterized by social and systemic modes of integration.

—Editor

Three Normative Models Of Democracy

I would like to sketch a procedutalist view of democracy and deliberative politics which differs in relevant respects from both the liberal and the republican paradigm. Let me remind you of the opposite feature of these two established models. I will then introduce a new proceduralist conception by way of a critique of the 'ethical overload' of the republican view. The last part of the essay further elaborates the three normative models of democracy by comparing their corresponding images of state and society.

According to the 'liberal' or Lockean view, the democratic process accomplishes the task of programming the government in the interests of society, -where the government is represented as an apparatus of public administration, and society as a market-structured network of interactions among private persons. Here politics (in the sense of the citizens' political will-formation) has the function of bundling together and pushing private interests against a government apparatus specialising in the administrative employment of political power for collective goals. On the 'republican' view, however, politics involves more than this mediating function; it is rather constitutive of the process of society as a whole. 'Polities' is conceived as the reflective form of substantial ethical life, namely as the medium in which the members of somehow solitary communities become aware of their dependence on one another and, acting with full deliberation as citizens, further shape and develop existing relations of reciprocal recognition into an association of free and equal consociates under law. With this, the liberal architectonic of government and society undergoes an important change: in addition to the hierarchical regulations of the state and the decentralised regulations of the market - that is, besides administrative power and individual personal interests - solidarity and the orientation to the common good appear as a third sourer of social integration. In fact, this horizontal political will-formation aimed at mutual understand MIK or communicatively achieved consensus is even supposed to enjoy priority, both in a genetic and a normative sense. An autonomous basis in civil society, a basis independent of public administration and market-mediated private commerce, is assumed is a precondition for the praxis of civic self-determination. This basis preserves political communication from being swallowed up by the government apparatus or assimilated to structures. In the republican conception, the political public sphere s along with its base in civil society, a strategic significance. These compiling approaches yield two contrasting images of the citizen.

According to the liberal view, the citizens' status is determined primarily according to negative rights they have vis-a-vis foe state and other citizens. As bearers of these right they enjoy the protection of the government, as long as they pursue their private interests within the boundaries drawn by the legal statutes - and this includes protection against government interventions. Political rights, such as voting rights and free speech, have not only the same structure as but a similar meaning to civil rights that provide a space within which legal subjects are released from external compulsion. They give citizens the opportunity to assert their private interests in such a way that, by means of elections, the composition of parliamentary bodies, and the formation of a government, these interests are finally aggregated into a political will that makes an impact on the administration.

According to the republican view, the status of citizens is not determined by the model of negative liberties to which these citizens ran lay claim as private persons, father, political rights - pre-eminently rights of political participation and communication - are positive liberties. They guarantee not freedom from external compulsion but the possibility of participation in a common praxis, through the exercise of which citizens can first make themselves into what they want to be - politically autonomous authors of a community of free and equal persons. To this extent, the political process does nut just serve to keep government activity under the surveillance of citizens who have already acquired a prior social autonomy in the exercise of their private rights and pre-political liberties. Just as little does it act as a hinge between state and society, for administrative authority is not at all an autochthonous authority; it is not something given. Rather, this authority emerge', from the citizens' power produced communicatively in the praxis of self-legislation, and it finds its legitimation in the fact that it protects by institutionalising public liberty. So, the state's raison d'etre does not He primarily in the protection of equal private rights but in the guarantee of an inclusive opinion - and will-formation in which free and equal citizens reach an understanding on which goals and norms lie in the equal interest of all.

The polemic against the classical conception of the legal person as bearer of private rights reveals a controversy about the concept of law itself. While in the liberal view tin- point of a legal order is to make it possible to determine in each case which individuals are entitled to which rights, in the republican view these 'subjective' rights owe their existence to an 'objective' legal order that both enables and guarantees the integrity of an autonomous life in common based on mutual respect: 'For republicans rights ultimately are nothing but determinations of the prevailing political will, while for liberals some rights are always grounded in a higher law of... reason.'

Finally, the different ways of conceptualising the roles of citizen and of law express a deeper disagreement about the nature of the political process. In the liberal view, the political process of opinion- and will-formation in the public sphere and in parliament is determined by the competition of strategically acting collectivities trying to maintain or acquire positions of power. Success is measured by the citi/nis1 approval, quantified as votes, of persons and programmes. In their choices at the polls, voters give expression to their preferences. Their voting decisions have the same structure as the acts of choice made by participants in a market. They license access to the positions of power that political parties fight over in the same success-oriented attitude.

According to the republican view, the political opinion- and will-formation occurring in the public sphere and in parliament obeys not the structures of market processes but the obstinate structures of a public communication orientated to mutual understanding. For politics, in the sense of a praxis of civic self-legislation, the paradigm is not the market dialogue. This dialogic conception imagines politics as contestation over questions of value and not simple questions of preference.

Proceduralist vs communitarian views of politics

The republican model as compared to the liberal one has the advantage that it preserves the original meaning of democracy in terms of the institutionalization of a public use of reason jointly exercised by autonomous citizens. This model accounts for the communicative conditions that confer legitimating force on political opinion- and will-formation. These are precisely the conditions under which the political process can be presumed to generate reasonable results. A contest for power, if represented according to the liberal model of market competition, is determined by the political values and interests that are at best aggregated with equal weight in the political process; politics loses all reference to the normative core of the public use of reason. The republican trust in the force of political discourses stands in contrast to the liberal skepticism about reason. Such discourses are meant to allow one to discuss value orientations and interpretation of needs and wants, and then to change these in an insightful way.

But contemporary republicans tend to give this public communication a communicatarian reading. It is precisely this move towards an ethical constriction of political discourse that I call into question. Politics may not be assimilated to a hermeneutical process of self-explication of a shared form of life or collective identity. Political questions may not be reduced to the types of ethical question where we, as members of a community, ask ourselves who we are and who we would like to be. In its communitarian interpretation the republican model is too idealistic, even with the limits of a purely normative analysis. On this reading, the democratic process is dependent on the virtues of citizens devoted to the public weal. This explanation of virtue had already led Rousseau to split the citizen oriented to the common good from the private man, who cannot be ethically overburdened. The unanimity of the political legislature was supposed to be secured in advance by a substantive ethical consensus. In contrast, a discourse theory interpretation insists on the fact that democratic will-formation does not draw its legitimating force from a previous convergence of settled ethical convictions, but from both the communicative presuppositions that allow the better arguments to come into play in various forms of deliberation, and from the procedure that secure fair bargaining processes. Discourse theory breaks with a purely ethical conception of civic autonomy.

According to the communitarian view, there is a necessary connection between the deliberative conception of democracy and the reference to a concrete, substantively integrated, ethical community. Otherwise one could inn explain, in this view, how the citizens orientation to the common good would be at all possible. The individual, so the argument goes, can become aware; of her co-membership in a collective form of life, and therewith become aware of a prior social bond, only in a practice exercised with others in common. The individual can get a clear sense of commodities and differences, and hence a sense of who she is and who she would like to be, only in the public exchange with others who owe their identities to the same traditions and similar formation processes. This assimilation of political discourses to the clarification of a collective ethical self-understanding does not sit well with the function of the legislative processes they issue in. Legal statutes no doubt also contain teleo-logical dements. But these involve more than just the hermeneutic explication of shared value orientations. By their very structure laws are determined by the question of which norms citizens want to adopt for regulating their living together. To be sure, discourses aimed at achieving self-understanding are also important for politics - I refer here to discourses in which the participants want to get a dear understanding of themselves as members of a specific nation, as members of a locale or a state, as inhabitants of a region, etc.; in which they want to determine which traditions they will continue; in which they strive to determine how they will treat each other, and how they will treat minorities and marginal groups; in short, discourses in which they want to be clear about the kind of society they want to live in. But these questions are subordinate to moral questions, being connected with pragmatic questions. Moral questions, in the narrow sense of the Kantian tradition, are questions of justice. The question having priority in legislative politics concerns how a matter can be regulated in the equal interest of all. The making of norms is primarily a justice issue and is gauged by principles that state what is equally good for all. And, unlike ethical questions, questions of justice arc not related from the outset to a specific collective and its form of life. 'The politically enacted law of a concrete legal community must, it" it is to be legitimate, be at least compatible with moral tenets that claim universal validity going beyond the legal community.

Moreover, compromises make up the bulk of political processes. Under conditions of religious, cultural and societal pluralism, politically relevant goals are often selected by interests and value orientations that are by no means constitutive of the identity of the community at large, hence for the whole of an inter-subjectively shared form of life. The political interests and values that stand in conflict with each other without prospects of consensus are in need of a balancing that cannot be achieved through ethical discourses - even if the outcomes of bargaining processes are subject to the proviso that they must not violate a culture's agreed-upon basic values. The required balance of competing interests comes about as a compromise between parties that may rely on mutual threats. A legitimate kind of bargaining certainly expends on a prior regulation of fair terms for achieving results, terms which are acceptable for all parties on the basis of their differing preference. While the debates on such regulations should assume the forms of practical discourse that neutralise power, bargaining itself well allows for strategic interactions. The deliberative mode of legislative practice is not just intended to ensure the ethical validity of laws. Rather, one can understand the complex validity claims of legal norms as the claim, on the one hand, to compromise competing interests in a manner compatible with tin- common good and, on the other hand, to bring universalistic principles of justice into the horizon of the specific form of life of a particular community.

In contrast to the ethical constriction of political discourse, the concept of deliberative politics acquires empirical reference only when we take account of the multiplicity of communicative forms of rational political will-formation. It is not discourse of an ethical type that could grant on its own the democratic genesis of law. Instead, deliberative politics should be conceived as a syndrome that depends on a network of fairly regulated bargaining processes and of various forms of argumentation, including pragmatic, ethical and moral discourses, each of which relies on different communicative presuppositions and procedures. In legislative politics the supply of information and the rational choice of strategies are interwoven with the balancing of interests, with the achievement of ethical self-understanding and the articulation of strong preferences, with moral justification and tests of legal coherence. Thus 'dialogical' and 'instrumental' politics, the two ideal-types which Frank Michelman has opposed in a polarising fashion, do-in fact interpenetrate in the medium of deliberations of various kinds.

Three Images of State and Society

If we start from this proceduralist conception of deliberative politics, this reading of democracy has implications for the concept of society. Both the liberal and the republican model presuppose a view of society as centred in the state - be it the state as guardian of a market-society or the state as the sell-conscious institutionalisation of an ethical community.

According to the liberal view, the democratic process takes place exclusively in the form of compromises between competing interests. Harness is supposed to be granted by the general and equal right to vote, the representative composition of parliamentary bodies, by decision rules, and so on. Such rules are ultimately justified in terms of liberal basic rights. According to the republican view democratic will-formation takes place in the form of an ethical-political discourse; here deliberation can rely on a culturally established background consensus shared by the citizenry.

Discourse theory takes elements from both sides and integrates these into the concept of an ideal procedure for deliberation and decision-making. Weaving together pragmatic considerations, compromises, discourses of self-understanding and Justice, this democratic procedure grounds the presumption that reasonable or fair results are obtained. According to this proceduralist view, practical reason withdraws from universal human rights, or from the concrete ethical substance of a specific community, into the rules of discourse and forms of argumentation. In the final analysis, the normative content arises from the very structure of communicative actions. These descriptions of the democratic process set the stage for different conceptualisations of state and society.

According to the republican view, the citizens' political opinion- and will-formation form the medium through which society constitutes itself as a political whole. Society is, from the very start, political society –societas civilis. Hence democracy becomes equivalent to the political self-organization of society as a whole. This leads to a polemical understanding of Politics directed against the state apparatus. In Hannah Arendt's political writings one can see where republican argumentation directs its salvas; in opposition to the privatism of a depoliticized population and in opposition to the acquisition of the legitimation through entrenched parties, the public sphere should be revitalised to the point where a regenerated citizenry can, through the forms of a decentralised self-governance, appropriate (once again) the power of pseudo-independent state agencies. From this perspective, society would finally develop into a political totality.

Whereas the separation would finally the state apparatus from society elicits a polemical reaction, from the republican side, according to the liberal view it cannot be eliminated but only bridged by the democratic process. The regulated balancing of power and interests has need of constitutional channelling, of course. The democratic will-formation of self-interested citizens is laden with comparatively weak normative expectations. The constitution is supposed to tame the state apparatus through normative constraints (such as basic rights, separation of powers, etc.) and to force it, through the competition of political parties on the one hand and that between government and opposition on the other, to take adequate account of computing interests and value orientations. This state-centred understanding of politics can forgo the unrealistic assumption of a citizenry capable of collective action. Its focus is not so much the input of a rational political will-formation but the output of sensible and affective administrative accomplishments. Liberal argumentation aims its salvos against the potential disturbance of an administrative power that interferes with the spontaneous forces of self-regulating society. The liberal model hinges, not on the democratic self-determination of deliberating citizens, but on the legal institutionalisation of an economic society that is supposed to guarantee an essentially non-political common good by the satisfaction of private preferences.

Discourse theory invests the democratic process with normative connotations stronger than those founa in the liberal model but weaker than those of the republican model. Once again, it takes elements from both sides and If fits them together in a new way. In agreement with republicanism, it gives' centre stage to the process of political opinion- and will-formation, but without understanding the constitution as something secondary; rather it conceives the principles of the constitutional state as a consistent answer to the questions of how the demanding communicative forms of a democratic opinion- and will-formation can be institutionalised. Discourse theory has the success of deliberative politics depend not on a collective acting citizenry hut on the institutionalisation of the corresponding; procedures and conditions of communication. Proceduralised popular sovereignty and a political system tied in to the peripheral networks of the political public sphere go hand-in-hand with the image of a decentred society. This concept of democracy no longer needs to operate with the notion of a social whole centred in the state and imagined as a goal-oriented subject writ large. Just as little does it represent the whole it. a system of constitutional norms mechanically regulating the interplay of powers and interests in accordance with the market model.

Discourse theory altogether jettisons certain premisses of the philosophy of consciousness. Thirst premisses either invite us to ascribe the praxis of civic self-determination to one encompassing macro-subject or they have us apply the rule of law to many isolated private subjects. The former approach views the citizenry as a collective actor that reflects the whole and acts for it; in the hirer, individual actors function as dependent variables in system processes that move along blindly. Discourse theory works instead with the higher level inter subjectivity of communication processes that flow through both the parliamentary bodies and the informal networks of the public sphere. Within and without the parliamentary complex, these subjectless forms of communication constitute arenas in which a more or less rational opinion and will-formation can take place.

Informal public opinion-formation 'influence' influence is transformed into 'communicative power' through the channels of political elections; and communicative power is again transformed into 'administrative power' through legislation. As in the liberal model, the boundaries between 'state' and 'society' are respected; but in this case, civil society provides the social basis of autonomous public spheres that remain as distinct from the economic .system as from the administration. This understanding of democracy suggests a new balance between the three resources of money, administrative power and solidarity, from which modern societies meet their need for integration. The normative implications are obvious: the integrative force of 'solidarity', which can no longer be drawn solely from sources of communicative action, should develop through widely expanded and differentiated public spheres as well as through legally institutionalised procedures of democratic deliberation and decision-making. It should gain the strength to hold its own against the two other mechanisms of social integration - money and administrative power. This view has implications for how one understands legitimation and popular sovereignty.

On the liberal view, democratic will-formation has the exclusive function of legitimating the existence of political power. Election results are the licence to assume governmental power, whereas the government must justify the use of power to the public. On the republican view, democratic will-formation has the significantly stronger function of constituting society ns a political community and keeping the memory of this founding act alive with well election. The government is not only empowered to exercise a largely open mandate, but also programmatically committed to carry out certain policies. It remains bound to a self-governing political community. Discourse theory brings a third idea into play: the procedures and communicative presuppositions of democratic opinion- and will-formation function as the most important sluices for the discursive rationalisation of the Decisions of an administration constrained by law and statute.

Rationalisation means more than mere legitimation hut less than the constitution of political power. The power available to the administration changes its aggregate conditions as soon as it emerges from a public use of reason and a communicative power which do nor just monitor the exercise of political power in a belated manner but more or less programme it as well. Notwithstanding this discursive rationalisation, only the administrative system itself can 'act'. The administration is a subsystem specialised for collectively binding decisions, whereas the communicative structures of the public sphere comprise a far-flung network of sensors that in the first place react to the pressure of society-wide problematics and stimulate influential opinions. The public opinion that is worked up via democratic procedures into communicative power cannot 'rule' of itself, but can only point the use of administrative power in specific directions.

The concept of popular sovereignty stems from the republican appropriation and revelation of the early modern notion of sovereignty initially associated with absolutist regimes. The slate, which monopolises all the means for a legitimate implementation of force, is seen as an overpowering concentrate of power - as the Leviathan. This idea was transferred by Rousseau to the will of the united people. He refused the strength of the Leviathian, with its classical idea of the self-rule of free and equal citizens, and combined it with his modern concept of autonomy. Despite this sublimation, the concept of sovereignty remains bound to the notion of an embodiment in the assembled, physically present, people. According to the republican view, the people are the bearers of a sovereignty that in principle cannot be delegated: in their sovereign character the people cannot have others represent them. Liberalism opposes this with the more realistic view that in the constitutional -rate any authority originating from the people is exercised only 'by means of elections and voting and by specific legislative, executive, and judicial organs'.

These two views would exhaust the alternatives only if we had to conceive state and society in terms of the whole and its parts - where the whole is constituted either by a sovereign citizenry or by a constitution. To the discourse theory of democracy corresponds, however, the image of a decentred society. To be sure, with the political public sphere the pro-reduralist model sets off an arena for the detection, identification and interpretation of those problems that affect society as a whole. But the 'self of the self-organising legal community here disappears in the subjectless forms of communication that regulate the flow of deliberations in such a way that their fallible results enjoy the presupposition of rationality This is not to denounce the intuition connected with the idea of popular sovereignty but to interpret it in intersubjective terms. Popular sovereignty, even if it becomes anonymous, retreats into democratic procedures and the legal implications of their demanding communicative presuppositions only in order to make itself fell as communicatively generated power.

Strictly speaking, this communicative power springs from the interactions between legally institutionalised will-formation and culturally mobilised publics. The latter for their part find a basis in the associations of civil society quite distinct from both state and economy alike.

Read in procedural terms, the idea of popular sovereignty refers to a context that, while enabling the self-organisation of a legal community, is not a t the disposal of the citizens' will in any way. Deliberation is certainly supposed to provide the medium for a more or less conscious integration of the legal community; but this mode does not extend to the whole of society in which the political system is embedded as only one among several subsystems. Even in its own proceduralist self-understanding, deliberative politics remains a component of a complex society which, as a whole, resists the normative approach practised in legal theory. In this regard, the discourse-theory reading of democracy has a point of contact with a detached sociological approach that considers the political system neither as the peak nor the centre, nor even as the formative model, of society in general, but as just one action system among others. On the other hand, polities must still be able to communicate, through the medium of law, with all the other legitimately ordered spheres of action, however these happen to be structured and steered.

(From *The Inclusion of The Other* by Jurgen Habermas, The MIT Prees 1998).

24

Judith Butler

Judith Butler (1956-) was born in Cleveland, Ohio to a family of Hungarian and Russian ancestry. Her mother was raised in Orthodox Judaism, later turning to Conservative, and finally to Reform Judaism. Butler's father belonged to a Reform Synagogue since his childhood. As a child and teenager, Judith attended both Hebrew school and special classes on Jewish ethics where she received her "first training in philosophy." She began the ethics classes at the age of 14 and that they were created as a form of punishment by her Hebrew school's Rabbi because she was "too talkative in class. Butler also stated that she was "thrilled" by the classes and chose to focus on Martin Buber. She also encountered the writings of Kant, Hegel, and Spinoza during these special sessions.

Judith attended Bennington College and then Yale University where she studied philosophy, receiving her B.A. in 1978 and her PhD in 1984. Her dissertation was subsequently published as *Subjects of Desire: Hegelian Reflections in Twentieth-Century France (1987)*. In her dissertation, Butler explores desire in Hegel's *Phenomenology of Spirit* tracing the ways in which Hegelian desire is appropriated by Kojève, Hyppolite, and Sartre. The published version of her dissertation also includes sections on Lacan, Deleuze, and Foucault.

She taught at Wesleyan University, George Washington University, and Johns Hopkins University before joining U.C. Berkeley in 1993. She will join the department of English and Comparative Literature at Columbia University as a visiting professor in the spring semesters of 2012 and 2013 and has the option of remaining as full-time faculty. In 2008 she received the Andrew W. Mellon Foundation's Distinguished Achievement Award for her contributions to humanistic inquiry. The prize money of $1.5 million is supposed to enable the recipients to teach and research under especially favorable conditions. Since 2006 Judith Butler has been the Hannah Arendt Professor of philosophy at the European Graduate School in Switzerland. She sits on the Advisory Board of the academic journal *Identities: Journal for Politics, Gender and Culture*. Butler is also working on critiquing ethical violence and trying to formulate a theory of responsibility for an opaque subject that works with Franz Kafka, Sigmund Freud, Michel Foucault and Fredrich Nietzsche.

Butler currently lives with her partner, the political scientist Wendy Brown. Butler identifies as an anti-Zionist Jew and is a critic of Israeli politics. Judith Butler is an American post-structuralist philosopher, who has contributed to the fields of feminist philosophy, queer theory, political philosophy, and ethics. In the late 1980s she held several teaching/research appointments, and was involved in post-structuralist efforts within Western feminist theory to question the presuppositional terms of feminism. Considered one of the most influential voices in contemporary political theory and as one of the most influential feminist theorists today, she is best known for her seminal work *Gender Trouble*. She was awarded the Theodor W. Adorno Award in 2012 for her work on political theory, on moral philosophy and gender studies.

Her research ranges from literary theory, modern philosophical fiction, feminist, gender and sexuality studies, to 19th- and 20th-century European literature and philosophy, Kafka and loss, mourning and war. Herself being Jewish, her most recent work focuses on Jewish philosophy, exploring pre- and post-Zionist criticisms of state violence. Politically, she is a member of the advisory board of Jewish Voice for Peace and a supporter of Boycott, Divestment and Sanctions against Israel. She identifies with a Judaism that is not associated with state violence, and emphasizes that Israel does not represent all Jews.

Judith Butler is the author of *Antigone's Claim: Kinship Between Life and Death, Hegemony, Contingency, Universality*, with Ernesto Laclau and Slavoj Zizek, *Subjects of Desire: Hegelian Reflections in Twentieth-Century France, Gender Trouble: Feminism and the Subversion of Identity, Bodies That Matter: On the Discursive Limits of "Sex",The Psychic Life of Power: Theories of Subjection, Excitable Speech: Politics of the Performance*, as well as numerous articles and contributions on philosophy, feminism and queer theory. Her recent project is a critique of ethical violence and an effort to formulate a theory of responsibility for an opaque subject that works with Franz Kafka, Sigmund Freud, Michel Foucault and Friedrich Nietzsche.

Gender Trouble was first published in 1990, selling over 100,000 copies internationally and in different languages. Alluding to the similarly named 1974 John Waters film *Female Trouble* starring the drag queen Divine, *Gender Trouble* critically discusses the works of Simone de Beauvoir, Julia Kristeva, Sigmund Freud, Jacques Lacan, Luce Irigaray, and, most significantly, Michel Foucault.

In this most influential book *Gender Trouble:* Judith Butler argued that feminism had made a mistake by trying to assert that 'women' were a group with common characteristics and interests. That approach, Judith Butler said, performed 'an unwitting regulation and reification of gender relations', reinforcing a binary view of gender in which human beings are divided into two clear-cut groups, women and men. Judith Butler notes that feminists rejected the idea that biology is destiny, but then developed an account of patriarchal culture which assumed that masculine and feminine genders would inevitably be built, by culture, upon 'male' and 'female' bodies, making the same destiny just as inescapable. That argument allows no room for choice, difference or resistance.

Judith Butler argues that sex (male, female) is seen to cause gender (masculine, feminine) which, in turn, is seen to cause desire towards the other gender. This is commonly regarded as a kind of continuum. Judith Butler's approach – inspired in part by Michel Foucault – is basically to smash the supposed links between these, so that gender and desire are flexible, free-floating and not caused by other stable factors. She suggests that certain cultural configurations of gender have seized a hegemonic hold, and calls for subversive action in the present: 'gender trouble' – the mobilization, subversive confusion, and proliferation of genders, and therefore identities. This idea of identity as free-floating, as not connected to an 'essence', but instead to a performance, is one of the key ideas in queer theory. Seen in this way, our identities, gendered and otherwise, do not express some authentic inner 'core' self but are the dramatic effect of our performances.

Judith Butler looks at psychoanalysis as a 'grand narrative', about how 'woman' as a unitary category is formed. Psychoanalysis is a story about origins and ends, which includes some aspects, and excludes others. This narrative 'gives a false sense of legitimacy and universality to a culturally specific and, in some cases, culturally oppressive version of gender identity'. Judith Butler understands gendered subjectivity 'as a history of identifications, parts of which can be brought into play in given contexts and which, precisely because they encode the contingencies of personal history, do not always point back to an internal coherence of any kind'. Gender, then, as the identification with one sex or one object is a fantasy, a set of internalized images, and not a set of properties governed by the body and its organ configuration. Rather, gender is a set of signs internalized, psychically imposed on the body and on one's psychic sense of identity. Gender, Judith Butler concludes, is thus not a primary category, but an attribute, a set of secondary narrative effects.

Judith Butler is careful, however, not to borrow the models Michel Foucault uses, thereby avoiding some of the gaps that occur in his thinking, namely his silence on the subject of women. Judith Butler is not willing to settle the debate on sexuality merely as the obtaining and disseminating of pleasures and how those bodies perform them. Rather, she takes bodies as always already gender indeterminate and destabilizes their performatives further to show how bodies are marked by gender, as well as race, class, sexuality, etc., and how these categories are also destabilized within the perfomative.

Judith Butler analyzes name-calling as both a social injury and the way in which individuals are called into action for political purposes. She cannot see a way to refuse the interpellating call, or chain of calls, outright, for it is through interpellation that the subject is constituted, and therefore, the 'I' who would oppose its construction is always in some sense drawing from that construction to articulate its opposition. Further, the 'I' draws what is called its 'agency' in part through being implicated in the very relations of power that it seeks to oppose. Judith Butler is interested in the concept of ambivalence because she sees it as a site of subversion. Her concept of ambivalence is closely related to Derrida's concept of *différance*. She defines it as the slippage between the call of the law and its articulation, from which one can reveal the false claim to naturalness and originality of hegemonic norms.

In *Antigone's Claim*, Judith Butler redefines Antigone's legacy, recovering her revolutionary significance and liberating it for a progressive feminism and sexual politics. Judith Butler's new interpretation reconceptualizes the incest taboo in relation to kinship and opens up the concept of kinship to cultural change. Antigone, the renowned insurgent from Sophocles' Oedipus cycle, has long been a feminist icon of defiance. What has remained unclear is whether she escapes from the forms of power that she opposes. Antigone proves to be a more ambivalent figure for feminism than has been acknowledged, since the form of defiance she exemplifies also leads to her death. Judith Butler argues that Antigone represents a form of feminist and sexual agency that is fraught with risk. She considers the works of such philosophers as Hegel, Lacan, and Irigaray, and she asks how psychoanalysis would have been different if it had taken Antigone – the "postoedipal" subject – rather than Oedipus as its point of departure. If the incest taboo is reconceived so that it does not mandate heterosexuality as its solution, what forms of sexual alliance and new kinship might be acknowledged as a result? The book relates the courageous deeds of Antigone to the claims made by those whose relations are still not honored as those of proper kinship, showing how a culture of normative heterosexuality obstructs our capacity to see what sexual freedom and political agency could be.

The crux of Butler's argument in *Gender Trouble* is that the coherence of the categories of sex, gender, and sexuality—the natural-seeming coherence, for example, of masculine gender and heterosexual desire in male bodies—is culturally constructed through the repetition of stylized acts in time. These stylized bodily acts, in their repetition, establish the appearance of an essential, ontological core gender. This is the sense in which Butler famously theorizes gender, along with sex and sexuality, as performative. The performance of gender, sex, and sexuality, however, is not a voluntary choice for Butler, who locates the construction of the gendered, sexed, desiring subject within "regulative discourses." These, also called "frameworks of intelligibility" or "disciplinary regimes," decide in advance what possibilities of sex, gender, and sexuality are socially permitted to appear as coherent or natural. Regulative discourse includes within it disciplinary techniques which, by coercing subjects to perform specific stylized actions, maintain the appearance in those subjects of the "core" gender, sex and sexuality the discourse itself produces.

A part of Butler's argument concerns the role of sex in the construction of natural gender and sexuality. Butler explicitly challenges biological accounts of binary sex, reconceiving the sexed body as itself culturally constructed by regulative discourse. The supposed obviousness of sex as a natural biological fact attests to how deeply its production in discourse is concealed. The sexed body, once established as a "natural" and unquestioned "fact," is the alibi for constructions of gender and sexuality, unavoidably more cultural in their appearance. On Butler's account, it is on the basis of the construction of natural binary sex that binary gender and heterosexuality are likewise constructed as natural. In this way, Butler claims that without a critique of sex as produced by discourse, the sex/gender distinction as a feminist strategy for contesting constructions of binary asymmetric gender and compulsory heterosexuality will be ineffective.

Butler emphasizes the role of repetition in performativity, making use of Derrida's theory of iterability, a form of citationality, to work out a theory of performativity in terms of iterability. Performativity cannot be understood outside of a process of iterability, a regularized and constrained repetition of norms. And this repetition is not performed *by* a subject; this repetition is what enables a subject and constitutes the temporal condition for the subject. This iterability implies that 'performance' is not a singular 'act' or event, but a ritualized production, a ritual reiterated under and through constraint, under and through the force of prohibition and taboo, with the threat of ostracism and even death controlling and compelling the shape of the production, but not insist determining it fully in advance.

In *Excitable Speech*, Butler surveys the problems of hate speech and censorship. She argues that censorship is difficult to evaluate, and that in some cases it may be useful or even necessary, while in others it may be worse than tolerance. She develops a new conception of censorship's complex workings, supplanting the myth of the independent subject who wields the power to censor with a theory of censorship as an effect of state power and, more primordially, as the condition of language and discourse itself. Butler argues that hate speech exists retrospectively, only after being declared such by state authorities. In this way, the state reserves for itself the power to define hate speech and, conversely, the limits of acceptable discourse. In this connection, Butler criticizes feminist legal scholar Catharine MacKinnon's argument against pornography for its unquestioning acceptance of the state's power to censor.

Butler revisits and refines her notion of performativity and focuses on the question of undoing "restrictively normative conceptions of sexual and gendered life". Butler discusses how gender is performed without one being conscious of it, but says that it does not mean this performativity is "automatic or mechanical". She argues that we have desires that do not originate from our personhood, but rather, from social norms.

Many scholars have praised Butler's work. She has been referred to as "a big-deal academic, and oft-cited academic superstar", "the most famous feminist philosopher in the United States," "the queer theorist par excellence," and "the most brilliantly eclectic theorist of sexuality in recent years." In addition, Lois McNay argues that, "Butler's work has influenced feminist understandings of gender identity." Others, such as Susan A. Speer and Jonathan Potter claim that her research has given new insight in several areas, especially in the concept of heterosexism. However, although Speer and Potter find Butler's work useful in this respect, they find her work too abstract to be usefully applied to real-life situations.

Others are more critical. Susan Bordo has chastised Butler for reducing gender to language, arguing that the body is a major part of gender, thus implicitly opposing her conception of gender as performed. Peter Digeser argues that Butler's idea of performativity is too pure to account for identity. Digeser doubts that pure performativity is possible, suggesting that in viewing the gendered individual as purely performed, Butler ignores the gendered body, which Bordo also argues is extremely important. He also argues that neither an essentialist nor a performative notion of gender should be used in the political sphere, as both simplify gender too much. Martha Nussbaum has argued that Butler misreads J.L. Austin's idea of performative utterance, makes erroneous legal claims, forecloses an essential site of resistance by repudiating pre-cultural agency, and provides no normative ethical theory to direct the subversive performances that Butler endorses. Finally, Nancy Fraser argued that Butler's focus on performativity has distanced her from "everyday ways of talking and thinking about ourselves ... Why should we use such a self-distancing idiom?"

Butler has become famous in some circles for her "impenetrable, jargon-ridden prose," which has also generated some controversy, according to Sara Salih. The author ascribes this to the fact that the concepts she writes about are "philosophically challenging, often counter-intuitive, and not always described in immediately accessible language." In 1998, Denis Dutton's journal *Philosophy and Literature* gave Butler First Prize in its "Bad Writing Competition," which claims to "celebrate bad writing from the most stylistically lamentable passages found in scholarly books and articles." Butler's 94 word long sentence, published in the journal *Diacritics*, received the award.

Butler responded to Dutton's criticism. She argued that writing clearly can make the author too reliant on common sense and as such make language lose its potential to "shape the world" and shake up the status quo. Stanley Kurtz, in turn, argued against Butler. "Bad Writing Has No Defense." Stephen K. Roney also responded that "many—indeed, most—generally recognized "great thinkers" have been clear and lucid in their writing [...] Is Butler claiming to be deeper than all of them?" Nussbaum's "The Professor of Parody" essay also raised the issue of Butler's style. Butler received the 2012 Adorno Prize and the prize committee has come under criticism from Israel's Ambassador to Germany. Butler got the prize because of her remarks about Israel and specifically her calls for a boycott against Israel.

Butler laments that those who are descendants of European Jews who were destroyed in the Nazi genocide it is the most painful insult and injury forthem to be called complicitous with the hatred of Jews or to be called self-hating. And it is all the more difficult to endure the pain of such an allegation when one seeks to affirm what is most valuable in Judaism for thinking about contemporary ethics, including the ethical relation to those who are dispossessed of land and rights of self-determination, to those who seek to keep the memory of their oppression alive, to those who seek to live a life that will be, and must be, worthy of being grieved. It is most important as a Jew to speak out against injustice and to struggle against all forms of racism. This does not make her into a self-hating Jew. Butler has never supported every organization that is arguably part of the global left – she is not unconditionally supportive of all groups that currently constitute the global left.

Butler's political views have ranged over a large number of topics, and have not been restricted to the Middle East or the State of Israel. Indeed, she has written about violence and injustice in other parts of the world, focusing mainly in wars waged by the United States. She has also written on violence against transgendered people in Turkey, psychiatric violence, torture in Guantanamo, and about police violence against peaceful protestors in the U.S, to name a few. She has also written against anti-Semitism in Germany and against racial discrimination in the United States.

It makes her into someone who wishes to affirm a Judaism that is not identified with state violence, and that is identified with a broad-based struggle for social justice.

—Editor

1. "Women" As The Subject of Feminism

For the most part, feminist theory has assumed that there is some existing identity, understood through the category of women, who not only initiates feminist interests and goals within discourse, but constitutes the subject for whom political representation is pursued. But politics and representation are controversial terms. On the one hand, representation serves as the operative term within a political process that seeks to extend visibility and legitimacy to women as political subjects; on the other hand, representation is the normative function of a language which is said either to reveal or to distort what is assumed to be true about the category of women. For feminist theory, the development of a language that fully or adequately represents women has seemed necessary to foster the political visibility of women. This has seemed obviously important considering pervasive cultural condition in which women's lives were either misrepresented or not presented at all.

Recently, this prevailing conception of the relation between feminist theory and politics has come under challenge from within feminist discourse. The very subject of women is no longer understood in stable or abiding terms. There is a great deal of material that not only questions the viability of "the subject" as the ultimate candidate for representation or, indeed, liberation, but there is very little agreement after all on what is that constitutes, or ought to constitute, the category of women. The domains of political and linguistic "representation" set out in advance the criterion by which subject themselves are formed, with the result that representation is extended only to what can be acknowledged as a subject. In other words, the qualifications for being a subject must first be met before representation can be extended.

Foucault points out that juridical system of power produce the subjects they subsequently come to represent. Juridical notions of power appear to regulate political life in purely negative terms- that is, through the limitation, prohibition, regulation, control, and even "protection" of individuals related to that political structure through the contingent and retractable operation of choice. But the subjects regulated by such structures are, by virtue of being subjected to them formed, defined, and reproduced in accordance with the requirements of those structures. If this analysis is right, then the juridical formation of language and politics that represents women as "the subject" of feminism is itself a discursive formation and effect of a given version of representational politics. And the feminist subject turns out to be discursively constituted by the very political system that is supposed to facilitate its emancipation. This becomes politically problematic if that system can be shown to produce gendered subjects along a differential axis of domination or to produce subjects who are presumed to be masculine. In such cases, an uncritical appeal to such a system for the emancipation of "women" will be clearly self-defeating.

The question of "the subject" is crucial for politics and for feminist politics in particular, because juridical subjects are invariably produced through certain exclusionary practices that do not "show" once the juridical structure of politics has been established. In other words, the political construction of the subject proceeds with certain legitimating and exclusionary aims, and these political operations are effectively concealed and naturalized by a political analysis that takes juridical structures as their foundation. Juridical power inevitably "produces" what it claims merely to represent; hence, politics must be concerned with this dual function of power: the juridical and the productive. In effect, the law produces and then conceals the notion of "a subject before the law" in order to invoke that discursive formation as a naturalized foundational premise that subsequently legitimates that law's own regulatory hegemony. It is not enough to inquire into how women might become more fully represented in language and politics. Feminist critique ought also to understand how the category of "women," the subject of feminism, is produced and restrained by the very structures of power through which emancipation is sought.

Indeed, the question of women as the subject of feminism raises the possibility that there may not be a subject who stands "before" the law, awaiting representation in or by the law. Perhaps the subject, as well as the invocation of a temporal "before", is constituted by the law as the fictive foundation of its own claim to legitimacy. The prevailing assumption of the ontological integrity of the subject before the law might be understood as the contemporary trace of the state of nature hypothesis, that foundation list fable constitutive of the juridical structures of classical liberalism. The per formative invocation of a non historical "before" becomes the foundational premise that guarantees a presocial ontology of persons who freely consent to be governed and, thereby, constitute the legitimacy of the social contract. Apart from the foundation list fictions that support the notion of the subject, however, there is the political problem that feminism encounters in the assumption that the term woman denotes a common identity. Rather than a stable signifier that commands the assent of those whom it purports to describe and represent, women even in the plural, has become a troublesome term, a site of contest, a cause for anxiety. As Denise Riley's title suggest, *Am I That Name?* Is a question produced by the very possibility of the name's multiple significations? If one "is" a woman that is surely not all one is; the term fails to be exhaustive, not because a pregendered "person" transcends the specific paraphernalia of its gender, but because gender is not always constituted coherently or consistently in different historical context, and because gender intersects with racial, class, ethnic, sexual, and regional modalities of discursively constituted identities. As a result, it becomes impossible to separate out "gender" from the political and cultural intersections in which it is invariably produced and maintained.

The political assumption that there must be a universal basis for feminism, one which must be found in an identity assumed to exist cross-culturally, often accompanies the notion that the oppression of women has some singular from discernible in the universal or hegemonic structure of patriarchy or masculine domination. The notion of a universal patriarchy has been widely criticized in recent years for its failure to account for the workings gender oppression in the concrete cultural contexts in which it exists. Where those various contexts have been consulted within such theories, it has been to find "examples" or "illustrations" of a universal principle that is assumed from the start. The form of feminist theorizing has come under criticism for its efforts to colonize and appropriate non-Western cultures to support highly Western notions of oppression, but because they tend as well to construct a "Third World" or even an "Orient" in which gender oppression is subtly explained as symptomatic of an essential, non-Western barbarism. The urgency of feminism to establish a universal status for patriarchy in order to strengthen the appearance of feminism's own claims to be representative has occasionally motivated the shortcut to a categorical or fictive universality of the structure of domination, held to produce women's common subjugated experience.

Although the claim of universal patriarchy no longer enjoys the kind or credibility it once did, the notion of a generally shared conception of "women", the corollary to that framework, has been much more difficult to displace. Certainly, there have been plenty of debates: Is there some commonality among "women" have a bond by virtue of their oppression alone? Is there a specificity to women's cultures that is independent of their subordination by hegemonic, masculinist cultures? Are the specificity and integrity of women's cultural or linguistic practices always specified against and, hence, within the terms of some more dominant cultural formation? If there is a region of the "specifically feminine", one that is both differentiated from the masculine as such recognizable in its difference by an unmarked and, hence, presumed universality of "women"? The masculine/feminine binary constitutes not only the exclusive framework in which that specificity can be recognized, but in every other way the "specificity" of the feminine is once again fully decontextualized and separated off analytically and politically from the construction of class, race, sex, ethnicity, and other axes of power relations that both constitute "identity" and make the singular notion of identity a misnomer.

My suggestion is that the presumed universality and unity of the subject of feminism is effectively by the constraints of the representational discourse in which it functions. Indeed, the premature insistence on a stable subject of feminism, understood as a seamless category of women, inevitably generates multiple refusals to accept the category. These domains of exclusion reveal the coercive and regulatory consequences of that construction, even when the construction, has been elaborated for emancipator purposes. Indeed, fragmentation within feminism and the paradoxical opposition to feminism from "women" whom feminism claims to represent suggest the necessary limit of identity politics. The suggestion that feminism can seek wider representation for a subject that it itself constructs has the ironic consequence that feminist goals risk failure by refusing to take account of the constitutive powers of their own representational claims. This problem is not ameliorated through an appeal to the category of women for merely "strategic" purposes for which they are intended. In this case, exclusion itself might qualify as such an unintended yet consequential meaning. By conforming to a requirement or representational politics that feminism articulates a stable subject, feminism thus opens itself to charge of gross misrepresentation.

Obviously, the political task is not to refuse representational politics-as if we could. The juridical structures of language and politics constitute the contemporary field of power; hence, there is no position outside this field, but only a critical genealogy of its own legitimating practices. As such, the critical point of departure is the historical present, as Marx put it. And the task is to formulate within the constituted frame a critique of the categories of identity that contemporary juridical structures engender, naturalize, and immobilize.

Perhaps there is an opportunity at this juncture of cultural politics, a period that some would call "post feminist", to reflect from within a feminist perspective on the injunction to construct a subject of feminism. Within feminist political practice, a radical rethinking of the ontological constructions of identity appears to be appears to be necessary in order to formulate a representational politics that might revive feminism on other grounds. On other hand, it may be time to entertain a radical critique that seeks to free feminist theory from the necessity of having to construct a single or abiding ground which is invariably contested by those identity positions or anti-identity positions that is invariably excludes. Do the exclusionary practices that ground feminist theory in a notion of "women" as subject paradoxically undercut feminist goals to extend its claims to "representation"?

Perhaps the problem is even more serious. Is the construction of the category of women as a coherent and stable subject an unwitting regulation and reification or gender relations? And is not such reification precisely contrary to feminist aims? To what extent does the category of women achieve stability and coherence only in the context of the heterosexual matrix? If a stable notion of gender no longer proves to be the foundational premise of feminist politics, perhaps a new sort of feminist politics is now desirable to contest the very reifications of identity as both as a methodological and normative prerequisite, if not a political goal.

To trace the political operations that produce and conceal what qualifies as the juridical subject of feminism is precisely the task of a feminist genealogy of the category of women. In the course of this effort to question "women" as the subject of feminism, the unproblematic invocation of that category may prove to preclude the possibility of feminism as a representational politics. What sense does it make to extend representation to subjects who are constructed through the exclusion of those who fail to conform to unspoken normative requirements of the subject? What relations of domination and exclusion are inadvertently sustained when representation becomes the sole focus of politics? The identity of the feminist subject ought not to be the foundation of feminist politics, if the formation of the subject takes place within a field of power regularly buried through the assertion of that foundation. Perhaps paradoxically, "representation" will be shown to make sense for feminism only when the subject of "women" is nowhere presumed.

2. The Compulsory Order of Sex/Gender/Desire

Although the unproblematic unity of "women" is often invoked to construct solidarity of identity, a split is introduced in the feminist subject by the distinction between sex and gender. Originally intended to dispute the biology-is-destiny formulation, the distinction between sex and gender serves the argument that whatever biological intractability sex appears to have, gender is culturally constructed: hence, gender is neither the causal result of sex nor as seemingly fixed as sex. The unity of the subject is thus already potentially contested by the distinction that permits of gender as a multiple interpretation of sex.

If gender is the cultural meanings that the sexed body assumes, then a gender cannot be said to follow from a sex in any one way. Taken to its logical limit, the sex / gender distinction suggests a radical discontinuity between sexed bodies and culturally constructed genders. Assuming for the moment the stability of binary sex, it does not follow that the construction of "men" will accrue exclusively to the bodies of males or that "women" will interpret only female bodies. Further, even if the sex appear to be unproblematically binary in their morphology and constitution (which will become a question), there is no reason to assume that genders ought also to remain as two. The presumption of a binary gender system implicitly retains the belief in a mimetic relation of gender to sex whereby gender mirrors sex or is otherwise restricted by it. When the constructed status of gender is theorized as radically independent of sex, gender itself becomes a free-floating artifice, with the consequence that man and masculine might just as easily signify a female body as a male one, and women and feminine a male body as easily as a female one.

This radical splitting of the gendered subject poses yet another set of problems. Can we refer to a "given" sex or a "given" gender without first inquiring into how sex and / or gender is given, through what means? And what is "sex" anyway? Is it natural, anatomical, chromosomal, or hormonal, and how is a feminist critic to assess the scientific discourses which purport to establish such "facts" for us? Does sex have a history? Does each sex have a different history, or histories? Is there a history of how the duality of sex was established, a genealogy that might expose the binary options as a variable construction? Are the ostensibly natural facts of sex discursively produced by various scientific discourses in the service of other political and social interests? If the immutable character of sex is contested, perhaps this construct called "sex" is as culturally constructed as gender; indeed, perhaps it was always already gender, with the consequence that the distinction between sex and gender turns out to be no distinction at all.

It would make no sense, then, to define gender as the cultural interpretation of sex, if sex itself is a gendered category. Gender ought not to be conceived merely as the cultural inscription of meaning on a pregiven sex (a juridical conception); gender must also designate the very apparatus of production whereby the sexes themselves are established. As a result, gender is not to cultural as sex is to nature; gender is also the discursive / cultural means by which "sexed nature" or a "natural sex" is produced and established as "prediscursive", prior to culture, a politically neutral surface on which culture acts. This construction of "sex" as the radically unconstructed will concern us again in the discussion of Levi-Strauss and structuralism in chapter 2. At this juncture it is already clear that one way the internal stability and binary frame for sex is effectively secured is by casting the duality of sex in a prediscursive domain. This production of sex as the prediscursive ought to be understood as the effect of the apparatus of cultural construction designated by gender. How, then, does gender need to be reformulated to encompass the power relations that produce the effect of a prediscursive sex and so conceal that very operation of discursive production?

3. Gender : The Circular Ruins of Contemporary Debate

Is there "a" gender which persons are said to have, or is it an essential attribute that a person is said to be, as implied in the question "what gender are you?" When feminist theorists claim that gender is the cultural interpretation of sex or that gender is culturally constructed, what is the manner or mechanism of this construction? If gender is constructed, could it be constructed differently, or does its contractedness imply some form of social determinism, foreclosing the possibility of agency and transformation? Does "construction" suggest that certain laws generate gender differences along universal axes of sexual difference? How and where does the construction of gender take place? What sense can we make of a construction that cannot assume a human constructor prior to that construction? On some accounts, the notion that gender is constructed suggests a certain determinism of gender meaning inscribed on anatomically differentiated bodies, where those bodies are understood as passive recipients of an inexorable cultural law. When the relevant "culture" that "constructs" gender is understood in terms of such a law or set of laws, then it seems that gender is as determined and fixed as it was under the biology-is-destiny formulation.in such a case, not biology, but culture,becomes destiny.

On the other hand, Simone de Beauvoir suggests in the second sex that "one is not born woman, but, rather, becomes one". For Beauvoir gender is "constructed", but implied in her formulation is an agent, a cogito, who somehow takes on or appropriates that gender and could, in principle, take on some other gender. Is gender as variable and volitional as Beauvoir's account seems to suggest? Can "construction" in such a case be reduced to a form of choice? Beauvoir is clear that one "becomes" a woman, but always under a cultural compulsion to become one. And clearly, the compulsion does not come from "sex". There is nothing in her account that guarantees that the "one" who becomes a woman is necessarily female. If "the body is a situation", as she claims, there is no recourse to a body that has not always already been interpreted by cultural meanings; hence, sex, could not qualify as a prediscursive anatomical facticity. Indeed, sex, by definition, will be shown to have been gender all along.

The controversy over the meaning of construction appears to founder on the conventional philosophical polarity between free will and determinism. As a consequence, one might reasonably suspect that some common linguistic restriction on thought both forms and limits the terms of the debate. Within those terms, "the body" appears as a passive medium on which cultural meanings are inscribed or as the instrument through which an appropriate and interpretive will determines a cultural meaning for itself. In either case, the body is figured as a mere instrument or medium for which a set of cultural meaning are only externally related. But "the body" is itself a construction, as are the myriad "bodies" that constitute the domain of gendered subjects. Bodies cannot be said to have a significable existence prior to the mark of their gender; the question then emerges: To what extent does the body come into being in and through the mark(s) of gender? How do we reconceive the body no longer as a passive medium or instrument awaiting the enlivening capacity of a distinctly immaterial will?

Whether gender or sex is fixed or free is a function of a discourse which, it will be suggested, seeks to set certain limits to analysis or to safeguard certain tenets of humanism as presuppositional to any analysis of gender. The locus of intractability, whether in "sex" or "gender" or in the very meaning of "construction", provides a clue to what cultural possibilities can and cannot become mobilized through any further analysis. The limits of the discursive analysis of gender presuppose and preempt the possibilities of imaginable and realizable gender configurations within culture. This is not to say that any and all gendered possibilities are open, but that the boundaries of analysis suggest the limits of a discursively conditioned experience. These limits are always set within the terms of a hegemonic cultural discourse predicted on binary structures that appear as the language of universal rationality. Constraint in thus built into what that language constitutes as the imaginable domain of gender.

Although social scientists refer to gender as a "factor" or a "dimension" of an analysis it is also applied to embodied persons as 'a mark" of biological, linguistic, and / or cultural difference. In these latter cases, gender can be understood as a signification that an (already) sexually differentiated body assumes, but even that signification exists only in relation to another, opposing signification. Some feminist theorists claim that gender is "a relation", indeed, a set of relations, and not an individual attribute. Others, following Beauvoir, would argue that only the feminine gender is marked, that the universal person and the masculine gender are conflated, thereby defining women in terms of their sex and extolling men as the bearers of a body-transcendent universal personhood.

(From *Gender Trouble*, by Judith Butler, Routelge, New York, 1999)

Bibliography

Ackrill, J.L. (1975): *Aristotle the Philosopher*. Oxford: Oxford University Press.

Allan, D.J. (1970): *The Philosophy of Aristotle*, Oxford, Oxford University Press.

Allen, J.W. (1967): *A History of Political Thought in the Sixteenth Centry*. London: Methuen.

Althusser, Louis. (1969) *For Marx* London: Allen Lane.

Anderson (1976): *Considerations on Western Marxism*: London. New Left.

Andrews, A. (1967): *The Greek Society*: Harmondsworth: Penguins.

Anglo Sydney (1969.) *Machiavelli: A Dissection*. New York: Harcourt, Brace and World.

Annas, J. (1977): *"Mill and the Subjection of Women"*, *Philosophy*, 52, pp. 174-194.

— (1981): *An Introduction to Plato's Republic*. Oxford: Oxford University Press.

Arblaster, A.(1984): *The Rise and Decline of Western Liberalism*: Oxford, Blackwell.

Aristotle (1962): *The Nicomachean Ethics*. W.D. Ross (Ed.): Oxford, Clarendon Press.

Arnhart, Larry (1981.) *Aristotle on Political Reasoning: A Commentary on the "Rhetoric."* Dekalb: Northern Illinois University Press.

Ashcraft, R. (1971): *"Hobbes' Natural Man,"* *Journal of Politics*, 33, pp.1077-1091. (Ed.) (1991): *John Locke: Critical Assessments*, 4 vols., London, Routledge.

— (1978) : "Ideology and Class in Hobbes Political Theory", *Political Theory*, 6, pp. 27-62.

—(1986): *Revolutionary Politics and Locke's Two Treatises of Government*. London: Allen & Unwin.

—(1987):*Locke's Two Treatises of Government*. London. Unwin & Hyman.

Avineri, S. (1972): *Hegel's Theory of the State*. Cambridge: Cambridge University Press.

—(1976); *The Social and Political Thought of Karl Marx*. New Delhi: S. Chand.

Ball T. (1984): "The Picaresque Prince: Reflections on Machiavelli and Moral Change," *Political Theory*, 12, pp 521-536.

Bambrough, R. (1965): *New Essays on Plato and*. Oxford, Oxford University Press. (Ed.) (1967): *Plato, Popper and Politics, Cambridge* University Press.

Barker, Ernest. (1959.) *The Political Thought of Plato and Aristotle*. New York: Dover Publications.

Barnes, J. (Ed.) (1992): *The Cambrdge Campanion to Aristotle*. Cambridge: Cambridge University Press.

Bathory, Peter Dennis. (1981.) *The Political Theory as Public Confession: The Social and Political Thought of St. Augustine of Hippo*. New Brunswick, N.J. Transaction Books.

Baumgold, D.(1988) *Hobbes' Political Theory*. Cambrdge Cambridge University Press.

Beiser, f. (Ed.) (1991): *The Cambridge Companion to Hegel* Cambridge, Cambridge University Press.

Bellamy, R. (Ed.) (1990): *Victorian Liberalism: Nineteenth Century Political Thought and Practice*. Cambridge: Polity Press.

—(1959): *John Stuart Mill and the Ends of Life*, London, Edgar G. Dunstan & Co.

—(1964): Hobbes, 'Locke and Professor McPherson,' *Political Quarterly*, October-December, pp. 444-468.

Bentham, J. (1962): *An Introduction to the Principles of Morals and Legislation*. New York: Russell & Russell.

— (1965): *Anarchical Fallacies*. Baltimore: Johns Hopkins University Press.

(1977): *A Fragment of Government*. J.H. Burns and H.L.A. Hart (Eds.) London: Athlone Press.

Berkeley: Univesity of California Press.

Berki, R.N. (1977): *The History of Political Thought: A Short Introduction*. London, Dent.

Bloom, A. (1968): *The Republic of Plato*. New York, Basic Books.

Bluhm, T. (1978.) *Theories of the Political System: Classical of Political Thought and Modern Political Analysis*. Englewood Cliffs: N.J.: Prentice Hall.

Bottomore, T. (1973) *Karl Marx*, Oxford: Basil Blackwell.

—(1981): *Modern Interpretations of Marx*. Oxford University Press.

Brinton, C, (1933): *English Political Thought in the Nineteenth Century*. London: Allen Lane.

Britton, Karl. (1969.) *John Stuart Mill: Life and Philosophy*. New York: Dover Publications.

Broome, J.H. (1963): *Rousseau: A Study of His Thought*. Oxford: Oxford University Press.

Brown, K.C. (Ed.) (1965): *Hobbes' Studies*. Cambridge Mass.: Harvard University Press.

Brown, Peter (1967.) *Augustine of Hippo: A Biography*. Berkeley: University of California Press.

Burke E. (1969): *Reflections on the Revolution in France*. C.C. O'Brien (Ed.), Harmondsworth: Penguins.

Burnham, J.(1943): The Machiavellians, New York, Double Day.

Butterfield, H. (1962): *The Statecraft of Machiavelli*. New York, Collier.

Canavan, F.P. (1960): *The Political Reason of Edmund Burke*. Durham: NC, Duke University Press.

Carnoy, M. (1984): *Statef and Political Theory*. Princeton: Nj, Princeton University Press.

Caver, T. (1983): *Marx and Engels: The Intellectual Relationship*. Brighton: Harvester.

—(Ed.) (1990): *The Cambridge Companion to Marx*. Cambridge: Cambridge University press.

Chabod, F. (1958): *Machiavelli and the Renaissance*. D. Moore (Trans.), New York: Harper & Row.

Chapell, V. (Ed.) (1994): *The Cambridge Companion to Locke*. Cambridge, Cambridge University Press.

Chapman, J.W. (1956): *Rousseau- Totalitarian or Liberal?* New York: Columbia University Press.

Charvet; J. (1974): *The Social Problem in the Philosophy of Rousseau*. London, Dent.

Classier, Ernst. (1963.) *The Question of Jean-Jacques Rousseau*. Bloomington: Indiana University Press.

Cobban, A. (1960) *Edmund Burke and the Revolt against the Eighteenth Century*. London: Allen & Unwin.

—(1964): *Rousseau and the Modern State*. London: Unwin University Books.

Cohen, G.A. (1978). *Karl Marx's Theory of History*: A Defense. Princeton: Princeton University Press.

Colletti, L, (1969): *From Rousseau to Lenin*. New Delhi: Oxford University Press.

Compleston, Frederick. (1955.) *Thomas Aquinas*. London: Search Press.

Condren, Conal (1985.) *The Status and Appraisal of Classic Texts* Princeton: Princeton University Press.

Conniff, J. (1977): *"Burke, Bristol and the Concept of Representation," Western Political Quarterly*, 30, pp. 329-341.

Connolly William E.(1993.) *The Augustinian Imperative: A Reflection on the Politics of Morality*. Newbury Park: Calif. Sage Publications.

Cook, I.(1998): *Reading Mill: Studies in Political Theory*. London: Macmillan.

Cornforth, M. (1968): *The Open Philosophy and the Open Society*. London: Lawrence and Wishart.

Cowling, Maurice.(1963.) *Mill and Liberalism*, England: Cambridge University Press.

Cranston, Maurice.(1957.) *John Locke: A Biography*. New York: Macmillan.

Crespigny, A. de and Minogue, K. (des.) (1975): *Cotemporary Political Thinkers*. London: Methuen.

Croce, B. (1969): *What is Living and What is Dead in the Philosophy of Hegel?* D. Ainslie New York, Russell & Russell.

Crossman. R. (1939): *Plato Today*. London, Allen & Unwin.

Davidson, W.L. (1957): *Political Thought in England: The Utilitarians from Bentham to Mill*, Oxford: Oxford University Press.

Davies, Brian (1992). *The Thoughts of Thoma, Acquiras* New York: Oxford

de Garzia Sebastian. (1989.) *Machiavelli in Hell*. Princeton: Princeton University Press.

Deane, Herbert A. (1963.) *The Political and Social Ideas of St. Augustine*. New York: Columbia University Press.

Draper, H. (1977): *Karl Marx's Theory of Revolution: State and Bureaucracy*. New York, Monthly Review Press.

Dunn, J. (1968): *The Political Thought of John* Locke. Cambridge

(1979): *Western Political Theory in the Face of the Future*. Cambridge: Cambridge University Press.

—(1984): *Locke*. Oxford Oxford University Press.

Durant T (1953): *The Story of Philosophy*. New York, Pocket Books.

Ebenstein, W. (1969): *Great Political Thinkers*. New Delhi, Oxford & IBH.

Elshtain, Jean Bethke. (1981.) *Public Man, Private Womans in Social and Political Thought*, Princeton: Princeton University Press.

—(1995) *Augustive and the Limist of Politics*, Indian: University of Notre Dame Press.

Elster, Jon. (1985.) *Making Sense of Marx*. New York: Cambridge University Press.

Evans, J. (1986): *Feminism and Political Theory*. New York: Alfred A. Knopf.

Figgis, John N.- (1963) *The Political Aspecty of st.Augustivis.*

Findlay, J.N. (1958): *Hegel: A Re-examination*. London: Allen & Unwin.

Finley, M. I. (1963): *The Ancient Greeks*. Harmondsworth: Penguins.

Foster, M.B.(1975): *Masters of Political Thought: Plato to Machiavelli*. Calcutta: Oxford University Press.

Foucoult, Michel- (1991) *Discipline and Punish* Harmondsworth: Penguin.

Freeman, M. (1980): *Edmund Burke and the Critique of Political Radicalism.* Oxford, Blackwell.

Gadamer, H. (1986): *The Idea of Good in Platonic-Aristotelian Philosophy*. New Haven: Yale University Press.

Gatens, M. (1991): *Feminism and Philosophy: Perspectives on Difference and Equality*. Cambridge, Polity Press.

Gauthier, D.P. (1969): *The Logic of Leviathan*. Oxford, Clarendon Press.

Gay, P. 91952): *The Dilemma of Democratic Socialism*. Eduard Bernstein's Challenge to Marx. New York, Columbia University Press.

— (1970): *The Enlightenment: An Interpretation*: 2vols., London Wildwood House.

Germino, Dante. (1972.) *Modern Western Political Thought: Machiavelli to Marx*. Chicago: Rand McNally.

Giddens, A. (1995): *A Contemporary Critique of Historical Materialism*. London: Macmillan.

Gilbert, Felix.(1965.) *Machiavelli and Guicciardini: Political and History in Sixteenth Century Florence*. Princeton: Princeton University Press.

Gilby, Thomas . 1958. *The Political Thought of Thomas Aquinas*. Chicago: University of Chicago Press.

Gilson, Etienne, 1960. *The Christian Philosophy of Saint Augustine*. New York: Random House.

Goldsmith, M.M. (1966): *Hobbes' Science of Politics*. New York, Columbia University Press.

Gough, J. W. (1950): *John Locke's Political Philosophy*. Oxford: Blackwell.

Gouldner, A.W.(1980): *The Two Marxisms: Contradictions and Anomalies in the Development of Theory*. New York: Oxford University Press.

—(1965). *Enter Plato: Classical Greece and the Origins of Social Theory*, New York: Basic Books.

Grabmann, Martin, 1963. *Thomas Aquinas: His Personality and Thought*. New York: Russell and Russell.

Gramsci, A.(1971): *Prison Notebooks*. London: Lawence & Wishart.

Grant, Ruth W. 1987. *John Locke's Liberalism.* Chicago: University of Chicago Press.

Gray, J. (1983a): *Mill on Feminism.* London: Routledge.

—(1983b): *Mill on Liberty: A Defense.* London: Routledge.

—(1989): *Liberalism: Essaya in Political Philosophy.* London, Routledge.

Grene, Marjorie. 1963. *A Portrait of Aristotle.* Chicago: University of Chicago Press.

Grimsley, R. (1973): *The Philosophy of Rousseau.* Oxford: Oxford University Press.

Habermas, Jurgen (1989)- *Theory of Communicative Action* Oxford: Polity Press.

—(1996) *Between Facts and Norms* oxford: Polity press

Hacker, A (1961): *Political Theory: Philosophy. Ideology: Science.* New York, Macmillan.

Haffman, S(1977): *Marx and Theory of Praxis.* London: Oxford University Press.

Hale, J.R. (960): *Machiavelli and the Renaissance Italy.* New York: Macmillan.

Halevy, E (1928): *Growth of Phisosophical Radcalism. M.* Morris (Trans.), London: Faber & Faber.

Hall, J.C. (1973): *Rousseau: An Introduction to His Political Philosophy.* Cambridge Mass: Harvard University Press.

Hallowell, J.H. (1960): *Main Currents in Modern Politival Thourht.* New York: Holt.

Hamburger, Joseph. 1965. *Intellectuals in Politics: John Stuart Mill and the Philosophic Radicals.* New Haven: Yale University Press.

Hampsher-Monk, I.W.(1987): *The Political Philosophy of Edmund Burke.* London.

(1992): *Modern Political Thought from Hobbes to Marx.* Oxford: Basil Blackwell.

Hampton, J. (1986): *Hobbes and the Social Contract Tradition.* Cambridge: Cambridge University Press.

Harrison, R. (1983): *Bentham.* London. Routledge.

Hart, H.L.A. (1982): *Essays on Bentham, Jurisprudence and Political Theory.* Oxford: Oxford University Press.

Hearnshaw, F.J.C. (Ed.) (1931): *The Social and Political Ideas of Some Representive Thinkers of the Revoutionary Era.* London: George Harrap.

Hegel, G.W.F.(1969): *Philosophy of Right,* T.M. Knox (Trans.) Oxford: Oxford University Press.

Heilbroner, R. (1980): *Marxism: For and Against*. New York: Oxford University Press.

Himmelfarb, Gertrfarb. 1974. *On Liberty and Libcralism: The Case of John Stuart Mill*. New York: Knopf.

Hobbes, T. (1991): *Leviathan*. R. Tuck (Ed.), Cambridge: Cambridge University Press.

Hook, (1962): *From Hegel to Marx: Studies in the Intellectual Development of Karl Marx*. New York: University of Michigan Press.

Hulliung, Mark (1983.) *Citizen Machiavelli*. Princeton: Princeton University Press.

Hunt, C. (1957): *The Theory and Practice of Communism*. London: Geoffrey Bees.

Hunt, R.N. (1975): *The Political Ideas of Marx and Engels*. London: Macmillan.

Johnston, David (1986.) *The Rhetoric of Levathan: Thomas Hobbes and the Politics of Cultural Transformation*. Princeton: Princeton University Press.

Jowett, b. (1905): *Aristotle's Politics*. Oxford: Clarendon Press.

—(1953): *The Republic of Plato*. Oxford: oxford university Press.

Kaufnam, W. (1965): *Hegel's Political Philosophy*. New York: Atherton.

Kellrer, Douglae (1984) *Herbert Marcouse and the Crises of Mavxism*

Kendall, Willmore.1941. *John Locke and the Doctrine of Majority-Rule*. Urbana: University of Illinois Press.

Kennedy, E. and Mendus, S.(1987): *Women in Western Political Philosophy*. Brighton: Harvester.

Kirk, R. (1960): *The Conservative Mind: From Burke to Eliot*. New York: Garden City.

Kitto, H.D.F. (1951): *The Greeks*. Harmondsworth, Penguins.

Klosko, George. 1986. *The Development of Plato's Political Theory*. New York: Methuen.

—1993 *History of Political Theory: An Introduction, Vol I: Ancient and Medieval Political* Theory. New York: Holt, Rinehart and Winston.

—1995 *History of Political Theory: An Introduction*. New York Holt: Rinehart and Winston.

Kolakowski, L. (1981): *Main Currents of Marxism*, 3.vols. Oxford: Oxford University Press.

Krammick I (1977): *The Rage of Edmund Burke: Portrait of an Ambivalent Conservative*. New York: Basic Books.

Kraut, R. (Ed.) (1993): *The Cambridge Companion to Plato*. Cambridge: Cambridge University Press.

Kymlicka, W. (1990): *Contemporary Political Philosophy: An Introduction.* Oxford: Clarendon Press.

Lamprecht, S.P. (1918): *The Moral and Political Phislosophy of John Locke.* New York: Columbia University press.

Laski, H.J. (1920): *Political Thought from Locke to Bentham.* Oxford University Press.

—(1936): *Rise of European Liberalism.* London, UNwin Books.

Laslett, Peter. (1963) *John Locke, Two Treatises of Government.* New York: Cambridge University Press.

Lerner, M. (1950): *Niccolo Machiavelli's The Prince and the Discourses: An Introduction.* New York: Random House.

Lessnoff, M.(1986): *Social Contract.* London: Macmillan.

Levinson, Ronald, B. (1953): *In Defense of Plato.* Cambridge Mass: Harvard University Press.

Lichtheim, George. 1964. *Marxsm: Historical and Critical Study,* New York: Praeger.

—(1971): *From Marx to Hegel and Other Essays.* London: Orbach & Chambers.

Lone, earl B- (1964) *Burke and the Nature of Politics.* Kentucky: Kentucky University Press.

Lord, Carnes (1982.) *Education and Culture in the Political Thought of Aristotle.* Ithaca: Cornell University Press.

MacIntyre, Alasdair. 1988. *Whose Justice? Which Rationality?* Notre Dame, Ind: University of Notre Dame Press.

—(Ed.) (1972): *Hegel: A Collection of Essays.* New York: Anchor.

Mack, MP (1962): *Jeremy Bentham: An Odyssey of Ideas.* New York: Columbia University Press.

Mackie, J.L. (1994): *Problems from Locke.* Oxford: Oxford University Press.

Macpherson, (1980): *Burke,* Oxford: Oxfoed University Press.

—(1973): *Democratic Theory.* Oxford: Oxford University Press.

—(1977): *The Life and Times of Liberal Democracy.* Oxford: Oxford University Press.

—(1964). *The Political Theory of Possessive Individualism: Hobbes to Locke.* England: Oxford University Press.

Manisfeld, H.C.(1979): *Machiavelli's New Modes and Orders.* Ithaca: Cornell University Press.

—(1989). *Taming the Prince: The Ambivalence of Modern Executive Power.* New York: Free Press.

Marcuse, H. (1954): *Reason and Revolution: Hegel and the Rise of Social Theory*. London: Routledge & Kegan Paul.

Marshall, J. (1994): *Locke: Resistance, Revolution and Responsibility*. Cambridge: Cambridge university Press.

Marx, K.H. (1975): *The Communist Manifesto*. Moscow: Progress Publishers.

—(1977a): *Selected Works*, I. Moscow: Progress Publishers.

—(1977b): *Selected Works, II*. Moscow: Progress Publishers.

—(1977c): *Selected Works, III*. Moscow: Progress Publishers.

Masters, R.D. (1968): *Political Philosophy of Rousseau*. Princeton: NJ Princeton University Press.

Maxey, C.C. (1948): *Political Philosophies*. New York: Macmillan.

Mazlish, B. (1975): *James and John Stuart Mill*. New Brunswick: NJ, Transaction.

Mazlish, Bruce. 1975. *James and John Stuart Mill: Father and Son in the Nineteenth Century:* New York: Basic Books.

McCloskey, H.J.(1971): *John Stuart Mill: A Critical Study*. London, Macmillan.

McIntosh, D. (1984): *"The Modernity of Machiavelli", Political Theory*, 12. May, PP. 184-203.

McLellan, D. (1969): *The Young Hegelians and Karl Marx*. London: Macmillan.

McNeilly, N. (1968): *The Anatomy of Leviathan*. London: Macmillan.

Mehta, Uday Singh (1992). *The Anxiety of Freedom: Imagination and Individduality in Looke's Political Thought*. Ithaca, N.Y.: Cornell University Press.

Meinecke, F. (1957): *Machiavellianism: The Doctrine of Raison d'Etat and its Place in History*. D. Scott(Trans.) London, Routledge & Kehan Paul.

Melzer, Arthur M. (1990). *The Natural Goodness of Man: On the System of Rousscau's Though*. Chicago: University of Chicago Press.

Meszaros, Istvan, (1970). *Marx's Theory of Alienation*. New York: Harper and Row.

Miliband, R. (1977): *Marxism and Politics*. Oxford: Oxford University Press.

Mill J.S. (1924): *Autobiography*. New York: Random house.

—(1950): *Bentham and Coleridge*. London: Fontana.

—(1976): *Utiltarianism, On Liberty and Considerations on Representative Government*. London: Fontana.

—(1985): *The Subjevtion of Women*. M. Warnock (Ed.), London: Dent.

Miller, James. (1984). *Rousseau: Dreamer of Democracy*. New Haven: Yale University Press.

Minogure K.R. (1973): *Hobbes' Leviathan*. New York: Everyman's Library.

Morcuse, Herbert (1955) *Eros and Civilisation* Boston: Beacon Press.

—1964 *One-Dimensional Man,* Boston, Beacon Press

Morrall, J.B. (1979): *Aristotle.* London: Hutchinson.

Mulgan, R.G. (1977): *Aristotle's Political Theory.* Oxford: Clarendon Press.

Niall Rudd (1998) trans. *Cicero: The Republic and the Laws. Oxford:* Oxford University Press.

Nietzsche, Friedrich-(1989) *Beyond Good and Evil:* New York: Vintage.

—(1988) *On the Geneology of Morals and Elco Homm,* New York: Random House.

Nozick, Robert-(1974) *Anarchy, State and Uopia,* Oxford: Blackwell.

O Gorman, F. (1973): *Edmund Burke,* London: Allen & Unwin.

O'Brien, C.C. (Ed.) (1968): *Burke's Reflections on the Revolution in France.* Harmondsworth: Penguins.

Oakeshott, Michael. 1975. *Hobbes On Civil Association.* England: Basil Blackwell.

Okin, Susan Moller. 1979. *Women in Western Political Thought:* Princeton: Princeton University Press.

Ollman, Bertell. 1971. *Alienation: Marx's Conception of Man* Cambridge Cambidge University Press.

Olschki, L. (1976): *Machiavelli the Scientist.* Berkeley: University of California Press.

Osborn, A.M. (1940): *Rousseau and Burke.* New York: Simon & Schuster.

Packe, Michael St. John. 1954.*The Life of John Stuart Mill.* New York: Macmillan.

Parekh, B. (Ed.) (1974): *Jeremy Bentham: Ten Critical Essays.* London: Croom Helm.

Parkin, C.W. (1969): "Burke and the Conservative Tradition", in *Political Ideas,* D. Thomson (Ed.), Harmondsworth: Penguins.

Parry, G.(1978): *John Locke.* London: Allen & Unwin.

—(1988): *The Sexual Contract.* Oxford: Polity.

Pelczynski, Z.A. (Ed.) (1984): *State and Civil Society: Studies in Hegel's Political Philosophy.* London: Athlone Press.

Pitkin, Hanna Fenichel.(1984). *Fortune Is a Woman: Gender and Politics in the Thought of Niccolo Nachiavelli.* Berkeley: University of California Press.

Plamentaz, J. (1963): *Man and Society. 2 vols.* London: Longman.

—(1966): *The English Utilitarians.* Oxford: Basil Blackwell.

—(1969): *German Marxism and Russian Communism.* London: Longman.

Plant, R. (1983): *Hegel.* Oxford: *Basil* Blackwell.

—(1991): *Modern Political Thought.* Oxford: Blackwell.

Plato (1955): *The Republic.* Harmndsworth: Penguins.

Pocock, J.G.A. 1975. *The Machiavellian Moment: Florentine Political Thought and the Atlantic Republican Tradition.* Prinveton: Princeton University Press.

Polin, R. (1953): *Political Philosophy of Thomas Hobbes.* Paris,

Popper, K.R. (1945): *The Open Society and its Enemies: 2 vols.* London Routledge & Kegan Paul.

Raab, F. (1964): *The English Face of Machiavelli: A Changing Interpretation* 1500-1700. London: Routledge.

Radhakrishnan, S. (1974): *Eastern Religions and Western Thought.* New Delhi: Oxford University Press.

Rainbow, Paul (1991)ed. *The foucault Reader* Harmondsworth: Penguin, Butler, Judith (1990) Gender Trouble London: Routwge.

Rawls, J. (1971): *A Theory of Justice.* Oxford University Press.

Rees, J. (1956): *Mill and his Early Critics.* London. University of Leicester Press.

Rees, John C. 1985. *Jon Stuart Mill's On Liberty.* New York: Oxford University Press. Robson.

Riley, P. (1986): *The General Will Before Rousseau: The Transformation of the Divine into the Civic.* Princeton: Nj, Princeton University Press.

Ring, J. (1985) *Mill's Feminism.* New York: Harvester Wheatsheaf.

Rogow, Arnold A. 1986. *Thomas Hobbes: Radical in the Sevrivec of Reaction,* New York: Norton.

Rosen, F. (1983): *Jeremy Bentham and Representative Democracy.* Oxford: Oxford University Press.

Rosenblum, N.L.(1978) *Bentham's Theory of the State.* Cambridge: Harvard University Press.

Rousseau J.J. *Social Contract and Discourses,* G. D.H. Cole (Trans.) London: Dent.

Russell, B. (1961): *History of Western Philosophy,* London: Allen & Unwin.

Ryan, A. (1965): 'Locke and the Dictatorship of the Bourgeoisie,' *Political Studies.* 13, PP. 219-230.

Ryan, A. (1970): *The Philosophy of John Stuart Mill,* London: Macmillan.

—(1984): *Property and Political Theory.* Oxford: Blackwell.

Sabine, George H. 1961. *A History of: Political Theory.* New York: Holt, Rinehart and Winston.

Salkever, S.G. (1990): *Finding the Mean: Theory and Practice in Aristotelian Political Philosophy.* Princeton: Nj, Princeton University Press.

Seligar, M. (1968): *The Liberal Politics of John of Locke.* London: Allen & Unwin.

Semple, J. (1992): *Bentham's Prison: A Study of the Panoptical Penitentiary.* Oxford: Clarendon Press.

Shklar, Judith N. 1969. *Men and Citizens: A Study of Rousseau's Social Theory.* London: Cambridge University Press.

Shumer, S.M. (1979): "Machiavelli: Republican Politics and its Corruption," *Political Theory*, 7. pp. 5-34.

Sibley, M.Q. (1981): *Political Ideas and Ideologies.* New Delhi: Surjeet Publications.

Singer, P. (1980): *Marx.* Oxford: Oxford University Press.

—(1983), *Hegel.* Oxford: Oxford University Press.

Skinner, Q. (1981): *Machiavelli.* Oxford: Oxford University Press.

—(1990): *The Fundations of Modern Political Thought, 2 vols.* Cambridge: Cambridge University Press.

Skorupski, J. (1998): *The Cambridge Companion to Mill.* Cambridge: University Press.

Smith, S.B. (1989): *Hegel's Critique of Liberalism.* Chicago: University of Chicago Press.

Sorell, T.(1986): *Hobbes.* London: Routledge.

Starobinski, J. (1988): *Jean-Jacques Rousseau: Transparency and Obstruction.* A. Goldhammer (Trans.) Paris.

Stephen, L.(1961): *Hobbes.* Ann Arbor University of Michigan Press.

Strauss, Leo. (1952). *The Political Philosophy of Hobbes: Its Basis and Its Genesis.* Chicago: University of Chicago Press.

Swanson, Judith A. (1992). *The Pubic and the Private in Aristotle's Political Philoso*phy, Ithaca: Cornell University Press.

Talmon, Jacob L. 1952. *The Rise of Totalitarian Democracy.* Boston: Beacon Press.

Taylor, C. (1979): *Hegel and Modern Society.* Cambridge: Cambridge University Press.

Ten, C.L. (1980): *Mill on Liberty.* Oxford: Clarendon Press.

Thomas. W. (1985): *Mill.* Oxford: Oxford University Press.

Thompson, Dennis, F. 1976. *John Stuart Mill and Representative Government.* Princeton: Princeton University Press.

Thorson, T.L. (1963): *Plato: Totalitarian or Democrat?* New Jersey: Prentice Hall.

Tocqueville, A. de. (19688): *Democracy in America. 2 Vols.*, J.P. Mayer and M. Lerner (ed.) London: Fontana.

Tuck, R. (1989): *Hobbes.* Oxford: Oxford University Press.

Tucker, Robert. 1972, *Philosophy and Myth in Karl Marx*. England: Cambridge University Press.

Tulloch, G (1989): *Mill and Sexual Equality*. London: Blackwell.

Tully, J. (1980): *A Discourse on Property: John Locke and His Adversaries*. Cambridge: Cambridge University press.

—(1993): *An Approach to Political Philosophy: Locke in Contexts*. Cambridge: Cambridge University Press.

Viroli, M. (1998): *Machiavelli*. Oxford: Oxford University Press.

Vlastos, G (Ed.),(1971): *Plato: A Collection of Critical Essays*. Noter Dame.

Volpe. G. della. (1978): *Russeau and Marx*. London: Lawrence and Wishart.

Von Leyden, W. (1982): *Hobbes and Locke: The Politics of Freedom and Obligation*. London: Macmillan.

Warrender, Howard. 1957. *The Political Philosophy of Hobbes: His Theory of Obligation*. Oxford, Oxford University Press.

Watkin, J.W.N. (1973): *Hobbes' Stystem of Ideas*. London: Hutchinson.

White, S.K. (1994): *Edmund Burke: Modernity, Politics and Aesthetics*. Thousand Oaks: Sage.

Whitefield, J.M. (1947): *Machiavelli*. Oxford: Oxford University Press.

Wilkins, B.T. (1967): *The Problem of Burke's Political Philosophy*, Oxford. Blackwell.

Willford, M. (1975): "Bentham on the Rights of Woman," *Journal of the History of Ideas*, 38.PP.167-176.

Wolfe, B. (1996): *Marxim: One Hundred Years in the Life of a Doctrine*. New York: Avon.

Wolin, Sheldon S. 1960. *Politics and Vision: Continuity and Innovation in Western Political Thought*. Little Brown.

Wollstonecraft, Mary (1999) *A Vindication of the Rights of Woman* (ed) by Janet Todd, Oxford; Oxford University Press.

Wood, Ellen Mieksins, and Neal Wood. 1978. *Class Ideology and Ancient Political Theory: Socrates, Plato, and Aristotle in Social Context*. Oxford: Blackwell.

Wood, N. (1984): *John Locke and Agrarian Capitalism*. Berkeley: University of California Press.

Yack, Bernard. (1993). *The Problems of a Political Animal: Community, Justice, and Conflict in Aristotelian Political Thought*. Berkeley: University of California Press.

Yolton, J. (1956): *John Locke and the Way of Ideas*. Oxford: Clarendon Press. (Ed.)(1977): *The Locke Reader*. Cambridge. Cambridge University Press.

Zeller, E. (1955): *Outlines of the History of Greek Philosophy*. New York: Meridian.

Index